STAN

HOW MANAGERS MOTIVATE

THE IMPERATIVES OF SUPERVISION

HOW MANAGERS MOTIVATE

THE IMPERATIVES OF SUPERVISION

William F. Dowling
Leonard R. Sayles
Columbia University
Graduate School of Business

Second Edition

McGraw-Hill Book Company
New York   St. Louis   San Francisco   Auckland   Bogotá   Düsseldorf
London   Madrid   Mexico   Montreal   New Delhi   Panama   Paris   São Paulo
Singapore   Sydney   Tokyo   Toronto

This book was set in Helvetica Light by Intergraphic Technology, Inc.
The editors were William J. Kane and Theresa J. Kwiatkowski;
the designer was Jo Jones;
the production supervisor was Dominick Petrellese.
R. R. Donnelley & Sons Company was printer and binder.

HOW MANAGERS MOTIVATE: THE IMPERATIVES OF SUPERVISION

90 EB EB 8987

Library of Congress Cataloging in Publication Data

Dowling, William F
    How managers motivate.

    Includes index.
    1. Supervision of employees. 2. Supervisors.
I. Sayles, Leonard R., joint author. II. Title.
HF5549.D63 1978   658.31′4   77-22788
ISBN 0-07-017668-X

For George Strauss

CONTENTS

ix
CONTENTS

PREFACE

For decades, managers and business educators alike have agreed that the first-line supervisor is the most critical member of the management team. Here is where the action is; where operating work gets performed. While there is no disagreement on the importance of face-to-face supervision, the subject has not attracted many major textbook efforts. There are probably thousands of courses within companies and colleges that seek to train young men and women to become effective supervisors. Most of these consist of more or less adequate collections of speeches, readings, articles, and notes. Given the quantity of first-class behavioral research that has been done in this area and the need for its application both in the classroom and in organizations, we sought to write a new type of text on face-to-face supervision.

Our objectives in developing this text are threefold: first, to include a broad range of research findings from the leadership and organizational behavior field; second, to express these in ways that would appeal to the reader because the text would contain lively first-hand examples of supervisors on the "firing line"; and third, to emphasize the actual behavior and analytical thinking required of supervisors, not abstract "principles" and traditional "theories."

We have sought to give equal emphasis to behavior and systems. New or prospective managers don't get much help from being told what attitudes they should adopt and what their feelings *ought* to be. Sentiments are a result of what happens to you, not the cause. Therefore we have consistently dealt with styles and patterns of behavior—how supervisors handle themselves with subordinates, colleagues, their bosses, the union—in a wide variety of situations. The particular situation determines what particular strategy will prove successful, rather than a memorized formula good for all seasons.

As many of the newer studies have shown, it is just as reasonable to expect that high-performance work groups *cause* employee-oriented supervision, as the reverse. There is no one "best" style. Technology and the kinds of jobs being supervised will have a profound impact on what the supervisor can and should do. The supervisor's job is not neatly compartmentalized into planning and doing, controlling and directing, and the other traditional categories. Instead almost every action the supervisor takes has elements of all these embodied in it, and is most likely to cue a subordinate as to what is wanted when least expected to do so!

We recognize in each chapter that the supervisor and the department are always part of a total system that includes the operations closely related in some work flow, often a variety of staff departments (that both service and control), perhaps a union, a boss, and the larger organization. For supervisors to play the "management game" successfully, the heart of the matter is to understand the importance of these interrelationships and dependencies. They must weigh carefully the impact of their actions and decisions on each one, as well as the role played by individuals they supervise and the group norms which have evolved. More often than not they must compromise and negotiate, accepting half a loaf, so to speak, rather than any ideal solution, if they hope to minimize conflict and provide a realistic accommodation between the goals they seek and the constraints that surround them.

Because our primary audience is managers-in-training, we have not sought to footnote any significant number of references. Footnotes, while useful and relevant to advanced work in the field, often discourage the new student or supervisor. We chose what we believe is a better road to impress the reader with the origins of the field. We have included brief selections from twelve scholars who have contributed greatly to modern management. By choosing people with broadly disparate backgrounds, we have sought to illustrate the breadth of knowledge and experience relevant to the job of the manager: psychology, sociology, anthropology, economics, engineering, to name the more important.

We are indebted to some great teachers, most of them friends and colleagues. While mentioning a few may do some injustice to the remainder, parsimony has been a guide in the preparation of the total work. Ms. Patricia Haskell, Professor George Strauss, Dr. Eliot Chapple, and the late Professors Robert McCloskey and Douglas McGregor have been among our instructors, although grades were given sparingly.

We especially want to thank the following teachers who read the manuscript and made many useful suggestions: B. A. Hindmarch, Purdue University-Calumet; Fred Luthans, University of Nebraska-Lincoln; Paul J. Wolff, Dundalk Community College; Margaret Fenn, University of Washington; Edward A. Nicholson, Wright State University; David H. Yoakley and Beve L. Sigal, Pensacola Junior College.

A book is the product of many hands. Mr. William J. Kane, our editor, provided us with a great deal of professional assistance, personal encouragement, and consistent good advice. Miss Penny Nathans skillfully clothed our "plot" and concepts in the continuing case which follows each chapter. Ms. Elizabeth Blair and Mr. William Wagel typed our many drafts conscientiously and with good cheer.

William F. Dowling

Leonard R. Sayles

1

THE SYSTEMS APPROACH TO SUPERVISION

LEARNING OBJECTIVES

1 Comprehend why a manager's view of the world will differ from that of subordinates.

2 Understand why the usual simple "pyramidal" description of an organization is inadequate in defining the supervisor's position.

3 Understand the difference between a human "systems" world of organizational relationships and a traditional "compartmentalized" managerial job.

INTRODUCTION

To be a manager is a formidable task. Look at the difficulties neighbors, families, and friends have in maintaining good relationships. Yet an organization expects that a manager will get to know the people working for him or her well enough not only to maintain good day-to-day relationships, but also to obtain their cooperation in performing difficult or tedious job assignments. It takes a psychiatrist years to determine the motivations of one individual, yet the manager is expected to understand the motivations of an entire work group.

While all this makes management sound like one of the most demanding professions, behavioral scientists over the years have made discoveries about how people react to work and supervision that make the manager's job a lot more doable than it first appears. Put another way, while it may be very difficult to understand everything about another individual and to live closely with that individual without serious conflict, people are more predictable in how they respond to their jobs and their organizational roles. In short, marital relations are both more demanding and less predictable than work relations.

In this book we will try to integrate what is known about the way people behave in organizations with what managers have to do to fulfill their supervisory responsibilities. Fortunately, there is no inherent conflict between the two.

To be successful, the manager needs two kinds of knowledge: self-knowledge and knowledge of the organization.

SELF-KNOWLEDGE

Self-knowledge is the easiest. It basically can be summarized this way: Don't confuse the way you feel with the way other people feel. Most managers assume that the way they view the world around them is the way their subordinates see the world. Thus in trying to analyze what is going wrong, why they're having a problem with Archie or Ellen, managers jump to the mistaken conclusion that reality is the same for everyone. "After all, I'm being realistic," is what most managers tell themselves. They then decide how to solve the problem based on their own perceptions, ignoring or denying the possibility that there could be another equally reasonable set of perceptions. In fact, it is almost impossible for two people occupying different roles or positions to see the world the same way.

Here's a case that makes a good point about self-knowledge (and its limitations):

Bill Handler was really angry this time. He had just finished asking Al Pfizer to skip his lunch period today (and either eat a sandwich on the job or go out later) in order to finish a rush order that Bill's boss, Shirley Carr, had especially requested be finished by 2 P.M. The job involved reviewing a number of accident claims in one set of insurance files, and Bill knew this was "duck soup" for an old hand like Al. But Al had simply mumbled something about having to stop at the bank today and some other important personal errands and that, after working hard all morning, he really needed a lunch break—after all it was what all employees received.

Bill thought to himself how right he had been to turn down Al's request for promotion to senior claims analyst. At the time he had done it because of Al's poor attendance record even though he had to admit that Al was one of the sharpest analysts around. But promotion ought to reflect a sense of responsibility as well as ability, and once more Al had showed that he couldn't "cut it." "He just doesn't care about his reputation," thought Bill.

If only Bill could have seen the situation from Al's perspective. Al watched Bill take over as supervisor of the department two years before. At the time he was wary because Bill, unlike his predecessor, Joan Crispo, was standoffish. Bill didn't mingle much with the others in the department, never joked around, and didn't seem to like Al much at all. Al reasoned that Bill was probably concerned that someone as experienced as he was—Bill had never seen an insurance claim before taking the job—would resent a "green" supervisor. He became more sure of it after the incident with the bike took place.

Al got the flu, and it seemed to hang on for days. He got a call from Bill after his third day out asking if he couldn't come back soon because work was backing up. Al told him the doctor had said to take a full week. As luck would have it, on the fourth day he had gotten restless, and since the weather was so beautiful, he had ridden his son's bike down the street to a repair shop, all of 10 minutes away from his house, to get the gears fixed. Just as he was turning into the shop, he caught a glimpse of Bill driving by.

When he went back to work on the following Monday, he had tried to explain, but he knew that Bill didn't believe him. He found just how damaging a few weeks later when a promotion slot to senior claims analyst opened up, a job for which Al was certain he was well qualified. After he had indicated he wanted to be considered for the post, Bill told him that the job required a real sense of personal responsibility, and while Al was a long service employee, his overall record was only fair.

Everyone in the department told Al he had been discriminated against and he ought to fight it, to file a grievance, to see Ms. Carr, not take it lying down, and so on. But Al was too humiliated at being passed over. He only hoped that Bill wouldn't stay around too long. At least his friends in the department had stuck by him.

So when Bill asked him to give up lunch, Al saw red. Imagine what all the others would say about his doing favors for the boss who had kicked him in the teeth. And what would they say about his going along with management's feeling that lunch time wasn't really theirs?

At this point there is little likelihood that Al will ever feel very motivated to go much beyond the minimum required by his job; this, in turn, will confirm Bill's view that Al is basically irresponsible, part of an antimanagement clique, and not qualified for promotion. In a sense, we're talking about a self-fulfilling prophecy. The way in which Al has treated Bill guarantees that Al, now and in the future, will live up to Bill's low expectations of him. The chapters to follow should help you acquire some knowledge and skills in how to avoid just this kind of destructive stalemate.

ORGANIZATION KNOWLEDGE

Supervisors need more knowledge than that derived by understanding that subordinates will view the world differently than their boss, that their own perceptions are not predictive of how others see the world. They also need to understand the special world of the organizations in which they perform their jobs.

Most managers start out with more false preconceptions than solid knowledge about the nature of modern organizations. They are deceived by the pyramids they have seen on formal organization charts, articles they have read, and the speeches on management they have heard. From these sources they draw conclusions such as:

1 It's the supervisor's job to get the work done through people over whom she has complete authority.
2 The authority of the supervisor is equal to her responsibilities. The supervisor controls all the resources she needs to perform the tasks for which she is held accountable by higher management.
3 The only person to whom the supervisor is accountable is the next manager in the chain of command, her boss.

Reality is far different. Subordinates have a good deal of power with which to counter the authority of the supervisor. They may have unions or other strong groups that can challenge almost any manager's orders as being unfair or even illegal. There are many assignments for which the manager must rely on the motivation and goodwill of the subordinate either because the work is complicated, is done out of sight, or lends itself to silent sabotage, delays, and deceptions. Work loads are often ambiguous, and adequate productivity frequently depends on the supervisor's use of persuasion and leadership skills and not on simply telling people what they must do.

The same distinction between myth and reality holds for the second statement. Almost no supervisors have authority equal to their responsibilities. Managers are dependent on outside groups to provide supplies, repairs, and data in the right quantities and at the right time. All these outsiders typically report to *other* managers with different goals and different perceptions from those of the supervisors.

Furthermore, many of these outsiders who have an impact on the manager's job also have some control or power not unlike that exercised by another boss. In other words, the modern manager is accountable to a variety of other managers (in addition to the next level boss) for such things as quality (to the quality control manager), quantity of output (to the production control manager), size of salary increases or disciplinary penalties imposed (to the personnel manager), for costs (to the accounting manager), and so on.

ORGANIZATIONS AS HUMAN SYSTEMS

Thus organizations function as much laterally—by negotiations and persuasions taking place between managers and their subordinates and between one set of managers and another—as they do hierarchically—by orders passing down the line. The manager gets things done by participating in a variety of interactions that involve subordinates, informal leaders, union representatives, staff departments, and service and support groups, as well as upper management.

The wide range of contacts required by the job means that managerial work does *not* follow neat timetables in which one task is finished before the next is begun. Instead, the manager operates by fits and starts. Just when he or she is planning to work out a problem involving a faulty invoice, an employee calls in sick and a replacement has to be secured from Personnel. In the meantime the invoice problem requires contacting the purchasing manager who is willing to authorize a change if Accounting has not yet approved payment for the bill.

But just as the manager is pursuing this down to what appears to be the finish line, another work problem requires intervention. In the midst of all this a work schedule change comes in the afternoon mail which involves some seemingly impossible levels of output, given the fact that next week three employees will be on vacation. On and on the day goes swiftly by with literally a hundred different calls, talks, meetings, and discussions with perhaps thirty different people.

If there is one constant in the manager's job, it is change—today won't be like tomorrow except that both will involve an extraordinary number of human contacts, mostly unscheduled, and with as many people outside the department as inside. This unpredictability means that managers must be alert to what their priorities should be today and not what they thought yesterday were going to be today's priorities. They must not get flustered because something new has to be started before something already started can be finished, and because other people don't appear to be acting rationally and fulfilling their commitments as the supervisor understands them to be.

After all, each individual in the system is also subject to pressures and demands from different sets of people and departments. As someone asks for more or gives them less, they will have to change what they can do, or are willing to do, in order to help you, the manager.

This highly interdependent world, in which individuals respond to different pressures and needs and thus don't always cooperate, is one in which the manager must learn to function, not by shouting orders and commands, but by understanding the system and how to function within it.

Thus the manager's job is unlike most other jobs. In other work you are used to having clear goals that you pursue pretty much on your own. In managerial work there will be many different goals, some of them conflicting with each other (for example, keeping subordinates satisfied, maintaining output, quality, servicing other departments, undertaking some longer-run change project, and so on). Moreover, the people you work with have different goals at different times. Some people are motivated to do first-class work, to get a sense of personal accomplishment; some want power and influence over their coworkers; others want to do the least amount of work possible and acquire as much leisure time as they can in the process; and still others merely want security and minimum risk. Managers need not only to understand themselves, as do all effective human beings, but also to understand the other people in the organization who affect their departments, including subordinates, superiors, and other supervisors.

There is always the danger that you will assume others are motivated the same way you are, that they share the same goals and the same values. Usually that's not true. There is a parallel danger involved in having a faulty model in your head that explains how things work in organizations. Most managers start with certain feelings about what causes what—often derived from past reading or experiences. They assume, for example, that offers of more money or threats of punishment are surefire ways to get more work, or they assume that work groups always seek to hold back individual output. While everyone needs to have some understanding of the world—what causes what—in order to function, it's even more important that these "models" be relatively accurate.

Therefore, much of this book will deal with cause and effect. We hope to provide you with a more realistic view of what makes things happen in the world of organizations—both good things and bad. This includes dealing with the impact of how jobs are structured and performance is measured, and with the effect of different styles of leadership on productivity.

In summary, people in organizations, like people anywhere, do things because they think a particular course of action will advance or protect their own interests. The manager has to know how subordinates view the world around them—what they *expect* will happen if they ignore the supervisor or increase their output, what risks they are willing to take for what possible rewards or punishments as they are defined by subordinates. While supervisors may be tempted to impose their own calculations of likely benefits versus likely costs for doing something, it's a mistake to do so. It's the employee's way of viewing the world that must be understood.

The manager must keep in mind all these points of view and different goals, as well as how the organization works. That's a tall order, and it's a different kind of knowledge than purely technical knowledge because human feelings and human systems are involved. Managerial work then consists of a never-changing array of tasks and actions designed to keep a complex system on target.

BIBLIOGRAPHY

Dill, W., T. Hilton, and W. Reitman, *The New Managers: Patterns of Behavior and Development,* Prentice-Hall, Englewood Cliffs, N.J., 1962.

Mintzberg, H., *The Nature of Managerial Work,* Harper and Row, New York, 1973.

Sayles, L., *Managerial Behavior: Administration in Complex Organization,* McGraw-Hill, New York, 1964.

2
MOTIVATING PEOPLE: HOW TO MATCH HUMAN NEEDS TO JOB DEMANDS

LEARNING OBJECTIVES

1 Determine the incentives available to any organization seeking to motivate employees.

2 Ascertain the existence of a hierarchy of incentives; some incentives motivate more than others.

3 See why any organization must supply a variety of incentives to meet the varying expectations of its work force.

4 Measure the supervisor's ability to dispense the incentives called for by the work situation.

5 Determine the extent to which money is a motivator.

6 Determine the extent to which the job itself defines and constrains incentives.

7 Define job enrichment and the conditions under which a job can be enriched.

You just set the work before the men and have them do it.
Henry Ford

When he was a teenager, Henry Ford's hobby was taking watches apart and then reassembling them. Legend has it that no watch he reassembled ever failed to tell the correct time. And, as everyone knows, he want on to perfect the assembly line and make a billion dollars. Henry Ford knew everything about machines—that's one side of the coin. The other side is suggested by the quotation above. He knew very little about what moves human beings. And it was his fantastically simplified view of human nature that more than anything else brought his company to the brink of bankruptcy in the latter days of his management. He really believed that all that was involved in the human side of management was to "set the work before the men and have them do it." If only it were that simple!

MAINSPRINGS OF WORK

Why do people work? Ask yourself the question. If there were a dozen persons answering it, we would guess that each one would list at least eight to ten reasons. And if each one were listing the reasons in order of their importance, no two lists would read exactly alike. People differ in the expectations they bring to their jobs and the satisfactions they derive from them. That's as you would anticipate.

The problem is that many jobs in both plants and offices are poor motivators as measured against any person's list of expectations and satisfactions. They offer a person a week's pay in return for services and very little more, for the nonmaterial rewards and satisfactions are slender.

This gap between the needs people bring to their jobs and the ability of their jobs to meet them is one of the central topics of this chapter. We will describe the principal needs that the majority of people bring to their jobs and the problems faced by higher management and supervision in trying to fulfill them.

WHY IS MOTIVATION IMPORTANT?

The problems of job expectation and satisfaction are important to even the most hard-boiled managers because, in the last analysis, management pays a heavy price for dissatisfying work—friction on the job, substandard output and quality, high turnover, absenteeism, and tardiness, to give only a partial list. The positive side of the motivation coin is of equal significance. The motivated worker is also the most productive worker, the worker who sometimes equals or excels any standards that bosses set or would contemplate setting.

Some years ago, Professor Argyris of Harvard wrote a book entitled *Personality and Organization,* in which he outlined the basic conflict between the demands of the healthy human personality and the requirements of the formal organization. It might better have been titled *Personality versus Organization* since, except for a few scientists and top decision makers, it was clearly in the nature of the organization to stunt the personality of those it employed and frustrate their desires for self-expression and self-fulfillment.

In this chapter, we're not going to be as grim as Chris Argyris was in his book. We can see that there is a substantial gap between what most people want from their jobs and what they're currently receiving, but we think that Argyris has substantially exaggerated the size of the gap. And we also believe, drawing on recent research in behavioral science, that it's possible to show how much of that gap can be bridged and the organization made at once more satisfying to the worker, more effective, and more profitable.

Simple People—Complex Methods

Many management thinkers have tackled the needs side of the job equation and come up with different, sometimes seemingly contradictory, answers to the question: Why do people work? Forty years ago, *scientific management,* the then dominant mode of business thinking, concentrated on the method, not the individual. The aim was simple: Divide each job into a large number of small, easy-to-learn tasks and devise the one best way for achieving each one of these tasks.

As for the worker, to quote Frederick Winslow Taylor, the founder of scientific management, "Each man must learn how to give up his own particular way of doing things, adapt his methods to the many new standards, and grow accustomed to receiving and obeying directions, covering details large and small, which in the past have been left to his individual judgment."

Taylor's thinking was eminently pragmatic. He based his conclusions on a series of experiments he had conducted at the Midvale Steel Company, a predecessor of Bethlehem Steel, where his approach had resulted in dramatic increases in productivity. The classic example involved an ironworker named Schmidt who, following Taylor's instructions, quadrupled the amount of pig iron he shoveled during an hour. What was in it for Schmidt? A 61 percent increase in wages and the satisfaction, to quote Taylor again, of being a "high-priced man." In other words, scientific management saw the worker, at least the hourly employee, as essentially a passive economic man with strong muscles and a weak mind only capable of absorbing the simple routines of mass-production technology—and incidentally, a person willing to accept a 61 percent increase in wages for a 362 percent increase in productivity.

Mass-production technology, for which scientific management provided a rationale, was enormously efficient. Few business executives questioned the theory when the practice worked so well. Scientific management probably reached its peak when Henry Ford outraged his partners by using some of the profits generated by the assembly line to give his workers—the year was 1914—the unprecedented wage of $5 a day. This historic move probably had its unselfish side, but primarily Ford was interested in getting the most work out of the best workers and he was appealing to them in the only terms that he thought had any meaning—economic ones. He had accepted completely the assumption that, in the specialization of industrial labor, a few people will do all the thinking while the rest will do the work. But let him be his own witness—his candor makes him a natural. "The average worker, I am sorry to say, wants a job in which he does not have to put forth much physical energy—above all, he wants a job at which he does not have to think."

The Power of Recognition

If it took Saint George to slay the dragon, it probably takes a psychiatrist to slay an engineer. At any rate, the human relations school of employee motivation, which pretty much has vanquished scientific management, got most of its impetus from the studies conducted at the Hawthorne works of the Western Electric Company under the guidance of Elton Mayo, an Australian psychiatrist turned Harvard Business School professor and practicing sociologist. The studies, conducted roughly over the five-year period 1927-1932, attempted to determine what made employees productive—Hawthorne management being convinced that its workers were far from realizing their potential. At the core of the Hawthorne research was the now classic study of the relay assembly workers. As Fritz Roethlisberger, an associate of Mayo, explained it,

> The idea was very simple: A group of five [women] were placed in a room where their condition of work (assembly of a telephone relay) could be carefully controlled, where their output could be measured, and where they could be closely observed. It was decided to produce at specified intervals different changes in working conditions, and to see what effect these inno-

vations had on output. Also, records were kept such as the temperature and humidity of the room, the number of hours each [woman] slept at night, the kind and amount of food she ate for breakfast, lunch, and dinner.[1]

Over a five-year period, Mayo and his associates collected and analyzed "literally tons of material."

What did the material prove? What were the correlations? At the level of physical environment, there were no correlations at all. But with the introduction of each variable, production kept increasing. The answer to the puzzle lay in the changing social environment. From an ordinary group of workers performing routine jobs with little or no recognition from management, they had been transformed into important people. "Their physical health and well-being became matters of great concern. Their opinions, hopes and fears were eagerly sought," observed Roethlisberger. Nor was this all. They were questioned sympathetically and at length about their reactions to working conditions by investigators—frequently in the superintendent's office. They could chat as they wished on the job, and they set their own production quotas.

Supervision was at a minimum, and the women were allowed to participate in a number of decisions that substantially affected their well-being. For example, at one point the women were given the choice between starting one-half hour later than usual or stopping one-half hour earlier. They chose the latter, and despite the fact that this reduced the working day by 10 percent, total production increased and hourly output increased sharply.

The immediate lessons drawn from the Hawthorne research at the Western Electric Company were fairly slight. The chief direct impact was an elaborate listening program—critics called it practicing "cow sociology." Employees were urged to discuss their problems with trained counselors in the apparent hope that the simple act of "blowing off steam" would relieve many of their tensions and dissatisfactions. However, this was only one ripple emanating from Hawthorne. The impact on motivation theory and management practice continues to this day. The emphasis on human relations in management stems from Hawthorne, including the major themes in most of the supervisory training classes attended by two generations of supervisors. Interpretations of Hawthorne varied with the interpreters. But one message everyone got: It was difficult, after Hawthorne, to view the rank-and-file

---

[1]F. J. Roethlisberger, *Management and Morale,* Harvard University Press, Cambridge, Mass., 1949, pp. 11-12.

employee as a pure economic being, to maintain that optimum output was a function of an appropriate wage scale with a minor assist from good physical working conditions.

In Search of Complexity

Not long after Hawthorne, Chester Barnard, the president of the New Jersey Bell Telephone Company, wrote a book, *The Functions of the Executive,* which still makes rewarding if difficult reading. In it Barnard argued that any organization secures the services of its employees by the incentives it offers them. Material inducements—salaries, bonuses, fringe benefits, and similar advantages—headed the list, not because he thought they were the most important but because they had been the incentives that had received the greatest emphasis—"relative to other incentives it is the material things which have been progressively easier to produce and therefore to offer. Hence there has been a forced cultivation of the love of material things among those above the level of subsistence."

The other incentives to which Barnard gave at least equal billing were the following:

Personal, nonmaterial opportunities for distinction
Desirable physical conditions
Ideal benefactions—what we more commonly think of as pride of craftsmanship or aesthetic satisfaction derived from work
Social compatibility or associational attractiveness, particularly with the members of a particular work group, including its boss
Conformity to habitual practices and attitudes
Feeling of enlarged participation
Condition of communion, which Barnard understood to mean the opportunity for comradeship and mutual reinforcement of personal attitudes

Barnard himself, perhaps influenced by the Hawthorne research but more likely reflecting his own experiences as a successful manager, emphasized the role of social compatibility. "Men often will not work at all and will rarely work well under other incentives if the social situation from their point of view is unsatisfactory." Money thus becomes a secondary incentive, one that only gets a chance to function once the employee views the social situation as satisfactory. We've traveled a long way from scientific management.

HIERARCHY OF NEEDS

The deemphasis on money and material things generally as a motivator has reached its apparent peak in the hypothesis of the needs hierarchies developed by two noted social psychologists, A. H. Maslow and Frederick Herzberg. The two hierarchies are separate but similar. In Maslow's, physical needs occupy the lowest rung, followed in ascending order by *safety* needs to be free from fear of deprivation, danger, and threat on the job and off; *social* needs to associate, to belong, to accept, to be accepted, to like, and to be liked; *egotistic* needs to obtain respect, recognition, and status; and finally, at the top, the need for *self-actualization* which Maslow defines as "the desire to become everything that one is capable of becoming."

In Maslow's research the implication is clear that needs are like a ladder to be climbed one step at a time, that if the satisfaction of a lower-level need such as safety or security is threatened, higher-level needs will be ignored. In some respects, however, Maslow doesn't appear to be as monolithic in his thinking as Herzberg. At least with higher-order needs, Maslow departs from the rigid hierarchy and admits that different people might place higher-level needs in a different hierarchy. One individual might rank esteem higher than autonomy, or vice versa.

Herzberg divides his needs into five job dissatisfiers and five job satisfiers. As dissatisfiers, he lists company policy and administration, supervision, salary, interpersonal relations, and working conditions, which correspond roughly to Maslow's physical and safety needs. His job satisfiers are achievement, recognition for achievement, work itself, responsibility, and advancement, which correspond to Maslow's social and egotistical needs and the need for self-actualization.

Herzberg, impressed by the analogy to preventive medicine, labeled his five dissatisfiers "hygienic factors." In his opinion, "A good hygienic environment can prevent job dissatisfaction but cannot create true job satisfaction or happiness."

What lends particular interest to Herzberg's theories, and what accounts in large measure for the recognition they have achieved, is the amount of empirical research that verifies and supports them. They began as the conclusion of a study conducted by Herzberg about twenty years ago among 200 engineers and accountants in the Pittsburgh area. Since then, he has repeated the study over seventy-five times in a wide variety of occupations from the sciences to housework—and the theory has checked out every time. Like "the Colonel's Lady and Judy O'Grady," the scientist and the blue-collar worker are brothers under the skin—they have the same basic job needs and so does the white-collar worker.

Let us assume—for the moment at least—that Herzberg is correct: Those who work with their heads have the same job needs as those who work with their hands. And let us further assume that Herzberg has correctly analyzed and ranked these needs. What are the practical implications of his theories for the supervisor who is charged with seeing that subordinates contribute as much as they are capable of to the effectiveness and profitability of the organization? In other words, having read Herzberg and been converted, where does the supervisor go from there?

The Supervisor's Dilemma

"Nowhere very fast" is an accurate although partial and not very satisfactory answer. One problem is exemplified by Maslow's observation that "the U.S. citizen is 85 percent satisfied in his physiological needs, 70 percent in his safety needs, 50 percent in his social needs, 40 percent in his ego needs, and only 10 percent in his self-actualizing needs." If to be satisfied is to be satiated, then the supervisor is going to get very little mileage from any efforts to make the employee's job safer and relatively little from efforts to improve the employee's pay. The big payoff in terms of effort and performance will come from making it possible for employees to realize more of their potential on the job.

Satisfaction and the status quo

In theory, this sounds fine. Applying it presents several obstacles. First, the supervisor must make sure that any favorable factors in the work environment stay that way. True, the status quo can't be used as a motivator with employees, but let current conditions deteriorate from the employees' point of view and the supervisor will be in serious trouble. We well remember a discussion we had several years ago about Eastman Kodak's bonus plan with the then vice president of industrial relations. The plan dates from the days of George Eastman (he died in 1932) and provides an annual employee bonus based on the combination of salary, seniority, and the size of Eastman Kodak's dividends. It was the industrial relations director's contention that the company didn't get an extra ounce of effort from any employee on account of the bonus—everyone had long since taken it for granted.

Water down the bonus? Scrap it altogether on the grounds that it provided no incentives to improve performance? Impossible. The negative consequences of tampering with it were difficult to predict, but no one in the company dared to risk them. Eastman Kodak was stuck with the bonus.

Similarly, the supervisor is stuck with the task of trying to maintain the positive elements in the status quo of his or her own little organization—whatever they happen to be. Maintaining them won't make employees a bit more effective, but failing to maintain them may motivate them to become less effective or even quit. In short, the supervisor must work hard at maintaining whatever elements are present of Herzberg's "good hygienic environment."

Satisfaction and employee perception

Another problem arises from the fact that any job, as viewed by an employee, can be and usually is both satisfying and dissatisfying at the same time—a phenomenon freely conceded by Herzberg. One reaction does not cancel out, preclude, or produce the other. The supervisor starts with limited resources—of time, energy, and money—as well as limited authority. If improved performance is desired, where should the supervisor's attention be focused? The answer, according to Herzberg, would seem to be on improving the job satisfiers rather than on removing the job dissatisfiers, with the qualification already made that the job dissatisfiers shouldn't increase while the supervisor's gaze is fixed in another direction.

Once again, behind the obvious answer lies a sticky wicket. At one level, the problem is one of definition, with Herzberg the villain or at least the source of ambiguity. He talks about motivation as lying at the root of any person's desire to excel in his or her work, and he criticizes monetary incentives for their alleged failure to motivate. The distinction, however, seems more semantic than real, for Herzberg describes the failure in these terms: "The promise of money can move a man to work, but it cannot motivate him. Motivation means an inner desire to make an effort." To the hard-pressed supervisor with a limited supply of the true motivators and an even more limited control over their disposition, the distinction between moving a person to work and motivating that individual to work probably would appear academic. Results are what concern the supervisor, and apparently it's possible to obtain the same results from decreasing the sources of job dissatisfaction as it is from increasing the sources of job satisfaction. The difference lies not so much in the way the employee performs as in the way one feels about one's performance—what is given freely and cheerfully in the latter case, is conceded as part of the work bargain in the former.

How Much Can the Supervisor Do?

A much deeper problem is the ability of the supervisor to dispense the several sources of job satisfaction defined by Herzberg: achievement, recognition for achievement, work itself, responsibility, and advancement. Boss and employee alike confront the same barrier—the job. Whether or not the supervisor is able to provide the five motivators depends more than anything else on the intrinsic nature of the job. No exercise is more futile than for supervisors to concern themselves with motivators that they are largely or totally unable to provide. On the classic assembly line where the moving machine determines the pace, not the worker, where the operation performed is simple, repetitious, and monotonous, where whatever knack that is needed to run the machine is acquired in days or weeks, not months or years, where promotions are few and far between—under circumstances such as these, it's ludicrous to harangue the supervisor about the necessity of developing a sense of achievement, of building pride in the work itself, of increasing the employee's responsibility on the job, or of motivating the employee to strive harder for advancement. The potential satisfactions just aren't there, and the gap between what the employee needs from the job, and what the job itself permits is large and unbridgeable. It's a great pity because people without satisfying jobs rarely have fully satisfying lives.

Of course, we chose the example of the assembly-line worker with due deliberate care. And we make no apologies. Hyperbole is a legitimate way of making your point as long as you don't pretend that it's anything else. In other words, few jobs are as barren of motivators as that of the production worker on a typical assembly line. In some factory operations, you have, at the other extreme, skilled craftspeople such as the tool and die maker, where a high degree of responsibility, achievement, and pride of workmanship are inherent in the job. Providing the tool and die makers are the skilled craftspeople they're assumed to be, the supervisor can take their job satisfactions and motivations for granted—they're built into the job.

The potential of many other jobs for providing satisfiers or motivators is greater than would appear on the surface. Take, for example, a half-dozen workers in a chair factory, whose job it was to bend several pieces of steel and attach them so that the end result would be a bridge chair. A "nothing" job with few if any possibilities for developing pride in the work itself? That's not the way these people felt about their job at all. As the best of ten or twelve teams engaged in the same work—theirs was the fastest and the most coordinated—each member of the team developed enormous pride in the superiority of his or her work group and its acknowledged position in the plant.

Two points are clear. First, the capacity of work to provide motivators and satisfiers, as defined by Herzberg, depends largely on the intrinsic nature of the job. What can the supervisor do to enhance the intrinsic satisfactions that an employee derives from his or her work? Providing the job is regarded as meaningful to begin with—quite a lot. Never underestimate the power of positive feedback—and here we're taking a leaf from B. F. Skinner. In Herzberg's terms, the supervisor can increase motivation by providing recognition for achievement.

We are reminded of the supervisor of a group of bank tellers who commented apropos of her group, "Why should I praise them? Good work is what we pay them for." The same supervisor, you will not be surprised to hear, was quick to blame whenever the performance of any of her subordinates fell below par.

Skinner would argue—and there is a lot of empirical evidence to support his thesis—that the woman's strategy was totally counterproductive. Censure and criticism do not change the behavior of most people. Actually, they are a form of recognition. The behavior will continue, while the source of censure and criticism will be resented. This resentment, in turn, will tend to express itself in additional undersirable behavior. Instead, contends Skinner, avoid censure and reinforce the desired behavior, that is, any improvements in performance, by praising them. He adds that to get the maximum motivational mileage, praise as soon as possible after the praiseworthy behavior has occurred.

The second point is that in factory work only a small number of jobs offer significant motivators and satisfiers, at least as defined by Herzberg. As a partial confirmation, consider a study by Dubin of "the central life interest" of industrial workers. On the basis of a forty-item questionnaire, he found that only 24 percent of the rank-and-file employees regarded work as a central life interest. For the satisfactions that made life meaningful or even bearable, workers had to look outside their jobs. Contrast this with a second study that found that 79 percent of the professional nurses queried regarded work as a central life interest, and with a third study of 331 supervisors—first through third levels—in six Michigan companies, in which 54 percent of the supervisors considered their jobs as a central life interest.

The figures, although gloomy, are not surprising. The nurse, after all, is a member of a profession with a deep sense of calling. The work itself continually provides a sense of achievement. Patients keep on getting better, at least partially, as a consequence of a nurse's efforts. In short, the job offers psychic satisfactions that are frequent, immediate, tangible, and significant. Under these circumstances, the surprising thing is that one nurse out of five did not regard his or her job as a central life interest. The figure is a measure, perhaps, of the degree to which some doctors make nurses feel that they are second-class citizens of the healing community.

Another surprise in the Dubin study was the finding that almost half the supervisors didn't regard their jobs as a central life interest. Again, we can hypothesize that this figure is an index of the degree to which authority, power, and initiative are centralized in the typical industrial organization and, as a corollary, it is an index of the degree to which lower levels of supervision lack authority and are unable to exercise initiative in meaningful ways. They are courtiers, not managers.

WHAT'S WRONG WITH A "HIERARCHY OF NEEDS"?

Let us relieve the gloom by pointing out what we consider the central flaw in the motivational theories advanced by Herzberg, Maslow, and company—their monolithic quality. They assume that all men and women have a universal set of needs in common—more than this, that these needs are shared to the same degree. In other words, human beings have the same needs hierarchy. They maintain that the relative standing of one need versus another reflects, not a basic difference in human nature but, instead, the extent to which a person's needs are currently being satisfied and the ability to concentrate on his or her higher needs, once any lower requirements are satisfied.

By contrast, we believe in the happy diversity of needs. Few people want the same things, at least to the same degree. And we reject as irrelevant the intellectual arrogance embedded in the notion of a needs hierarchy. "Better Socrates dissatisfied than a pig satisfied," thundered John Stuart Mill. The supervisor, however, is not dealing with a race of heroic men like Socrates, but with real people and real needs. The supervisor's problem is how to meet these needs within his or her always circumscribed abilities.

Furthermore, we feel there is a tendency for men and women with a certain set of job needs to seek a job where these needs are congruent with the demands of the position. The big question, and one we don't pretend to answer, is the extent to which the process of matching job needs to job demands is a conscious one and the extent to which people learn subconsciously and over time to adjust their needs systems to the opportunities afforded by their jobs.

Take Kornhauser's study, for example, in which he compared a similar group of auto workers with employees with more complex jobs over which they exercised more control. He found that the auto workers showed a diminishing amount of initiative in relation to their work activities along with less personal ambition and less desire for personal growth. His general conclusion: "Factory employment, especially in routine production tasks, does give evidence of extinguishing workers' ambition, initiative, and purposive direction toward life goals."

We suspect, however, that with most people, both factors play a part in the matching process. People initially seek out a job that satisfies their needs as they understand them. As time passes, they readjust their personal needs system to inflate the needs that the job can satisfy and downgrade those which the job simply isn't equipped to fulfill. Not that we've come full circle from gloom to euphoria. The matching of job needs to job demands is neither automatic nor uniformly successful. Each organization has its quota of round pegs in square holes, and as Aldous Huxley warned, "Round pegs in square holes tend to have dangerous thoughts about the social system and to infect others with their discontent."

WATER SEEKS ITS OWN LEVELS

In attempting to demonstrate our thesis that most people seek jobs with a capacity to satisfy their particular set of needs, we have to rely pretty much on anecdotal evidence (of which there is a sufficiency), personal observation, and common sense. If we could marshal large bodies of statistics to serve as heavy artillery for our thesis, we would. Lacking such support, we take what comfort we can in the absence of any impressive statistics that would tend to refute our thesis.

Let's begin with simple needs and simple demands—those of the happy morons at the Utica knitting mill cited by Argyris. They performed their jobs with such a high degree of efficiency that management expressed surprise that they were considered subnormal. (The classification "moron" is assigned, according to *Webster's Third New International Dictionary,* to a person "with a potential mental age of between eight and twelve years who is capable of doing routine work under supervision.") In addition, their attendance was good and their general behavior compared favorably with that of any other group of employees.

Are we saying that some jobs are fit only for morons? And are we implying that only morons could find satisfaction in holding down such jobs?

Not quite. Taylor might well have answered yes to both questions; at least, that's a reasonable inference from his comment that "one of the very first requirements for a man who is fit to handle pig iron as a regular occupation is that he should be so stupid and so phlegmatic that he more resembles an ox than any other type." All it required of a worker to perform one of the minute tasks made possible by the subdivision of labor into the smallest discrete elements was enough ability to "execute punctiliously the orders given, down to their minutest details."

What Makes a Job Beautiful?

We will not go as far as Taylor would probably go—but for somewhat different reasons. We agree that there are many positions, including the overwhelming majority of assembly-line jobs, where the work itself could provide a challenge and offer positive satisfactions to few persons above the level of morons. Our point is, instead, that many of the people occupying these jobs, although far from morons, are not unhappy on their jobs, are not living lives of quiet desperation, and are not round pegs in square holes. Since the work itself provides few satisfactions, employees seek their satisfactions elsewhere on the job. Take, for example, the analysis of workers in a public utility made by Dr. Harry Levinson, then of the Menninger Clinic. He found a clear correlation between the kind of work a person did and the expectations that were brought to the job: The bulk of employees in routine, unchallenging positions valued job security, the noncompetitive character of operations, the informality of work activities, and the opportunity to develop close personal relationships—exactly the benefits afforded by the jobs they were in. The only workers who emphasized expectations having to do with their specific work were the relatively few with highly individualized work responsibilities: the chemist in the power plant or the clerk who worked alone in the company office in a small community with few opportunities for interpersonal contact.

In other words, we reject the idea that the person with a routine job is, of necessity, unhappy, frustrated, and bored. Many are, of course—but many more are not. We tend to study the components of such a job, then shake our heads in dismay and say, "No one should be doing that." What we have done is to universalize our own feelings and needs—we have confused ourselves with Everyman. What we haven't done is to remember that the beauty of the job is in the eye of the beholder.

We agree with Professor Sexton of Notre Dame, who sampled the reactions of 200 electronics workers performing routine, semiskilled functions and found that routine work actually promotes freedom on the job. What's the explanation of that apparent paradox? The task is not monotonous unless the individual is forced to concentrate on it, Sexton emphasizes. A routine job rather quickly becomes a task performed automatically—or at least without conscious thought—such as dressing, eating, or walking. Because the sense of monotony presumes thought, the routine job loses its monotonous character early in the game. The worker is free to daydream or talk with fellow employees, and usually neither gossip nor fantasy life interferes with doing an acceptable day's work.

More than one organization has experienced unwelcome, as well as unexpected, difficulties in transferring its clerical employees to more responsible jobs because of the advent of the computer. Management's thinking made surface sense: The computer did take over many routine clerical duties. The people who formerly performed these duties were retrained and then moved to new jobs which were, in almost every instance, more challenging and responsible—and in most instances, somewhat better paid. In the majority of cases, the upgrading process succeeded, but with a significant minority, it failed. The upgraded employees actually seemed to miss their dull, monotonous old jobs. They resented the continuous attention that they had to give to their new duties and felt that the extra pay fell short of compensation for their extra effort.

We challenge the behavioral scientists to say that the employees were wrong. Most behavioral scientists, of course, would be repulsed by the prospect of performing a clerical job. But most such scientists have different aptitudes, different temperaments, and most important, different value systems.

Choosing the Right Company

At one level, a person's value system or need system (the two are practically interchangeable) is revealed by the initial selection of X company over Y company as a place to work. Of course, we're presuming the freedom to choose between alternatives, a freedom which exists except for the rare case of the person with limited abilities living in a community with limited opportunities—a community dominated by one industry or one company—and even this person has mobility. Freedom is the price of a bus ticket.

One side of this largely unconscious process of selection is that safe people—people preoccupied with safety needs—gravitate toward safe companies. They want the company that, in comparison with other employers, offers stability, job security, and the status of being affiliated with an organization that has real clout in the community. Leading banks, the electric light company, the local telephone company, and any large and long-established manufacturer are typical institutions to which they are drawn. Among the factors which do not attract them to an employer are an unstructured job situation in which duties and responsibilities are loosely defined, the chance to move ahead fast but at considerable risk to both job security and peace of mind, and the chance to grow with a fledgling enterprise if, as, and when it grows.

Contrast the typical employee of a firm such as Polaroid, that operates on the frontiers of scientific knowledge, with the typical employee of AT&T. We're not denying Polaroid its share of safe types or Ma Bell its quota of hard drivers and risk takers, but we're talking about the average, not the exception. We still maintain that there is a major difference between the two, a difference of organizational climate that, in turn, determines the organizational image and reputation of the two enterprises. The individual who is attracted to one would probably not be drawn to the other, and if the wrong choice is unwittingly made, it is likely to turn out to be an instance of the round peg in the square hole.

When Levinson argues about how important it is for the supervisor to accept and gratify the legitimate dependency needs of subordinates, he's talking about an organizational setting that is apt to attract people with strong dependency needs in the first place and to foster their further development—for example, a public utility company.

The question of why people are attracted to some types of organizations rather than to others also illustrates the impact of culture on a worker's system of needs. Among lower- and lower-middle-class men of Irish descent in the northeastern United States, for example, there existed for two generations a tradition of regarding three institutions as the logical route to status and recognition (we're omitting the Catholic church as a special case): the police force, the power and light company, and the telephone company.

The source of the mystique is unclear. Certainly it had little or nothing to do with pay. We suspect it was a survival of the class system and the acceptance of class distinctions as part of an obscure but unchanging and unchallengeable natural order. The jobs themselves may not have been much, but the occupants felt a glory that gave them some of the prestige they felt was occupied in the community by the institutions they served—and sometimes loved. When they talked about the company, you could hear the capital letters.

At times, the cultural impact may lighten the task of the organization and the supervisor. A longtime Sears executive, James Worthy, a man of great sophistication in personnel matters, for instance, praised and explained Southern employees in these terms: "A great many of these young people have had religious upbringings which, together with parental admonitions, emphasized the rightness of hard work and the moral obligation of the employee to give his employer a full day's work for a full day's pay." Lest we start a new wave of industrial migration south of the Mason-Dixon line, let's hastily add that this is an accurate description of a South that is rapidly disappearing, not the South as it is becoming.

WHAT'S THE MATTER WITH MONEY?

So far, we've talked a lot about the plurality of human needs and the different ways in which they are satisfied on the job. And we have stressed that many people seek jobs and that many more accommodate themselves to jobs which afford few of the satisfactions delineated by Herzberg and Maslow, yet they remain reasonably content and reasonably productive for years or even decades. These satisfactions run the spectrum from job security to the freedom to daydream, the opportunity to develop meaningful interpersonal relations, the pleasure of working for a superior who is both boss and parental figure, and the reflected glory of association with a powerful and prestigious organization. Most workers, of course, bring to their jobs a complex of needs and expectations which, in turn, they find satisfied to a greater or less degree. Happily, in our society—at least, until a person is well into middle age—those who find few of their major needs satisfied in their current jobs are in the position to leave, fortified by the knowledge that they can find other and hopefully more satisfying positions.

Up to this point, we have omitted any evaluation of the motivator that previous generations regarded as the mainspring of performance and that this generation, among academics at least, has banished to the sidelines—money. Have we been intimidated by the current vogue among behavioral scientists to downgrade or dismiss money as a motivator? Possibly, although we don't think so. We've been deterred much more by the difficulty and complexity of the subject and by the problems involved in distinguishing between illusion and reality and of separating the two.

Does Money Motivate?

A few instances stand out where it is difficult to deny that the worker puts a very high value on money, indeed.

The classic ratebuster on an incentive job works furiously from start to finish, has no time for sociability, usually incurs the active hostility of coworkers and the passive antagonism of the supervisor (by implying that higher management may get the idea that the supervisor should make the other employees do as much work), and ends the day with little energy to spare. All this is evidence that the size of a paycheck means a lot to the ratebuster. In fact, the only other likely motivator is whatever satisfaction the ratebuster derives from being the winner of a race which, typically, no one else cares to enter—cold comfort, we should think.

In one sense, we would agree that money has ceased to be an effective motivator—the ratebuster being the exception, not the rule. The reasons were neatly summed up by Lawrence Appley, formerly chairman of the board of the American Management Association: "A person who is born into a world of legislated and sizable security benefits must have a different point of view from one who is not. An individual who starts work in a world of great organized union strength must have a different point of view from one who does not. That individual who expects, receives, and is accustomed to high pay unrelated to quantity or quality of work done must think different from one who does not." Mr. Appley exaggerates when he talks about high pay unrelated to the quantity or quality of work—but not by much. In other words, to a degree undreamed of by any previous generation, the basic financial needs of most workers are satisfied from their very first day on the job.

An obvious objection arises: Aren't unions forever demanding more and more money for their constituents, who already have all the money they need? Are we claiming, then, that the unions are misrepresenting the needs of their members? Not really. The process at work, a pretty complex one, has been encapsulated best by Argyris. Many elements of the work situation frustrate employees, and they respond by asking for more money—"wages for dissatisfaction," Argyris calls them. Unions press their demands and management reinforces the importance of the dollar drive by the publicity campaign that inevitably follows any wage increase. In turn, the worker feels more strongly than ever that the answer to any job dissatisfaction is more and more money.

Several factors are at work here. One is cultural lag. When Samuel Gompers, the founder of the American Federation of Labor, summed up the goal of the organization in behalf of its members as "more," he was talking primarily about money in an era when the value of wage increases was real rather than largely symbolic. Unions and managements both are conditioned to argue about money—the union usually has a pretty good idea as to what the company can afford, and the company usually has a pretty good idea as to what the union will settle for. Bargaining about recognition, restructuring of jobs, and making work more meaningful are complex, nebulous, and unfamiliar activities. By contrast, money talks in terms that everyone understands. Yes, but money, at least as it is seen in nine-tenths of the wage increases granted to the rank and file or exacted in their behalf, doesn't talk loudly enough. Increases that weren't sufficient by and large to make any real differences in the recipient's standard of living, increases that were granted to everyone irrespective of merit, increases that were sought in the spirit of exacting revenge and granted in the spirit of offering a bribe—all these work against the raise providing any real satisfaction for the employee and any real incentive to do a better job. We have never heard of a case where a blanket increase led to better performance. At best, it maintained the status quo.

We know of only one company, Lincoln Electric of Cleveland, Ohio, that has used money as an incentive on a really large scale with its rank-and-file employees. (Many companies do it with their top brass.) Over the past thirty years, Lincoln workers have consistently earned twice as much money as workers performing similar jobs in competing companies and have turned out more than twice the output per worker. One reason why Lincoln has not had any imitators is the shortage of workers preoccupied with money almost to the exclusion of other on-the-job needs and satisfactions—in other words, a shortage of ratebusters. Most experts agree that only about one worker out of ten is strongly motivated by money. And if Edward E. Lawler III, a top authority on compensation and motivation, is correct in his profile of such workers, they are going to be in increasingly short supply. According to Lawler, "The employee is a male, young (preferably in his twenties), his personality is characterized by low self-assurance and high neuroticism. He comes from a small town or farm background. He owns his own home and probably is a Republican and a Protestant." On several counts, the profile of a vanishing American. Still 10 percent of the work force adds up to a lot of people, in fact several million of them. Therefore the failure of organizations to imitate Lincoln cannot be explained primarily on the basis of the shortage of employees fueled by pecuniary incentives. Apparently the same top executives who respond to the challenge of a 100 percent bonus with the right performance do not believe that many rank-and-file employees could be similarly motivated. Or perhaps there is something unseemly about the idea of the man or woman on the production line earning $35,000 or $45,000 a year. We can only speculate.

We're realists. We know that there is nothing about the potential contribution of average workers to justify making them millionaires. However, we think that management collectively is missing the boat by its failure to view money as an incentive with the rank-and-file workers because of its preoccupation with a wage policy whose principal purpose is to achieve equitableness and minimize frictions. We agree with Gellerman that "money may well turn out to be the costliest motivator of them all, but money may also prove to be the most potent motivator of all, at least in certain circumstances, and when used on a sufficient scale."

We are suggesting that management try using money on jobs where the worker's efforts have a large and direct impact on productivity, on jobs where most workers are realizing only a portion of their potential, and on jobs that offer few other satisfactions. We are also proposing that management be willing to utilize the lion's share of any productivity gain as an incentive bonus— 45 percent more productivity might, for example, yield a 40 percent bonus. Most so-called incentive systems now in effect don't work because (1) the standards are so tight that it takes extraordinary effort to effect any substantial increase and get a meaningful bonus, (2) workers are afraid the system will be revamped to their financial disadvantage if large bonuses are given constantly, or (3) an individual fears social ostracism by the work group if he or she produces too much. The approach we have in mind would take care of the first two objections. The potential for earning large bonuses would be built into the system—we wouldn't advise this use of money as an incentive where workers were already producing 80 percent of their capacity or more. There should also be built-in guarantees that the incentive system would remain the same as long as the production process was unchanged. And with the first two objections erased, the work group probably wouldn't object to rapid raises in output. But we don't think the expectation of a 5, 10, or even a 15 percent pay increase will motivate a person. Our guesstimate is that money as a motivator begins with the 20 percent increase.

JOB DEMANDS DEFINE INCENTIVES

Now that we've finished discussing the principal incentives, we can see their importance to our central thesis: the interrelationship between the needs the employee brings to the job and the demands the job imposes. The nature of the job sets limits to the possible satisfactions one can derive while holding it. Many people derive satisfaction from their work by the subtle and largely subconscious adjustment of their needs structure to accommodate those satisfactions permitted by the job, while others buck the job and derive satisfaction from beating the system—seeing how little they can do for a week's pay. Still others quit in disgust and get another job.

In any case, the job itself defines the satisfactions anyone can derive from it and sets limits on the incentives even the wisest and most socially conscious managements can provide. Returning once more to our favorite horrible example, let's consider the moving assembly line. Listen to one assembly-line worker: "The job gets so sickening day in and day out plugging in ignition wires. I get through with one motor, turn around, and there's another staring me in the face. It's sickening." Excessive specialization of the kind we've just described deprives the employee of almost any chance to be independent, to do quality work, or to achieve a feeling of accomplishment. Work that has been so subdivided and simplified that it takes almost no time to learn and requires no attention provides little or no interest.

There's also little opportunity for advancement in the typical assembly-line job. Most such positions require similar levels of skill and reward the worker with similar pay. Many workers hold on to their dreams of advancement or a business of their own for a while, but by age 40, they've said goodbye to Horatio Alger.

Even on the social side, the assembly line, at least in an automobile plant, affords few satisfactions. Workers are restricted to a very small area and can only talk with those directly on either side, or occasionally across the line. Moreover, since most workers dislike the job or feel, at best, indifferent to it, they're not particularly interested in making friendships which carry over after their shift is over. Most of them want to get away from every aspect of the job at quitting time.

What makes the jobs endurable?

The pay is considerably higher than it is in most semiskilled jobs that are more interesting. The jobs make limited physical and minimal mental demands on the occupant, leaving the worker comparatively fresh for his or her real life once the shift on the assembly line is finished. And there's always the freedom to fantasize, since assembly-line jobs make few demands on the employee's attention span.

Of course, not all mass-production workers wear blue collars. In many clerical operations, the eye can take in literally hundreds of desks and work tables. The jobs are minutely described, broken down into mechanized short-cycle tasks requiring such tools as card-punchers or typewriters, and they are time-studied just as their counterparts on the factory floor. Also, there's the same continuous pressure to make the standard.

Small wonder that many clerical employees derive few satisfactions from the job itself. For example, here's part of a self-description provided by an office worker in a large insurance company: "As an operator, I had to complete 720 units in four hours with no more than eleven errors. This quota was often very difficult to meet, especially on nights when the packs were of more than average difficulty. The job was extremely boring." Whatever satisfactions the person derived were social and associational. For the vast majority, the jobs are temporary positions which they soon expect to leave.

CONTINUOUS-PROCESS AUTOMATION: AN EXCEPTION

Continuous-process automation affords significant exceptions to the lack of built-in satisfactions in fragmented blue- and white-collar jobs.

Continuous-process automation occurs in industries, such as chemicals and petroleum, in which the product flows continuously from entering raw material to finished product through a number of interlinked stages. In these plants, the employee spends much time monitoring gauges and control instruments and handling breakdowns, start-ups, and changeovers. The skills required are not necessarily greater, but as Walker commented in his study of an automatic rolling mill, they are different in kind: "of the head rather than of the hand; of logician rather than craftsman; of nerve rather than muscle; of pilot rather than manual worker; of maintenance man, not operator." The work cycles are long, and the employee retains some control over the work rhythms. In breakdowns, it frequently takes a great deal of skill to remedy the stoppage, and in between, employees derive satisfaction from being responsible for keeping some very complex and expensive machinery in good working and running order. Employees also see themselves progressing on career ladders that naturally evolve as they gain experience and express a willingness to accept responsibility. The top crew-chief positions involve enormous responsibility and challenge.

Let's consider the case of the worker's soup described by Blauner as an illustration of the difference between the auto assembly line and continuous-process technology. A chemical operator mentioned that he often warmed up a can of soup on a hot plate in the automated control room— *a procedure requiring perhaps 10 minutes*. What if the soup is ready when the operator is about to make his round of instrument readings—something that takes 30 minutes? "You can eat the soup first and do the work later, or you can take the readings earlier than scheduled, in order to have the soup when it's hot" was the operator's reply. The auto-assembly-line worker, by contrast, who wanted a bowl of soup would have to wait for his allotted relief time, purchase his soup from a vending machine, and probably gulp it down on the run on his way back from the lavatory—relief times being both fixed and brief.

In summary, continuous-process automation is the opposite of Taylorism and the specialization of labor. The latter tries to make the job something that anyone can do by breaking it down to its smallest common denominators and, ideally, assigning one element to one worker. Continuous-process automation, on the other hand, looks at the work process as a whole and utilizes the actual abilities of the rank-and-file worker to integrate jobs, not fractionate them.

IMPROVING THE QUALITY OF WORKING LIFE

So far, we have talked about the limits imposed by technology on the satisfaction of employee needs as if they were immutably fixed and could not be changed. The truth is much different. Many organizations have redesigned jobs within the framework of the existing technology in order to make them more meaningful to their employees, or have made other changes in the circumstances of work intended to make the job more interesting or to give the employee more initiative or control.

Why have they taken the trouble? Social consciousness or philanthropic instincts have played little or no part in most managements' decisions.

The growing dissatisfaction of a better-educated, more youthful work force with higher job expectations than can be fulfilled by the monotonous, simplistic, programmed jobs into which many of them have been slotted has given rise to the by now notorious "blue-collar blues"— although obviously such jobs are not the monopoly of blue-collar occupations. Improvement in the quality of work life over the past five years has assumed the status of an international movement. Symposia, conferences, dozens of books (including *Work in America*, with the imprimatur of the U.S. Deputy of Health, Education, and Welfare), and hundreds of articles have depicted the present situation, frequently in melodramatic terms, or have described the success stories in which jobs have been made more meaningful in terms that sometimes have been Pollyannaish or just plain wrong.

Just how discontented is the work force? How real are the blue-collar blues? Do they exist largely in the minds of their self-appointed champions and representatives? It's hard to tell. Empirical data on attitudes are thin and contradictory. The best estimate is that there is overall some increase in discontent, although not nearly as much as some of our secular theologians would have us believe. Furthermore, there are pockets of major discontent where you would expect them— among younger, better-educated workers performing routine duties.

Maybe, as one of the authors of this book has argued, young workers resent the discipline enforced by assembly-line work more than they do the job's lack of meaning. Still the discontent is real. Turnover in one automobile plant, for example, exceeded 100 percent in a single year. When General Motors designed its Lordstown, Ohio, plant and pared the average time per job activity to 36 seconds, it claimed that employees would not work any harder (because of added improvements, including robots that performed some especially onerous tasks)—merely faster. The employees themselves apparently felt otherwise. For a while, the assembly line had to be shut down for a half day in order to repair the defects, some of them certainly consciously inflicted, that appeared on cars that went to final assembly during the first half of the day. As one worker put it, "You're always waiting for the line to break down." Sometimes reality justifies revolt.

Of course, Lordstown is an exaggerated case of work division and speedup, as auto assembly lines in general are extreme instances of the division of labor in industry. Extreme but not unique. Many jobs possess the same characteristics of working on an automobile assembly line, only to a lesser degree. They, too, are repetitive, monotonous, meaningless, rigidly programmed, and devoid of challenge. And in some organizations, management has attempted to make these jobs more meaningful—with varying degrees of success—because it was convinced that the time, effort, and expense would pay off on the bottom line.

The other satisfactions and incentives present in any job situation— including money as it's presently used (we would argue, misused)— are real enough. But at best they are motivators to stay on the job, to show up for work most days, to contribute what the employee defines and what the company pretty much has to put up with as a fair day's work. On the other hand, if you make the job itself more interesting and more challenging, if you give the worker more control over the job and more responsibility for performing it, you might actually provide the motivation to do more work, better work—or both.

Of course, there are limitations to management's ability to make the job more meaningful. In some cases, reversing the process of the division of labor would be technologically unsound. No dividend gained from motivating workers can offset the savings lost. To advocate the introduction of job enrichment would be to deserve the retort Theodore Roosevelt made to union leaders who objected to using steam shovels instead of men with shovels in building the Panama Canal: "Should we dig it with teaspoons?"

Companies, such as IBM and Texas Instruments, that have been in the forefront of job enlargement have discovered in their operations a number of "stupid" jobs where job enlargement doesn't pay. In consequence, IBM uses job enlargement or job enrichment, as one IBM spokesman put it, "whenever we can"—in other words, wherever management is convinced it will pay dividends.

We may be faced with an unfortunate paradox: The very jobs that would appear to need job enrichment the most, i.e., jobs on the auto assembly line, may be uneconomic to enrich. One expert has estimated that applying job enrichment would push the cost of today's economy car to over $10,000. What about the Swedish auto companies Volvo and Saab-Scania that have introduced the team system in assembling auto engines? (Volvo also uses this system in assembling car bodies.) The analogy probably doesn't hold. The two Swedish companies faced an average absence rate—approximately 25 percent daily—that made the smooth operation of any machine-paced, continuous assembly line almost impossible. In short, the lines were constantly breaking down. Also, the operations are vastly different in size: Volvo, the larger of the two companies, assembles about one-seventh the number of cars at its Kolmar assembly plant as General Motors assembles at Lordstown. Edward N. Cole, former president of General Motors, who knows something about the requirements of mass production and has visited both Volvo and Saab-Scania, describes them as job shops and dismisses the analogy. At least under present conditions, it would appear that the economies made possible by the minute division of labor on the auto assembly line would continue to more than offset whatever productivity is lost because some employees resent the job and do poor-quality work or quit and have to be replaced.

Job Enrichment

What changes in work methods and procedures do we have in mind? Nothing we're talking about is very new. Many companies have tried one or all of them with a considerable measure of success.

Let's begin with job enlargement and a story about the late Thomas Watson of IBM. He approached a middle-aged woman on the assembly line in Endicott, New York, in the early 1940s and asked her an unusual question: "What don't you like about your job?" "Doing the same thing over and over again," was her frank response—Mr. Watson had apparently caught her off guard. It led IBM to pioneer job enrichment and make most IBM operators responsible for both setup and inspection of their jobs. The result: generally improved operator efficiency, fewer errors, and fewer inspections.

In other instances, IBM enlarged the scope of the actual production job. For example, it decided it would get better results at its Lexington, Kentucky, typewriter plant by having one person put together an entire tab mechanism for the machines rather than the six who had done the job previously.

Why does it work?

The explanation for the improvement you won't find surprising. Since specialization uses only a small portion of most workers' abilities, many employees respond to job enrichment because it makes their tasks more interesting and intellectually more challenging. If you make the workers responsible for quality, as IBM has done, you also give them autonomy and develop their sense of responsibility.

Texas Instruments in its "Meaningful Work Program" has gone several steps beyond IBM with job enlargement. In addition to doing their own testing and inspecting, many TI workers daily set their own quality and quantity goals—with results that management finds very satisfactory. In some instances, TI has experimented with giving workers almost complete control over jobs, delegating to them responsibilities for planning, organizing, and controlling their work that are usually monopolized by management. These experiments have, at times, produced spectacular results.

One such success occurred with a group of women assembling a complex instrument. At the beginning of the experiment, it took an average of 138 hours to assemble a single unit. In a problem-solving meeting, the women came up with many ideas for improving work methods, including a rearrangement of the assembly procedures. All of them were adopted. Subsequently, they set their own production standard for the unit—86 hours. Unknown to them, industrial engineering had determined on a standard of 100 hours. They made it in 76 hours. After a second problem-solving session and the introduction of still more employee suggestions, the goal was reset at 65 hours—this time, they did the assembling in 59. Later, they got the assembly time down to 32 hours. Some improvement from 138 hours! Nor was this the only benefit. Absenteeism, turnover, learning time, employee complaints, and trips to the health center all fell off.

Some reservations
Not all attempts at job enlargement have worked out nearly so well—at Texas Instruments or anywhere else. At times, most of the problem lay with some of the employees whose jobs were being enriched. They liked their old routines and disliked their new responsibilities. The duller-witted among them probably found the old job as much of a challenge as they could handle, and the rest were lazy, indifferent, or had been conditioned too long to adjust successfully to the change.

In one survey of assembly-line operators conducted by Professor Kilbridge of the Harvard Business School, he found that over half the sample preferred smaller assembly tasks, 37 percent were indifferent to the size of the task, and only 12 percent preferred larger tasks. Mechanical pacing was not distasteful to the majority of workers with whom he talked. What we can't know, of course, is to what extent their reactions were based on anxiety about the unknown and how different their reactions might have been had their jobs been enriched and had they been asked to make a before-and-after comparison. Another study of assembly-line workers at a pharmaceutical plant found that they liked their jobs on the assembly line, but two years after the change to a whole-job approach wherein each employee secured the materials, performed nine operations, and did the final inspection, employees indicated their reluctance to return to the old method.

Also, as Professors Turner and Lawrence of the Harvard Business School have warned, managements shouldn't introduce job enlargement and simultaneously diminish other job satisfactions. They cite an instance where fifteen workers on a rotary conveyor were given work stations surrounded by high banks of parts, and each was assigned to assemble the total product according to a carefully predetermined method and sequence. This particular form of job enrichment emphasized variety at the expense of autonomy and the opportunity to interact with coworkers—and it failed, for obvious reasons.

Sometimes the problem with job enlargement lay in an overall climate that didn't support the enrichment of the job. Foulkes quotes an official at Texas Instruments on the reason why its Meaningful Work Program sometimes succeeded but sometimes failed: "Many times the behavior of top and middle management ran counter to the value of the Meaningful Work Program and thus TI was not getting the necessary mileage out of the program." The point he made could be generalized to include any effort at job enrichment. The program must be consistent with the overall plant or office system, of which it, after all, forms only a part. If the employees, for example, are given more so-called responsibility but their supervisor insists on inspecting every piece of work, they will see the program for the empty gesture that the supervisor has made out of it, and the consequences for motivation and performance are more likely to be negative than positive.

Finally, companies need to remember that cultural factors can influence the way in which an employee will respond to job enrichment. In general, urban workers appear to be more alienated from their jobs than workers from rural settings and therefore are less likely to respond positively to efforts at job enrichment.

Professors Turner and Lawrence conducted a study that determined the reactions of a large number of workers to six "requisite task attributes": (1) variety, (2) autonomy, (3) required social interaction, (4) opportunities for social interaction, (5) knowledge and skill required, and (6) responsibility. They expected a positive relationship between these six attributes and employee satisfaction and attendance on the job. Their actual findings were quite different. Only workers from factories in small towns exhibited the reactions they had expected. In urban settings, reported satisfactions were less with jobs that scored high on the six factors (combined into a Requisite Task Attribute Index), while attendance was unrelated.

A subsequent study by Hulin and Blood developed the same general thesis. When workers were alienated from the middle-class work ethic (defined in part as "a belief in the intrinsic value of hard work, a striving for the attainment of responsible positions"), as was likely to be true of Lawrence and Turner's urban workers, they would be unlikely to respond positively to attempts at job enrichment. With growing urbanization, the implication is clear: The appeal of job enrichment may already have peaked. Perhaps. Certainly organizations need to be reminded that job enrichment is not for everyone. With urban workers, especially those in factories, they should consider a modification in their overall strategy of job enrichment, emphasizing factors such as autonomy and loose supervision and playing down others such as variety and responsibility.

INDIVIDUALIZE JOB ENRICHMENT

We just said that job enrichment is not for everyone. And we weren't guessing. What happened at Motorola when employees were given the chance of remaining on the traditional assembly line or assembling the whole product on a bench by themselves? Half of the sixty workers chose to stay on the assembly line—remember that we are talking about an urban plant setting. At Saab-Scania, where three-person teams do the final assembly on engines, they had this option: Each worker could assemble one-third of the engine (a 10-minute operation) or the whole engine (a 30-minute operation). (Incidentally, the comparable time for each job task on the assembly line at Saab-Scania had been 1.8 minutes.) Only a minority chose to assemble the entire engine. A comparable experiment at assembling entire truck engines was abandoned at the employees' request because they found the task too complex (there were 1500 parts) and too time-consuming. Each engine took 6 hours to assemble.

The classic case is that of Non-Linear Systems, a small West Coast electronics manufacturer. The president, Andrew Kay, had the assembly line dismantled and made each worker responsible for the total product on which he or she was working from setup to inspection. With what result? Only a minority of the employees wanted the responsibility for putting a whole instrument together. Most of them preferred something in between their previous small jobs and the new vastly expanded responsibilities that they had been assigned. To solve the problem, Kay reorganized the production groups and left the decision on the span of responsibility up to the individual worker. Of course, what we have no way of knowing is whether the story would have been different if Kay had increased the amount of responsibility gradually.

Nevertheless, after five years the experiment ended in failure. Factory departments continued to exercise a large degree of autonomy in scheduling work, but many other participative features were scrapped: Direct supervision was provided; specific duties and responsibilities were assigned; standards of performance and quality were re-established; authority was delegated to be commensurate with responsibility; and remuneration was related to effort.

Why was the experiment abandoned? Because it failed to live up to expectations. One important point: Productivity per employee hour had not increased. In fact, while overall output had increased by 30 percent, the number of employees had increased by 42 percent over the same period. A behavioral scientist employed by Non-Linear Systems from the beginning of the experiment commented, "I think we know now that human relations don't have a lot to do with profit and productivity."

These three stories point to two morals, the obvious one being that people vary considerably in their response to job enrichment. The other moral suggests an ideal goal for job enrichment: Let the employee decide whether he or she wants his or her higher-order on-the-job needs to be satisfied and in what ways. Forcing someone into an enriched job is likely to have the reverse of the hoped-for results—increased absenteeism, poorer quality, and lower output.

Employee participation in determining the shape of job enrichment runs into a couple of roadblocks, both of them ultimately ideological rather than logical. First, the "high priest" of job enrichment (United States branch of the faith) Fred Herzberg says that it should not be done because "direct involvement (by employees) contaminates the process with human relations hygiene." Second, wherever it has been done, the results were disappointing. Certainly most attempts at job enrichment in the United States have been unilaterally imposed with little or no employee participation. As one employee caught up in a job enrichment program commented, "They're dictating to me again, but this time about how I should take more responsibility and initiative for changing the organization's goals."

The picture is complicated. In Europe, where employee participation in determining the content of job enrichment programs has been the rule rather than the exception, some programs, like Volvo's, have succeeded while others have failed. In his study of eight radical experiments on job redesign, all of which featured much employee participation in determining the form of job enrichment, Richard Walton found that six experiments reported quality improvement and more efficient production due to decreased scrap, less downtime, or more efficient methods. Also, most companies reported reduced turnover and absentee rates. Of the six success stories, however, only two occurred in the United States—Corning Glass in Medfield, Massachusetts, and Gaines Dog Food in Topeka, Kansas.

38

What can be said about the relationship between employee participation in a job enrichment program and its long-term success? Nothing conclusive. Certainly Fred Herzberg's dictum is unwarranted. We suspect that it arose more through the fear of offending many managements by associating job enrichment with the modification of what is traditionally regarded as management prerogatives. Herzberg, after all, is a consultant as well as an academic, and job enrichment has proved to be a highly salable concept. It does appear that the success of job enrichment programs over the long run depends more on factors outside the unit experimenting with the job enrichment program. Walton lists six crucial factors: (1) internal consistency in the original design, (2) continued support from levels of management above the experimental unit, (3) continued service of leaders, operators, or consultants directly associated with the project, (4) absence of stress and crisis that lead to more authoritarian management, (5) good relations between the innovative unit and other parts of the organization, and (6) diffusion to other parts of the organization.

A NEW APPROACH TO JOB ENRICHMENT

The most recent, the most comprehensive, and, we believe, the most convincing approach to job enrichment is the one recently developed by Professor Richard Hackman of Yale and his associates. They have identified five core characteristics of jobs that will motivate people to be high performers as well as five strategies for endowing jobs with these five dimensions.

The five core dimensions are

1 *Skill Variety.* Obviously the degree to which the job requires the employee to utilize a number of skills and abilities.
2 *Task Identity.* The degree to which the job involves the completion of a whole and identifiable task. It is clearly more meaningful, for example, to assemble a complete toaster than to endlessly attach electrical cords.
3 *Task Significance.* To take an extreme case, it is more significant to work on the space module for a moon landing, even on a lowly job, than it is to fill small boxes with paper clips.
4 *Autonomy.* The degree to which the worker has discretion in scheduling work and deciding how to carry it out.
5 *Feedback.* Does the employee get frequent answers—answers that

can be trusted—to the question, "How am I doing?" In other words, feedback is most powerful when it comes directly from the work.

The five parallel strategies for changing the job to make it more meaningful are

1 *Form natural work units.* These can promote the employee's sense of "ownership"—a sense of continuing responsibility for an identifiable piece of work. Doing so plugs in two of the core dimensions: task identity and task significance.
2 *Combine tasks.* Wherever possible, combine fractionalized tasks to form larger job assignments. At the Corning Glass plant in Medfield, for example, each hot plate is now assembled from beginning to end by one operator. Again, task combination fosters task identity.
3 *Establish client relationships.* Wherever possible, put the employee in direct touch with the user of the product or service. This expands three core dimensions—feedback, skill variety, and autonomy. For example, let the employee handle customer complaints or requests for information directly rather than going through the supervisor.
4 *Vertical loading.* Give the rank-and-file employee responsibilities and controls traditionally reserved for a supervisor. For example, give an employee greater discretion in setting schedules, deciding on work methods, checking on quality, and so on. Obviously, autonomy is the core dimension expanded by vertical loading.
5 *Open feedback channels.* The high payoff from this strategy comes by enabling the worker to learn about performance while doing the job rather than from management on a when-they-think-of-it basis. Job-provided feedback is more immediate and objective than supervisor-supplied feedback. Moreover, it increases the employee's feeling of personal control over his or her work.

Does the strategy work in practice? Hackman and others cite one example of a nothing job, a keypunch operation, at the Travelers Insurance Company with no skill variety, nonexistent task identity, invisible task significance, and no autonomy or feedback. Job changes included all five strategies for increasing the core dimensions. Each operator was given the continuing responsibility for certain accounts, and each operator was given direct contact with clients in other departments. In addition to client feedback, each operator was given additional sources of feedback—for example, an operator receives directly on a weekly basis a computer printout of his or her errors and productivity. Under vertical loading, operators set their own schedules and planned their own work as long as they met predetermined standards.

All in all, twenty changes were made in the job—with highly gratifying results. Among other benefits, productivity rose almost 40 percent, the number of operators with poor performance dropped from 11.1 percent to 5.5 percent, while absenteeism dropped 24.1 percent. Over the short run, at least, the substantial enrichment of a nothing job had paid off handsomely.

Hackman and his associates offer a few caveats. They concur with the other experts that not everyone wants his or her job enriched. People with low growth needs are likely to resent and resist having themselves or their jobs stretched. The question is whether low growth needs reflect some innate psychological predisposition or are more the reflection of ten or twenty years spent on a stultifying job. Hackman favors the latter reason, although he concedes that it is not known whether the growth need can be reactivated after years on a growth-depressing job. In any event, he is all for an organization giving the employee a chance to find out.

Hackman also recognizes that many organizations are not in a position to change jobs to provide all the core dimensions wherever they are missing. His general belief is that a job can be low in two or three dimensions and still be perceived by the employee as meaningful if it is sufficiently high in the other dimensions. And he picks out vertical loading as the most crucial of the five job design strategies, because "In some cases, where it has been impossible to implement any other changes, vertical loading alone has had significant motivational effects."

WHAT CAN THE SUPERVISOR DO
ABOUT JOB ENRICHMENT?

At first blush, not very much would appear to be the correct answer. Most of the job enrichment strategies advocated by Hackman, for example, involve decisions outside the scope of the typical supervisor's authority. Travelers' effort at enriching the keypunch operation was a joint undertaking by the administrative services department and an outside consultant. To be sure, the supervisors were consulted on the design changes, but they had no responsibility for the overall program.

Supervisors, however, can do something about job enrichment. First, they must always be on the alert for trouble signs in their departments—high turnover, restricted output, poor quality, excessive absenteeism, and so on. Whenever such conditions exist, they should ask themselves whether the nature of the job itself is likely to be at least one of the reasons why subordinates are unproductive and unhappy. The checklist below should help the supervisor in answering this question.

Checklist on Job Enrichment

Natural work units

1 Does the job correspond to a natural unit of work—one in which the employee can develop a sense of continuing responsibility?
2 Is there any basis for identifying the job with the person or department for whom it is performed?
3 Is work assigned randomly or naturally—in ways that promote task identity?

Combining tasks

1 Are there fractionalized tasks that can be combined into larger work units?
2 Are there tasks such as setup, inspection, verification, or checking that can be added to the existing work units?
3 Are there possibilities for assigning the responsibility for a new, larger task to a small team of workers?

Establishing client relationships

1 Do we know who the "client" for the workers' services is?
2 Can we establish direct contact between the worker and the client?
3 Can we set up criteria by which the client can judge the quality of the product or service that he or she receives?
4 Can we see to it that the client has a way of communicating his or her evaluations directly to the employee?

Vertical loading

1 Can we give the worker more responsibility in setting schedules, deciding on work methods, and helping to train and advise less experienced employees?

2 Can we give the worker more control over his or her time—when to stop and start work, take breaks, and so on?

3 Can we encourage workers to come up with problem solutions on their own rather than relying on their bosses or staff departments for the answers?

4 Can we provide the workers with more information about the financial aspects of their jobs?

Feedback channels

1 Can we place quality control close to the workers so that they get frequent direct feedback about their performances?

2 Can we provide the worker directly with standard summaries of performance records?

3 Can the computer be used to provide the workers with individual performance information that they currently receive at best second-hand?

4 Can we see to it that workers correct their own errors?

The supervisor who goes over the checklist only to find that most of the five core dimensions are largely or wholly missing from the job would do well to consider their absence as a likely source of discontent. The likelihood is increased, obviously, if other frequent sources of discontent are absent—factors such as poor working conditions, below-average pay scales, inequitable promotion policies, and so on. In other words, if the job rates high on Herzberg's hygienic factor, the chances are good that job impoverishment is the problem, and some form of job enrichment the probable solution.

Supervisors, as we have seen, are strictly limited in the initiatives they can take on their own to enrich their subordinates' jobs. But they can do something. For example, usually supervisors are free to take steps such as having workers correct their own errors, letting workers set their own breaks, encouraging workers to handle their own job problems, and providing workers directly with a copy of their performance records.

As for the rest, the supervisor is the expert on his or her own operation. It's the supervisor's responsibility to let higher management know what's wrong in his or her department and to offer some suggestions on what should be done to correct the situation. And it's an ostrich-like higher management that refuses to give these sentiments and recommendations a respectful hearing.

Job Rotation

Job rotation, as a technique for making the job more interesting and employees more valuable, is not restricted to blue-collar workers. The Boston Safe Deposit and Trust Company, for example, uses it with many clerical employees. Moreover, many companies practice it in their management-training program for recent college graduates.

An unusual case

Some applications of job rotation seem far out—but they work. Take the case of the Steelcraft Manufacturing Co., which sent draftspersons to Toronto for a week to call on architects and try to sell them on specifying its products—metal doors and frames. How did these draftspersons make out as sales representatives? They batted .500—in half the cases they were able to convince the architects to specify Steelcraft's products.

There was also a substantial bonus. The draftspersons returned to their drafting boards with a better understanding of what the firm's sales representatives were talking about when they described customers' needs, likes, and dislikes. They're no longer drawing doorways in a vacuum.

Job rotation, then, is another important technique for increasing job satisfaction and efficiency—under the proper conditions. Once again, it's necessary to hedge. Job rotation won't be appreciated and won't work with many employees if they are deeply rooted in their jobs and regard them almost as a piece of personal property, or if they work on jobs that demand no attention so that they can daydream to their hearts' content. Polaroid, where participation in the job-rotation program was optional, found that many workers—in fact, more than a majority—elected not to participate.

The truth is, there are people who would keep digging holes and filling them up again if they enjoyed the company of their fellow diggers.

The Right-sized Job

Most people get a feeling of accomplishment from completing a whole job. But if the work unit takes too long to complete, the goal is too far away to be much of a motivator. And if the natural unit is too small (such as, say, tightening a bolt), the units are too trivial to be meaningful and completing one of them doesn't give anyone a sense of accomplishment.

The question inevitably arises—how large is an optimal unit? One study suggests that it should last from an hour to an hour and a half, depending on the situation. Think of your own household chores. You may have maintained a minimal level of interest in mowing the lawn, for example, by the device of dividing it into small sections as you went along.

Many companies have applied a similar technique called "Short Interval Scheduling" (SIS) to jobs where the work is repetitive and the time required for the task is relatively short and fairly constant. SIS is a technique that replaces the usually weekly or daily job assignment with a series of smaller, short-term performance goals. The length of the interval varies according to the type of work assigned. For example, a typist might finish eleven letters and envelopes per hour, a maintenance electrician might take four hours to modernize a load center, or a draftsperson might need three hours to complete two detailed drawings of specific units. But within any category, the interval will be the same for all employees.

Employees get a sense of achievement every time they complete an assignment in less than the scheduled time, which usually happens several times a day. Some managements let the worker who finishes ahead of time sit back and take it easy, with leisure as a reward. Others offer some form of bonus pay for extra production.

CONCLUSION

Why do people work? What needs to they have that are gratified on the job? To secure the means of subsistence, to enjoy the banter and support of their coworkers, to be identified with an organization far more powerful than themselves, to make a meaningful contribution to a product they think of as important, to test their abilities on a challenging task—these are a partial catalog of the needs people hope to satisfy by work.

The potential for satisfying this galaxy of needs varies greatly from job to job. We think it's useful to distinguish between needs satisfied *on the job* and needs satisfied by *the job itself*. In a Michigan survey of 401 men, 80 percent said they would continue to work even if they inherited enough money to live comfortably, and one-third identified the socializing aspects of work as what they would miss most if they did not work. On many jobs where the work itself is trivial and monotonous, there are continuous opportunities for socializing. In other words, the absence of satisfactions from the job itself are offset, to a greater or lesser extent depending on the individual employee, by the satisfactions found on the job. Also, it's difficult to generalize about the satisfactions employees derive from the job itself. People with dull wits may find a job challenging that a more intelligent person would deem intolerable. It does indeed take all kinds to do the world's work.

Of recent years, many managements, for economic reasons, have become more and more concerned over the large number of situations in which the job itself offers minimal satisfactions. The problem, oversimplified, is that on-the-job satisfactions almost never motivate a worker to make more than an acceptable contribution—many companies have resigned themselves to a 60 percent day. Only when employees derive positive satisfactions from the job will they exert themselves and come close to realizing their full job potential. Hence, many organizations have redesigned the jobs—made them more varied or more complex, or have given the worker more control over the job and more responsibility. In fewer instances, the jobs have remained the same, but the employees have been rotated from job to job.

How have these efforts worked out? Have they accomplished their goal of motivating the worker to more and better performance?

Success stories are frequent—apparently they outnumber failures. We say apparently because the perpetrators of success tend to see that their stories get maximum exposure, while the sponsors of failures usually do their best to obscure the results.

George Strauss raises the question: "Can we ever expect workers to find self-actualization on an assembly line or in a dog food factory?" His answer is negative. We think he is both right and wrong, right as to the assembly line and wrong as to the dog food factory which enriched the jobs of all its employees in all five core dimensions, particularly that of autonomy. It's also true, as we have seen, that not all workers want more meaningful jobs, and particularly true that not all workers want more autonomy and the corresponding increase in responsibility that goes along with more autonomy.

The worker in Sweden and the Netherlands, in contrast, places a higher value on autonomy than the worker in the United States. Therefore, job enrichment that features increased autonomy for the employee will be more appreciated and lead to more job satisfaction than comparable efforts would in the United States. Here Huey Long's concept of a satisfying job, with allowances for the regional overtones, and the hyperbole, still makes sense: "There shall be a real job, not a little old sowbelly black-eyed pea job, but a real spending money beefsteak, gray Chevrolet/Ford in the garage, new suit, Thomas Jefferson, Jesus Christ, red-white-and-blue job for every man." The employee did then and still does, although to a progressively decreasing degree, define a satisfying job in terms of how much it pays. For a measure of the difference, take the definition of a dissatisfying job by Malin Lofgren, a 12-year-old Swedish schoolboy: "A bad job is one where others make all decisions, and you have to do what the others say."

There's another factor that explains the difference between success and failure in many job enrichment efforts. Was the supervisor's job correspondingly enriched? Was he or she given new assignments and new responsibilities to take the place of those that were assumed, in whole or in part, by subordinates? If not, there's going to be trouble. The supervisor whose job has been impoverished as the result of enriching subordinates' jobs most probably will fill the day by exercising the kind of close supervision that makes a mockery out of the best-designed, most well-intentioned job enrichment program.

As for the big picture, it's changing—and most people would agree that it's changing for the better. The assembly line hasn't vanished, but it's in full decline.

Blauner estimates that assembly-line workers in all industries make up no more than 5 percent of the total work force. In fact, there are probably more white-collar workers in clerical assembly jobs than there are assembly-line workers in factories. The crucial trend is away from low-skilled manual occupations of every kind that offer few intrinsic on-the-job satisfactions and toward jobs that provide, along with at least an adequate level of pay, a measure of satisfaction and reward from the work itself. The auto assembly line, where the level of pay substitutes for the absence of other satisfactions, is fast becoming unique.

One final word about an almost forgotten person—the rank-and-file employee's boss. We've pretty much neglected this subject, in large part, because we're going to have so much to say about the boss in the pages that follow. We've stressed the importance of the demands inherent in the job in defining and limiting the satisfactions possible from the job—and we're not about to retract our emphasis. The supervisor works within the same framework as subordinates, but within that framework, there is much he or she can do to increase or diminish whatever satisfactions employees derive from the job. His or her actions, in fact, add a dimension to the motivational picture. All other things being equal, loyalty, affection, and respect for the supervisor can motivate employees to turn in a better performance. Reverse the picture and the supervisor's actions will act as a demotivator.

Take Elton Mayo's classic study of workers in a Southern California aircraft factory. Absenteeism was generally high throughout the plant and production generally low. A few departments in which the opposite was true stood out. When Mayo investigated, he found the explanation to be the way the supervisors in the successful departments managed: They spent most of their time facilitating the work of their subordinates, acting as buffers between them and higher management, listening sympathetically to whatever complaints they had. In short, the supervisor always has an impact on motivation and performance. Sometimes it's decisive.

THE ARROW PLASTICS COMPANY: A CASE STUDY

The Arrow Plastics Company, located in Traverse City, Michigan, is a small (200 employees), family-owned business with a record of forty years of profitable operation. Using injection-molding equipment, it manufactures both high-volume and custom-order small plastic parts for use by equipment and computer manufacturers. The company recently hired a new supervisor, Greg Horning, who is in his midtwenties and a graduate of a technical institute with course work in industrial engineering. This is Greg's first management position, and the case which follows each of the book's chapters describes his first six months on the job as supervisor of the custom-molding group.

Greg's work group, injection molding, is a part of the production department headed by Steve Phillips. Work flows from mixing (mixers, pelletizers, extruders; headed by Joe Barber) to molding to shipping. His group includes a day crew and a night-shift crew, but Greg spends most of his time with employees who work on days. Among the key employees are:

Molders:
Alfred Cameron
Henry Creegmore (who had expected to be named supervisor and who is very influential among the work group)
Phil Martello (union steward)
Ted Kilpatrick (the most senior employee)
Rick Cohn (the youngest employee)
Inspectors:
Jeannette Greely
Helen Kowalski

The other parts of the organization with which Greg must work, the staff departments, are the following:

Industrial engineering: Frank Granto, manager
Personnel: Albert Sykes, manager
Maintenance and materials handling: Ed Brisco, manager

THE EDUCATION
OF GREG HORNING:
JANUARY 15

Greg Horning thought he knew what he was up against when he had been hired to supervise the injection-molding department at Arrow Plastics. Steve Phillips, the production manager, was not an overly communicative man, but Greg had gotten the picture. Phillips had decided to go outside the department—in fact, outside the plant altogether—to replace the old supervisor when he had retired. The crew had been spoiled under him, and Phillips wanted fresh young blood to turn it around.

"The shop puts out 85 percent of standard now," Phillips told Greg. "Without busting a gut, they should be making 110 percent. That's what I'm counting on you for—to get that extra 25 percent."

It was a challenge, but Greg would be able to use all the knowledge he had been cramming into his head in technical school for the past two years—he felt he could handle it.

Things had gotten off to a bad start. When Phillips had brought him into the shop on the first day, Greg had realized immediately that there was no love lost between the production manager and the men in injection molding. Phillips had introduced Greg curtly and left. The crew had listened sullen and silent, then turned their blank, unfriendly faces toward the new supervisor.

Greg hadn't expected that hostility to be directed toward him. It made him feel defensive and extremely young. He said something about having a lot to learn and counting on their help and the importance of teamwork.

"If we all play on the team," he finished lamely, "we can make this the smoothest running operation at Arrow Plastics." The crew faced him with the same unenthusiastic expressions. He hadn't blamed them—he hadn't believed what he'd said to himself. Trying to smile, and muttering something about learning how the records were kept, he escaped into his office.

And that's where he stayed during much of the week that followed. He was going to be sure of his ground before he made any moves. Reading through the records and reports that were available and watching the workers through the glass partition that separated his office from the floor, he observed the places where procedures were not being followed and where bottlenecks in the operation occurred.

There were plenty. He decided that he would start off with an obvious one—the location of the two women in the group. Jeannette Greely and Helen Kowalski, who checked the pieces that the men produced, were working close to each other rather than to the machines they inspected. By moving the women closer to the machines, he would cut down on movements and waste motion by as much, perhaps, as 25 percent. He would also cut out their steady stream of conversation. They talked constantly—Greg couldn't measure what that did to their efficiency, of course, but he was sure it didn't help.

There was no hesitation from either woman in rejecting Greg's plan for their new job stations.

"It'll never work, Mr. Horning," Jeannette declared flatly. "Now, look," Greg said, "and by the way, call me Greg—it makes much more sense than the way it is now. You see, you'll both be much nearer to your machines. The operators will be only a couple of yards away instead of 70 feet—in case you have to ask them anything."

"But you don't understand," Helen said, with a determined look. "Jeannette and I—we have to check back and forth with each other a lot. When I'm not sure if I should reject a piece, I ask what she thinks. And she asks me."

"Two heads are better than one, as they say," Jeannette added in support.

"No, no. There's no need for that." Greg's voice rose and took on an edge—he was no longer trying to be persuasive. "The standards are clearly spelled out and you women are both experienced. Of course, there will be borderline cases, but you should bring those to me, anyway. That's one of the reasons I'm here."

Greg paused, looking from Jeannette to Helen. Neither of them said anything. They had been given an order and their tight, glaring looks were sufficient to tell Greg what they thought of it. Well, he hadn't expected them to be very enthusiastic over the idea—they'd have to fit all their gossiping in at lunch—but they'd just have to get used to it.

"So we'll try it my way for a while," he said more heartily. "Once you get used to it, I'm sure you'll see how sensible it is." Starting back toward his office, Greg added, "And don't forget, my door is always open if you have any problems."

Feeling more confident now that he had taken his first step, Greg decided to go right on to the next. He stopped at Henry Creegmore's machine and asked him into his office.

"Please sit down, Henry," Greg said. Then, picking up a single-spaced mimeographed page from his desk, he handed it to Creegmore. "Does this read the same as your copy, Henry?" Greg had received job descriptions for the whole crew from the industrial-engineering department three days ago; this was a description of Creegmore's job. Glancing at the paper and then looking fixedly at the wall behind Greg, Creegmore answered.

"I guess it's the same."

"Well, I just wanted to make sure of that, Henry, because I have the impression that you don't always follow the job description."

"And?" Now Creegmore focused directly on Greg's face. Greg shifted in his chair.

"Well, Henry," he answered, "I think you should. I want you—and the others too—to stick to the descriptions from now on. After all, industrial engineering has put a lot of work and study into figuring out what's the best way to do the job. When people do things their own way instead of sticking to what the description says, production falls off."

"You've watched me and you see I'm doing things that aren't in the rules, you say. Well, how do you know my way isn't better?" Creegmore was studying the wall again.

"I don't know that, Henry. But if you feel what you're doing is an improvement, why don't you describe the changes to me in detail? I'll be happy to talk it over with industrial engineering."

"Yeah. That's nice. Very nice." Creegmore stood up and leaned over just slightly toward Greg. "Tell me. Just what makes you so certain that the industrial engineers have the right answer to everything? You accept everything they say as gospel, just like that?"

"That's their job," Greg snapped. "So, I'll take their word, at least until someone proves they're wrong. And my crew will take their word too, and follow their instructions until I tell them differently. Have I made myself clear?" Greg had raised himself up out of his chair and was leaning over the desk. Creegmore looked at him for an instant, then stepped back.

"Quite clear," he answered, his voice quiet and hard. "You're the boss. Do you have anything else you want to say to me?"

"No, Henry," Greg said, "I guess not." But, as Creegmore started toward the door, he went on. "Henry, I hope you see that I'm just trying to get this shop running more efficiently."

Without answering or looking back, Creegmore opened the door and went out.

QUESTIONS

1 If you had been in Greg's shoes, how would you have handled the opening remarks to the crew?
2 How impressive do you find Helen and Jeannette's objections to Greg? Were their reasons only rationalizations?
3 Do you feel that Greg could have handled Creegmore in a way that would have made him happy to accept his criticism? How?
4 On balance, do you feel that Greg did anything right in his encounters with the crew?

BEHAVIORAL EXERCISE

Try to recall two or three jobs which you have had and list the aspects of each job that provided you with satisfaction and the kind of satisfaction it was (for example, social experiences, sense of personal accomplishment, feeling of being useful, and so on). Also list what you didn't like about these jobs and why. Then try to rank the relative importance of the "satisfactions" and the "dissatisfactions." If you're doing this in a group, exchange lists and try to explain to each other why the lists differ and ask to what extent the lists differ because each of you is different (and likes and dislikes different things). Also discuss to what extent the differences are due to differences in the jobs. (Note: be sure to ask yourself how your reaction to the job would have been different if you thought you would be doing the same job indefinitely.)

BIBLIOGRAPHY

Davis, L., A. Cherns, and Associates, *The Quality of Working Life,* 2 vols., The Free Press, New York, 1975.
Dowling, W., "Job Redesign on the Assembly Line: Farewell to Bluecollar Blues?" *Organizational Dynamics,* 2: 51-67, Autumn 1973.
Maher, J., ed., *New Perspectives in Job Enrichment,* Van Nostrand Reinhold, Princeton, N.J., 1971.
Porter, L., E. Lawler, and R. Hackman, *Behavior in Organizations*, McGraw-Hill, New York, 1975, Chaps. 2-4.

READING

PREFACE TO THE SELECTED READINGS

At the end of each chapter, we're including a few pages written by a classic management thinker on an aspect of the topic you are studying. Which raises the question—who is a classic management thinker? But first, a comment that is not a criterion. Compared to philosophy, political science, psychology, and history, to use some examples, few first-rate minds have concerned themselves with management. Maybe it reflects the citation given each year to all graduating MBAs at the Harvard Business School that refers to management "as the youngest of the professions." Of course, no work of permanent literary or intellectual worth has emerged from the oldest of the professions either. Anyway it makes the anthologist's chores lighter.

Not to beg the question: A classic management thinker is a person, first, whose work is intrinsically first-class. He originated, not regurgitated, and what he had to say was a contribution then—and now. Second, he has achieved wide recognition among his peers and among the book-reading wing of management. Third, there is pleasure in reading him, whether it's for his preciseness, the breadth and depth of his thought, the elegance of his simplicity, or in some cases, such as Taylor and McGregor, his eloquence. Passion is not the monopoly of priests, poets, and politicians.

For each reading, in the brief space allocated, we will attempt to say a few words as to what makes him a significant thinker. Our purpose, beyond introducing the men and their ideas, is to stir some of you to read further in these men who thought deeply at what they were about.

Whitehead said, "the justification of a university was to serve as a connection between knowledge and the zest of life." We are addressing ourselves primarily to the same public about whom Whitehead was speaking. We hope that these excerpts and the book as a whole have a like justification and fulfill a similar purpose.

What Is Scientific Management?*

FREDERICK WINSLOW TAYLOR (1856-1915)

Poor Taylor. He has had a terrible press for the past generation and, as the tone of his testimony in the selection would indicate, he was very much on the defensive back in 1912. He was the

---

*Reprinted by permission of the publishers from Frederick W. Taylor, *Scientific Management*, Harper and Bros., New York, 1947, pp. 77-80.

Excerpt from testimony of Frederick W. Taylor at hearings before the Special Committee of the House of Representatives to Investigate the Taylor and Other Systems of Shop Management, January 25, 1912, pages 1387-1389.

prototype of all efficiency experts, the father of time-and
motion study, the man who dehumanized factory work by breaking
each job down into the smallest possible components, thereby
robbing it of the slightest interest or challenge for any sentient
worker.

Not at all, Taylor would have responded—and did on many
occasions. The division of labor permitted laborers to devote all
their energies to performing the work at hand: thinking was practically excluded. Furthermore, because the worker was on incentive,
the more he produced, the more he got paid. Of course, management got higher profits because of the increased productivity. In
Taylor's system there were no losers: Time-and-motion study ensured that things were done "the one best way" at the "one best
speed"; the worker was spared the burden of thinking about what
was being done and made more money to boot; management had
the satisfaction derived from efficient planning—and larger profits.

Taylor's ideas had tremendous appeal and wide application: the
lesson of the famous Schmidt, who weighed in at 130 pounds, but
nonetheless, using Taylor's methods consistently loaded 47 tons of
pig iron per day versus the prevalent 12.5 tons, was not lost on a
generation of employers. Scientific management became the religion
of efficiency, with Taylor as high priest, and Henry Ford as lord
high practitioner.

What went wrong? Why did the movement run out of steam? To
what extent were its deficiencies inherent in Taylor's ideas? A few
suggestions. Taylor's view of the laborer—and for that matter the
executive too—as a purely economic animal was always a partial
view. His belief that the increased wages made possible by the
division of labor would more than offset any loss caused by a
shrinkage of the intrinsic interest of the job was never as generally
palatable as Taylor assumed and became progressively less acceptable to the better-educated blue-collar worker with higher
expectations in the two generations after him. In short, there were
never as many Schmidts as Taylor had assumed and they became
in increasingly short supply.

Beyond that, Taylor's ideas were appropriated by many so-called
efficiency experts who in the name of scientific management did
institute speedups and exploit workers—by almost anyone's standards. Scientific management, and Taylor, got an undeserved bad
name in the process.

Most important, technology passed Taylor by. The times had
been ripe for Taylor in the 1890s. One hundred years before, Eli
Whitney of cotton-gin fame had put forth pretty much the same
ideas, but he was decidedly premature. Today it's only in assembly-line operations, which now account for a small fraction of total

factory production, that the minute division of labor still makes economic sense. In other words, the same logic of efficiency that once carried the day for Taylorism has dethroned it.

Taylor belongs more to the past than any other of our classic thinkers. However, his is an important voice of a past that is still with us. On this ground alone he is worth reading. The task is easy; all his key works have been assembled in *Scientific Management*, Harper and Bros., New York, 1947.

Scientific management is not any efficiency device, not a device of any kind for securing efficiency; nor is it any bunch or group of efficiency devices. It is not a new system of figuring costs; it is not a new scheme of paying men; it is not a piecework system; it is not a bonus system; it is not a premium system; it is no scheme for paying men; it is not holding a stop watch on a man and writing things down about him; it is not time study; it is not motion study nor an analysis of the movements of men; it is not the printing and ruling and unloading of a ton or two of blanks on a set of men and saying, "Here's your system, go use it." It is not divided foremanship or functional foremanship; it is not any of the devices which the average man calls to mind when scientific management is spoken of. The average man thinks of one or more of these things when he hears the words "scientific management" mentioned, but scientific management is not any of these devices. I am not sneering at cost-keeping systems, at time study, at functional foremanship, nor at any new and improved scheme of paying men, not at any efficiency devices, if they are really devices that make for efficiency. I believe in them; but what I am emphasizing is that these devices in whole or in part are not scientific management; they are useful adjuncts to scientific management, so are they also useful adjuncts of other systems of management.

Now, in its essence, scientific management involves a complete mental revolution on the part of the workingman engaged in any particular establishment or industry—a complete mental revolution on the part of these men as to their duties toward their work, toward their fellow men, and toward their employees. And it involves ths equally complete mental revolution on the part of those on the management's side—the foremen, the superintendent, the owner of the business, the board of directors—a complete mental revolution on their part as to their duties toward their fellow workers in the management, toward their workmen, and toward all of their daily problems. And without this complete mental revolution on both sides scientific management does not exist.

That is the essence of scientific management, this great mental revolution. Now, later on, I want to show you more clearly what I mean by this great mental revolution. I know that it perhaps sounds to you like nothing but bluff—like buncombe—but I am going to try and make clear to you just what this great mental revolution involves, for it does involve an immense change in the minds and attitude of both sides, and the greater part of what I shall say today has relation to the bringing about of this great mental revolution. So that whether the details may be interesting or uninteresting, what I hope you will see is that this great change in attitude and viewpoint must produce results which are magnificent for both sides, just as fine for one as for the other. Now, perhaps I can make clear to you at once one of the very great changes in outlook which come to the workmen, on the one hand, and to those in the management on the other hand.

I think it is safe to say that in the past a great part of the thought and interest both of the men, on the side of the management, and of those on the side of the workmen in manufacturing establishments has been centered upon what may be called the proper division of the surplus resulting from their joint efforts, between the management on the one hand, and the workmen on the other hand. The management have been looking for as large a profit as possible for themselves, and the workmen have been looking for as large wages as possible for themselves, and that is what I mean by the division of the surplus. Now, this question of the division of the surplus is a very plain and simple one (for I am announcing no great fact in political economy or anything of that sort). Each article produced in the establishment has its definite selling price. Into the manufacture of this article have gone certain expenses, namely, the cost of materials, the expenses connected with selling it, and certain indirect expenses, such as the rent of the building, taxes, insurance, light and power, maintenance of machinery, interest on the plant, etc. Now, if we deduct these several expenses from the selling price, what is left over may be called the surplus. And out of this surplus comes the profit to the manufacturer on the one hand, and the wages of the workmen on the other hand. And it is largely upon the division of this surplus that the attention of the workmen and of the management has been centered in the past. Each side has had its eye upon this surplus, the working man wanting as large a share in the form of wages as he could get, and the management wanting as large a share in the form of profits as it could get; I think I am safe in saying that in the past it has been in the division of this surplus that the great labor troubles have come between employers and employees.

Frequently, when the management have found the selling price going down they have turned toward a cut in the wages—toward reducing the workman's share of the surplus—as their way of getting out whole, of preserving their profits intact. While the workman (and you can hardly blame him) rarely feels willing to relinquish a dollar of his wages, even in dull times, he wants to keep all that he has had in the past, and when busy times come again very naturally he wants to get more. Thus it is over this division of the surplus that most of the troubles have arisen; in the extreme cases this has been the cause of serious disagreements and strikes. Gradually the two sides have come to look upon one another as antagonists, and at times even as enemies—pulling apart and matching the strength of the one against the strength of the other.

The great revolution that takes place in the mental attitude of the two parties under scientific management is that both sides take their eyes off of the division of the surplus as the all-important matter, and together turn their attention toward increasing the size of the surplus until this surplus becomes so large that it is unnecessary to quarrel over how it shall be divided. They come to see that when they stop pulling against one another, and instead both turn and push shoulder to shoulder in the same direction, the size of the surplus created by their joint efforts is truly astounding. They both realize that when they substitute friendly cooperation and mutual helpfulness for antagonism and strife they are together able to make this surplus so enormously greater than it was in the past that there is ample room for a large increase in wages for the workmen and an equally great increase in profits for the manufacturer. This, gentlemen, is the beginning of the great mental revolution which constitutes the first step toward scientific management. It is along this line of complete change in the mental attitude of both sides; of the substitution of peace for war; of the substitution of hearty brotherly cooperation for contention and strife; of both pulling hard in the same direction instead of pulling apart; of replacing suspicious watchfulness with mutual confidence; of becoming friends instead of enemies; it is along this line, I say, that scientific management must be developed.

The substitution of this new outlook—this new viewpoint—is of the very essence of scientific management, and scientific management exists nowhere until after this has become the central idea of both sides; until this new idea of cooperation and peace has been substituted for the old idea of discord and war.

This change in the mental attitude of both sides toward the "surplus" is only a part of the great mental revolution which occurs under scientific management. I will later point out other elements of this mental revolution. There is, however, one more change in viewpoint which is absolutely essential to the existence of scientific management. Both sides must recognize as essential the substitution of exact scientific investigation and knowledge for the old individual judgment or opinion, either of the workman or the boss, in all matters relating to the work done in the establishment. And this applies both as to the methods to be employed in doing the work and the time in which each job should be done.

Scientific management cannot be said to exist, then, in any establishment until after this change has taken place in the mental attitude of both the management and the men, both as to their duty to cooperate in producing the largest possible surplus and as to the necessity for substituting exact scientific knowledge for opinions or the old rule of thumb or individual knowledge.

These are the two absolutely essential elements of scientific management.

3

SELECTION, ORIENTATION, AND TRAINING

LEARNING OBJECTIVES
1 Know how to separately assess a job applicant's technical proficiency, aptitudes, and motivation-personality characteristics.
2 Be able to perform a productive preemployment interview and aid a potential employee to decide whether or not the organizational position is one for which he or she would be both suited and satisfied.
3 Know the importance of and how to handle orientation.
4 Be able to apply the principles of learning and reinforcement theory to facilitate employee training.
5 Learn how perceptive managers can counter the minority employee's fear of failure and discrimination. Know what supervisory behavior is likely to be interpreted as distrust and discrimination.
6 Learn how to provide nondiscriminatory employment opportunities.

In many ways managers control their destiny. By helping to determine who will work in the department and by influencing the employee's first experiences, managers go a long way toward determining the skills and motivation of the work force. Therefore selection, orientation (helping the new employee to adjust), and training are critical managerial skills.

WHO MAKES THE HIRING DECISION?

Organizations vary substantially in terms of who has the authority to hire. In a large organization, the personnel department may do advance screening, and only send to the supervisor applicants who do reasonably well on tests and whose formal applications show relevant experience. Personnel may also undertake the reference checks. In addition, the supervisor's boss may want to interview an applicant that the supervisor wants to hire. In some cases higher levels of the organization are much involved in hiring but will hire only an applicant previously approved by the supervisor. In any event, the supervisor plays a key, if not predominant, role in the hiring process.

Selecting the New Employee

How does the manager predict how a job applicant will actually behave on the job? A good question. The answer is that it can't be done with precision, but a lot can be learned about how to do it well.

Background

What is relatively easy to discover is the kind of training the employee has had through formal schooling, extra courses, and previous jobs. While the objective facts tell the manager a good deal about the prospective skills and experiences the applicant has been exposed to, they need judicious interpretation.

Course titles and job titles can be misleading or ambiguous, so the manager must seek to ascertain more specifically what technical skills and knowledge the job applicant has acquired. The following are possible questions a supervisor can ask an applicant.

You did drafting at Corbett's. Tell me something about the kind of drawings you actually did.

What elements did they cover in that computer languages course that you took?

Tell me what a typical day was like as an assistant to the toy buyer?

Technical tests and reference checks

In most cases the manager needs to go beyond the applicant's statement for information. For many jobs there are standardized *achievement* tests that involve sampling the individual's skills by means of written questions or actual tasks. Thus the ability to program, read blueprints, calculate discounts, and the like can be "tested" by school-like examinations or by having the applicant actually do some job-oriented tasks, such as typing a sample letter.

When an applicant has had previous job experience, performance should be checked with former employers. Since letters of reference often are vague or even deliberately inflated, it's best to call or visit with someone who has worked closely with the applicant. Here the manager should be careful not to ask broad, general questions such as, "Would you tell me what you think of Ms. Lucido's laboratory skills." Instead, ask questions that require judgment and discrimination.

What tasks did Ms. Lucido excel at and what tasks did she have difficulty performing?

What was her relative rank in her group as to quality and quantity of work?

Reflecting on her work in your organization, what kind of job would she do best; what jobs should she avoid?

Of course, some of these questions will also get at personality and motivational characteristics, but more of that later in this chapter.

Aptitude tests

There's an important distinction between what people already know and what their potential is to learn. Therefore many jobs require applicants to take various kinds of intelligence tests. Usually the employer is not interested in knowing (or paying the high cost of measuring) an applicant's actual I.Q., but instead wants to know whether Jane or Bill is relatively good at quantitative tasks, logical tasks, or understanding written ideas. There are a great variety of relatively short tests that can predict whether an individual will be good at learning new tasks involving numerical or word manipulation, programming, accounting, and so on.

Predicting motivation is far more difficult. Will the individual extend himself or herself and *try* to learn? Does he or she want to succeed? And, of course, related to motivation is: Can this individual work well in this organization? Motivation is situational. Some of us would stretch ourselves to perform well in the accounting department but would "goof off" or sulk if we wound up in Data Processing.

Personality and motivation tests

While many tests do a good job of predicting skills and knowledge, most tests do not do as well predicting personality or motivation. To be sure, there are personality tests designed for use in preemployment, but they are unreliable. As we shall discuss later, current governmental regulations also forbid the use of any selection procedure that may discriminate against any segment in our society. Because personality tests are frequently unreliable, it may be difficult to justify their use.[1]

Nevertheless, a manager has good reasons for wanting to know how an individual will fit into the work situation. Someone who has the right qualifications but after hiring turns out to be absent often, frequently hostile, or unwilling to be cooperative with fellow workers will be a source of endless trouble and decreased departmental effectiveness.

Interviewing

Interviewing is widely utilized to observe the applicant "in action." A manager needs skill in getting the other person to be open, and self-restraint in order to resist the impulse to stereotype the applicant. One key point is to avoid dominating the conversation. The manager should watch carefully to see how the other person engages in give and take. Is the applicant able to be somewhat flexible—at times giving a lengthy explanation, at other times being brief and to the point? (Difficult personalities show themselves in constant long-windedness or in the inability to be more than curt or laconic.)

A good interviewer also probes for past behavior, inducing the applicant to describe personal reactions to authority, pressure, and challenges in previous job or school situations. Some helpful questions are:

---

[1]This can also apply to those aptitude tests we previously discussed unless the employer can prove (1) that the aptitude being measured is absolutely essential to job performance, and (2) that the test does a good job of measuring that aptitude. For example, many intelligence tests may provide a reasonable assessment of intellectual ability, but intellectual ability may not be an absolute requirement for the job.

What parts of your previous job did you do least well; what things did you like least about it?

What part of that assignment would you have liked to have spent more time on? What part did you find challenging? What part did you find boring?

Nondirective interviewing

In developing such questions, the interviewer has to use so-called nondirective skills to get the respondents to be as free and open as possible in their replies. To do this a manager should:

1 Use broad, open-ended questions that can't be answered by simple, short answers, such as "yes" or "no".
2 Keep the respondent talking by adding, when he or she stops, phrases such as, "That's very interesting; would you tell me more about what happened?" or "You say that you never went back to that customer again" (simply repeating the last phrase the respondent used, but in the form of a question). Such actions show you're interested, but do not provide the other person with clues as to what you want to hear, what pleases you, or what subjects should be avoided.
3 Avoid showing positive or negative emotion. Maintain a pleasant, reassuring, but noncommittal, posture. Be careful not to indicate shock or pleasure by facial or eye movements.
4 Refrain from interrupting, but keep mental notes of the areas you want to probe in depth and get the applicant to go into those areas whenever there is a natural pause in the conversation—using probes like those described in (2).

The manager must try to avoid jumping from question to question. It takes time to learn how another person thinks. Most people will reveal much more of themselves if they are allowed to ramble and keep talking. Then the manager will be able to see more of how the applicant views himself or herself. Does the applicant rationalize failure, or are difficulties always the "other person's fault"? Are the expressed goals realistic or daydreams? Is ambition backed by real drive? Is the applicant comfortable answering some questions with "I really don't know," or "That's something I have no experience with." Also an effective, ambitious, interested applicant will want to ask the manager questions and explore the job, the organization, and the potential in the situation. How thoroughly an applicant does this gives the interviewer some idea of what is important to the applicant and how well an applicant can anticipate the problems in a new situation.

Note: These nondirective techniques also will prove useful in interviewing the applicant's previous employers to learn more about what he or she was like on those jobs.

We'll have more to say about nondirective skills in Chapters 8 and 9.

Observation

One of the best ways of predicting behavior and personality is to put the person to work for a trial period and observe his or her performance carefully. The applicant could work as a part-timer for a few days or weeks, or would fill in when someone is absent. Government departments use "probationary periods" (from three months to a year), during which time the new employee can be terminated without much formality.

Needless to say, the manager has to watch himself or herself as much as the applicant. Most of us are prone to make snap judgments about other people, quickly developing strong likes or dislikes and often for extraneous reasons.

> Wow, did I ever make a mistake in hiring Chris Fubrico. He was very neatly dressed, real conservative, and couldn't have been more polite, and I like that kind of person. They're my kind of people. Well the minute Chris goes to work he starts bossing everyone in the department, barking out demands like a master sergeant.

This is called "stereotyping" or the "halo effect." Certain elements in the other individual's mannerisms or appearance can cause you to classify someone as "good" or "bad," and lead you to ignore the total person.

Promotion or Demotion?

In predicting job success, it is important to know how well the position fits the expectations and aspirations of the applicant. Often times managers are too anxious to get the best-qualified applicant who, in fact, may be overqualified for the job. The technician who has lost a $300 a week job may be willing to take a $200 job, but the chances are (after a period of unemployment) he or she will be looking around for another job very soon. The college graduate may accept a low-level clerical job, but being overqualified can lead to quick boredom and poor performance, even before the person almost inevitably quits. Ideally, the position should represent something of a promotion and be consistent with the applicant's previous training and experience.

Self-Selection

Who picks whom? Does the organization select the applicant or the applicant select the organization? Obviously it should be both. It's important for the manager to know that the applicant wants this particular job because it fits the individual's view of who they are and where they want to go. This is very different from taking a job simply because it's available or because the boss offering it is very persuasive. Thus the supervisor has an important responsibility: to give the applicant an "unvarnished," clearly understandable view of what the job entails. The supervisor should inform the applicant:

1 *What* is the actual work to be performed—what skills will be needed, roughly how will time be allocated, and what kinds of problems can arise.
2 *How* the job is performed—who will be the applicant's coworkers (and what the status relationships will be, who will outrank whom), what pressures and strains there will be, who will be giving orders, and who can be called on for help.
3 The relationship of this job to other jobs as far as promotion is concerned: where does it lead (if anyplace), and what has been the past record of promotions for those working in this position.
4 The pay and privileges that go with the position.

After giving a clear, unglamourized description of what's involved, the manager ought to be very observant as to how interested the applicant really appears. The manager ought to note carefully what questions the applicant asks about the job to assess what worries him or her. Is he or she confident that the job fits any longer-range career interests?

ORIENTING THE NEW EMPLOYEE

As a supervisor it is important to empathize with a new employee. After all a new job frequently induces anxieties. The individual may feel lost and vulnerable unless the supervisor both understands and seeks to allay these insecurities. Some newcomers will quit, and others will develop poor work habits and antagonisms that will bias their work performance for years to come (on the doubtful premise that they will stick around that long). Listen to Jane Fellows describe her first week in a large bank.

It was my second job— ever. The boss seemed cold and unavailable. He gave me some pamphlets to read, a brief description of my job, and then disappeared. Most of my fellow employees ignored me; they all seemed to have close friends and lots of gossip and work problems to exchange. I really wondered if I'd made a mistake quitting teaching for this. I was scared to turn in my first analysis; I was sure I had left some key item out for which I would be criticized. I didn't know where to get some additional data I needed. I wasn't even sure where the cafeteria was. What a miserable start!

Well, if that's the new employee's point of view, what are the supervisor's responsibilities? The most important is to be sure that what the employee first learns about the job and the organization is accurate; unlearning is painful and costly.

It took me weeks to get Rhoda to accept only a half-hour lunch. She spent most of her first day with Hal and Betty, both of whom told her they frequently took an hour or so for lunch to go shopping. That's a violation of a clear rule, and I've reprimanded them for it. But the damage was done.

Therefore the manager, not employees, should be the source of information about the new job.

Have Frequent Contact with the Employee

There are a number of reasons for giving special attention to the new employee through increased contact. (Managers soon learn that new employees take time—that's one of the many reasons why turnover is costly and even why some supervisors hesitate to terminate an unsatisfactory employee.)

The employee should get to know a manager as a person and not simply as a position on an organization chart. This knowledge can only come through interacting—by spending time together. One of the most unnerving aspects of a new job is not knowing the personality, whims, likes, and dislikes of the person who is going to have a major impact on your life.

It's going to take time to give him or her a realistic view of the job, the group, and the organization. We'll talk more about training later in this chapter, but obviously the manager has to think through both the kind of questions a new employee will have (which will in part relate to previous experiences) and how the job is actually performed:

Bill, I know you've had a good deal of experience as a programmer, and you've worked on DS-60's before. Our maintenance work differs a little here from what you're likely to find in most companies. We don't wait for complaints or new projects, our own group is constantly initiating efforts to improve existing programs. Also here, unfortunately, you can't work directly with the machine room . . . .

In describing the job, remember to give as much emphasis to the "externals" as to the "internals." Provide a behavioral view of the job. Make it clear "who does what with whom, when, where, and how frequently"; from whom materials, requests, and other pressures will come; to whom the new employee will be sending items; and from whom the employee can expect aid, service, and assistance. Then add the "internals," the technical knowledge, skills, standards, and information needed to do the job.

One very clear conclusion from a number of studies is that the manager should be realistic about the job. Nothing is more damaging than excessively optimistic descriptions as:

> If this works out, you can expect a promotion in from six to twelve months (when, in fact, most employees don't get promoted for several years).
> You'll rarely have to work without an assistant or clean out that sump (when, in fact, there's often a shortage of people and the sump is always getting plugged).

Employees remember both promises and the more attractive features they were told about. When these turn out to be untrue, employees feel cheated. It's much better to err on the side of conservatism and to let the good "possibilities" come as pleasant surprises.

Showing enthusiasm
The new employee is quick to detect the degree of confidence the manager has in his or her potential performance—how pleased the manager is that they have joined the organization. Although managers should be cautious about promising unrealistic job benefits, there is no reason to be restrained in expressing pleasure about the new relationship. Nothing will do more to ensure reasonable confidence in the employee concerning his or her ability to do the job and get along with the new supervisor. Here is a good example:

> I wanted you to know, Phyllis, how pleased I am personally that you've joined my department. You know we looked quite a long time before settling on a replacement. I liked your previous experience, and I have great confidence in how you'll handle this assignment. You appear to be ideally suited to what this job calls for.

Introduction to Informal Organizations

Studies of informal organizations reveal that employees who do not find a home in a social group are more likely to leave a job. The informal group, as we note in Chapter 5, plays a critical role in the life of both the employee and the organization. While the manager can't "make friends" for an employee, there's a lot one can do to get the newcomer off to a good start. Introduce him or her with gusto and compliments:

"Bill has handled some of the biggest rigs in the business," or "I know from her employment record that Sally has managed to learn about as much about tear tests as anyone we've ever had here."

Beyond the formal introductions there are two more important details of orienting the new employee to the group. Most relevant is the introduction to the informal leader or leaders. This can accomplish two objectives: (1) It tells the employee something about the structure of the group and who is critical to get to know and gain acceptance from, and (2) it also extends some recognition to the status of the leader. In fact, the supervisor can ask the informal leader to take some responsibility in introducing the newcomer and showing him or her some aspects of the job and the organization.

TRAINING THE NEW EMPLOYEE

The supervisor often makes a choice. Hiring well-trained, well-rounded applicants means they can do the job or several jobs in the department with no additional preparation. Such employees, however, may be costly and hard to find. Meanwhile, applicants with potential, but who lack immediately useful skills, "cost" less in direct salary but may well require on-the-job training. And because some jobs will be unique to a particular organization, even well-qualified workers may be asked to undertake a new-to-them assignment. Therefore, regardless of how the supervisor makes the salary-preemployment-preparation trade-off, he or she needs to know something about how to train a new employee.

Training incorporates the general principles of how people learn, something managers need to learn if they are going to be successful training new employees.

Motivation is essential

Learning requires effort. It won't occur unless the employee sees some purpose, some advantage to be gained, some need to acquire new skill and knowledge. It may help if the individual first determines what he or she doesn't know or can't do, and what problems he or she might have on the job. These can be an impetus to learn.

Understanding helps

Knowing the underlying purpose of what you're going to learn to do is critical. At work this means the supervisor should demonstrate how the job to be learned fits into other jobs, why it has to be done in the prescribed way, how the process works overall, and so forth.

Break the job into reasonable segments

After demonstrating the total job in proper sequence and putting it all together, the manager-trainer has to break down the total job into reasonable steps. A complex operation cannot be comprehended all at once. What are sensible break points depend both on the job and on the existing skills of the individual. Ideally the managers should break the job down into natural units, for example, where new materials or adjustments are necessary, where the pace or sequence changes, and so on.

Demonstrate and request questions

The manager needs to demonstrate each segment accompanied with a running explanation of what is being done, why, and how.

> Note how I'm placing the test material in the receptacle curled end out. . . . It's important that it always be placed that way or the readings will be inaccurate. It's also important that the heating element be off while this step is going on. . . . See how I double check that the switch is off with my left hand while separating the test portions with my right hand? Keep your eyes on the meter, and if the indicator goes above "5" on the scale, stop and redo step 1.

Rather then simply asking if that's clear or asking for questions, it's better to ask trainees to explain in their own words the how, what, and why of the job. Of course, questions should be encouraged about steps that seem unclear, difficult, or just plain foolish.

Encourage spaced repetition

The best way to learn is not by verbalizing but by doing. So as quickly as possible the trainee should begin performing each of the segments.

Repetition is obviously important. A new swimmer may quickly learn the proper kick and stroke, but it takes countless repetition before the kick and stroke can be done effortlessly and synchronously. Repetition needs, however, to be spaced. You don't learn to swim by doing those motions over and over for hours on end. It's practicing an hour a day for a week that does the trick.

Provide positive reinforcement

As the trainee exhibits some measure of success, immediate and positive feedback is crucial from the manager-teacher. Play down the negatives (what's wrong or left out) and overstate the accomplishment. Positive reinforcement serves as a powerful psychological encouragement to repeat the successful effort. As we will discuss later under Controls in Chapter 7, early reinforcement should be on a one-to-one basis—each successful completion of a segment rewarded by a laudatory or encouraging comment. This inspires quicker learning, but retention—durability of learning—depends on random reinforcement. Therefore once the segment can be done successfully, the manager should periodically try to observe and commend its performance in order to imprint it permanently.

Stress overlearning

This random reinforcement is part of the overlearning process. Even though the individual appears to know how to do the task, it's important to have it repeated and reinforced beyond the proof-of-having-learned-it stage to be sure the learning will be retained. The results of this are easy to see. A good driver, deprived of an auto for years, can still get behind the wheel and drive off because of the earlier overlearning. Therefore on complex jobs, the manager should seek to be sure that the individual, during the early days on the job, gets a chance to practice even the more rarely used elements.

HIRING AND HELPING "MINORITY" EMPLOYEES

The manager must recognize that there are some special problems and techniques involved in employing what we will call "minority" employees. Although the principles of selection, orientation, and training we've just discussed still apply, the manager has to make an extra effort to assist these newcomers.

Who are "minority" employees? We shall use that term here slightly differently than it is used in everyday speech. By "minority" we refer to any employee who feels different from the majority of the work force and thus susceptible to discrimination—which can be anything from personal rejection to unfair recognition in pay, continuity of work, and opportunity for promotion.

Over the past decade, the United States has moved vigorously to make discrimination in employment for reasons of race, religion, sex, and even age illegal. Organizations face severe penalties if they persist in engaging in unfair employment practices. Such practices include not only discrimination in hiring but in failing to provide adequate promotional opportunities for minority-group members.

The implications of this federal policy for the supervisor are quite unambiguous. Management is going to insist that the supervisor both hire and be successful in motivating blacks, women, Spanish-speaking workers, and others who might have been treated unfairly in the past.

Problems of the Minority Employee

Many minority employees start work with real handicaps stemming from earlier experiences. For example, some blacks will not have the language or arithmetic skills of equivalent-aged whites because of inferior schooling. They will not have learned on previous jobs (perhaps because they had no previous "real" jobs except casual labor) the importance of coming to work on time (9 A.M. to 5 P.M. for real), of avoiding absenteeism, meeting precise performance standards, and following orders.

Similarly, in the past, women were less likely to learn, in or out of school, about technical subjects—machine design, accounting, electricity—and were less likely to value power and assertiveness. But today women are most likely to be anxious about entering a "man's world" where they are perceived as outsiders, tolerated at best, ridiculed at worst.

Both black and women workers require special treatment because of their own expectations (that failure is likely) and the potentially adverse reactions of both the manager and their coworkers to their minority status. Their orientation requires both self-awareness and some additional supervisory behavioral skills on the part of the manager.

Need for Self-Awareness

Women's groups often use the term "consciousness raising." It used to be called "sensitivity training." This term simply means that a manager (or anyone else for that matter) can't develop successful relationships without being aware of his or her own biases, perceptions, preconceptions, and hidden beliefs.

Here are some common myths managers often have about a new employee who may be black or female.

> Blacks don't want to work; they're lazy.
> Women are too emotional to take a job with any pressure; they're always ready to break down and cry.
> Most blacks are dumb; they can't really learn anything technical.
> Women work for kicks or to provide a little something extra for their families, and you just know they're not going to be permanent employees.

In some cases the manager may not even be conscious of how deeply felt are these prejudicial beliefs. Nevertheless they surface the moment the new black or female employee enters the door. Thus the manager needs to know that a large share of women who work are, in fact, the sole source of support for themselves and/or their families, and that blacks have the same capacities as whites. Poor motivation is often the result of a dual handicap: inadequate early training and continuous discrimination.

Confronting Negative Expectations

The most important task of the manager is to change the negative expectations of minority employees. Typically, minority employees anticipate failure because of previous unhappy experiences. Expecting to fail, they are initially less responsive to the requests of the manager. At times they may become hostile or truculent by interpreting things the manager and the work group do as being discriminatory, even when they're not. In other words the minority employee provides a self-confirming prophecy: "I think I'm going to fail, there's no use trying hard . . . the boss will 'fail' me."

This self-confirming prophecy is most often fulfilled because the new employee detects latent prejudice on the part of the new manager: "The minute I met him I knew he had no respect for blacks; he figured he was stuck with me because top management said I had to be hired to fill some minority quota. But I knew I'd never get a break from him." There are many studies that show that employees, like pupils in school, respond to supervisory expectations. When they detect lack of confidence and prejudice, they respond with poor performance.

Often the poor performance results also from conflict and confrontation. Here is a typical scenario:

Supervisor (to new employee): "Jane, when you've finished with that first assignment I gave you, would you go over to the typing pool and pick up those reports they're preparing for us."

Jane (to herself): "There he goes; while I'm not a typist; he sees all women as typists and someone to run errands."

Jane (to the supervisor): "Really, Harold, running errands wasn't listed as part of the job description you gave me when I was hired."

Supervisor (to himself) "Another troublemaker, expecting to be treated as someone special just because she's a woman."

Supervisor (to Jane): "Jane, don't get legalistic; I need those reports, and I want you to get them; you're getting me angry!"

Jane: "Well you're getting *me* angry! That's not my job and you know what you can do with your reports."

From now on Jane will be convinced that Harold is another male chauvinist pig, not to be trusted; and Harold will assume that Jane is another testy woman with a chip on her shoulder. Who's at fault? We don't think that's a good question. Anyhow, there's probably no conclusive answer.

What is clear is that the minority employee begins work with trepidations and anxieties that can easily be converted into overt hostility. Any new employees starting with low self-confidence and often low self-esteem—meaning plenty of insecurity—are just waiting to find something to prove they aren't going to make it. Then when that occurs, they become uncontrollably angry. Their hostility in turn generates an equal reaction from the boss, and the relationship is injured, perhaps permanently.

The supervisor, having the greater status, security, and power, obviously also has the responsibility to do things that will avoid this vicious spiral. This requires special attention and special training.

Special Attention

Needing self-confidence and tolerance, the minority employee requires a supervisor's extra attention. Here is an example of what we mean by "a very successful supervisor."

When Henry Phillips was hired, I knew that I would have to be both tactful and patient. This was his first real job, other than pickup day-laboring. I spent several hours with him the first couple of days, both assuring him of my confidence in him, explaining what the job required in great detail, answering his questions, and aiding him to do the job. All went well for a few days, and then he arrived two hours late one morning. I suppose I was tempted to throw the book at him as he just waltzed in like it didn't make any difference. Instead, I went over and first told him that he had made a good beginning, coming in four days on time. This was his first "miss," and I reminded him how important it was to have everyone here at the same time because a lot of the work depended on people working closely together. I let him make what excuses he wanted to and ended the discussion with an encouraging remark about his output. A week later, he was out a whole day. I went through a similar routine, including reminding him that if he was ill, he should call and report it. Otherwise it was a rule that all employees had to report five days a week.

I guess the tardiness and absenteeism continued for about six weeks. Each time I'd explore the reasons with him, reemphasizing why it was necessary to live up to the procedures management had established, and each time I found something specific to compliment him on. Gradually he did learn that we wouldn't tolerate his being casual in his working habits. But I just know if I'd yelled or threatened he would have become sullen or even more resistant to my supervision. After all, in his eyes I was "Whitey," the oppressor, and these were all new habits. As he got to know me and feel more self-confident, his behavior gradually improved, and he became a very satisfactory employee. Now he's the best I have.

Behavioral conditioning

By reading carefully what this manager is telling us, we can see that he has learned, or knows intuitively, what we will describe in Chapter 7 as "reinforcement" in talking about controls and appraisals. It is especially important when dealing with insecure employees to place stress on positive reinforcement. Discipline or threats of reprisal are likely to have negative effects—temper outbursts, a desire to get back at the boss, or quitting the job. Patiently feeding back encouragement to the employee based on what he or she has learned to do successfully and reminding them about what still remains to be done to meet the total job requirement are what's called for. This takes conscious effort on the part of the manager to avoid the more obvious emotional reaction and temptation: "She let me down; she's just as I thought she would be—inadequate. The only thing she will understand is discipline; I'll show her who's boss here!"

Proper reinforcement requires frequent contact and feedback and prompt response on the part of the supervisor. Unfortunately this takes time and it takes overcoming the temptation to wait, to avoid another annoying encounter, to just hope the problem will go away by itself.

How long does it take? Obviously there are individual differences, but managers must expect to devote extra time and effort to new minority employees for at least a month, perhaps two or three. Well-established attitudes and bad habits can't be unlearned in a day or a week.

Listening Is Different Too

Whenever the manager deals with someone with a different background, there are certain to be some misunderstandings. There is no way of determining how employees perceive their jobs, their troubles, their ambitions, or their relationships with you without your being willing to listen. This poses special problems in communications because of differences in language or word usage.

> Last week I called Joan Hadley into the office to talk about why her efforts to get the mistakes in the Frank account cleared up still hadn't come to anything. I began by saying that the accounting department had thanked me a dozen times over for sending them a blonde instead of the usual bearded programmer, but they were still unhappy at why the printout was wrong. Before I could finish with a suggestion of what I thought might be wrong and get her views, she began berating me for treating her like a sex object. I was flustered; I had only meant to say that I didn't think this was a terribly serious problem, and she thought I was playing around. But as I began to listen to her concerns, I finally realized that Joan wasn't angry with me but was describing all those other bosses who had thought of her as nothing more than a cute, young thing without brains or guts.

In this context communication means more managerial time, more frequent contact—at least for the first few weeks, sometimes months—and more concentration on getting behind the words to the intentions of the speaker. Here's an example.

> When Bill said the work I had given him was really "busting him wide open," at first I didn't know whether he was pleased or angry. So I simply repeated "busting you open, you say" and then was silent to see what he would fill in. . . "Yeah, I am really busting a gut to get on top of this; it's the toughest assignment I've ever been given. I'm pleased you think I can handle this kind of problem, but I want you to know it's going to take longer than you first estimated to finish. You don't know what you got me into!"

You can be sure there will be a more frequent need to ask questions or to complain and vent frustrations. The supervisor, as the higher-status person, may have to go out of his or her way by being very accessible in order to help overcome either the timidity or the fear of rejection that inhibits social initiative for many minority-group members.

> Man, I've learned, stay away from those boss types. The less you say, the less they got on you.

The Limits of Conformity

Helping the employee to learn the job and the relevant work rules and organizational procedures does not involve demanding complete conformity from the employee. The supervisor has to learn to accept individual differences in language, styles of dress, hair length, and other personal characteristics. There was a time when organizations felt quite free to prescribe almost everything an employee could say and do, even to what they could do off the job. Few employees will stand for that today; they insist on the right "to do their own thing."

There may, however, be some legitimate limits. A job that requires dealing with the public may also require an employee to be neatly groomed and to wear suitable clothes. Working around whirring machinery may require that long hair either be tied back or put in a snood. But unless these personal styles impinge on required job performance, the supervisor is well advised to allow as much individual freedom as possible. After all, what you consider attractive, suitable, or seemly depends on the culture in which you were raised. Just as all of us don't like to eat 1,000-year-old eggs, all of us don't have to like wedged-sole shoes or jive talk.

Relations with the Work Group

Three problems which the supervisor must cope with that involve the work group and the new minority employee are favoritism, integration, and sponsorship.

Favoritism

To some old-timers, and perhaps to the supervisor, this special treatment will appear to be favoritism, even *reverse discrimination*. For example, it becomes important for the supervisor to communicate to the work group that the minority employee didn't get hired just because of being black or female. It's also important that the supervisor recognize—and communicate—that it's quite legitimate to provide more help and assistance, for a limited period of time, to those who have heretofore received more neglect and unfair treatment than the average. The typical employee has never experienced the sense of hopelessness, rejection, and being "out of it" that most minority-group members have experienced.[2]

Integration

There is also a good deal of evidence that the supervisor who insists that there will be no group censure or ostracism can be successful. Both by his or her own behavior as boss and by responding firmly and quickly to any evidence of group discrimination the manager can halt hazing and other forms of discrimination.

> I noticed that Judy never got the help that other employees got when the equipment started acting up. Also, the group frequently gave her wrong advice. I even saw them hide her adjusting kit. I called in the group leader and several other key employees and told them that this was intolerable to me. Judy was a new, promising operator, and in a group as small as ours, an important part of everyone's job was to build teamwork. Those who didn't could no more be expected to be recommended for merit increases than those who turned out defective work. I felt strongly that if I didn't move quickly and firmly, the group would develop woman baiting as one of their norms and that I wouldn't stand for it.

Of course, normal orientation procedures can also facilitate integration: Introduce the new employee to the group leadership early, openly express confidence in the new employee, and assist him or her in getting acquainted with some of the more obvious group norms and customs. (For example, "I tipped off Henry the first day that his fellow workers had a few habits he ought to know about. It's considered a little uppity to wear a machinist's coat. Almost no one eats in the cafeteria; they bring their lunch and play cards over near the files, and at the end of the day they take turns filing away the drawings.")

Sponsorship

Another means of support for the new minority employee is sponsorship. The manager should help the new employee find a "buddy" who will take the responsibility of aiding her or him in finding a place in the

---

[2]As part of the dominant majority "culture," most of us have experienced minority status only when we travel in a foreign country. We call this "culture shock" because it is shocking to be ignored, not to understand a language, to have behavior patterns that are considered strange and unacceptable—to be a "foreigner," an outsider. If you have traveled to another country and culture, try to remember how upsetting it was at first when you couldn't communicate easily and felt that you were constantly doing the wrong thing.

group. This may be the time to make use of the informal leader—to give the leader recognition and responsibility—if, of course, he or she is willing. Or it may be more appropriate to find someone who is reasonably empathetic with the problems the newcomer is facing. The important criterion is simply that the sponsor be someone already well accepted and outgoing enough to take the social initiative in making introductions.

Summary

Minority employees may expect failure; that's why their performance and perseverance are often below par. The supervisor must take the initiative in reversing this habitual pattern by being willing to invest a good deal of time and use patient positive reinforcement in contrast to negative discipline which is demoralizing and self-defeating.

A manager who does the job right will be perceived by the employee as a big help in meeting his or her sought-for goal of stable and satisfying employment. A fruitful relationship between the minority employee and the manager will result from the aid, support, and encouragement that the manager provides, along with a desire to hear out the inevitable problems and frustrations the minority employee is going to experience.

CONCLUSION

The organization usually gives managers a large say in the hiring process because the skills and motivation of employees will be an important determinant of the success of the operation in meeting its goals. Moreover, if managers can't select the employees that they believe they need, it is illogical and unfair to hold them responsible for the goals their departments are expected to meet.

Getting good employees in turn requires knowledge about selection techniques, including the differences between achievement and aptitude tests. It also involves learning how to evaluate previous job experiences and how to conduct interviews to assess personality strengths and weaknesses.

After hiring, motivation will partly depend upon successfully integrating the new employee into the work group and providing him or her with a realistic and complete overview of the job and its relationship to the larger organization. A knowledge of learning principles is important in training employees to realize their full on-the-job potential.

We have defined minority employees as employees who have been at a disadvantage in previous education and job exposure, or employees who sense a status gap between themselves and the majority group. Minority groups require special treatment. New federal legislation as well as sensible management policies compels the supervisor to devote extra time and pay special attention to understanding these more sensitive employees. In some ways they require a degree of "reverse discrimination" to make up for their earlier years of deprivation.

THE EDUCATION OF GREG HORNING: JANUARY 17

Greg got back from the weekly management meeting and found a young woman waiting for him at his desk. "I'm Sally Phipps, she said. "Personnel sent me here. I'm applying for the job you have open for an administrative assistant."

"Fine, fine," said Greg, turning off the smile he automatically gave when he saw an attractive woman waiting. "I'm very anxious to get someone who's really qualified; I have no patience with people who just want to collect a pay check. By the way, is it Miss or Mrs. Phipps? You know, are you married? How important is this job—looking for extra money, or do you really need it?"

Sally looked dismayed and started to say something explosive, but she caught herself. "I don't really think my marital status is relevant, but for your information I am married, and if I didn't want to work, I wouldn't be applying for the job."

"OK, let's get right down to it. The job requires a really first-rate typist, someone who isn't put off by reading accounting, that is, cost accounting reports, who can do arithmetic quickly and accurately, write occasional letters for me when I just tell you roughly what I want said, can run out and get me coffee, answer the phone, and 100 other things I can't think of. How's your typing speed?"

Sally looked dismayed again. "I guess I'm slow, Mr. Horning, but I can't tell whether you want to hire a clerk or maid, or someone with professional . . ."

Greg interrupted to say that, of course, it was difficult to describe any job as it really was. "In a week or so you'd get the hang of it, I'm sure. You look bright enough. Now about that typing?"

"Personnel was a little vague about the salary; they said there was a range, and you would have to make the final decision," Sally countered.

"Not so fast; salary is the last thing after we find out if you're qualified. What about working overtime? Of course, there's extra pay, but I know that some husbands get angry when the little woman isn't home on time to fix dinner. If we get in a bind, could you stay an extra hour or two?"

Again, Sally had to control herself. "My job is *my* business, Mr. Horning, but aren't you going to ask what previous experience I've had, what I can do and have done? We seem to be talking about small details."

"Of course," Greg said with a slight flush. "Tell me about your last job."

Sally looked pleased for the first time. "I worked for a senior editor in a publishing company. It was really a great job, but unfortunately my boss got dropped in a cutback. I had a great deal of responsibility for maintaining all his contacts with both authors and production. This meant that I . . . ."

Again Greg cut in to say, "Well I hope you're prepared for the change; this place is a lot dirtier than any publishing office and a lot more rough and ready. But anyhow, do you like people? My assistant has to be able to work with all the people who work in my department, as well as to field questions from a lot of other departments."

Sally again started to warm up to the conversation and the chance to talk about her previous job. "I certainly do. In fact, I really hated to lose that publishing job. I had a great many friends and before I left they gave me a wonderful party, and . . . ."

"Fine, fine," echoed Greg again. "But this job is not all people. There's lots of data here to be worked with, and I know that lots of women are put off by numbers. How's your math?"

Sally answered more glumly now than when she was reminiscing about her last job. "Figures don't frighten me."

"There's another thing I should mention," Greg said in a much lowered voice. "Some of the men around here may try to get fresh; doesn't mean anything of course, but you've got to be able to take some teasing without calling for 'Women's Lib' to file a case. You know what I mean, don't you?"

"No, I guess I don't know what you mean," was Sally's rejoinder. "I'm getting more confused about the job and the organization and what you really expect. And what did you say the pay was?" Sally was scowling by now.

"I thought I was being pretty clear, and I certainly am trying to be honest with you Miss, err Mrs. Phipps. Why don't you just come right out and tell me whether it sounds like the kind of work you can do or not? There's no use beating around the bush. I'm busy and I'm sure you are too. Let's be honest with each other."

80

QUESTIONS

1 How much did Greg learn about Sally's qualifications and how much did Sally learn about the exact nature of the job and what would be required of her?

2 Indicate where Greg did a poor job of interviewing and its effect on Sally's responses. Where was he demeaning?

3 Make a short outline of the topics (and sequence) which Greg should have covered with Sally.

4 At what point should Greg have encouraged Sally to ask questions. What could he have learned from her questions?

BEHAVIORAL EXERCISE

Assume that you are hiring an assistant. You are manager for customer complaints in a department store with one central city unit and three suburban units. You are an overworked supervisor of the "complaint desks" that are located in each store and deal with the various merchandise departments. These departments keep complaining that too much customer-damaged merchandise is being accepted by the complaint desks.

Decide what you want the assistants to do, and what qualifications you think they should have. Then undertake several employment selection interviews with a colleague or classmate to judge who would be best suited to the position based on her or his interests, personality, and past experience. Afterwards, ask each one what they thought the job that you were describing would be like, and evaluate how close their perception was to what you thought you were saying.

BIBLIOGRAPHY

Bass, B., and J. Vaughn, *Training In Industry: The Management of Learning*, Wadsworth, Belmont, Calif., 1966.

Fear, R., *The Evaluation Interview*, 2d ed., McGraw-Hill, New York, 1973.

Goldstein, A., and M. Sorcher, *Changing Supervisory Behavior*, Pergamon, New York, 1974.

Nierenberg, Jesse, *Breaking Through to Each Other: Creative Persuasion on the Job and in the Home*, Harper & Row, New York, 1976.

Strauss, G., and L. Sayles, *Personnel: The Human Problems of Management*, 3d ed., Prentice-Hall, Englewood Cliffs, N.J., 1972, chaps. 19-20 and 24.

Taylor, B., and G. L. Lippitt, *Management Development and Training Handbook*, McGraw-Hill, New York, 1975.

READING

The Supervisor as Trainer*

MASON HAIRE (1916-   )

Mason Haire was one of the distinguished social scientists brought to Massachusetts Institute of Technology (MIT) by Douglas McGregor in the late 1940s to help build the interdisciplinary faculty that pioneered in developing the field now called organizational behavior. Like McGregor, Haire was a psychologist but his interests spanned a wide range of subjects, from staff planning in the personnel field to organization design. He undertook quantitative studies of changing ratios of staff to line personnel, encouraged students to undertake field experiments, and wrote one of the most influential textbooks in management theory: *Psychology in Management*.

　　He was born in Iowa in 1916 but spent most of his academic career in Cambridge, Massachusetts, receiving his doctorate from Harvard and, of course, teaching and consulting at MIT.

The superior's job is to get help from his subordinates. He has subordinates because he is responsible for more work than he can do himself. He is successful only if, and to the extent that, he is able to enlist their cooperation and to direct their efforts toward the productive aims of the organization. In the process of directing their efforts and teaching them what needs to be done, he is bound to be a trainer. A large part of the difference between an old and new employee, or between a good and bad employee, is apt to be in the way in which he does his job. The superior's objective, then, is to train him in the kinds of attitudes and the kinds of skills that will insure production. In the early stages of association it is almost impossible for the subordinate to have any sort of interaction with the superior without some sort of training taking place. The subordinate learns certain kinds of things about the job and the plant and the superior. This kind of training always takes place in on-the-job interaction, and it is inevitable that the superior will be a trainer. The only question is whether he will do it consciously and properly, or without paying attention to it and haphazardly.

　　We also say that the superior must help the subordinate to achieve a new and stable organization of the work place and of the job. He must help him to make sense of his part of the world and the particular sense he makes of it will have a great deal to do with his attitudes, with his morale, and with his productivity. He must be helped to learn what is expected of him, what his resources are, what the rules and values of the organization are, and the like. He

*Mason Haire, *Psychology in Management*, McGraw-Hill, New York, 1956, pp. 96-97.

must be helped to achieve a coherent organization of the environment which will include himself, his job, his superior, and his future goals. In doing all these things the leader is inevitably a trainer.

In still another sense, the superior is inevitably a trainer . . . the superior controls most of the values in the work situation and, through his administration of these values, is constantly supplying rewards and punishments to his subordinates.

Further, in considering the Law of Effect, we say that the behavior of the subordinates tends to be modified in the direction of repeating behavior which seems to lead to reward and eliminating those behavior patterns which seem not to. Because of this, and because of the dependence of the subordinate on the superior, the leader *is* training all day and every day. He is, whether he likes it or not, continually using the Law of Effect and shaping behavior by the administration of rewards and punishments, and consequently it behooves him to be aware of it and do it carefully. The leader cannot escape his role as a trainer, and although he often tends to ignore it, he continues to function as one. Consequently it is important to be aware of the function as explicitly as possible, so that he may use his training function to shape behavior toward the proper ends rather than at random.

4

ADAPTING TO JOB REQUIREMENTS

LEARNING OBJECTIVES
1 Learn to describe the boundary or interface of jobs—those elements which are vital to effective work flow and coordination.
2 Recognize the significance of work flow to productivity.
3 Assess, for a given subordinate and job, how much delegation is desirable, and how different patterns of delegation can be maintained.
4 Determine how much programming is desirable for a given job and know what factors in job design are likely to discourage or inhibit coordination.

What is a job and how is it supervised? On the surface these look like simple questions. You expect to hear answers like this: A job consists of a series of duties which the employee is supposed to perform in a prescribed fashion—and the supervisor makes sure that these duties are performed! But this really isn't an answer.

WORK FLOW AND THE SYSTEMS APPROACH

Modern management recognizes that the supervisor's major emphasis should be not on individual jobs but rather on the *interrelationship* of jobs. After all, the purpose of work is not so much to complete a task or an assignment as to complete goods or services. A file clerk may work incredibly hard, but if no one else can retrieve the material that has been filed, the clerk's work has not been useful. Even an engineer or a technician who energetically and conscientiously solves a problem in equipment failure may not be working effectively from the point of view of the total organization if the solution creates problems for others, as for those who must repair or use the equipment in the future.

Experienced supervisors concentrate on the interrelationship of jobs, on how employees work as a team. Good teamwork means that each person does the job in such a way as to complement or fit into the work of other employees. Evidence of poor teamwork—everyone is out for himself or herself, completing the task but not caring about how it affects fellow workers. For example, you might hear this:

Hey, Mary, you're dropping metal filings all over the place and they're getting on my tools and gauges!

Look, Barney, don't bother me. I'm behind on my schedule for the day. It would take me half an hour to readjust this machine to stop spraying those filings.

Another way of saying this is to note that emphasis had shifted to the *flow of work,* the movement of material or papers or communications from work station to work station. The ideal that every supervisor seeks is to keep this movement *continuous* and *regular.* Such continuity, the absence of breakdowns between work stations, is the primary source of efficiency—not speed or sweat. This is one of the major conclusions and implications from the substantial emphasis on automation in recent years. Automation provides this continuity and regularity. It is the manager's job to keep things going, which really means to be concerned with the interrelationships between and among jobs more than with the individual job. To put this in another way, the supervisor ought to concentrate primarily on the *system,* on how jobs feed into one another and impact one another.

How the supervisor achieves and strengthens these interrelationships will be the focus of this chapter. Let's look first at jobs that can be individually programmed; that is, the method of doing the job can be precisely specified in advance. Then we will try to cope with the more difficult task of the supervisor's relationship to less programmed work.

PROGRAMMED INDIVIDUAL WORK

The coordination among jobs such as those found in a good deal of manufacturing can be accomplished by explicitly defining in advance what each worker must do. The typical assembly line "works" because some engineer has carefully thought through the tools, motions, and placement of each employee. Each worker's job is designed in advance so that if everyone does precisely what he or she has been told, the work will progress smoothly from job station to job station through to completion (as shown in Figure 4-1). This is what we mean by the word "programming."

Of course, we have described this in Chapter 2 as the source of monotony and dissatisfaction: the requirement that a job be performed as some supervisor or industrial engineer has prescribed. The supervisor's job, then, is to make sure that the employee is adequately trained and is capable of doing the work. She or he sees that the job is actually being performed as planned.

How Much Programming for the Employee?

Jobs differ, of course, in how much programming they require for their effective performance. Some jobs can be learned in a few minutes, others require weeks, still others, years of training. Often what seems like a simple job may require many weeks of practice to perfect. Thus even a simple assembly-line job may not be done with adequate

FIGURE 4-1 Programmed work

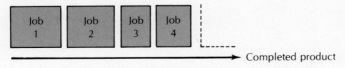

Each job is designed so that it is separate from
every other job, and yet nothing is left out:
everything that needs to be done is assigned to
someone. Thus there are no overlaps or gaps between jobs.

86

speed and accuracy for a number of weeks because all the muscle movements, the hand-eye coordinations, take time to integrate into smooth, semiautomatic actions. The same is true of any athletic ability. You can learn to swim in a few hours, but becoming a good swimmer may take months or even years of practicing the same few motions.

Organizations sometimes have a choice of how much employee programming is required. In what we call mass-production industry, jobs have been meticulously subdivided (providing the morale problems we have already discussed) and the employee can learn these in quite rapid order. On the other hand, many technical jobs (in construction, maintenance, and printing, for example) have not been so finely subdivided, so much more training is required either before the employee is hired (in schools or apprentice programs) or after hiring. In either case, these employees will be more expensive and valuable because of the complexity of their programming.

And then you find professionals like chemists and lawyers whose internal programming is the most complex of all. They have learned great varieties of problem-solving and diagnostic techniques which tell them how to handle a wide range of problems. Similarly, social workers, nurses, and managers themselves have this type of programming. These jobs usually are found in services and areas where technology has not progressed to the point that jobs can be minutely subdivided and aided by machines.

THE SUPERVISOR'S ROLE WHERE JOBS ARE PROGRAMMED

Where jobs can be well defined and are reasonably independent, the supervisor functions in the following ways:

1 He or she may help to define the jobs: the specialization that will divide up larger tasks into small, programmed units. As we have said, it may be difficult and expensive to find and hire fully trained craftspeople or professionals. However, if you supervise a medical laboratory, for example, you may be able to define the activities necessary to do a particular blood test so that a willing new employee with no knowledge of biology or chemistry can do this specific test.

2 Then the supervisor helps train the individual employees to do the job, using patience and understanding, and encourages them to practice, to ask questions, to learn to cope with all the problems that may occur, and to understand a few of the underlying principles, since this "theory" will help them to know what to do when.

3 After the employee has demonstrated his or her competence, the supervisor makes periodic checks to be sure the job is being done as prescribed and with adequate quickness and concern for quality. How can this best be done?

Sampling

Although we shall look more intensively at this whole subject of controls in Chapter 7, it is worth noting here that most supervisors learn how to *sample* the behavior of the employee. The objectives are to:

1 Avoid the implicit pressure and even distrust communicated by continuous watching, as well as the cost in supervisory time.
2 Avoid having the employee "show off" when the supervisor is watching.
3 Distribute observations sufficiently broadly so the boss gets to see all the various parts of the job, but at different times of the day.

In practice, this means a supervisor may walk by when an employee is finishing some work and thus have a chance to observe the last stages. Later in the day, he or she manages to come by at a time when a new job is just being started, and at some other point finds the time to look at the middle portions. Of course, all the observations need not take place within one day, and the better trained and more able the employee appears, the more widely spaced the checks. Where an employee seems to be having troubles, shows some incompetencies, has quality problems, and such, more frequent observations are made. (As for what the supervisor does when he or she observes that the employee is not doing the job as prescribed, see Chapter 6.)

Delegation and Technology

Even when the employee is well trained, highly motivated, and working on a job with a reasonable amount of programming, there will be subjects or problems on which the supervisor wants to be consulted. The manager doesn't want the subordinate handling these things alone. How much leeway the subordinate has versus how much the supervisor wants to be involved is often called the *amount of delegation*. Let us see if we can discover what determines how much or how little delegation the supervisor gives subordinates.

How much the supervisor intervenes is a function of the technology and the amount of training the subordinate has, but the relationship is a somewhat complicated one.

Amount of training

In some industries, as we have noted, it pays management to hire a well-trained employee who is, in fact, already "programmed." Both advanced education and experience can prepare an employee to handle a wide variety of problems without calling on the supervisor. Thus you can hire a lawyer or an engineer or even a well-trained bookkeeper, give her or him a broad assignment, and have some confidence that she or he will know what to do in a broad range of cases and with a wide assortment of problems on the job, most of which you couldn't predict anyhow. In a sense, the company is trading a higher salary for lower costs of supervision (and also of equipment). For the most part (although the relationship is never a perfect one), the better trained and/or more experienced the employee, the less supervision is required.

Complexity of the job

On many jobs, if the supervisor is to intervene effectively, it will be necessary for the subordinate to spend a great deal of time informing the boss on what has already been learned, what has been going on, and what the unique circumstances of the case are. Thus, an engineer faced with a technical problem may not be able to get help from a superior without spending hours explaining all the things already tried, the special properties of the immediate situation, and exactly what is trying to be accomplished. "Bringing the boss on board" is costly in terms of both managerial and employee time.

Availability of limits of discretion

Some technologies allow the supervisor to say, in effect, "You handle all the easier problems and bring me the more difficult ones." This assumes that "easy" can be defined in meaningful terms. For example, an insurance claims adjuster may be told to handle all cases up to claims of $500. Or a sales representative may be permitted to extend credit to a customer so long as the amount is not over $100. A machinist may use some discretion about waiting for material or repairs as long as the time involved is under 15 minutes, and a secretary may be encouraged to handle all telephone requests for information that come from certain specific departments in the organization.

Patterns of delegation

When the job goes outside these explicitly defined limits, the employee has the responsibility of calling in the supervisor. However, we are really oversimplifying the use of "limits of discretion" in defining the amount of leeway delegated to subordinates. The supervisor actually has a broad array of choices open in defining when subordinates should act on their own, in terms of their own internal programming, and when she or he, the supervisor, should be called in. Here are most of the possibilities. (See if you can think of a realistic situation to fit each category.)

1 Within these limits, you take action based on your best judgment. Don't contact me.
2 You take action, but keep me informed as to what you did (after the fact, in other words).
3 In these kinds of situations I want you to look into the problem and inform me of what you intend to do. You can go ahead as long as I don't say not to.
4 (Same as point 3) but delay any action until I have given positive approval.
5 In these situations, I want you to assess the situation and the problems and let me know what are the possible actions that should be taken. Tell me the relative pros and cons and recommend what action I (the supervisor) should take.
6 (Same as point 5) but just give me the facts. I'll make the decision on my own.[1]

Obviously, the lower-numbered alternatives are most suited to jobs being handled by employees with more internal programming. But note that all depend upon the ability of the supervisor to predefine, to specify in advance, the limits within which the subordinate acts *alone* as compared to where the boss must be involved.

Ambiguous Jobs

The supervisor needs to distinguish between those jobs for which explicit guides for performance are available and those which are inherently ambiguous. For example, a typist's job is reasonably objective. You can assign a specific quantity, observing the speed and the quality of performance. But ask an employee to clean up his or her work area and you can anticipate that there will be very substantial differences in interpretation. How clean is clean? Do the corners have to be scrubbed? Should furniture be moved or just cleaned around?

Two extremes are dangerous. Start telling an employee in too much

---

[1]For this list we are indebted to Harvey Sherman, *It All Depends*, University of Alabama Press, University, Ala., 1966, pp. 83-84.

detail how and what should be done and serious resentment can build up very quickly.

> My boss told me to go to our upstate branch tomorrow and do some sales-planning work with the branch manager. He said it would be a good idea to leave on the 5:55 plane this afternoon, stay at the Corgan Hotel, rent a car at the airport to get to the hotel and to the office, and ask for the 10 percent company discount.
>
> I've done this dozens of times in the past. What does he take me for? Can't I be trusted to use my own judgment as to how to get there? I was so angry when he finished I asked him if he wanted to buy my ticket too!

On the other hand, no specifications for the job can be disastrous unless the employee is very experienced. In any case, the more ambiguous the job, the more the supervisor must rely on previous training, knowledge, and motivation. The last is the most important because such jobs will always have aspects which are difficult to judge, where the employee works alone and must use some discretion as to how much work to do and how carefully to do it.

Imagine the problem of hiring a gardener to maintain the land around a house. How free of weeds should the flower beds be maintained? How straight should the borders be cut, and how often? How often should the grass be cut and fertilizer be used, and what amount of trimming and what shaping are satisfactory for trees and shrubs? When should the lawn be rolled? Should the sidewalks be edged? There is really no end to such questions, which is what makes such relationships difficult, to say the least.

Except for the most rigidly controlled assembly-line type of job, it is hard to find jobs which do not have some significant discretionary component. It is much too easy to ignore this—to accept the commonplace assumption that most people work best when they do precisely what they are told and that consequently there is little room for discretion in modern organization. The facts are really just the opposite: Most jobs have a substantial, unprogrammed content, and the supervisor must be concerned with how well this is performed. Look at the kinds of decisions file clerks may well have to make on their own:

> How to rate concurrent demands for filing service coming from several sources at the same time, that is, how to decide which should be met first.
>
> Whether to go to the supervisor and ask for assistance to meet a temporary flood of work, or to get temporarily into arrears.
>
> When to open new files for correspondence which was previously filed under a bulging "miscellaneous" category.

Whether particular documents are or are not intended for filing in this center.[2]

In appraising the effectiveness of the employee, the manager may well want to concentrate on these unprogrammable elements. While obviously the file clerk has to be able to do the programmed parts (if she can't or won't she may have to be discharged), the difference between an average and an excellent file clerk will be found in how the discretionary elements are performed.

UNPROGRAMMED WORK

Many managers tend to overestimate the degree to which jobs under their jurisdiction are programmable. Many jobs which seem very simple and precise on closer examination turn out to be much more variable. The variability usually results from the fact that some jobs are not as separable as the supervisor thought. Let us take an example.

Two employees perform simple computational tasks on weekly sales reports. In order to do their work, they must periodically go to some central files to take accounting records which they then work with at their desks. Obviously, there will be times when one of them wants to keep a specific record out and use it for a while. Similarly, they will face the problem of who handles what files, and there will also be many times when one of them has some information or some skill that the other can use, for example, when a mistake is discovered.

We have seen many cases in which the supervisor's efforts to develop rigidly programmed job descriptions and rules of procedure are self-defeating. By attempting to preprogram the job, productivity may decrease as well as motivation. For example, the supervisor may insist that

1 Each employee does his or her own work and cannot ask for help.
2 Each employee must do exactly one-half of each day's files.
3 No accounting record can be kept for more than 15 minutes and an employee can have only one record out at a time.

---

[2]Interestingly, a study of new managers identifies one of the most successful as a young engineer who was assigned the job of maintaining a file of reports for a vice-president. His initiative in converting this routine, uninteresting "dog-work" type of job into a challenge—by developing original indexes and techniques for updating the file—made a superb impression on his boss. It was an important step in his rapid promotion in the company. Cf. W. R. Dill, T. L. Hilton, and W. R. Reitman, *The New Managers,* Prentice-Hall, Englewood Cliffs, N.J., 1962, pp. 39ff.

Leonard R. Sayles, *Individualism and Big Business,* McGraw-Hill, New York, 1963, p. 156.

The result: Some files will be easier than others, so it's likely that one employee will be idle while the other works. Useful information cannot be exchanged. Many times they will need to make several extra trips to the files because of the time limits, and because they cannot pass things back and forth.

This is a very simple work situation and purposefully so. In practice, most jobs have a much wider variety of "motions" associated with them. Employees have to learn to do these motions in such a way as to complement and not interfere with the way their fellow workers are doing their jobs. Thus, clerks in a store must learn to allocate customers, help each other find merchandise, and handle certain complex sales-slip problems. Even an assembly-line worker may discover ways of doing the job that make it easier for the employee next in line to do the job.

It is always amazing to the outside observer to note how frequently the formal rules of procedure for any job have to be modified in the light of special circumstances. While Beth and Joe are not supposed to help each other, now that Joe occasionally has to work on very large pieces, Beth's help in getting the parts into the machine can save ten or twenty minutes or prevent the need to call for a special laborer. Similarly, many times employees are told not to repair their machines— that is the job of maintenance workers. An alert employee, however, can spot certain things and make minor adjustments that will save a good deal of maintenance time. Even when this isn't practical, by watching carefully when the equipment appears to malfunction and reporting this to the mechanic who comes to fix it, the worker saves the mechanic a good deal of diagnostic time. Again, this isn't in the formal job description!

In all these cases, the supervisor's attention is drawn to the *interface* of the job. He or she wants to see how jobs intermesh, which workers help each other, and which make work difficult for one another. Unlike programmed work, the supervisor recognizes that these jobs do overlap and that employees must decide on the spot how to handle the overlap (for instance, the need to share files or a common work space). And there are always aspects of the work that are left out of any job description, but alert, efficient employees will do certain things even though they are not formally part of their jobs (like tipping off the maintenance worker when the machine begins malfunctioning). The aspects of interfacing jobs are sketched in Figure 4-2.

Semiautonomous Groups

There are times when the supervisor makes little or no effort to divide work among a group of interrelated workers. In effect, the whole group

Some jobs have certain amount of overlap; there are tasks that cannot easily be assigned to any specific job in advance of the actual work situation.

FIGURE 4-2 Unprogrammed work

is told, "Your job is to complete this task, and in doing so, you are going to have to develop your own division of labor, deciding who should do what and when." This approach is particularly useful where supervision is difficult, the employees are facing unpredictable and changing circumstances, and they have somewhat similar status.

The situation that fits this description is found in certain kinds of heavy construction or mining work. The group is held responsible for total performance, but there may still be some rudimentary division of labor within the group. A famous study of small mining crews in England found that the workers had separate tasks to do, but that a number of unpredictable and unprogrammable factors (water leakage, rock slides, and more difficult terrain) required them to help each other a great deal. Similarly, during the war it was noted that radar crews plotting the approach of enemy planes were more effective when they learned to supplement each other's efforts—to fill in the blanks, you might say.

Now the supervisor is acting much like the coach of a good athletic team. Each person has a position to play, but the important thing is how they play together. This can't be predetermined by any abstract formulas. A good second baseman is good because of close coordination with the shortstop and the third baseman, and each one's strengths and weaknesses are taken into account in what the others do. And what each player does depends on where the ball is hit; there isn't a fixed pattern. They learn by practicing as a team, not as individuals.

The more critical that teamwork is, the more a supervisor must consider how disruptive replacing any one member by another will be and what impact these actions might have on individuals. Obviously, any part cannot be influenced without influencing the whole.

Job Design to Facilitate the Flow of Work

Once we see that the primary objective for the supervisor is to manage the jobs under him in such a way that they feed smoothly into one another, we can establish some critical criteria for job design.

One common problem is that a job requires a lower-status employee to get a higher-status employee to do something. For example, one of the duties assigned to the mail-room clerk was to go to the book-keeper's office to request that certain statistical information be prepared quickly for the use of the personnel office. Whenever the mail room clerk would ask one of the bookkeepers to stop what he was doing and get this information for personnel, he would be greeted by a crescendo of complaints about how busy everyone was and how he was interfering and to come back later, etc.

The problem of status

Most people are not used to having their actions impacted by people they believe are doing less important work. (The same reluctance can be observed in the community. Apartment dwellers resent being told by the building superintendent, whom they often call the janitor, how to handle their rubbish or when to use the laundry room.) Whenever a job requires that a lower-status person push or initiate or make demands on a higher-status employee, you can expect problems. Good job design tries to eliminate this by having workers of relatively equal status make demands of each other or having the initiator be of higher status (as suggested in Figure 4-3).

Handling pressure

Another criterion, similar to the one above, is that the supervisor should try to avoid creating jobs which require too much responding to others.

Bob Allen's job was to pass out certain tools and jigs in a small shop in which every worker was on a piecework incentive. The company was short of some of this equipment, and he could not keep the workers supplied. But many employees believed the toolroom personnel just used favoritism. In any case, there were constant pressures from the employees to move more quickly, to find parts, to give them something so they wouldn't be delayed. The pressure was so bad that Bob quit after a few weeks and so did the next three people who filled his job.

FIGURE 4-3 Status and flow

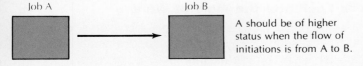

Job A   Job B

A should be of higher status when the flow of initiations is from A to B.

Particularly where such pressures are unpredictable and erratic and the jobholder can't reverse them, the supervisor can expect to have difficulty getting someone to hold the position or to hold it without constantly losing his or her temper or becoming morose. Obviously, some personalities are better than others in taking pressure from other workers, just as some waiters or waitresses are very good at "fielding" customer demands. This is a good technique that a supervisor can teach some employees—turning around the pressure so they are initiating to their would-be tormentors. Here is how a first-class waitress does it as the number of customers she must serve increases and the kitchen is getting delayed:

> *Waitress to table 1,* even before the customers can ask for service: Let me at least give you some water while you're waiting; it will take a while because the kitchen is so busy. But don't worry—I won't forget you. (And she walks off.)
> *Waitress to table 2,* whose occupants have already said they are in a hurry: Why don't you order the prime ribs? They're ready to serve and there's no delay. And if you'll give me the vegetable orders all together, that will save some time, too.

There's a woman who knows how to take the initiative and turn around a job in which the other person usually does most of the initiating! The toolroom worker could be taught some of these devices to equalize the interaction pattern, too.

In fact, a good rule of thumb is that the supervisor should try to have most of the jobs designed so that an employee can initiate to others roughly as much as she or he is initiated to. Look closely at how many people, how frequently, come to that individual in getting their jobs done. Then see if the supervisor can build into the employee's job the need and the opportunity to go to others with requests of about the same quantity. Of course, this is much harder to do for service positions, where the major component of the job is to be responsive to others.

Studies in hospitals have shown that maids, for example, quit more frequently when they work by themselves because everybody, including nurses, aides, doctors, patients, has requests to make of them. Equally menial tasks performed by laundry personnel in the same hospitals don't create this problem, because the laundryworkers interact with people of their own status and there are not many requests made directly to them—except by their supervisor and by a fellow employee when there is a work-flow relationship.

ACTIVE COORDINATION—INTERDEPENDENT JOBS

Job design, training, and delegation are passive methods of supervision since they are really "before the fact." The supervisor must also be actively engaged in making sure that employees properly coordinate their work where jobs are interdependent.

Of course, there are some systems which make it easier for one to do this. An assembly line is really acting as a supervisor's impersonal coordinator. It tells an employee *when* to do something—as the work passes in front of him or her—and as long as the individual reacts to the timing of the line, the work will be coordinated with that of other employees who are responding similarly. Some studies have suggested that an impersonal supervisor—such as an assembly line— creates less worker resistance to its "orders" than do the *personal* requests of a boss. This is really the purpose of an assembly line—to tie together the efforts of a large number of employees who are part of a single work-flow system. The line is timed so that each job can be completed and moved to the next station in time for that worker to do a task. Naturally, each task has to be thought through so that the worker has adequate time to do the job.

Other jobs can be coordinated by the clock: "Every hour, take a sample from the 302 vat up to the laboratory." There are also built-in coordinating points within the job: "Whenever you process an order from the Middle Atlantic states, telephone Donna Jenkins in sales and give her the order number and the total."

Groups of employees can develop their own coordinating mechanisms and may be required to do so when their jobs are interdependent. (For the supervisor's role in developing a group spirit and group identification, see Chapter 10.) Singing and chanting provide a beat by which a group can be responsive to the same stimulus. Like a conductor's baton or a metronome, the tempo of the song helps to keep people doing things in unison and mutually responsive. Watch a football team coming out of a huddle chanting or calling out numbers and you will see the adept responsiveness of a well-coordinated group, each of whose members moves in response to this common source of timing. The same techniques apply at work. Crews doing heavy work or work that requires each to move in response to the other will often say,"Now all together, when we say one, two, three . . . PULL! OK, one, two, three . . . *Again!*"

Obviously, being able to see each other is a help or maybe an absolute requirement of coordinating two jobs. For example, in a plant assembling washing machines, the body was built on a line located on a balcony, and the workers at the end of that line were supposed to slide the body down an incline to the first floor. At that point, the group that was building the frame was to attach the body to the frame. The bodyworkers were told to slide their unit down as soon as the frame assemblers had attached the previous unit and passed it along their main-floor line. Unfortunately, the two groups could not easily see each other, and the balcony group frequently slid its work down the slide before the next group was ready or held back too long and interrupted the pace of the frame assemblers. There was constant squabbling between the two groups, each claiming the other went out of its way to be difficult or to interfere with their own work pace. In fact, it was simply that these jobs were designed in such a way that the employees ought to be able to see each other and time themselves accordingly: dynamic coordination.

Barriers to Easy Give-and-Take Relationships

We have seen that most jobs require employees to collaborate even though their actions, at first glance, appear to be quite independent of one another. Why doesn't this cooperation always appear spontaneously among people who must work together over an extended period?

One obvious reason: New employees haven't had time to learn personal idiosyncrasies and how they can best do the job so as to facilitate the work of the other workers. Therefore the supervisor can expect, when one or more employees are temporary or new, that there will be a substantial quantity of inept coordination. One hears comments like:

> Hey, Joe, I can't handle these cartons if you are going to keep sliding them every which way.
>
> Nearly all those computer mistakes are your fault because you keep writing the serial number in the middle of the form instead of in the upper right-hand corner where the punch-card operator looks for it.
>
> I'm getting tired of doing your work for you. From now on, you just get your own fixtures from the toolroom.
>
> Whenever you get a customer who starts to dawdle, you drop her and then try to beat me to the next one who looks like a real buyer, and that's not taking your turn!
>
> You'll have to clean that grease off the floor yourself. My job is just to do mechanical maintenance work, and I can't help it if some of the grease we put on drips down.

These are workers who are physically or psychologically colliding with one another, each defining his or her job in such a way that it clashes with the jobs of the others. Usually, informal groups serve to rub away these rough edges that each person may have around his or her own conception of the job. Through subtle and not so subtle pressures, the group encourages its members to help one another, to extend themselves a little, and to refrain from doing their job in such a way that satisfies only themselves, but this takes time.

Of course, where groups can't form easily, this type of mutual aid isn't likely to be forthcoming. If a supervisor has an employee working in an out-of-the-way location or in a spot where he or she identifies with another group, coordination difficulties can be expected.

Colliding interests

Often two supervisors will have to spend a great deal of time untangling coordination problems when each supervises a part of what is essentially an integrated operation. In a clerical department we observed, one supervisor handled clerks who processed sales orders when they first came from the mail room. Two other supervisors were responsible for clerks who checked the correspondence for mathematical errors, the warehouse instructions from which the merchandise was to be shipped, and the credit status of the customer. All three supervisors were constantly fighting over whose fault it was that a customer's order could not get through these various stages in a single day (as the company required).

The problem was that each group did things for its own welfare and the flow of work was impeded. Group 1 would often wait until they had a large batch of orders before delivering them to group 2, which introduced one kind of delay. If someone was absent in group 2, the other employees might or might not pitch in and help out, depending on whether groups 1 and 3 had recently done them a favor or had insulted them.

The chances are good that people who are separated from each other by physical or group boundaries will blame one another for whatever work problems they have rather than try to seek ways of overcoming them. In the large office just described, it is likely that the 2s began to say that the 1s were just unfriendly, not to be trusted, and always tried to do things in the least convenient way. This is another example of the general tendency to have the stranger become a scapegoat for your own difficulties.

Under these circumstances, one often sees *self-confirming* prophecies at work. I forecast that Mr. B is not going to be very helpful when

I have to go over to his department to get some help. Believing he will not be cordial, I speak to him rather sharply or with some hostility in my voice. Detecting this feeling or this pressure, B is likely to be discourteous or reluctant to extend himself to help me, which confirms my initial prophecy: B is no good!

Gradually, a kind of cold-war iron curtain is built between two such employees or two such groups, and then the supervisor really has a difficult time getting work done because, whenever they must collaborate, there will be trouble. It is therefore the supervisor's job to try to detect the sources of these problems.

Where the supervisor has everyone who must engage in close coordination under her or his jurisdiction, the group can be built into a social unity in which these aggressive feelings cannot flourish. Where communication is difficult, such feelings tend to fester until workers are either not talking at all to one another or are actually and purposefully sabotaging one another's work.

Checking the intersections

The supervisor will be wise to watch the point at which two jobs intersect when checking to see how the work is progressing. This is the most crucial point in the work flow, the point at which the most difficulties are likely to occur, personal as well as technical. To do this, the primary rule of *work-flow* supervision should be kept in mind: Is employee A doing the job in such a way that it complements and assists employee B and vice versa? Put another way, the supervisor is observing whether work is moving smoothly between work stations, since this is the major determinant of productivity.

He or she will be able to observe such problems as these:

1 B never appears ready when A brings him the work.
2 B has to undo some of the things A gives him because they make it difficult for him to proceed with his steps.
3 B is frequently rushing A to finish so that he can begin his work.
4 B complains to A that the quality of A's work is such that it makes it more difficult for him to do this.

Of course, the supervisor is just as likely to see any of these reversed so that A is the one with the problem. In either case, such observations suggest that the supervisor must intervene and seek to identify the work-flow problem. Investigation may disclose:

1 A personality problem: A and B rub each other the wrong way and can't seem to learn to be mutually responsive.

2 A job-design problem: A's or B's job has not been designed to fit well into the other's. Or one or the other has inadequate or too much time.

3 A training problem: A or B needs more training as to the method of doing the job so that the work is mutually complementary.

The Supervisor Ensures Coordination

Thus the supervisor's task is to make sure that both the workers and the machinery under his or her jurisdiction operate at their maximum capability. Specifically, the supervisor's responsibilities are to:

1 Make sure that jobs are designed in such a way as to feed into one another, so that if worker A does her job in the prescribed fashion, it will facilitate the efforts of worker B. (Here is a good example of the opposite: Shelf workers in a grocery warehouse were told to do the job of putting new stock on the shelves as rapidly as possible, which meant that they pushed the older merchandise to the back of the shelves when placing new cans in stock. The pickers, who took food from the warehouse to the store shelves, on the other hand were told always to bring the older merchandise first. This meant that they had to first remove the new cans, then reach way in back for the older cans, and then replace the newer merchandise. The two sets of jobs were designed in such a way as to frustrate the real objectives of the work-flow system.)

2 Ensure adequate training, given the amount of delegation that will be provided. Where employees are going to be delegated a rather substantial amount of autonomy, meaning fewer supervisory check-ups, more on-the-job or previous training and experience will be required.

3 Observe the "intersections" between jobs and detect breakdowns in the flow of work.

OVERVIEW

It is easier to supervise jobs which can be made very independent and those which can be programmed. On these, the job of the supervisor is to make explicit through *training* the task or tasks required, and then to make sure by periodic *sampling* that the subordinate is doing the job as prescribed.

A complication is added when a job contains some elements in which the supervisor personally wants to participate or get involved. Then the *delegation* decision arises, and the supervisor must establish clear criteria which enable the subordinate to know when a matter can be handled alone and when the supervisor must be consulted. Obviously, a number of employees doing the same job may differ in the amount of discretion and tasks which they are delegated. The better-trained, more experienced, and more able employees are encouraged by the supervisor to take on more tasks. This saves supervisory time and can give employees greater job satisfaction in assuming more responsibility. Less delegation is given to those who are less well prepared or able.

It is a time-saver for the supervisor to give as broad responsibilities as possible to employees and to check the quality of work performed *after* completion. This way sampling and checking performance are used at times when it does not interfere with other supervisory duties. However, to require an employee to check with the manager *before* beginning a task or while doing the task is much more time-consuming—for both employee and manager. This is another compelling reason encouraging fuller delegation, giving employees more autonomy in doing their work. Whenever the supervisor must get involved during the job cycle, scarce supervisory time is going to be expended.

On jobs which are *not* independent of one another, where employees' work is interdependent, the supervisor's job changes. Many supervisors are misled into concentrating on individual job performance, but work efficiency depends upon completed activities—something "going out the door," so to speak. Even though certain employees may work diligently and almost to the point of exhaustion, if their work does not fit in with the work being done by others, much of their efforts are probably wasted.

Thus, where jobs are interdependent, the focus of supervisory action shifts from the individual job to the flow of work, the interrelationships among jobs, the work *system.* The supervisor is concerned with the smoothness with which work progresses from one employee to another and with identifying and correcting whatever serves to block or inhibit that smooth flow of work.

It will sometimes be matters of personality, although supervisors often are misled into thinking two or more employees can't work together effectively when job-design factors are responsible. Usually the pressures of the work group serve to iron out personal idiosyncrasies that get in the way of cooperative efforts. The alert supervisor can spot job-design barriers to teamwork. These may include communications problems. If workers have to collaborate, they must engage in a good deal of give and take, usually much more than the supervisor recognizes.

> Betty and I do the final design drafting. Each of us knows what we are supposed to do and our jobs are pretty well separated, at least in the boss's eyes, since I handle the electrical and she does the mechanical. But, boy, heaven help us if we can't keep going back and forth to each other's board. There are countless things the engineers left out or aren't clear on that one or the other of us has more information about. Also, each will be doing things that the other ought to know about if the final plans are going to be clear. We used to work in separate rooms and I would save up problems to check with her, but then I would forget some and on others I just couldn't wait because I wanted to get on with the drawing. As a result, a lot of stuff had to be done over. Now we just yell across to each other and have developed a real helping spirit. She not only answers my questions but also gives me a hand on some of the tougher interpretations.

Many managers are guilty of underestimating the amount of effort that must be placed on the *interface* or boundary between jobs. This give and take cannot be programmed because its quantity and quality depend on personality factors as well as on a hundred little things that affect how a job is performed. Thus a supervisor's efforts must be concentrated on looking at the total process of cooperation and coordination, not on individual, separated jobs. And the supervisor must also seek to identify the environmental or structural factors (like physical proximity providing ease of communication) that facilitate or inhibit group efforts.

Four Types of Jobs: Four Types of Supervision

We have talked about four types of jobs and their distinctive supervisory requirements. The categories (as illustrated in Figure 4-4) are these:

1 Programmable individual jobs: Here the supervisor (S) concentrates on the "inside" of the job: Is the employee doing the various elements correctly, sequentially, with adequate speed, and without interfering with others?
2 Programmable interdependent jobs: Here the supervisor, while having some concern with correct job performance, watches the boundary between the jobs to make sure that there is adequate mutual assistance, complementarity, and a smooth flow of work.

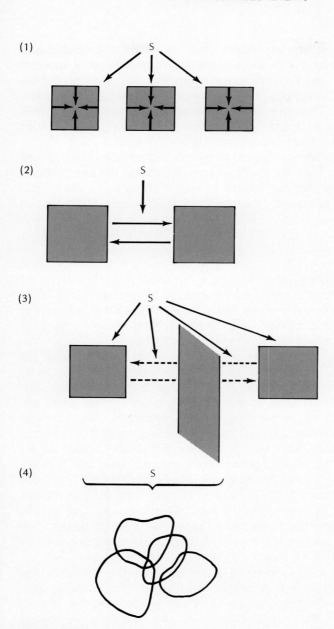

FIGURE 4-4 Four supervisory approaches

3 Nonprogrammable interdependent jobs in which the employees cannot easily communicate or are parts of separate work groups: The supervisor should anticipate spending a disproportionate amount of time resolving conflicts and disagreements between these employees. They are not close enough to evolve an easy give and take and mutual assistance. The supervisor sometimes will also have to act as a link or coordinator between them.

4 Nonprogrammable group tasks: Here the supervisor concentrates almost entirely on the total task and only slightly on the interrelationship between jobs and the "inside" of jobs. "The group's the thing." His or her job is to develop the group's capacity and willingness to work as a team.

A FINAL NOTE

It is worthwhile to obtain some historical perspective on the types of jobs that the supervisor in the United States will be managing. In 1900, the chances were one out of three that a supervisor would be handling farm laborers, probably as the owner. It took a third of our labor force to grow the products we needed for food and clothing.

By 1975, however, agricultural workers made up no more than 3.5 percent of the labor force. We had 50 percent of our work force in factories—the blue-collar workers—in the 1920s, but today these employees (who are more likely to be handling programmed jobs) are down to one-third of the work force. At the same time, the numbers and proportions of white-collar workers have been steadily increasing to where, today, they comprise 50 percent of the work force. To be sure, many of them perform routine, programmed jobs, but a large proportion, including some professionals, are highly trained. They are both able to and demand the autonomy to determine for themselves the best way of doing their jobs. In fact, there are now 12.5 million professionals and another 1 million managers and administrators, almost perhaps 25 percent of the work force, and this segment is increasing each year.[3]

At the same time, more and more of the work is being done outside of factories: in schools and government bureaus and hospitals and laboratories. This is the age of the white-collar worker and the professional because our technology has shifted from orientation toward extractive and production industries to focus on service and consumption.

---

[3]*1976 Employment and Training Report of the President*, U.S. Government Printing Office, Washington, D.C., 1976, p. 234 (Table A-15).

THE EDUCATION OF GREG HORNING: JANUARY 19

Greg looked up in surprise to see Alfred Cameron standing outside his office. He had already pegged Cameron as a follower—Creegmore's usually—he rarely acted on his own initiative.

"Come on in, Alfred," Greg called out. "I hope you haven't been out there long. It slows us down, you know, taking time out to talk. Why didn't you call me? I'd be glad to come out to see you at your machine if you need me for something."

"Well, it's not exactly that I need you," Alfred said. Greg had not asked him to sit down and he stood beside Greg's desk, shifting his weight from one foot to the other. "You see, it's this new mold brace. I wanted to ask you about it. See, I found out I can lock it in with an extra clamp. It improves the tolerances that way. And then I don't get Helen coming around all the time, all excited, bringing me back pieces. So I was wondering if. . ."

"That's fine, Alfred," Greg interrupted. "If it works, that's just fine. But, look. What about right now? Your machine is turned off and we're wasting time. You know we need every piece we can get out to fill our orders and get them delivered on time."

"Oh, that's all right, Greg, my machine is going and Henry is watching out for it. See, we spell each other all the time so we don't waste time if one of us has to step away for a minute." Alfred smiled now, feeling more confident. "Now as I was saying, you know, about that extra clamp. . ."

But Greg cut him off again. "I've spoken to some of the others about this, Alfred, and as long as you're in here, I might as well make it clear to you too. I don't want any of you doing anyone else's job. The description that you have from industrial engineering tells you exactly what you should be doing. They've worked out a fair work load for each person. It's very carefully set up. How can Henry do what he's supposed to do when he . . . Now, you see what's happened, Alfred? What's going on out there, anyway?"

Greg had gone over to the window that opened onto the floor as he was talking. "Would you just look at that? You see, Alfred, it proves what I was telling you. Henry isn't watching your machine at all. He isn't even paying attention to his own—dammit. He's way over on the other side of the room shaking his fists at one of the materials handlers."

"Oh, I know what that's about, all right," Alfred began explaining eagerly as he looked out. "See, they've been putting our supplies in the wrong place. And Henry keeps telling them and telling them, but it doesn't do any good. Those people! You ask them to do something and they've always got an excuse. 'The night workers won't like it,' they say. Or it's not their job and it's too much trouble and they can't be bothered or . . ."

"All right, Alfred, don't worry about it—it's not your problem or Henry's either. Go back to work and don't leave your machine alone again. If you need me, call me over or wait until there's a break or a changeover when the setup man is there."

"Okay, Greg," Alfred muttered. "I guess we can talk about that clamp idea some other time, maybe?" But Greg, looking out at the floor again, didn't seem to hear. Alfred fumbled with the door handle for a moment, then left.

Creegmore was back at his machine by the time Alfred came out. They exchanged a few words and looked over at Greg, then both men returned to their work.

But Greg was disturbed. Creegmore had no business fighting with the materials handlers; that was something he should have brought to his supervisor's attention. But too much time had been wasted already for one day and Greg decided not to make an issue of it.

Another thing was bothering Greg—what Alfred had said about Helen returning unsatisfactory pieces to him. That just didn't sound right to Greg. Going out on the floor, he went over to Helen and asked, "What do you do, Helen, when you feel the work you're getting from a machine is defective?"

She was in her new location, breaking the flashes off a batch of completed gears. This was another aspect of the job the women did; before sorting and packing the orders for shipping, they cleaned the extra bits of plastic from the edges of the pieces. Helen finished up the gear she was working on and put it in the box beside her before she answered.

"Well, I go right over to whichever operator it is and tell him he'd better keep his eyes open and stop doing wrong the thing he's doing wrong."

"But, Helen, how do you know what he's doing wrong? You're not a methods person or a setup man. That's not your job and you're not trained to do it."

"But we've always done it this way, Greg. Jeannette and I know bad work when we see it and the men know we do. Now take Rick—you know he likes to race and sometimes . . ."

"No, Helen," Greg interrupted. "That's not the point. Of course, you can spot bad work. But what I'm talking about is you wouldn't know *why* it was bad. You see, that's my responsibility. I'm the one who has to maintain the quality in this department, so I should be called in on these things. From now on, Helen, when you or Jeannette spot a bad piece, I want you to call me over. That way, I'll be able to see what's going wrong and figure out how to fix it."

Helen had gone back to the gears she was working on. "All right, Greg," she said without looking up. "If that's what you want, that's what you'll get."

Greg got it. Coming back from lunch a few days later, he found a box of several hundred tape drives on his desk. There was a note beside the box: "I thought you would want to see these pieces. They're no good. Helen."

A hell of a help that was. She hadn't said what was wrong with them and he couldn't tell. Greg started out to the shop, then realized that the women were still out to lunch.

"Of all the . . ." Greg muttered out loud in frustration. "When are they going to realize I'm doing all this for their own good?" He took a piece out of the box and slammed it down on the desk.

QUESTIONS

1 Comment on Greg's handling of Alfred's suggestion.
2 Under what circumstances should Greg allow Alfred and Henry to help each other and when not?
3 How do you evaluate the desirability of having Henry talk with materials handlers and Helen "correct" the molders?
4 How can Helen make Greg's job almost impossible?
5 What is the delegation problem here?

BEHAVIORAL EXERCISE

Identify a job with which you are familiar—either because you've seen it in action or you've actually worked on it—and try to describe precisely how this job relates to every other job around it. That is, try to make explicit what the jobholder should do with each person who has something to do with the job, when, how, where, how often. You should try to give a complete, detailed, and behavioral description of the job. The objective is to tell someone who has never worked on this job exactly how he or she is to relate to everyone with whom some relationship is necessary and how to conduct these relationships. The result will be a much more complete "work flow" analysis of a job than management ever provides, and you should be able to see how complicated human relations can be, even on the most seemingly simple of jobs. (Be sure to include people who provide materials, ideas, questions, assistance, potential interference, and so on.)

BIBLIOGRAPHY

Chapple, E., and L. Sayles, *The Measure of Management: Designing Organizations for Human Effectiveness*, Macmillan, New York, 1961, chap. 2.

Homans, G., *The Human Group*, Harcourt, New York, 1950, chaps. 3-10.

Taylor, C., *In Horizontal Orbit: Hospitals and the Cult of Efficiency*, Holt, New York, 1970.

Whyte, W., *Organizational Behavior*, Dorsey Press, Homewood, Ill., chaps. 9 and 11.

READING

From Kitchen to Customer*

WILLIAM F. WHYTE (1914-   )

Perhaps the best-known field worker and writer in the organizational
behavior field has been William F. Whyte, who is a professor at the
New York State School of Industrial Relations at Cornell. Following
on the anthropological field-work success of the bank wiring-room
part of the Western Electric studies (in which researchers sat back
and watched and became part of the furniture), Whyte instituted
studies in such diverse locales as Chicago restaurants, Oklahoma
oil refineries, a midwest steel container plant, and a fine-glass
products plant in New York State. His detailed and vivid descriptions of work groups and worker-supervisor relations have been
captured in his books: *Human Relations in the Restaurant Industry,
Money and Motivation, Men at Work,* and *Pattern for Industrial
Peace.* Both Sayles and Strauss worked with him in some of his
research studies at Cornell, and all three with Chapple share this
emphasis on observation rather than questionnaires. Chris Argyris of
Yale, whose work in human relations has also become very famous,
was a student of Whyte's.

Thus Whyte and his students have emphasized the importance
of field work as distinct from abstract theorizing. Whyte's work
shows that managerial activities differ substantially depending upon
the nature of the technology. Oil refineries do not pose the same
challenge as restaurants, and the manager better comprehend the
pattern of relationships among employees, among managers, as
between staff and line managers, necessary to maintain coordination. His work emphasizes the actual give and take required among
people to fulfill the requirements of the underlying technology.

In recent years, Whyte has returned to his earlier anthropological
interests and has been studying the problems of a developing
country: Peru. His work there illustrates the significant applicability
of management theory to a wide variety of social and political
problems, not just business. Whyte's broad interests make it difficult
to categorize his work; it includes both sociology and anthropology,
and business and public administration.

The girls themselves blamed the downstairs countermen for much of
their difficulty. Their explanation was simply that the downstairs
countermen had difficult personalities, whereas Sam, the chief upstairs counterman, was very easy to get along with.

---

*Reprinted from William F. Whyte, *Human Relations in the Restaurant Industry*, McGraw-Hill,
New York, 1948, pp. 72-75.

There are several things wrong with such an explanation. In the first place, all the downstairs countermen had been with Jessup's for years, and were very highly regarded by the management. This would not prove that they had "pleasant personalities," but it does show that we are not talking about the unstable short duration employees upon whom so many of management's problems were blamed. Furthermore, the men were known to get along well with each other. Then, comparing them with the upstairs men, we can say that while Sam equalled them in experience, his various co-workers were inexperienced and—according to the waitresses—difficult to get along with.

When we hear that an individual has a good personality, we should ask, good to whom? We must recognize that the same individual may be easy to get along with in one relationship and very difficult in another. This discredits the personality explanation.

The layout of the counter was very important. While men, being on the average taller than the girls, could look down at them across the counter, the girls had to stand on tiptoe to talk effectively with the men. Even then a counterman could step back or bend over and drop out of sight. This enabled the men to ignore the waitresses or else to drop verbal bombshells across the counter when they were least expected.

When everything was running smoothly, there was no need for countermen and waitresses to talk with each other. Hours or even days could go by in which there was virtually no contact between them. This meant that the countermen were not accustomed to responding to the waitresses. And since the height of the counter was a bar to informal conversation, nearly all the talk that went across the counter was in the nature of gripes, demands, protests, and indignant denunciations. While the total amount of interaction was small, such frictions were not balanced by any informal adjustment, and the waitresses found the situation very hard on their nerves.

Upstairs the situation was quite different. Sam had his formula to take the pressure off himself, and through his informal ties with the girls, established outside of working hours, he built up relationships through which it was possible to adjust many of the conflicts arising out of the nervous tension. Even when there was trouble with one of his coworkers, Sam was there to smooth things out. The girls were able to tell him of their troubles, and he told them of the problems he was facing, so that they were not left in the dark as were the girls downstairs.

This does not mean that the low service counter is superior from a human-relations point of view. Sam's adjustment with the girls was something that had simply grown up between them. It was not determined by the layout of the counter or by the policies of management. If, for example, Lew had been substituted for Sam, then surely there would have been trouble at that counter. We can only say that a waist-high counter makes possible an informal adjustment—or a pitched battle.

When we ask whether a high or a low counter is better, we must also ask, better for whom? The men behind the high counter found it an ideal arrangement and would have been very much upset if the barrier had been lowered. The waitresses took the barrier for granted and complained only of the personalities of the men behind it.

What can management do in this situation? Any move by supervisors that results in better coordination of production with service will automatically lead to more harmonious relationships. Since restaurants differ so much from each other, we cannot undertake to work out any detailed plan in this general study. We can only point to this as one of the key problems of the industry and suggest that it needs the most thoughtful attention of restaurant people.

The point of contact between waitresses and pantry people also deserves special supervisory attention. In Jessup's restaurant, when supplies did not come up, the waitresses felt frustrated not only because they were delayed but also because they could not understand what was going on. When they demanded the attention of the countermen, this only created friction. If the pantry supervisor had been able to step in between the two groups, explain the situation to the waitresses, and let them blow off steam to her, it seems likely that the flood of tears could have been avoided. It may be worth while to experiment in developing a go-between role for the pantry supervisor.

Before we leave the service pantry, we should look at the social role of the insignificant-looking spindle. It serves to fend off from pantry people a good deal (but not all) of the pressure exerted by waitresses. Where we have men (unaccustomed to taking orders from women) behind the counter, it seems likely that the spindle makes the difference between a workable system and one that would blow up.

There are still other ways of handling spindles in the counterman-waitress relationship. We observed one restaurant in which the waitresses handed all their written order slips to a pantry supervisor (male), who in turn placed them on the proper spindles where they were picked up and acted upon by fry cooks and countermen. Completed orders were placed in warming compartments where they were picked up by the waitresses. If the girls had any complaint about the service they were getting, they did not speak directly to the men behind the counter but turned instead to the supervisor, who explained the situation or took other appropriate action. Under this system, the men behind the counter had to respond to only one man, the supervisor, and contact between waitresses and pantry workers was completely eliminated.

The spindle is also of great importance where we have middle-aged counterwomen and young waitresses. Where the counter is waist high, there is a temptation for waitresses to call in their orders instead of taking the time to write them out. The dessert-pantry woman in one restaurant frequently allowed waitresses to dispense with the slips, but she stood on her rights when she was dealing with a waitress who was less than half her age and seemed to enjoy ordering her around. "If you want desserts," she said once, "you'll have to learn to write them out. I positively will not serve you any more unless you do." Later the pantry woman said, "I can't stand that kid. She's too fresh for me—snippy little thing."

To sum it up, wherever the people on the receiving end of the orders are related to the order givers as males vs. females, or older vs. younger, then it is important for the pantry people to have some impersonal barrier to block the pressure from themselves. Even when such differences are eliminated, the use of spindles makes the job easier for the pantry people.

5

GROUPS AND THE INVISIBLE ORGANIZATION

LEARNING OBJECTIVES

1 Explain why employees join informal groups.

2 Define the concept of norms and describe the types of norms common to most informal organizations.

3 Diagnose the sources of conflict between the formal and the informal organization.

4 Describe cohesive groups and how they got that way.

5 Analyze group leadership—the role and function of the leaders in an informal organization.

6 Spell out the ways in which the supervisor can deal effectively with the informal organization.

7 Determine the guidelines for using group participation.

At first glance, the title of this chapter resembles a paradox wrapped within an enigma. If the groups we're talking about are informal, that is, unrecognized by the formal organization and have no legal status, how can we link them to the development of an organization, and an invisible organization at that—one that lacks the formal authority both to make rules and to enforce them? These are two indispensable attributes of any organization. If the informal group lacks both of them, why bother spending time studying it?

INVISIBLE STANDARDS

To start unwrapping the enigma, let's take the case of Hank Brewster. At home in his basement workshop, Hank is a whiz with a lathe—very fast and very accurate. But on the job, it's a different story. He's still accurate—he hasn't changed in that way. But speed is a different story: Hank works at about half the pace he consistently makes in his home workshop.

How come? After his first few days in the department, a couple of the people took him aside and "wised him up." "There's no sense in killing yourself, kid. A fair day's work around here, for your job, is twenty to twenty-five borings an hour." That was the essence of their message. And because Hank was eager to be accepted by his co-workers, he not only got the message—he also took it very much to heart. Over the past two years, Hank's production has deviated very little in either direction from the norm set by the informal—what we call the invisible—organization.

In another instance, the worker who always makes sure the safety guard is in its proper position on the power saw in his home workshop will leave the safety goggles in his locker. Why is he cautious at home and careless on the job? The same reason as in the case of Hank Brewster: At home he is conforming to his personal values, and at the plant, he is adjusting to the standards of the informal organization.

A couple of things may strike you about these hypothetical but true-to-life illustrations. First, in both cases the employee, in conforming to the standards of the informal organization, is in conflict with his own value system. Second, his behavior also conflicts with the norms of the formal organization—obviously, management wants higher production and wouldn't have issued safety goggles unless it wants them worn on the job. Evidently, the informal organization within the informal group sets up norms that can motivate employees, on occasion, to behave in ways that contradict both their own value system and that of the formal organization. All of which suggests that the reasons why employees form informal groups must be many and powerful.

Let's take time for a definition and a qualification. In the case of the informal group and the informal organization, it's easy to tell which is the chicken and which is the egg: The informal group always comes first, but not all informal groups achieve organizational status, a state in which the group develops explicit standards along with explicit sanctions to make these standards stick. The qualification is that even in the most cohesive group, not all the members live up to all the standards all the time. However, a pretty high batting average on conformity is the price of membership, at least in any group deserving of the designation "informal organization."

WHY EMPLOYEES JOIN INFORMAL GROUPS

The propensity of employees to become members of an informal organization, at first glance, looks surprising when you consider that they are already members of a formal organization with a specified role and specific duties, explicit channels of communication, and a definite line of command. What more could they need?

A good deal more—obviously. Looked at one way, and a quite legitimate way it is, employees develop informal groups to meet needs that are left unsatisfied by the formal organization. To what needs are we referring?

Friendship

First, not in order of importance but because it's the simplest need and the one that comes most readily to mind, is friendship, companionship—call it by whatever name you will. Humans are social beings who spend about half their waking hours at work. They need and enjoy the social contacts with their fellow workers—joking, sharing experiences, getting their opinions off their chests, obtaining a sympathetic hearing to their troubles when necessary.

Take the case of the supervisor of a word processing department who learned the importance of sociability—what sociologists prefer to call interaction—the hard way. The woman felt that the typists did entirely too much gabbing, but none of her verbal admonitions took. Finally, she decided on a drastic step and, with the office manager's permission, had plywood partitions installed between the workplaces. What happened? By Monday noon all work had ceased and a delegation of the typists informed the supervisor that they would not return to work unless the partitions were removed. She had no choice but to yield to the ultimatum. Yes, sociability does count.

And in the group context, it counts even more. The adage is

wrong—familiarity *doesn't* breed contempt. Quite the reverse. Usually, the more people interact with one another, the friendlier their feelings toward each other become. To say it another way, in the informal group, which is characterized by a high frequency of interaction between the members, companionship becomes an increasingly attractive reason for membership as progressively friendlier feelings develop between the members.

Identification

Linked to it but separate from friendship as a motive for joining an informal group is what we call *identification* or sense of belonging—and what Barnard rather grandly called "the condition of communion." We all need to belong, to associate with others in purposes and goals that may encompass and also transcend our individual self-interest. Of course, the formal organization has its goals and purposes. The problem is, at least in an organization of any size, that these purposes appear abstract, remote, and meaningless to the average employee. What rank-and-file worker can identify with a chairman of the board and his purposes?

However, one can and does identify with one's immediate work group, which is a reason one becomes affiliated in the first place. Let's take an example from the military to illustrate our point. Studies conducted during World War II showed that bravery and the willingness to make sacrifices have little to do with a person's grasp of the overall objectives of the conflict, a commitment to them, or a devotion to the triple abstraction "honor, duty, country." On the contrary, they have almost everything to do with the individual soldier's loyalty to an immediate group—a desire not to let any buddies down. George Homans, in his classic study of the human group, summed it up thus: "That both self-interests and something else are satisfied by group life is a truth that is the hardest for the hard-boiled—and half-baked—person to see. As Mayo says, 'if a number of individuals work together to achieve a common purpose, a harmony of interests will develop among them to which individual self-interest will be subordinated. This is a very different doctrine from the claim that individual self-interest is the primary human motive.'"

Thus, one reason why Hank Brewster went along with the production quota laid down by the informal organization was that, in general, he had, as an employee, subordinated his personal goals to those of the group. He had, as it were, exchanged the satisfactions of independence for those of association and, typically, he felt better for it.

117

GROUPS AND THE INVISIBLE ORGANIZATION

Production

Another motive for Brewster's going along with the group in setting production quotas suggests another reason why employees form groups: to attain protection for the membership, especially protection from what the members feel are impositions and encroachments by management. This time the adage works—in unity *does* lie strength. Although it's true that employees may occasionally band together to defend themselves from another work group, nine-tenths of the time the enemy is management and the protection the workers seek is from management's demands for additional output, longer work hours, higher quality, restriction of customary privileges, and other constraints. Many organizations, for example, introduce changes in work methods at a faster pace than the individual employee can comfortably adjust to. On their own, employees can accomplish little. Conform or quit are their alternatives. However, when the group as a whole objects and the supervisor faces the prospect of slowdowns, discreet sabotage, or a concerted campaign to put him or her in a bad light with superiors, he or she is likely to do whatever can be done to make the introduction of the work methods compatible with the group's ability or, to speak more precisely, its willingness to accept them.

Getting back to Hank Brewster: An individual employee may have a personal concept of what constitutes a fair day's work. As long as it remains a personal concept, it will avail an individual little if it's contrary to management's definition. Over the comparatively short run, the employee has to bend or be bounced. Once again, the group is in a different position. With a concerted opposition to its standards of what constitutes a fair day's work, management faces an altogether unpleasant alternative: Fire the whole group or live with its production quotas. Just as long as the standards set by the group permit what management feels is a reasonable output and a reasonable rate of return, and when the group is relatively difficult to replace, most managements elect to put up with its standards. We've come a long way from the joys of undiluted ownership and unregulated enterprise as exemplified by Colonel Borden of Fall River, Massachusetts, a lord of the loom, who, when his workers demanded a ten-hour day, replied, "I saw that mill built stone by stone; I saw the pickers, the carding engines, the spinning mules and looms put into it, one after the other, and I would see every machine and stone crumble and fall to the floor again before I would accede to your wishes." Against such an attitude and such a man, any group would be helpless. However, we repeat—we've come a long way.

Exploitation

We've been talking about protection against management as one reason why employees join groups. Less frequently, they join in order to exploit the strategic advantages inherent in their work position. Whereas the posture of most informal groups toward management is defensive, theirs is offensive. By presenting a united front to management, they seek to gain—and are frequently successful in gaining—advantages not enjoyed by the rest of the work force, such as looser standards, more discretion over work methods, more overtime, and other concessions. To cite a flagrant example, in one plant the automatic screw-machine operators were the only hourly employees to enjoy a paid lunch hour—a case of discrimination which surely rankled the less favorably placed and hence less favored members of the work force. Such groups, generally small in number but positioned so they can disrupt overall operations at will, usually aren't hostile to management. They're often high-producing groups, composed of clear-eyed opportunists bent on using their strategic advantage as a lever to extract whatever benefits they can from management.

Assistance

Nor are these the only reasons why employees join groups. When the employee has a problem, it's natural to ask for help from a member of the group instead of from the boss. The assistance given is usually just as valuable, and the employee has been spared the tension and embarrassment frequently involved in admitting failure to the supervisor. In the bank wiring room of Western Electric, members of the group frequently helped each other even though the rules forbade it. The fact that helping and being helped made them feel better was the simple but adequate explanation the workers gave as to why they violated the rule.

Groups also help to facilitate the use of creativity and initiative even when the job requirements are rigid and the jobs themselves simple and undemanding. This exercise of initiative is sometimes desirable from management's viewpoint. Exchanging jobs in the bank wiring room, for example, even though contrary to the rules, probably made a positive contribution to morale and efficiency. On other occasions, such as when a group puts its heads together in order to beat a complicated incentive formula, it exercises its creativity at management's expense. The key point is that on jobs which provide little intrinsic opportunity for the use of initiative or creativity, employees manage, under the umbrella of group sanction, to exercise both. The individual employee wouldn't risk it alone, most such expressions being clearly contrary to the rules or outside them. However, with group approval and support, the risk is less and the satisfaction greater.

HOW GROUPS BECOME ORGANIZATIONS

In our discussion, we're restricting ourselves to work groups whose members share common job interests. We've neglected friendship cliques because they are of secondary importance to the supervisor and to the organizational process in general. Given the parameters of our concern, it's fair to state that all informal groups have the potential to become informal organizations and that all aspire to this goal. Not all of them make it. As we indicated previously, a work group that has achieved organizational status is one that has norms or standards accepted by the group, plus an effective procedure for punishing members who violate them. In short, a norm is more than an ideal. Conformity to the norm almost invariably results in rewards, and non-conformity almost invariably ends up in punishments.

What type of norms are we referring to? Do all groups have the same norms? A double-barreled reply would be that the things groups care about—that become embodied in their norms—show striking similarities among groups, but that the content of the norms themselves shows equally striking diversities. The informal organization usually develops norms that cover chiseling, squealing to management about a coworker, standards of behavior between group members, and quality and quantity of work. This list is by no means exhaustive, but it does include the areas most frequently subject to norms. Within the areas, the norms vary widely. What passes for officious behavior in an informal organization of electronics workers might be totally acceptable among a group of coal miners. In an informal organization composed largely of skilled craftspeople, quality norms typically will be very high. Among semiskilled workers, they will be much lower. Between plants and sometimes even within the same plant, there will be significant differences between output norms: One informal organization may progressively restrict productivity while another may sanction increasingly higher output. Instances of both practices abound.

Output control deserves special mention because it's the one type of norm found in every informal organization. And for good reason. As one of the authors of this book wrote in an earlier study of industrial work groups—and the thesis is also valid for white-collar work groups:

"Output control is a basic objective of group action as well as an essential element in maintaining group stability. Not only the relation of the members to one another but the durability of the worker's relation to his job depends on the efficiency of the process." He cited instances of "runaway" output where group controls were feeble, and young and low-status employees exceeded the production and earnings records of their "betters." "The results were calamitous for the internal status hierarchy of the department and ultimately for the effectiveness of the formal organization."

Norms

Because output control is the prototype of all norms, we should get a viable insight into the overall process of the formation of norms once we understand—*really* understand—in even one instance how the norm of output control has been determined. Back to the bank wiring room! (We make no apologies for the backtrack. After fifty years, the Hawthorne studies, and the bank wiring room study in particular, are still the most systematic, exhaustive, and illuminating investigations of informal work groups.) In the bank wiring room, the wiremen decided that 6,000 or 6,600 completed connections a day, depending on the type of equipment being wired, were a proper day's work—a figure well below what management considered a desirable norm. That the norm represented what many of the wiremen had been used to reaching, that it reflected a depression atmosphere in which the fear was very real that too much output might result in one or more members of the group losing their jobs (some workers in the plant had been laid off prior to the development of the norms), that it indicated a measure of thankfulness at not being unemployed when so many were, together with a sense of resentment at the supervisor for pressuring them for more output—all these elements illuminate but don't fully explain the quota. We know that the operators frequently stopped wiring when they had finished their quotas even though it was not official stopping time. And we also know that the concept of a day's work was related to a variety of fears—that the rate might be cut, that it might be raised, that the "bogey" might be raised, that someone might be laid off, or that the supervisor might bawl out the slower men. All these fears somehow contributed to the formulation of a specific production quota.

We say somehow. The process is mysterious and will remain so largely, as Homan states, because the process was subconscious. "The behavior of the employees could be described as an effort to protect themselves against such changes in routines and human associations: to give management the least possible opportunity of interfering with them. When they said that if they increased their output 'something' was likely to happen, a process of this sort was going on in their minds. But the process was not a conscious one. It is important to point out that the protective function of informal organizations was not a product of deliberate planning. It was more in the nature of an automatic response." In other words, the group decides what the finish line should be after it starts to run the race—norms emerge from activities with a previous track record, but the decision is reached via a subconscious consensus.

Sanctions

With sanctions, we're on more solid ground. The process by which the punishment is matched to the crime may be just as elusive as the process by which the norm that occasioned the sanction evolved, but the sanctions themselves are usually visible. One worker summed up the informal organization's ability to control its members as follows: "You have your choice between standing in with the group and standing in with the boss. And if you don't go along with the group, the gang can make it mighty unpleasant." That it can. The informal organization's most potent disciplinary weapon is rejection or ostracism. The employee who doesn't conform will end up on the outside looking in. Initially, discipline may be mild—a warning to fall into line. If this doesn't bring the worker back into the fold, he or she can expect to be cut off from the group's social activities—lunching together, bowling after work, exchanging small talk at coffee breaks. If the group considers the recalcitrant employee a real threat to its stability, it may take more extreme measures, such as spreading malicious rumors or sabotaging tools. Ultimately, it may try to get the worker fired or make life so miserable that he or she quits.

Because output control is the sacred totem among norms, you would expect an exceptionally severe handling of deviance, and you'd be correct. The typist who persists in averaging eighty words a minute when the group feels that sixty words is a fair pace stands an excellent chance of being ejected from the group. A worker's equipment may be "adjusted" while he or she is away, or coworkers may withhold information or be slow in delivering supplies. In a plant, if the group thinks it unwise to produce more than 500 units a day, steps will be taken to control the worker who consistently produces 600. Such steps can be drastic up to and including "binging"—pounding a ratebuster's arm until it's so sore that the deviant output can't possibly be maintained. In the bank wiring room, on one occasion, a worker identified as W. 8 told W. 6, one of the two men who consistently exceeded the group standard, "If you don't quit, I'll binge you." When W. 6 persisted, W. 8 struck him and then chased him around the room. W. 6, momentarily chastened by this experience, quit his own wiring, saying, "I've got enough done." Then he went over and helped another wireman.

GOAL CONFLICTS

In our discussion of the norms evolved by the informal organization, two facts stand out: Some of the norms developed by the informal organization may be in conflict with either the employee's personal norms or the norms of the formal organization—sometimes with both. And yet, time after time, the norms of the informal organization take precedence. The employee forsakes any personal preferences and risks retaliation—whatever steps the boss may take to bring her or him into line—from the representatives of the formal organization.

Conflict between Groups

Let's add another dimension to the problem. There are also conflicts *between* groups, and they frequently coalesce around the differences between the group norms. Conflicts between work groups that share the responsibility for the same product are inevitable—mistakes will happen and buck-passing is a universal phenomenon. The extra measure of exacerbation is provided by the fact that cohesive groups (groups that have achieved informal organization) are peculiarly suspicious of outside groups. We're talking about something that you may have observed yourself as a member of a group—or will if you think about it. The more friends like each other when they're in a group, the more they tend to dislike outsiders. As stated in the hypothesis formulated by Homans: "The greater the inward solidarity, the greater the outward hostility." The bank wiremen, our tried and tested examples, found themselves, after they had developed cohesiveness, antagonistic to the men who hadn't taken part in the study and who had remained in the department. The study group claimed that the stay-behinds were discriminating against them in various small matters.

What we have is the potential for a circular and vicious pattern: The members of a cohesive group start off with a chip on their collective shoulder via-à-vis other groups; the first possibility for a conflict with the other group is joyously embraced and blown up out of reasonable proportion; the other group retaliates in kind; both groups treat the other as an enemy—and the group that started it all basks in the dubious satisfaction of a self-fulfilled prophecy.

To take a hypothetical example, a work group on the night shift of a belt factory finds that the bins contain a lot of defective material. They all leap to the conclusion that the day shift is trying to make them look bad. Actually, the handlers had delivered a batch of material too late for anyone on the day shift to inspect it. So, in retaliation, the night group works only on the good material and leaves the defective material in the bins for the day shift. The day shift, in turn, takes one look at the bins and swears to get even "with those miserable idiots on the night shift." So it goes.

The problem would be compounded if the day shift, for example, has the responsibility of inspecting work done by the night shift—as sometimes happens—and evaluating the quality of the work performed. If the quality norms of the two groups are different, as they will almost certainly be, it would be difficult to exaggerate the resentment and retaliation that might ensue.

Conflict between Informal and Formal Organizations

As we've indicated, an even more serious kind of outsider-insider conflict occurs between the informal organization with its goals and the formal organization with its goals—what the sociologists like to call the problems of suboptimization. We've said enough about them already to indicate the gravity and frequency of the problem. Let's just give one simple illustration by way of example.

The shelf-fillers in a supermarket had developed their own procedures for doing the work, one of which was tackling the aisles in rotation, with the entire store being worked on within each six-day period. Logical and neat? Perhaps. However, the system contained two aspects that delayed customers and even prevented the filling of orders: An unexpected run on an item might denude the shelves even though refills were no farther away than the store basement. More serious, each Saturday, hordes of shoppers found at least one aisle jammed with crates and cartons a good part of the day. In short, the two prime norms of the formal organization, sales and service, were under attack by the work procedures developed by the shelf-fillers.

Whether or not the store manager could successfully buck the norms and keep the aisles cleared and the shelves filled would depend on a number of factors—the unity of the group, how much these norms meant to its members, their attitudes toward the manager, the skill used in dealing with the group and its leaders, the ability to replace some or all the shelf-fillers if necessary—and we've sketched only the most obvious factors. The manager just might decide to put up with the crowded aisles and give the customers such specious apologies as "Sorry, we're temporarily out of stock." But this would be a weak manager.

THE MAINSPRINGS OF COHESION

We've just stated that the store manager's getting his or her way with the shelf-fillers would depend in part on how united they were, on whether they had formed a cohesive group. The statement is true as far as it goes, but we haven't said very much. We've also seen that groups differ greatly in the degree of cohesiveness they achieve, a fact of prime importance for the plant or office supervisor and his or her relationship with the informal groups. But why are some groups cohesive and others disunited? Why do some groups develop norms and a capacity to attain them despite resistance from within and pressure from without, while other groups have few if any norms and lack the stamina to defend those they do possess? As with most questions involving the human behavior in an organization, there is not one answer but several, all of them interrelated.

Status

Status plays a part. The member of a high-status group is keenly conscious of being part of an elite, with privileges, pay, and deference that set it off from the rest of the community. The employee naturally identifies with the rest of the group. This was so with the mandarin class in Imperial China and it is so today with the diemakers and patternmakers, the mandarins of the industrial work force.

Close contact

Smallness of group size helps. We've already seen how constant, face-to-face contact develops strong feelings of loyalty and friendship. In short, the small work group tends to be cohesive. Another obvious by-product of the constant interaction in the small work group is ease of communication. And exchanging views, developing a consensus, and making strategic moves to defend or extend their norms all require frequent interaction among members of the group.

Communication

The key determinant of ease of communications, however, is not geographical proximity. In the typical assembly line, workers are physically close to each other, but the structure of the line limits each employee's interactions while working pretty much to the people immediately preceding and immediately following him or her on the line. In some steel mills and foundries, the noise level makes verbal interactions almost impossible, so the employees are reduced to communicating simple messages by banging a hammer against a steel plate. On the other hand, widely scattered workers, such as maintenance workers and materials handlers, communicate with ease and frequency because the nature of their jobs requires frequent interaction. We even know of one highly cohesive group of electric utilities substation operators who never saw one another but whose work required them to communicate constantly by telephone.

Similar work
Performing the same or similar work creates a sense of common economic self-interest among group members. This, in turn, leads to frequent interaction and the development of feelings of friendship and identification which transcend the bonds of self-interest and lay the basis for an informal organization. Similar jobs, of course, don't always contribute to cohesion—witness the sometimes frantic competition of store clerks for scarce customers. Our hypothesis is that similarity of jobs among members of a work group is a cohesive factor unless the higher earnings of one member of necessity result in lower earnings for another—except where, although the members are pitted in direct competition with one another, even the minimum earnings appear sufficient to motivate the group. We recall, for example, a chat with one of the bartenders at the King Cole Room at the Saint Regis Hotel in New York. He confided that they each made at least twenty "purple fish" ($20,000) a year. And those were 1946 dollars. Presumably, competition for tips among such affluent employees wouldn't inhibit the development of group cohesiveness.

In exploring the mainsprings of cohesiveness, we have thus far done most of our digging within the group itself. If only cohesiveness were that simple!

Common background
We have overlooked secondary but influential factors such as the behavior of the supervisor. She or he can discourage cohesiveness by fostering competition between group members, encourage it by nurturing and rewarding cooperation between members (as discussed in Chapter 4). Then there are influences of age, sex, marital status, and ethnic, cultural, and religious orientation. No one of the last six is very influential by itself. But if you combine several—for example, if you

have a work group composed predominantly of middle-aged, married, female, Irish-Catholic high school graduates such as you would find among many groups of light assembly workers in electronics plants along Route 128 in Massachusetts—you have a combination of factors that would contribute to the development of cohesion.

Power—the Mystique of Success

Contribute to the development of cohesion is right, but such a group would probably not become cohesive because it would lack the most important requisites for the development of group cohesiveness— power and the mystique of success. In an earlier study, one of the authors of this book determined, after extensive research, that the most cohesive groups studied were those who possessed the heaviest clout—the greatest power—within the organization and therefore presented the strongest threat to the formal organization. Their members' skills were indispensable and next to impossible to replace. Their position in the technology of the organization was such that if they decided on a work stoppage—though they were usually few in number—they would paralyze the entire operation and nullify the efforts of ten, a hundred, or even a thousand times as many workers. The patternmakers and diemakers are two such groups. So are the automatic screw-machine operators, the cutters in the clothing industry, and the "ding men" who make the final repairs on the metal body on an automobile assembly line. Slightly less powerful and even more aggressive and cohesive are such groups as metal polishers, in-plant truckers, and welders. Apparently, they have more need to throw their weight around.

The relationship that exists between power and cohesiveness is a complex one. The groups, high in status and power but recognizably not at the top, are like Avis—they have to try harder. As for the groups at the top with few demands left to satisfy—objectively speaking, management has more gripes against them than they have against management (witness the paid lunch hour for the screw-machine operators cited earlier); they tend to become complacent and somewhat lax in chastising deviations from their norms. They develop a measure of toleration for eccentric behavior, one of the hallmarks of a well-established group or class.

The success mystique is almost self-explanatory: The more powerful the group, the more successful it will be. Power contributes to cohesiveness and also to success, which in turn reinforces the sense of cohesiveness. With many such groups, it would take nothing less than a revolution in the technology of the production process to weaken their power position or undermine their cohesiveness.

To reformulate our definition of cohesiveness: All other things being equal, the smaller the group, the more similar the work performed, the greater the ease of communications between members, and the higher its status, the more cohesive the group will be. Some things being more equal than others, however, we add the codicil that a highly cohesive group depends on its being in a position, by virtue of the state of technology, to exert continuous and effective pressure on management in pursuit of its goals. In short, in a power struggle it has management at an overall disadvantage. Sometimes, giving in to its requests will appear less costly to management than the risks involved in refusal.

GROUP LEADERS—AND HOW THEY ACHIEVE LEADERSHIP

Most groups, certainly all cohesive groups, develop leaders—and leaders come in many sizes. Selection of informal leaders is a complex and varying process. In some instances, the informal leader is the functional head of the work group, a person with quasi-supervisory duties who is frequently known as the crew chief or "straw boss." Of course, the crew chief doesn't have to be accepted as the informal leader, but because management and the union (where there is one) turn to the leader in dealing with the group, it's hard for the members to reject that individual. Any attempt to do so would result in a real donnybrook, tear the group apart, and cause no end of trouble for the manager.

In other cases, informal leaders—and we stress the plural because a work group seldom has a single leader—evolve as the result of natural selection. But different leaders perform different functions. In a group concerned with adjusting the small parts that go into telephone equipment, for example, one leader dealt with any outsiders while another handled the enforcement of standards of output and behavior. One was, in effect, foreign secretary, and one was home secretary. In other groups, leadership is even more specialized. One person may deal with management, another with the union, and a third with maintaining internal unity. In part, this division of responsibility reflects a recognition of the strengths and weaknesses of the people involved, but it also reveals the fact that opinion in the group is rarely unanimous on all matters. Some of the leaders' actions in negotiating with management may be unpopular with a strong minority of the group. Diffusion of leadership may be necessary to maintain group cohesion.

Cohesive group—conforming leader

What kind of men or women are the informal leaders of the work group? In a really cohesive group, they are its most representative members. They may also be more articulate, more personable, or more gregarious, but these qualities count as nothing if they do not also conform—and conform more completely than most—to the norms of the informal organization. In the bank wiring room, for example, the leader (in this case there was one clearly identifiable leader) conformed to the norms more rigidly than any other member of the group. As Homans wrote of Taylor, the group leader, "He is not the most, but the least free person within it." Leadership was thrust upon him, and this was the only route to power the group would tolerate.

Uncohesive group—the best line wins

Other groups, with less cohesion, are suckers for the charismatic leader, the strong personality with an overpowering ego who imposes personal purposes upon the group. Some loosely cohesive and erratic groups align themselves for no rational reason under the banner of a particularly aggressive individual with a promising line. The same group for no more rational reason may transfer its allegiance overnight to a slightly more aggressive individual with a presumably even more promising line. And some groups are so weak and so disorganized that they have no recognizable goal and no identifiable leader.

When you look at the situation closely, there are only two legitimate roles for any leader of a group. They were identified almost two hundred years ago by Edmund Burke in his letter to the Electors of Bristol: A leader either reflects the views of those he represents as closely as possible—the mirror theory of representation—or else he feels that it is his duty to mold them, educate them, and represent their potential and presumably better sentiments, not necessarily their current beliefs. (The latter point of view was espoused by Burke himself.) When the group is intelligent and united, the leader must either bow to its will or persuade it to change its mind through an appeal to reason. When it's disorganized, with its power weak and its position unclear, the leader can manipulate the members and leadership belongs to the most skillful demagogue among them.

DEALING WITH THE LEADERSHIP

Most groups have leaders. How does the supervisor deal with leaders? Again, there is no single, simple answer. Let's first take a look at two minicases. You could label them "right way" and "wrong way," but if you did, you would be more wrong than right.

The Shipping Room Gets Its Comeuppance

Bert Fogarty, the supervisor of shipping, was hopping mad—the superintendent had just bawled him out about the productivity of his crew.

"Those characters must just sit around on their butts all day," he had said. "They handled 20 percent less work last week and earned 10 percent more overtime. What are you doing, Fogarty, anyway—telling them to conserve their energy until three o'clock so they can earn more overtime?"

A properly chastened Fogarty cornered his crew and told them: "All this business of coming in ten to fifteen minutes late in the morning and coming back ten to fifteen minutes late from lunch stops here and now. Anyone who's late—one minute late—gets no overtime. Understand?"

Three weeks later, Bert looked over the production sheets and permitted himself a slight smile—he wasn't an expressive man. Production up 10 percent. "Well, it worked and I should have done it before," he mused to himself.

The Drafting Room Delivers a Message

Tom Hilson, the supervisor of the drafting room at Pioneer Astrodynamics, looked at the summary work sheets for the week. Just as he thought, output was down. Sure, there was an unusually large number of new workers—four out of twenty in the past four months. But to Hilson, that wasn't the whole story. "These characters drift in one at a time—it's not nine but nine-thirty with many of them, and the real goof-offs have the guts to come in at ten. Not that I don't appreciate that the bums get a phony round of applause from the rest of the people. They don't like it much better than I do."

Hilson slept on it, then acted. He called the drafting room together: "We're way over budget and we've got to make it up. One way is to make sure that everyone starts to work on time. From now on, there's no such a thing as being 'a little bit late.' " That was the essence of Hilson's message.

Three weeks later, Hilson looked at the records and moaned softly. Tardiness had declined all right—by 30 percent. But look at the other figures—absenteeism up 20 percent, completed work down by 15 percent—plus his feeling that interest in the projects at hand wasn't what it should be or even what it had been. Just yesterday, Jill Welsh, the best-liked person in the drafting room, had approached him and, after a couple of petty questions (probably a pretext for their conversation), dropped the remark that "Everyone really resents your getting on their backs to be on time. We'd all be a lot happier if you would relax a little." Jill's inflection rose a bit on "relax a little." She was a pretty subtle woman.

"So I should relax a little." Hilson looked at the sheet again and pursed his lips.

Why did Bert Fogarty succeed and Tom Hilson fail? After all, their problems were similar and their approaches to solving it were much alike, too. Fogarty *acted* tough while Hilson merely *talked* tough—an important distinction, but not, we think, the reason why one supervisor was successful and the other was not. The real explanation lies in the different nature of the two work groups.

Fogarty faced a group of shipping-room employees, people at the bottom of the plant's power and status totem pole—with easily acquired skills, low pay, and undesirable jobs. Such a group, which an author of this book has previously dubbed "apathetic," is characterized by passivity, lack of cohesion, and little or no recognizable informal leadership. Here, getting tough works: Fogarty, with threats, was able to cow the group into submission.

Not so with Hilson. Merely talking tough resulted in a surface compliance with his request, together with a tacit resistance that was far more damaging to the efficiency and productivity of the drafting room than the tardiness problem which had caused him to act in the first place. The shipping room folded under pressure, whereas the drafting room stiffened its resistance under pressure and fought back—it was that kind of group. The members had a sense of themselves as professional employees with distinct skills that were much in demand. They combined pride of technique with the knowledge of being valued as a group and difficult to replace. They had also, apparently, developed an informal leader—Jill Welsh—a factor which Hilson was either unaware of or preferred to ignore.

Hilson made two mistakes, one major and one minor. His minor mistake was in failing to recognize and use Welsh as a medium of communication to the group instead of trying to "bull his way through." His major error was in failing to appreciate that you can't bully or intimidate this kind of group. After all, the group with its mock applause was already applying a type of censure to the ten o'clock stragglers who were violating an apparent group norm—showing up before nine-thirty was OK, but later than that was taboo. We suspect that wisdom, for Hilson, would be to swallow a bit of pride, take Welsh's advice, and see what the records of completed work looked like in two or three weeks' time. Worse things can happen to a supervisor than having people a little bit late if output can be raised in the process.

Respect the Group Leaders' Position

We said that Hilson made an error in not recognizing Welsh as the informal leader of the drafting room and using her as a means of communicating his views to the group. In general, how should the supervisor treat the informal leadership of a cohesive group? "Respectfully" is a good one-word answer. "Share leadership with the informal leaders of the group" is a more precise and accurate answer, but one calculated to enrage many supervisors or at least arouse their opposition. They resent sharing their leadership. Some even overreact and end up repressing and destroying their capabilities for leadership. Either they become laissez-faire managers incapable of giving guidance, or they turn into "bureaupaths" who guide only by citing directives or statements from higher authority.

The psychological threat of sharing authority with the informal leadership is a real one for many managers. But consider the alternatives. Take the story of two supervisors (not in industry), one who worked with the group through its leadership and one who did not—in this case, through ignorance, not choice. They were social workers in charge of recreational centers in a slum area, and they faced a similar problem. The younger boys were supposed to leave the centers at 9 P.M. to make way for an older crowd who hung around outside and generally made a nuisance of themselves. One social worker pleaded with them again and again, in the interests of fair play, to go away and leave the center alone—but always to no avail. The other social worker faced the problem just once and solved it promptly. How? He went outside and said to the ringleader, "Listen, Joe. The time's up. Be a good fellow and take your gang out of here." This is a simple but dramatic illustration of the advantages of working through the informal leader. Of course, this wasn't the first contact between the successful social worker and Joe. He had made a regular practice of working through him at the recreation center.

It's true that in a nonunion situation, it's possible for the supervisor to pick off the informal leaders of a group one by one by getting them transferred or fired. However, in the end, you have at best a resentful but cowed mass of individuals who docilely follow orders. At the same time, they usually show a lack of initiative or teamwork, and their performance is likely to be substandard in most respects. Enough said.

Identify the Group Leaders

Assuming that it's desirable to work through the informal leaders, how does the supervisor, particularly the new supervisor, identify the leaders of the informal group? How does a manager make sure that he or she isn't being taken in by appearances—by the person who talks all the time or the one who clowns and kids and is therefore the center of attention? The answer—there's no substitute for close observation. The supervisor should look for the people the other employees go to when they have something on their minds—they are usually the same people who make the most sense when the supervisor is talking to them. One supervisor, somewhat uncertain of who the group leaders were—"the heavies," she called them because they carried the most weight with her crew—went around and asked each employee whom he or she wanted to work with on a special job. The two workers who got the most votes were, she figured, the two whom everyone listened to the most—and that's the way it turned out. The key determinant, proved by continuing observation, is who has influence over the group, who sets the pace. Most cohesive groups contain a few people of whom it can be said, "if they say go, it's usually go."

Work through Informal Leaders

How does the supervisor work with the informal leaders? Let's assume that a supervisor has thought up a rearrangement of work stations that would reduce motion and save time. He or she should try it out on the informal leadership before announcing it to the group. They may have objections that hadn't been anticipated and can't be answered. In any event, the assistance of informal leaders will be needed to sell the change to the group.

Equally important: Before the formal announcement of any change, the supervisor should let the informal leaders know in advance. Their feedback may reveal information that may be passed on to higher management, and there's a better chance in having their help in getting the change accepted if they have been taken into the supervisor's confidence.

The supervisor might extend recognition to an informal leader by asking for help in breaking in a new employee, confident that the new worker will be clued in to the group's norms as well as to the formal rules and regulations. If the supervisor has a disciplinary problem with an employee, she or he should try airing it with an informal leader. Because the leader has the confidence of that employee, the supervisor may receive a new insight into the problem. If the leader agrees with the boss's diagnosis of what's wrong, she or he may see that the group itself brings the person into line.

One thing the supervisor shouldn't do is to show favoritism toward the informal leaders, do special favors for them, or give them easier or higher paid assignments. Nothing can undermine their leadership position more quickly. The supervisor should extend recognition to the leaders and reinforce their status with the group by consulting with them—nothing less but also nothing more.

THE SUPERVISOR VERSUS THE INFORMAL ORGANIZATION

We've described in some detail how the supervisor of a closely knit group should work through its informal leaders and share authority with them. But what if the supervisor faces an informal organization with several norms, including one on output, that are opposed to the norms of the formal organization? What should the supervisor do then? How should the leaders of such a cohesive group be treated?

Emphasize the Positive

First of all, it is necessary to put the group into perspective. True, all cohesion in a group means is that the members will adhere closely to the group's standards, whatever they are. However, from the manager's viewpoint, cohesive groups have many positive characteristics. Morale is higher in a cohesive group, and turnover and absenteeism are usually lower. Members tend to work smoothly together, so the manager escapes the bickering, bad feelings, and poor workmanship frequently found in a disorganized group. Supervision is easier, too. The manager doesn't have to transmit orders and information to every member individually or consume time with formal meetings. Informal leadership can be depended on to act as the unofficial but effective channel of communication. Under many circumstances, then, the manager will want to encourage cohesiveness within the group, not try to suppress it. As for the informal leader, if one doesn't exist already, it will be necessary for the supervisor to invent one, or at any rate to develop whatever leadership potential is on hand within the group.

This holds true with groups that develop only a slight degree of cohesion on their own. Walker, Guest, and Turner found, in their study of workers on an automobile assembly line, for example, that the most effective managers were those who fostered group cohesiveness by delegating informal responsibility to the leaders of the group or by allowing the group—with guidance, to be sure—to establish informal systems of job rotation. Comparing many work groups, an author of this book found that those with the highest degree of cohesion ranked substantially above the apathetic groups in overall plant performance and cooperation.

All well and good—but cold comfort to the supervisor with a cohesive group that has enshrined low output as its number one norm. A little more perspective on the problem is needed before we talk about solutions. What about the output of the isolated employee who has to rely on pressures from the boss, the urge to make more money (provided she or he is on incentive pay), and the dictates of conscience in determining how much work to turn out? Most employees who fall into this category have undistinguished output records (the minority of ratebusters who somehow manage to exist even in cohesive groups being the spectacular exception). Deprived of the pleasures of group association and saddled with jobs that are for the most part intrinsically of little interest, these employees settle for making a minimal contribution to the organization.

Cohesive groups show a different output pattern. S. Tawley, director, The Institute of Social Research of the University of Michigan, found that highly cohesive work groups were likely to have output records that diverged in either direction from the plant averages. A similar study of output among groups of clerical workers emerged with the same conclusion. High productivity among cohesive groups is something you would expect. After all, restriction of output is born, in part, of fear, and the cohesive group with the ability to protect and advance its interests and to win justifiable grievances can afford to be productive. If management should take advantage of high output to raise standards, for example, the group could fight back and probably win.

A norm of low output is more difficult to understand. In some cases, the norm may be vestigial, a hangover from the days when the group forged its original cohesion largely in the successful effort to resist what it thought were unreasonable encroachments by management. Attitudes, once formed and institutionalized in low output norms, are difficult to change, even though the facts which prompted and justified them may have disappeared. Another factor which may partly or totally account for the low output norm in a cohesive group is the supervisor's attutude. He or she may have what one team of researchers called a "frozen group." They referred to a group made up of people who had decided (1) that management's plans for them were based on the conviction that they, like the machines they operated, would do no more nor less than they were told to do, and (2) that like machines, they were not expected to know more when they retired than when they were hired. Under such circumstances, decided the researchers, the group leaders had instinctively decided that their only chance to feel human was to stick together and give the company as little work as possible.

The Employee-centered Approach

To the extent that management's attitudes as symbolized and interpreted by the supervisor are the reasons for the low output norms of a work group, what should the supervisor do to turn things around? Sometimes the group's restriction on output is simply one way in which it expresses its frustration and discontent. The restriction gives the employees the chance to revenge themselves for what they see as deprivations. The implication is that the manager who recognizes the employees' needs and tries to meet them is less likely to have a department of restricters. Take the study of absenteeism and productivity made during World War II by Elton Mayo in an aircraft plant in Southern California (referred to in Chapter 2). Mayo found that absenteeism was high and productivity low. But there were some departments where absenteeism was phenomenally low and productivity was phenomenally high. What was the explanation for the difference? These were departments in which the development of team spirit was the central objective of the managers in charge. They devoted themselves to facilitating the work of their employees and to listening to whatever complaints or suggestions the employees might have. As a result, the employees felt that they were important rather than taken for granted, and as a group they exerted pressure to raise output, not to restrict it.

Consider another study made several years later by Rensis Likert and Daniel Katz of the University of Michigan. They examined the relationship between productivity and supervision in twenty-four departments of a large insurance company, twelve of which were low-producing and twelve, high-producing. As all the employees did similar work and had similar backgrounds, the researchers looked to the environment for the explanation of the disparity in production. The key difference, they found, was the supervisor's approach to managing his department. The supervisors seemed to fall into one of two categories: There was the employee-centered supervisor who considered managing people rather than expediting production to be his main job. And there was the production-centered supervisor who considered his main job to be getting the work done and viewed his workers as merely the tools for accomplishing that objective. He supervised with strict controls, while the employee-centered supervisor gave his subordinates more leeway and responsibility in handling their jobs. Significantly, the researchers found that the employee-centered supervisor was likely to be in charge of a high-producing group, while the production-centered supervisor's department was usually a low producer.

We're talking about the fact that, under the right conditions, the supervisor can accomplish wonders simply by practicing what two generations of experts have identified as good human relations. In a leaderless, disorganized group, the supervisor who cares about the employees, who presents their grievances to higher management, who listens sympathetically to their complaints, will be able to build cooperation and teamwork where little or none has existed before. And she or he will be the leader of the group in fact as well as in name.

The cohesive group asks much more of its supervisor, however. Tea and sympathy are not enough. Its members have already developed cooperation and a sense of teamwork among themselves. The group doesn't need to be made to *feel* important—it already *is* important, with the fruits of its victories over management and the supervisor to prove it. In other words, the successful supervisor must tailor his or her approach to the type of group under supervision and to the amount of functional power the group wields in the organization. Politics has been defined as the art of the possible, and management should be subject to the same definition. The manager who perceives the power situation realistically and makes the necessary concessions to circumstances is living out the spirit of that definition. One caveat: There is no sure formula for turning low-producing groups into high-producing ones, even though a generation of theorists and practitioners has been systematically overturning stones in its search for one.

Share the Decision-making Power

Caveat aside, there are things the supervisor can do to help get the support of the cohesive group. One set we have already discussed at length. In addition, the supervisor's real power should be shared with the leadership of the group—recognize, consult with, and be influenced by its leaders on just about any question of consequence. By so doing, he or she saves time and energy, expedites workable solutions to pressing problems, and permits the realistic adjustment of potential conflict situations. And under certain conditions, the manager should go even further and share power with the entire group. Because the group and its leadership are as one, group decision making can be resorted to without undermining the position of its leaders—or even seeming to try.

You may be surprised at the scope of decisions made with employee participation that have turned out to the advantage of all concerned. For example, take the touchy area of sales goals. The chemical department of McKesson & Robbins at one point enabled each sales representative to play a major part in setting individual sales goals for the forthcoming year. It gave this approach most of the credit for a substantial increase in sales volume per person after the system was first introduced. The sales representatives have consistently set high goals for themselves, in some cases higher than the goals their managers have thought reasonable and attainable.

Again, take performance appraisal—a real hot potato because it's linked, whether people admit it or not, to salary increases and promotions. Yet, in the personnel department of a large chemical company, each professional on the staff rates each member's performance including his or her own, and the results of the ratings are open to discussion among the group. The personnel director is not bound by the group consensus, but on several occasions the group's final rating has persuaded a member to change his or her initial evaluation.

The same department has made the annual budget subject to group participation and one year reduced expenditures by 30 percent in the process. The biggest cost variable in the department, next to salary, was travel. So the department head asked each member of the group to answer these questions: Where do I need to go? Where do I want to stay? For how long? How much do I need to spend? Then, the group as a whole set travel and training allowances on a per person, per year basis. The person with above-average training or travel needs is offset by the one whose budget need is below average. The group tackles each major budget item in a similar fashion.

Not that the successful application of group decision making is restricted to cohesive groups. We're arguing only that the approach is especially suited to such groups because the possibilities of achieving a consensus are the greatest. Thus the supervisor can frequently achieve results that couldn't be accomplished in any other way, since the groups have a built-in tendency to resent pressure and reject outside influence even—or maybe even more—when the sources of pressure are their own bosses.

Take the case of the industrial engineers in a metal-plating plant who were repeatedly frustrated in their efforts to figure out an equitable way of dividing up the women's work. Every time they made a suggestion, the women were quick to prove that it was unfair to someone. Finally the women asked, "Why not let us decide?" In a short while they had worked out job allocations that even the engineers agreed were superior to their own recommendations. In the solution there were no losers. The women had the satisfactions of exercising greater control over their jobs and of accomplishing something on their own. Management got a better decision and one that was more likely to be followed—employees are more apt to obey rules they set down themselves.

Guidelines for Group Participation

Participation by the group is no panacea, however. Let's consider some of the ground rules for successful group decision making and also some of the problems. Let's assume, for a moment, that you're a manager with little or no experience in holding group meetings of the problem-solving variety. Your experience has been limited chiefly to information-giving meetings in which you have offered people a chance to ask questions or even raise objections. But that's as far as you've ever gone. Now you're thinking of holding a problem-solving meeting with your subordinates and you're looking for some guidelines. We offer four that have helped many managers in setting up and running such a meeting.

1 Select a problem where the acceptance of the solution by the group is at least as important as the quality of the decision. Management, for example, doesn't care how vacations are scheduled, so long as jobs are covered and the time allotments are not exceeded. No vacation schedule will fail to alienate some people, so the manager who passes this responsibility on to the group prevents a headache. And, because the group has made the decision, it's more likely to be implemented by all the members.

2 Set clear limits to the area of discussion. You will obviously want to keep the group from encroaching on areas of decision making that higher management has decided are not its concern. Suppose management is interested in refurbishing the women's lounge. You, as the supervisor, might say, "We have $500 allowed us. How should we spend it?" This is obviously vastly preferable to asking the question, "How much should we spend?" The chances of management's figures and the group's figures being the same or even coming close are small.

3 Make it crystal-clear whether you're asking the group for suggestions on how to solve the problem or delegating the solution to the group. Both approaches are valuable. But the group that thinks it's making the decision will be frustrated and embittered if you end up the meeting by vetoing its solution, which you have never thought of as more than a suggestion.

4 Don't confuse the cause of the problem with its solution, at least not at a problem-solving meeting. You might, for example, begin a meeting by saying that the question is: "How do we get production back to acceptable levels?" After much talk, the group may zero in on tardiness as the cause of the problem. Fine, but you're only halfway home. At this point you might want to ask a loaded question such as, "Well, what do you think we should do about tardiness?" or "What do you think is a reasonable time to come to work?" You know what the solution is, but you want them to name it because, if they make the decision, it's more likely to stick.

But what if they decide that starting work 15 minutes late consistently is OK? Then you will have learned a valuable lesson and the dangers of letting the group decide. You misjudged the temper of the group, not realizing that it was unable to come up with a solution that management would be willing to accept. Your bosses will feel you have made a mistake in holding that sort of meeting, and you will lose face with the group because you won't be able to go along with its decision. In other words, always know how much rope you have before you give it to the group, or you may be hung with it.

One note of caution: Successful group participation, whether formal or informal, depends in large part on the climate of the organization and the attitudes of the supervisors. Several years ago, Professor Mason Haire, then at the University of California, and his associates surveyed 3,000 managers in fourteen countries, including the United States. Most managers in these countries viewed the ordinary individual as preferring to be directed, wishing to avoid responsibility, and having little talent for leadership. If the organizational climate is hostile to group participation, the supervisor shouldn't try for it. Any efforts will probably fail and the supervisor will end up frustrated and in worse favor with the group than before he or she began. Group decision making is a delicate organism—you don't grow Jeffersonian practices in a Hamiltonian climate.

If the supervisor adopts group participation as a gimmick but really doesn't believe in it, catastrophe is on its way. "It is better to be feared than loved," said Machiavelli's prince. Maybe so. But the manipulation game is a dangerous as well as a shoddy one. Experience shows that employees sooner or later see through the pretense and, in the resulting atmosphere of resentment, the manager's position becomes almost intolerable. The manager is more despised than feared, more resisted than obeyed.

CONCLUSION

We've seen why groups develop and the important role they play in the on-the-job existence of most employees. We have explored some of the internal workings of groups—how their leaders emerge and how their norms develop. We have noted also that the mysterious, spontaneous, and seemingly inevitable development of informal organizations is simultaneously a boon, a spur, and a thorn to those responsible for running the organization. Without cohesive groups the organization would be hard-pressed to retain or motivate many of its most valued employees, but once it has them, it faces competition from the groups for their allegiance to their coworkers or to management.

How to reconcile the two allegiances? That's the challenge and the problem. The supervisor who shares power with the informal leadership and who involves the group directly in consulting and in making decisions will plaster over many differences between the organization and the group. The drives for status, recognition, power, initiative, and protection against pressure, which led many members to affiliate with groups in the first place, will be satisfied by the joint action of management and the group. In other words, group decision making is a mechanism for channeling energies into working with management that might otherwise be used in combating it.

Observers have long recognized the swing position of the first-line supervisor: Caught in the middle, he or she represents management to the worker, and the worker to management. We would argue that the supervisor of a cohesive group, proud of its skills and independence and conscious of its position and power, will best serve management's interests by devoting most of his or her energies to representing the group to management, an activity which a supervisor alone is equipped by function and knowledge to do. In other words, the supervisor must somehow persuade management that the price of performance is to let the group have some autonomy—that management should place results ahead of prerogatives.

We don't want to sound like a Pollyanna. Given the proper encouragement, most of the time cohesive groups and management can reach an agreement. However, there will be other times when agreement between superiors and subordinates, between the groups and management, may be impossible—and output controls might be one of the issues involved. There are times when every manager must go contrary to the wishes of the group that he or she supervises. Call it what you will—the demands of a higher loyalty, bowing to the dictates of authority, or simply the price of survival.

THE EDUCATION OF GREG HORNING: FEBRUARY 15

Greg had sent out for lunch so that he could stay in his office and think this thing out. The turkey sandwich he had ordered tasted as if it had been made with yesterday's bread and he threw it, half-eaten, into the wastebasket. The session with Phillips that morning had pretty much killed his appetite, anyway.

Not that Phillips had told him anything he didn't already know. Instead of production increasing to anywhere near the projected goal of 110 percent during Greg's first month, it had fallen 5 percent and was now down to 80 percent of standard.

Greg took a sip of his coffee and began to pace back and forth in front of his desk. That only made his office seem smaller and more closed in. That was it. He felt so boxed in. The way Phillips had talked down to him that morning had made him feel like he was a kid in school again and hadn't prepared his lesson. But he *had* done his lesson, step by step, following all the rules. It's just that the answers kept coming out wrong.

It was the attitude of the group. They treated him like a kid, too. Of course, he was only twenty-three and fresh out of school. He had tried to be friendly, and he had assumed that they would realize increased production was as much in their interests as it was in his. Maybe that had been his mistake. After all, why should he have expected people who get paid a straight hourly wage to understand that? They were taking advantage of him. Well, he'd just have to put the screws on them; make them work harder. If Phillips was going to be tough with him, he'd have to be tough with them. Greg Horning was not going to get boxed in. He broke his pacing in the middle of a turn and strode out of his office into the shop.

The operators were all at their machines. Helen and Jeannette were just coming in. Phil Martello jerked his head around when Greg's office door slammed.

"I'd like your attention for a moment. I have something I want to say to you." The women stopped, immediately silent, just inside the door. Everyone looked at Greg and he realized that he had spoken louder than was necessary. He began again, more slowly and quietly.

"I don't know whether or not you know it, but our department is doing very badly. Our job is to get the work out and we're not doing it. Production's going down, in fact. We've dropped 5 percent since I've been here. You've got to work harder and get more out. Maybe you don't realize that or maybe you're trying to make me look bad. I don't know. But we're all out of jobs if we don't keep up with the competition."

Greg looked at the faces of the workers. They were all as passive and expressionless as the turned-off machines in the room. Just like when he had come in that first day. Phil Martello was opening and shutting his mouth in an elaborate yawn and Rick Cohn was nodding slightly but regularly to some rhythm that was going through his head. What was the matter with them? Couldn't they understand anything?

"OK, if you don't care, I do," Greg snapped. "We're going to increase the output of this department and we're going to start doing it now. Now, let's all get back to work."

Greg strode back to his office and slammed the door again. The group outside his window watched him for a few minutes before they returned to their machines. He was pacing back and forth in front of his desk.

Greg realized during the days following his talk to the group that it had made no difference in their performance. If anything, they were more openly hostile. Sometimes he regretted having said anything to them at all. Sometimes he wondered if taking a different tack would have been more effective. Sometimes—and this seemed strange to him—when he went back to that afternoon in his mind, all he could see was Rick Cohn's rhythmic head. That head, with all that hair, bobbing easily to some unheard beat. The boy irritated Greg, and yet he found himself intrigued by him.

Rick was unpredictable and inconsistent, and Greg didn't understand what made the boy tick. But there was no denying that he was bright and that he could produce. Greg could remember several days when Rick had turned out a great deal over standard.

Gradually an idea began to form around the image of Rick's bouncing head. If only Greg could get him on his side, get him to set a higher standard for the group. That rhythm that Rick responded to— none of the others understood it any better than Greg did himself. Rick was less tied to the group than anyone else; he was the only one in there who was younger than Greg, and he hadn't been in the plant too much longer than Greg either.

Greg decided that it was worth a try. He called Rick into his office one day, early in the afternoon.

"I've been watching you, Rick," he said with a smile that was tighter than he had planned, "and I think you've got potential. Those times when you've produced, *really* produced, I mean—don't think I haven't noticed it. It's the kind of thing we need around here. I know it's hard to keep it up all the time, especially with the relaxed pace of some of the others. But I think you can do it. No telling what it could mean for you. A bright boy like you, if he puts out, isn't going to stay with that machine for too long. There are places to move with this company, but I don't have to tell you that. Let's give it a try—what do you say?"

Rick looked at Greg a long time before he said anything. It made Greg feel uncomfortable. Finally he began to speak, softly, and in time with the beat that sometimes moved his head.

"Gee, that's cool of you, man. I mean to tell me I'm good. A guy digs that, if you know what I mean. But I think you've got me all wrong. I mean, sure man, some days I really turn out the stuff. You know, some days you wake up and you feel great and you think you can do anything. So you get in here and here's this machine. So you say, 'OK, machine, it's just you and me. We're really gonna make it today.' And you turn it out. But let's face it, man. It's a game. You know what I mean? And some days you feel like playing and some days you don't. Some days you wake up and you just know you're gonna win. But you don't make any promises. How do you know what you're gonna dig tomorrow? It might be a whole new thing by then. You know what I mean?"

"Well, I suppose I do, Rick," Greg answered. But there was more than a few years and a few inches of hair between these two young men. Greg had plans, goals, places to go, things to achieve. He didn't think it was all a game. He knew what he would "dig" tomorrow. He didn't know what Rick meant at all. Still, this was the closest he had come to anyone in the group. He just couldn't let him go without some kind of link being established between them.

"OK, Rick, OK—it's like you say, but let's also say that starting next week you change places with Kilpatrick. Now, you don't have to make any promises. It's just that you've done good work and you deserve the break. And if you wake up next Monday and feel like winning, you do it big—for both of us. What do you say?"

"Well, OK, man. That's cool. But who knows if I'm even gonna wake up Monday mornings. You know what I mean?"

Rick's response to his offer had not been what Greg had expected. Still, given Kilpatrick's track record, he felt it was a worthwhile move. What did he have to lose? He was putting Rick on a machine that had longer runs and fewer changes. A really good worker could turn out a lot of work there. Even if he wasn't consistent, Rick would certainly produce more than Kilpatrick. He was pretty old—almost retirement age—and he was inefficient. It was just as well to have him on a machine with shorter runs and more setup time—a machine that would have lower output, anyway. Greg wrote up the notice of the change and went right out to put it up on the bulletin board.

After finishing a report later in the afternoon, Greg got up from his desk, stretched, and strolled over to the window. Out on the floor, he saw all the men, except Rick, grouped around Creegmore's machine. They were huddled together; Creegmore had his hand on Kilpatrick's shoulder; there were wide gestures and long looks toward Rick and toward him.

He started to go out, then stopped. They had read the notice. So what. If they wouldn't play ball with him, he wasn't going to play ball with them. Sure, Kilpatrick was an old-timer—but he just wasn't shaping up. None of them were, so they'd just have to take their lumps.

As Greg watched, the group broke up; shaking their heads and gesturing, the men went back to work. Except Creegmore. Greg saw him go over to Rick and take his arm. The boy stopped working, but he did not look up. Creegmore's hand was tight around Rick's arm and he bent his head forward as he talked.

Once again, Greg started to go out on the floor. If Creegmore was threatening Rick . . .

But as he got to the door, he saw their faces. Creegmore looked the way Greg had felt when he'd had Rick in his office. And Rick was smiling—the way he had smiled at Greg when he'd said, "But you don't make any promises. How do you know what you're gonna dig tomorrow?"

QUESTIONS

1 Why do you feel Greg's appeal to the group to turn out more work fell as flat as it did?

2 Using the terms developed in the chapter, how would you characterize the group Greg had to deal with? Why?

3 Do you think it would have made any difference to productivity if Greg had set a higher standard for the group?

4 How would you evaluate Greg's reasons for switching Rick and Kilpatrick?

BEHAVIORAL EXERCISE

Try to recall an informal group of which you were a member. It could have been at work, in school, or just in the community. List its norms and describe its social structure; that is, who were the leaders, who had the relatively higher status, and who had the lower status and why? How could an outsider have observed these status differences (in terms of how people dealt with each other)? How did the group change over a period of time and why? Were there conflicts with other groups and why? Analyze any instances of "role conflict" where members of this informal group had conflicting "pulls" because of their membership in other groups. What was the impact of this group on other organizations or groups—where was it constructive, where was it damaging? If you had been in the position of having to supervise such a group, what would you have done to increase the likelihood that they would be cooperative with you?

BIBLIOGRAPHY

Dalton, M., *Men Who Manage*, Wiley, New York, 1959.

Homans, G., *The Human Group*, Harcourt, New York, 1950.

Homans, G., *Social Behavior: Its Elementary Forms*, rev. ed., Harcourt, New York, 1974.

Sayles, L., *Behavior of Industrial Work Groups*, Wiley, New York, 1958.

Whyte, W., *Street Corner Society: The Social Structure of an Italian Slum*, rev. ed., Univ. of Chicago Press, Chicago, 1955.

READING

Norms*

GEORGE CASPER HOMANS (1910-   )

Intellectually, George Homans is a hybrid. A would-be poet who majored in English literature at Harvard, he has ranged widely in his attempt to deduce universal principles about the behavior of human beings from frequently reluctant data. He studied social psychology with Elton Mayo, and as a young man, he wrote an excellent introduction (with Charles Pelham Curtis) to Pareto, whose principles he embraced briefly as an antidote to Marxism. His historical research culminated in his study *English Villagers of the Thirteenth Century*. Although he is best known as a sociologist and as the author of a classic in the field, *The Human Group*, published twenty-five years ago, he lacks a degree in sociology. His member-ship in the Society of Fellows, a frankly elitist organization (a kind of platonic academy on the banks of the Charles River), exempted him from any requirements for an advanced degree. Among its other alumni are B. F. Skinner, William F. Whyte, McGeorge Bundy, and Arthur Schlesinger, Jr. In forty-five years, he has gone the course from aspiring poet to being what he calls "an ultimate psychological reductionist," a self-confessed believer in that branch of behavioral psychology whose chief seer is Skinner.

What general principles has Homans ended up with? In wrestling with the data on medieval villages, kinship patterns in primitive societies, and interpersonal relationships within small groups in industry, what has he found that they have in common? Homans' general conclusion is that "the ultimate explanatory principles in anthropology and sociology, and for that matter in history, were neither structural nor functional but psychological." As one of the unhappily rare instances that demonstrates this thesis, he cites the fact that tribesmen in a variety of primitive societies tended to be "distant" from anyone set in authority over them. The reason is clear: Persons in authority had frequent recourse to punishment or the threat of punishment in controlling their subordinates, but people as people tend to avoid both punishment and its source—a basic proposition of Skinnerian psychology and a proposition that lies at the core of the problems between superior and subordinate in any organization.

Finally, Homans is clear to note that he differs from Skinner in that Skinner, the great behavioral psychologist, is not a great social psychologist. In essence, Skinner has not been very concerned with the problems involved in applying his theories in the workaday world. His attitude seems to be that somehow, because his theories

---

*George C. Homans, *The Human Group*, Harcourt, New York, 1950, pp. 122-125.

are true, they must ultimately prevail—the delusion of prophets from Mohammed to Marx. Homans has been more concerned with the problems involved in applying his theories "since my Puritan background taught me that nothing valuable could be obtained without hard work, the facile solutions came under moral suspicion."

What do we mean by norms? Sociologists and anthropologists are always saying that such and such behavior is, in a particular group, "expected" under such and such circumstances. How do they know what is expected? Sometimes the members of a group will state quite clearly what the expected behavior is, but sometimes it is a matter of inference. The process of construction by which social scientists determine the expectations of a group—and the process must be complex—seems to be taken for granted by the less sophisticated among them in their textbooks and popular works. Here we never take such things for granted, though we may not spend much time on them. Suppose, for example, three men are in a room. One goes out, and one of the two that remain says to the other, "I don't believe we've met. My name is Smith." Or, in another variation of the same scene, a man comes into a room where two others are already standing. There is a silence, and then one of the two says, "I'm sorry. I should have introduced you two, but I thought you had met. Mr. Jones, this is Mr. Smith." From observing several events of this kind, the sociologist infers that, in this particular group, when two men are in the presence of one another and have not met before, the third man, if he has met both, is expected to tell each the other's name, but that, should he fail to do so, each is expected to act on his own account and tell the other his name. The sociologist's inference may be confirmed when he reads in a book of etiquette current in this group, "When two persons have not met before, their host must introduce them to one another." Inferences of this kind we shall call *norms*. Note that most norms are not as easily discovered as this rather trivial one, and confirmation by a book of etiquette or its equivalent is not always possible. The student should turn to *Management and the Worker* and run over the material from which the inference was reached that about 6,600 or, according to the type of equipment being wired, 6,000 completed connections were considered in the Bank Wiring Observation Room the proper day's work of a wireman. For example, Mueller (W2) said in an interview:

> Right now I'm turning out over 7,000 a day, around 7,040. The rest of the fellows kick because I do that. They want me to come down. They want me to come down to around 6,600, but I don't see why I should.

In few works of social science are the norms, whose existence the sociologist often appears to assume so lightly, traced back to their referents in word and deed as carefully as they are in the Roethlisberger and Dickson book. We have already seen what some of the other norms of the Bank Wiremen were, in such matters as squealing, chiseling, and acting officiously.

A norm, then, is an idea in the minds of the members of a group, an idea that can be put in the form of a statement specifying what the members or other men should do, ought to do, are expected to do, under given circumstances. Just what group, what circumstances, and what action are meant can be much more easily determined for some norms than for others. But even this definition is too broad and must be limited further. A statement of the kind described is a norm only if any departure of real behavior from the norm is followed by some punishment. The rule of the Bank Wiremen that no one should wire much more or much less than two equipments a day was a true norm, because, as we shall see, the social standing of a member of the group declined as he departed in one way or another from the norm. Nonconformity was punished and conformity rewarded. A norm in this sense is what some sociologists call a sanction pattern. But there are many other statements about what behavior ought to be that are not norms and are often called ideals. "Do as you would be done by," is an example. In an imperfect world, departure from the golden rule is not followed by specific punishment, and this is precisely what gives the rule its high ethical standing. If a man lives by it, he does so for its own sake and not because he will be socially rewarded. Virtue is its own reward.

We have defined norms as the expected behavior of a number of men. This is justified: each of the Bank Wiremen was expected to wire about 6,000 connections a day. But some norms, though they may be held by all the members of a group, apply to only one of them: they define what a single member in a particular position is supposed to do. A father is expected to treat his children, a host, his guests, a foreman, his men in certain special ways. A norm of this kind, a norm that states the expected relationship of a person in a certain position to others he comes into contact with is often called the *role* of this person. The word comes, of course, from the language of the stage: it is the part a man is given to play, and he may play it well or ill. A man's behavior may depart more or less from the role, and if the real behavior of enough persons in enough such positions over a long enough time departs far enough from the role, the role itself will change. For instance, our notion of the way a father ought to behave toward his children has changed greatly in the last century, as circumstances have made the patriarchal role of fathers on small, subsistence farms no longer appropriate for many fathers today.

One point must be made very clear: our norms are ideas. They are not behavior itself, but what people think behavior ought to be. Nothing is more childishly obvious than that the ideal and the real do not always, or do not fully, coincide, but nothing is more easily forgotten, perhaps because men want to forget it. A possible objection to the word *norm* itself is that we may easily confuse two different things: norm A, a statement of what people ought to do in a particular situation, and norm B, a statistical, or quasi-statistical, average of what they actually do in that situation. Sometimes the two coincide, but more often they do not. In the same way, the word *standard* suggests, on the one hand, a moral yardstick by which real behavior is judged and, on the other hand, in the phrase *standard of living*, a certain level of real behavior in the field of consumption.

6

ADMINISTERING POSITIVE DISCIPLINE

LEARNING OBJECTIVES
1 See how the supervisor can administer discipline in a way that motivates rather than demotivates.
2 Consider what's wrong with punishment.
3 Appreciate the virtues of the "hot-stove" approach—predictability, flexibility, and impartiality.
4 Make a case for the single-penalty approach—nothing short of discharge.
5 Study the context of discipline and how it limits the supervisor's freedom of action.
6 Understand the guidelines for order compliance.

What do we mean by positive discipline? For a hint of the answer, consider two tales: one of savages and the other of civilized persons.

Among the Xingu Indians in Brazil, there is no equivalent word for punishment; no one punishes, not even the chief of the tribe. Yet the tribe has its methods for dealing with those who violate its laws.

Take, for example, what happens when an Xingu steals something. The tribal elders send a man at dawn to make a speech in front of the thief's hut. His remarks are couched in general terms—no names are mentioned, and the thief is not identified. Then the speaker departs and the village is silent. The method is almost always successful: The thief returns what he has stolen. And if he doesn't, the punishment is left to his own conscience and his diminished ego. He is aware that the whole village knows he is a robber, although no one will breathe a word.

Our second tale concerns the Luddites, English textile workers who took to smashing power looms with heavy hammers as their way of protesting against the introduction of machinery. The outraged establishment—the year was 1813—passed a bill imposing the death penalty on Luddites caught destroying frames and looms. Byron protested that only two things were wanting to convict and condemn a person under the bill: "twelve butchers for a jury and a Jeffreys [a notorious hanging judge] for a judge."

However, reluctance to enforce the decree was not caused by a deficiency of the legislation. What was in error was the apparent assumption behind it: that a sufficiently severe punishment would prevent the crime. Actually, in the English law of the period, the punishments were frequently more criminal than the crimes. Stealing a loaf of bread was a hanging offense and so were countless other acts that we would regard as minor crimes. What happened as a consequence of these punitive laws? The hangman worked overtime and a large proportion of the population so resented the savage punishments that they became accomplices to crime. But we lack any evidence that the penalties acted as a deterrent.

Our two tales encompass a couple of morals as well as a partial definition of positive discipline. The dual morals are pretty clear, we think. The first is that the prime function of discipline is not to make the punishment fit the crime but to administer it in a way that will prevent a particular offender, at least, from committing the crime again. The second shows that the effectiveness of the discipline has nothing to do with the severity of the punishment. If anything, the ratio is inverse. Incidentally, there's more in Webster than lexicography: The last definition given of discipline is "punishment."

You may feel that our analogies are farfetched. What do the Luddites and the Xingus have to do with constructive discipline in an office or plant in the 1970s in the United States? Quite a lot, we feel. We confess that we deliberately chose our exotic examples, at least in part, to illustrate the universality of our points. However, let's turn to something more familiar and consider a typical case of how a disciplinary situation evolves in a company setting.

A FEW SHORT BEERS

"That damn Reardon must have stopped off for some beers again at Cronin's," Rickey Allen swore to himself, looking at his watch. It was seven minutes after the end of the lunch period and still no Reardon.

Rickey was in charge of the pickling operation in a Midwest wire mill. Tom Reardon, who worked on one of the pickling tanks, was one of Allen's best workers—except for one failing. He frequently had lunch at a neighborhood bar. And when he did, he took his time getting back on the job.

Just then Allen was called to the phone. When he came back a few minutes later, he spotted Reardon all right—with a big grin on his face, shooting the breeze with Joe DiBona on number four station.

Rickey wasted no time in getting within earshot of Reardon and DiBona. "Quit the yacking, Tom, and get back to work," he ordered. "You're ten minutes late already."

The grin on Tom Reardon's face froze and a flush crept up his cheeks.

"Lay off, Rickey. I put in a hell of a morning's work and I'm entitled to a little break."

"That's not the point, Tom, and you know it. You're making a habit of coming back to work with half a load on, goofing off, and holding up the rest of the guys—that's the point."

"The hell you say," Reardon shot back. "You can't crucify a guy for having a few short beers. It's a free country and if I want to have a couple of beers with my lunch that's my business."

"And it's my business to see that you're at the pickling tank and working when you're supposed to be," Allen retorted. "Now get over to that tank—pronto."

Reardon didn't budge. He just jutted his jaw out as the flush deepened toward purple.

"Wait a minute, Rickey, just you wait a minute! You're making a big production about always being where you're supposed to be. The way you talk you'd think that you were always around when we needed you.

When we had trouble with the 380 wire last week, we had one hell of a job flushing you out. It seems you were with your buddies in production control—probably settling the affairs of the nation," Reardon added sarcastically after a short pause.

"I was there on department business—and you know it," Allen shouted.

"I know no such thing," Reardon roared back.

"You're insubordinate, Reardon. Get your gear and check out. I'm suspending you for the rest of the day. Maybe that'll get the message through your thick skull about who's running this shop."

Commentary on "A Few Short Beers"

One message of our little vignette is that Rickey Allen wasn't running his department by the end of the conversation. He had abdicated control and let his temper take over. The case is an all too typical escalation of the disciplinary situation. The boss observes a laxity, usually (as with Rickey Allen) not for the first time. And of itself, the offense is not earthshaking. Reardon was, after all, only seven minutes late coming back from lunch. He wasn't drunk, just talkative. And he was an outstanding worker who had done his customary good job all morning.

Yet, as often happens and for reasons that usually defy rational analysis, this time the supervisor, in this case, Rickey Allen, flipped. His approach to Reardon was emotional and harsh, while Reardon's resentment was instant and equally harsh—a kind of emotional reflex. His resentment, in all likelihood, had three bases: He naturally resented Allen's approach; it was apparently the first time he had been reprimanded for coming back a little late—the first time is not the time to talk tough; and finally, Reardon knew he was good, and good people know they don't deserve to be on the receiving end of this kind of treatment.

From here on, things went the only way they usually go under such circumstances: Anger begets anger, accusations lead to counteraccusations and to a conclusion in which both parties are losers. In our case, of course, as the man who started the chain reaction, Rickey Allen was primarily at fault—the real spree was his. We say "primarily" because, ideally, Tom Reardon should have returned a soft answer and (with luck) turned away wrath. But in the real world, seldom does it happen that way. The burden of guilt rests with the one who strikes the first blow, hurls the first insult, raises the initial provocation.

Like most supervisors caught in a similar dilemma, Rickey Allen had a second chance—all it takes to succeed are magnanimity, common sense on both sides, and luck. If Rickey came in the next morning and sincerely apologized to Tom for losing his temper, assuming Tom hadn't quit already (part of what we meant by luck), and if he was willing to discuss, calmly and rationally, two questions (Tom's occasional tardiness after lunch and his own absences from the department), the situation just might resolve itself satisfactorily. In a union plant, however, the whole sorry mess would probably be beyond redemption. Tom Reardon would have immediately contacted the steward, who would have been delighted to file a grievance he was bound to win. To accuse a subordinate of "having half a load on," with no proof and in front of a third party, is to ensure the reversal of whatever penalty the supervisor imposes. However, the fact that Rickey had his emotions on so loose a leash indicates that he was probably functioning in a nonunion setting.

We dwelt, in our case, on the negative side of positive discipline (negatives are always more dramatic), on an instance where the offense was minor, the penalty excessive, and the manner of handling it calculated, if not guaranteed, to make the offender both repeat the particular offense and broaden the scope of the offenses. In short, our case was a distillation of what the supervisor shouldn't do.

CONDITIONS OF COMPLIANCE

Let's reverse the coin and try to be constructive. How can the supervisor administer discipline in a way that motivates, not demotivates— that is positive, not negative? In other words, to return to our basic theme, how should the supervisor behave when discipline is called for and she or he wants both to stop whatever laxity has occurred and to maintain the subordinate's overall performance at its current level or improve it? Little is accomplished if the manner of handling the problem has convinced subordinates that it's altogether too risky to repeat the offense if they want to keep their jobs, but at the same time has motivated them to seek out more protected areas in which they can play saboteur. This is a fairly frequent outcome of a disciplinary encounter.

Timing

To suggest a few guidelines: To start off, supervisors shouldn't procrastinate in administering discipline. The longer they postpone reproof or punishment after they have observed the violation, the more likely they are to get a "who—me?" reaction from the violator. Sure, the employee has done something wrong. Nonetheless, that individual is almost certain to resent some superior playing cat-and-mouse games.

Take Charley, who has been warned by his boss, not once but several times, to keep the guard down on his machine. However, because he has a "it-can't-happen-to-me" outlook, the guard never stays down much longer than the boss remains in clear view. However, the day comes when the boss catches him unawares but says nothing. Therefore Charley concludes he hasn't been noticed. Not so. The boss hasn't quite made up his mind what to do—besides, it will do Charley good to "sweat it out." At the end of the shift four or five hours later, the boss lowers the boom with a two-day layoff. Not too harsh perhaps, under the circumstances, but that's not how Charley looks at it. The delay has given him a chance to build a case, in his own mind, that the boss bears him a grudge, otherwise he would have looked the other way or acted on the spot.

Like most useful guidelines, this one has its exceptions. For example, if the boss breaks up an argument between two of his men and he knows one of them is a wise guy and a bully, that's not the correct psychological moment to talk to him. The man is in no condition to listen, and things are almost certain to get worse as he responds to the boss's words with threats or abuse. Furthermore, as we saw with Rickey Allen, if the boss is angry, it's no time for him to talk over a problem with an employee. He should wait until he cools off before talking. Also, sometimes the man's guilt isn't clear or it takes time and consultation to establish the penalty. What's the proper course under these circumstances? The supervisor should notify the man on the spot that he's well aware of what's going on, but it's going to take a little time—spelled out, whenever possible (24 hours, 48 hours, or whatever)—to determine the facts and to fix the punishment.

Tone
The next prerequisite is to administer discipline impersonally. A tall order, certainly. The disciplinary interview is inevitably an emotionally charged situation in which the violator tends to feel resentful even if guilty, and the supervisor feels angry or at least righteously indignant, in part as self-protection from any guilt feelings at having to hurt someone else. The best thing to do is to approximate the impersonal, that is, to administer discipline in a way that will do minimum damage to future relations with subordinates.

A supervisor shouldn't hesitate to speak in very specific terms of what the employee has done wrong. If one is hesitant to discuss the matter, this will probably fog the issue or even raise doubts as to its existence. And one shouldn't be apologetic about either the rule or the penalty imposed for breaking it. Even if the supervisor has reservations about the rule, the least appropriate place to lobby against it is during a disciplinary interview. The apologetic approach is bound to be interpreted in ways that will defeat the purpose of the discipline. Subordinates will conclude—and correctly—either that the supervisor doesn't agree with the rule, is being hypocritical in enforcing it, or simply lacks the guts to back it up, or possibly all three.

In setting the tone of the disciplinary interview, supervisors want to avoid personalities as they would the plague. Phrases such as "I've really gone out on the limb for you" or, even worse, "How could you do this to me?" have no place in this discussion. They get across a dual and dangerous message: The supervisor is judging the whole person, and things between them are never going to be the same again.

How does the supervisor set the stage for the relatively impersonal disciplinary interview? First, the problem is stated as clearly, precisely, and unemotionally as possible. Then the subordinate is encouraged to take as much time as he or she needs to tell his or her side of the story—not of *why* it happened but of *how*.

Once the employee's story is heard, the supervisor imposes the penalty, again in the lowest key. Then the supervisor sits back and listens to the employee's objections as to why he or she is being unreasonable, unfair, arbitrary, and otherwise unethical. If the job has been done properly, the boss can afford to disregard the substance of the objections and take them in stride as a necessary, even salutary case of "blowing off steam" and a precondition of accepting the penalty. People complain about the penalty when their grievance is at being caught.

The next, and most important, stage is where the supervisor abandons impersonality and reverts to the customary helpful role. Let's assume that a two-day layoff has just been given to a worker who offered no better explanation for habitual tardiness than a faulty alarm clock or a poor memory about setting it. The supervisor wants the tardy worker to suggest a plan for getting to work on time—get up a half-hour earlier every morning, join a car pool, move closer to the plant, buy a new and noisier alarm clock. If the employee comes up with the solution, it's more likely to be followed. Of course, if the worker has no plan, then it's up to the boss to come up with one.

Follow-through

The supervisor isn't out of the woods yet. Once a subordinate has been disciplined, it's crucial that he or she be treated the same as before reproof. The boss may feel like avoiding the employee for several days after the interview. That's only human. But this temptation should be overcome. Instead, one should go out of the way, if necessary, to find some occasion to be friendly, to get across the message: "It was the act I was punishing; you, I like and respect. The past is past, and the only things that matter are the present and the future."

In talking of positive discipline, we should perhaps define it a little differently. It is discipline that simultaneously reinforces the rule and motivates the violator to comply with it and the other company rules in the future. As we have seen, it rests on a good deal more than the fairness of the penalty. Timing, tone, and manner are a large part of the battle. The boss who takes a morally superior tone or who plays judge and treats the penalty as a reprisal is not administering positive discipline. Above all, the supervisor must remain impersonal. As Cummings and Sholl wrote in *Personnel,* "There is all the difference in the world between falling down on the job and being accused of being a loafer, of committing an unwise act and being told you're a fool. The employee will remember and instinctively resent any downgrading aimed at him personally."

The Problem of Consistency

Part of the problem is that, among various punishments, the most that can be argued is that some are more unfair than others. Obviously, it's unfair when one supervisor, all other things being equal, imposes a penalty harsher than that imposed by another supervisor in the same plant for the same offense. And it's a common occurrence, at least in many nonunion plants where the grievance procedures and practices are rudimentary and the communications flow is constipated, that rules are made on high by managers with little or no understanding of the informal standards that exist at the level where the rules are broken and presumably are enforced.

We use the words "presumably are enforced" because, when a lot of people feel a rule or a law is unreasonable, they will refuse to obey it—witness our experience with the not so noble experiment of prohibition and our present problems with people smoking pot. At the same time, a division of opinion usually arises among the law enforcers over a law or a regulation that is widely held to be unreasonable. To some, a rule is a rule and it's their duty to enforce it, in sorrow and anger perhaps, but enforce it they will. Others will either ignore the violation although they are aware of it, or recognize the violation but somehow neglect to impose the penalty even when it is mandatory.

Consider, for example, what happened during a simulation session at one of the Bell System's operating units. The instructor described a situation in which a supervisor caught someone working on a telephone pole without a safety belt. The official penalty for the violation was a layoff. Twenty-five percent of the supervisors in the session said they would look the other way and ignore the violation. In 60 percent of the simulated cases where the supervisor discussed the violation with ths worker, the worker admitted it, but in only 15 percent of these cases did the supervisor lay the worker off. Obviously, the rule had broken down. Most of the supervisors felt that either the rule or the penalty was unreasonable and they refused to enforce it. However, we believe that, in real life, the percentage of supervisors who would prefer not to catch the violator would be much higher than it was in the simulation exercise. This way, they would minimize the possibility of getting into hot water with higher management for not punishing the offender.

Also, in real life the grapevine would have been at work exposing inconsistencies in the enforcement of the rule and contributing to a vicious cycle. The greater the inconsistencies of application, the less respect for the rule itself and the fiercer the resentment at those who followed the letter of the rule. In the end, we suspect, higher management would face two choices: either to set up a system of continuing surveillance to make sure that a largely discredited penalty was enforced, or to yield as gracefully as possible and modify the penalty. In the meantime, there are three lessons that an employee caught violating the regulation and punished as prescribed might learn from the episode: (1) The violation must not be repeated, (2) he or she must be sure not to get caught again, and (3) the supervisor is unfair and unreasonable. We think lessons (2) and (3) are the ones the average employee would learn from the experience.

What's the Matter with Punishment?

Let's look a little deeper at the problem of penalties and punishments. When we maintained that all punishments are unfair, we meant that it's important to recognize that a penalty is not the consequence of violating a rule but, instead, of being caught violating the rule. The distinction is crucial. Getting away with murder is difficult in the literal sense because of the resources the community brings to bear on a capital crime, but this is not so with most lawbreaking or rule violation. The relationship is like that between the total iceberg and the visible portion—with two-thirds submerged and unseen. (See Figure 6-1.) And it's one big reason why discipline is so difficult to administer. More often than not, it appears to be punitive even when it isn't—and in terms of consequences, appearances count more than reality. The employee interprets the punishment not as the end result of the remorseless turning of wheels by an even-handed justice but as a personal act based on the superior's desire to get even, to show who's boss, or simply because "she's got it in for me." This is rationalization, of course—for every boss who is unfair, ten appear to be. Punishment, in other words, contains within itself inherent elements of unfairness that cause the penalizer to appear unjust because, for the few who are caught and disciplined, the many who are equally guilty but undetected go scot-free.

Are we building up to the conclusion that, because all punishment contains an element of injustice, all punishment should be discontinued because it contributes nothing to positive discipline? In fact, its contribution is negative: Largely due to the aspect of unfairness, any punishment breeds resistance, encourages subterfuge, and undermines the employee's willingness to make future contributions to the organization.

Would that it were possible to dismiss the case for discipline or even the occasional imposition of penalties for wrongdoing. With all the problems involved, some of which were just considered, discipline and punishment still play a necessary role both in the community at large and within the corporation.

What Discipline Should Accomplish

What does discipline accomplish? Why are penalties sometimes necessary? Managers who discipline subordinates accomplish four things:

FIGURE 6-1 The iceberg phenomenon

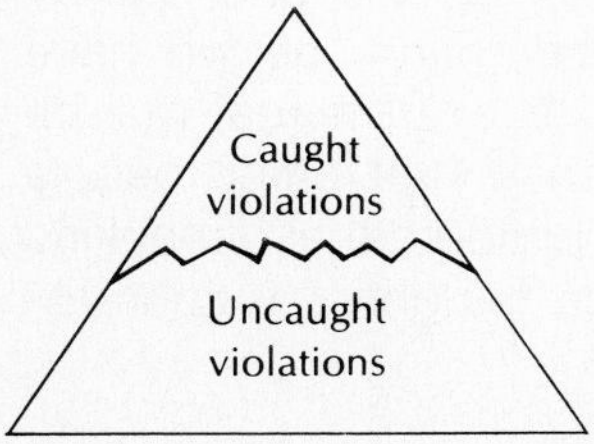

1 They strengthen the rule and express their confidence in it by their enforcement. Rules, like muscles, atrophy through disuse.

2 They correct the individual's breach of the rules and warn that they must comply with them in the future or face more serious consequences.

3 They remind the person's coworkers of the existence of the rule and of the gravity with which it is regarded. Occasional references to the possibility of discipline help some people to obey the rules of the game. As one worker put it, "If you can sneak nuts and bolts out of the plant in your lunch box, you start trying to take spare parts and accessories out next. It's much better if you know that they are going to check your lunch box every night and you can't take out the smallest thing. Then you don't get into bad habits."

4 Finally, disciplining the violator reassures the vast majority who respect the rules not because they fear punishment but because they believe in doing things right. Time out for introspection. Haven't you ever resented the overly lenient superior who let someone else get away with murder, though it didn't happen to be your particular temptation? And haven't you ended up breaking the rule yourself when such indulgence was continued.?

We know of a case in an advertising agency where a particularly sharp copywriter took advantage of her presumed indispensability and started coming in thirty to fifty minutes later each day than the other copywriters on the staff. But not for long. After waiting for a few weeks to see whether their coworker was going to be disciplined and brought into line, the other copywriters felt free to break the rules too. Now all the copywriters arrive at least a half-hour after the nominal start of the working day. The moral is obvious: If the violator isn't disciplined, the rest of the group, out of resentment at management or a natural desire to improve their lot, will imitate the offender. An illegal perquisite is still a perquisite—with its currency undevalued.

Most people in an organization tend to obey most of the rules most of the time. Supervisors' roles would be insupportable if employees didn't—they would have to spend four-fifths of their time and energy spotting and correcting infractions. On the other hand, as we have suggested, the way of the transgressor seems to exert a real pull on many people—all they need is tangible evidence that other people have gotten away with it. D. H. Lawrence quipped that "mankind invented sin in order to enjoy the feeling of being naughty." Rulebreaking perhaps affords analogous attractions.

All totaled ...

We have seen the case for punishment: Without the felt presence of other worldly sanctions, the existence of formal rules and the occasional imposition of penalties perform a therapeutic function, not in terms of what they accomplish in reforming the rulebreaker but in terms of what they do to prevent more dutiful employees from succumbing to temptation. In short, punishment does fulfill a preventive function, although not the one usually ascribed to it.

On the other hand, we're acutely aware of the deficiencies in any punishment. It is almost always resented; it frequently does permanent damage to the relations between superior and subordinate, and it very infrequently results in a change of attitude by the employee toward the offense for which he or she was punished. Precautions are merely redoubled against being caught again.

THE "HOT-STOVE" APPROACH—
PREDICTABILITY, FLEXIBILITY, IMPARTIALITY

One possible way of restating the problem of how to achieve positive discipline is to determine the conditions under which the employee feels the least resentment toward punishment. Some we have already dealt with in talking about the tone and manner in which discipline should be administered. These and others were incorporated into what the late Douglas McGregor of MIT called "the hot-stove rule." The process of effective discipline is similar to what happens when you touch a hot stove—the reaction you get is immediate, without warning, impersonal, and consistent.

The last conditions are the most important. When a superior enforces discipline, it must be done in such a way that the act and the discipline seem almost one. The employee therefore feels that the discipline is directed not against her or him but against the act—hence the need to administer discipline impersonally and impartially. If the boss does a good job, the employee will still feel resentful but also somewhat guilty and foolish about any resentment—akin to the woman who kicks the stove that has burned her hand—her animosity probably will be neither deep nor lasting. She will feel, after a time, that the boss was performing a reluctant duty and only doing what a boss is paid to do—enforce the rules.

One element in the hot-stove rule deserves closer examination. It is consistency. The supervisor, of course, doesn't administer discipline in a vacuum. Other managers are handing out penalties to their subordinates for similar violations. We believe that managers should have a good deal of leeway in the kind of penalties they prescribe and we're against drawing up and posting standard and compulsory penalties for each violation. Carried to its logical extreme, for example, a mandatory discharge for stealing would mean that the employee who takes a box of paper clips would receive the same penalty as someone who rifles the safe. In short, no two offenses are really the same, nor are any two offenders.

On the other hand, in the interests of fairness and consistency, managers should get together among themselves and agree on a range of punishments. Any manager who goes outside the limits should be subject to severe discipline. But what if managers can't or won't agree on the same penalties? Then top management may feel that it's necessary to extend the list of fixed and formal penalties to include every infraction in the book. Consistency isn't perfect justice, but it's still justice.

Consistency contains the seeds of possible injustice, but it appeals to a strong need in almost every individual. Most of us want to know the limits of permissible behavior. And most of us tend to be unhappy and insecure in a situation where we are unsure what is expected of us. Child psychologists, for example, have found that children usually are not happier when they are given absolute freedom. One reason they get into so much mischief is that they are trying to find out how much they can get away with. Many adults are obsessed with the same question—they have to know the answer to "How far can I go?"

Consistency doesn't mean, however, that you determine the penalty only on the basis of the offense and ignore the history of the person who committed it. Consider, for example, three men who have been caught shooting craps behind the machines instead of working. The first man, a two-year employee with a barely satisfactory performance record, was given a three-day layoff a few months before for the same offense. He's discharged. The second man is also a short-term, not particularly distinguished employee, but he has no previous gambling record. He gets a three-day layoff. The third man, also without a gambling record, is an above-average worker with fifteen years' service. He's given a written warning. A higher consistency has governed management's decisions here. The key point about consistency in handing out penalties is that if two persons with approximately the same personal histories commit the same offense, they should be treated equally. In summary, the goal to be sought in administering justice with consistency is a blend of predictability, flexibility, and impartiality.

DISCIPLINE WITHOUT PUNISHMENT

With all its virtues, the hot-stove rule contains an inherent weakness. Every time the manager follows it, future relationships with a subordinate are put on the line. At best, resentment is minimized—but not eliminated. Let's revert once more to definitions. Punishment is the last definition of discipline given in Webster. What's the first? "Training which corrects, molds, strengthens or perfects." We'll risk a definition of our own: Discipline is the well-tempered reprimand, one that the object accepts without resentment and that conditions future behavior. We've pretty much concluded that punishment doesn't pay and we're interested only in discipline that prevents future wrongdoing.

In meting out punishment the manager has to remain impartial and impersonal in order to defuse a potentially explosive situation; in administering a reprimand the manager can and should tailor the approach to the personality of the individual. Because a manager's basic role is that of a counselor and not that of a judge, she or he has much greater freedom of action.

An Individually Tailored Approach

Let's consider several examples of discipline without punishment, with the only thing in common between them the fact that each one worked. Take Daredevil Dan, who operated his forklift truck as if the main aisle of the plant were the Indianapolis Speedway. One morning, what the manager had long been expecting happened: Dan dropped and ruined half a shift's work of finished material. The manager could have fired him or given him a stiff layoff. However, Dan, except for his speeding, was a first-class operator.

He could have embarrassed Dan by making a snide remark in front of the whole crew, such as "I think we're going to trade in your lift truck for a perambulator." Clever enough to get a yack from the boys and certain to wound a show-off like Dan. But the manager reasoned it would accomplish the opposite of his objective. Being a show-off, Dan would probably drive more wildly than ever just to show everyone that the boss's cracks didn't bother him a bit.

What to do? The manager got Dan in private and cut him down with a couple of withering sentences: "Everyone's been telling me what a fool I am for letting you run that jeep. But I've been insisting that you were going to grow up one of these days." He left it at that. He gave Dan the opportunity to "grow up" without making him feel that he had to prove to the rest of the crew that he was unaffected by criticism.

Furthermore, the manager assumed that Dan had a better side and appealed to it by putting on record his previous expressions of confidence. Dan, happily, rose to the occasion and was content to prove his mastery of the lift truck without endangering life and property.

Another case was a clerk-typist we'll call Lazy Leona, whose problem simply was that she was unambitious and bridled at the suggestion of hard work. However, her basic skills were excellent and her supervisor, although sorely tempted, decided against firing her. Motivating her was practically out of the question, the supervisor concluded. Counseling, an appeal to Leona's sense of fairness and responsibility, was bound to fail—she didn't have any, and such a session would probably result in tears, resentment, and mutual recrimination.

Discipline in Leona's case consisted of a four-pronged attack on the problem: (1) The supervisor gave Leona plenty to keep her busy and checked her progress regularly. (2) She gave her additional chores that forced her to work harder, although no harder than most of the clerks, to get time for her additional tasks. (3) She spelled out standards and set a time limit each time she gave Leona a nonroutine job. (4) She moved Leona's work station to a spot among a hardworking group who, by example and/or pressure, would probably help Leona to turn in a fair day's work. In short, the supervisor gambled on having Leona either shape up or quit and, in this case, her gamble paid off.

Then there's Superior Sam, an intelligent man and first-class operator whose problem was that the job was too easy for him. He frequently got bored and his favorite way of relieving boredom was to go visiting other workers in his own department and some of his buddies in other departments. Something had to be done. Yet when he was working, Sam was tops. Obviously, the management had to crack down on Sam, but it had to do it in a way that would spare his feelings and not give him the impression that he was being singled out and persecuted.

Sam was a reasonable man—that was the core of insight on which the manager based his strategy. The first step was to get the facts. He took notes on the time Sam actually spent doing the things he was supposed to do. Next, he made up a facsimile time card showing how much time Sam would have lost for the week if the time card were real and the time he spent away from the job were being deducted. Finally, he confronted Sam and let the evidence speak for itself. There were no histrionics, no verbal accusations, and everything was played in a low key. And Sam being Sam and basically rational and responsible, the approach worked.

We recall another case where a manager had a similar problem with Gregarious Georgia, an amiable, not too bright subordinate who spent a good deal of time visiting other departments. The manager could have built up a case against this woman (incidentally, a good worker when she worked) and eventually thrown the book at her. She preferred to handle the case differently. Whenever she suspected where the subordinate was visiting, she tracked her down, sneaked up on her, and told her in piercing tones, "Go back to work!" Undignified? Yes. Time-consuming? Yes. However, the boss maintained good relations with the woman. And after having been startled out of her wits on several occasions, the subordinate quit visiting around.

A Problem-solving Approach

Another alternative the manager should consider, particularly when there are several violators, is the problem-solving approach. We know of one example where tardiness among office employees had been averaging a high 10 percent. Management could have taken the route of cajolement, warnings, and eventual punishment of the outstanding offenders. Instead, the managers met with their employees and agreed on a tardiness target of 3 percent. During the next two years, the tardiness rate never exceeded that target. We doubt if any other approach would have accomplished as much—and this with no resentment or bad feelings among the employees. The target, after all, was self-imposed.

As we asserted at the beginning of this section, one advantage of choosing the path of discipline without punishment is that the supervisor can vary his or her repertoire. He or she may be gentle with one person and tough with another or appeal to reason in one case and, with deliberate care, use emotion in a second. What works with the Superior Sams of this world will fail to make a dent on the consciences of the Gregarious Georgias.

Obviously, the well-tempered reprimand—maybe it's more accurate to call it the tailor-made reprimand—doesn't always succeed. Daredevil Dan may continue to speed down the floor risking his life and limb. Lazy Leona may neither quit nor meet any of her deadlines. What then? Should the manager fall back on the traditional progression of penalties, oral admonition, written warning, layoff, and discharge, always bearing in mind the hot stove at each step?

THE SINGLE-PENALTY APPROACH

We would argue that each manager should consider the merits of what we call the single-penalty approach, under which the only penalty imposed on an employee is discharge. Put that way, it sounds as punitive as hell—but it's actually the reverse.

The approach, to our knowledge, was developed first in a Douglas fir plywood mill with several hundred hourly paid and unionized employees and a history of bad union-management relations and excessive recourse to arbitration. An analysis of all disciplinary cases over a three-year period showed not a single favorable result from any of the penalties imposed. This led logically to the conclusion that punishment doesn't pay and that a new system of discipline should be substituted for the old.

But what new system? Management wanted one that was oriented toward the future, not the past. It wanted to avoid future trouble, not to apportion the proper punishment for a particular violation. "We feel that if we condemn an individual we give up all hope of changing him," said John Duberman, industrial relations director of the mill at the time the new approach was developed.

The new policy consisted of five basic steps:

1 With the first offense, the foreman issued the employee a casual, friendly reminder on the job.
2 If there was another episode within four to six weeks, the foreman had the employee come into his office for a serious but friendly chat.
3 A further episode within six weeks involved a repetition of step 2, but with a difference: First, the foreman in charge of the shift was also present, and second, the possibility was raised with the employee that he might find the kind of strict discipline necessitated by the working conditions of a plywood mill distasteful. Also, the employee was reminded that vocational guidance was available at the personnel office. Afterwards, a summary of the conversation was incorporated in a letter sent to him.
4 Another episode within six to eight weeks of step 3, and the employee was called into the foreman's office, sent home for the rest of the shift with pay, and asked to mull over whether he thought he could live up to the company standards. At the same session, he was told that another occurrence of the same offense within a reasonable time would lead to termination. Duberman emphasized that "during steps one to four the employee is reminded of the requirements without any implication that if he does not conform, he deserves condemnation and punishment."
5 Termination without discussion.

Did the approach work? The answer is in the affirmative, at least during the period that Duberman reported on. In the first seven months, only three people went to step 4, of whom two quit after a period of a few weeks, while the third saw the light and reformed. There were no terminations, and moreover, the morale of foremen and superintendents had measurably improved. Asserted Duberman: "For the first time they felt they had a strong, reliable, and fair tool to deal with unsatisfactory work performance and breaches of discipline."

We're willing to accept Duberman's claims because the policy developed at the plywood mill meets so many of what we feel are the preconditions for positive discipline. We're only surprised that variations on the policy have not been more widely adopted. Apparently it takes the complete bankruptcy of the traditional disciplinary approach, plus the documentation of the bankruptcy, to persuade most managements to break the "cake of custom" and search around for a more effective alternative.

Achieving Positive Discipline

When we flag this policy as fulfilling the requirements for positive discipline, we have in mind principally four points:

1 The discussions between boss and subordinate in steps 1 to 4 put the emphasis where it belongs, not on fixing punishment and accepting blame but on the simple reminder of the rule, an attempt to understand why the employee violated it, and hopefully a statement of his or her intent not to repeat the violation.

2 The policy avoided souring the relationship between the superior and subordinate as long as there was any realistic possibility of salvaging him or her. We feel strongly that to forgo the intermediate penalty of the disciplinary layoff or suspension connotes a hard head, not a soft heart. The person who is laid off may return chastened and repentant, a mood that usually passes quickly. More likely, the individual comes back to work in an even nastier mood than when he or she departed.

3 The policy postpones punishment until everyone, with the possible exception of the employee being dismissed, acknowledges that it's the only solution to the problem. We've seen the impact on the rest of the work force of what is regarded, wrongly or rightly, as an unfair discharge—transfers, quits, and silent sabotage by the remainder of the work crew are apt to follow. Supervisors should remember that, even though the person dismissed is gone, the manner of dismissal remains, perhaps to plague them.

4 The policy takes into account the existence in any work force of irredeemable troublemakers—admittedly, in another work situation they might not be beyond redemption at all—and the necessity of getting rid of them once their disruptive pattern has been established beyond doubt. In other words, every plant or office has its small quota of "rotten apples" who must be weeded out if the department is to remain efficient and the other employees are to avoid contamination by example. Justice Holmes upheld a Virginia statute requiring compulsory sterilization of certain mental defectives with the comment, "Three generations of imbeciles are enough." A similar ruthlessness in weeding out employees is justified after a certain number of sufficiently serious offenses.

DISCIPLINE HAS A CONTEXT

So far we have written as if supervisors operated in a vacuum—as if the decision on whether or not to discipline and how much is theirs alone, and that they are free agents in the disciplinary process with plenary power and responsibility. Such is typically not the case. The average manager, in imposing discipline, has limited discretion and is subject to being overruled. And, in many cases, the first-line manager has little or no power over certain categories of discipline. Under some circumstances, the only discretion one has is whether or not to look the other way.

What keeps supervisors from disciplining any subordinate in any way they can think of? The first limitation on their freedom to administer discipline is internal—their own personality set. If this seems like a paradox, it's real enough. By and large, the aggressive, dominant supervisor, for example, belongs to the Papa Knows Best School and identifies very strongly with authority and the rules that buttress it. An attitude toward discipline tends, in turn, to be highly legalistic. To the supervisor, a rule is there to be enforced, irrespective of the consequences or what a less rigid personality would judge to be extenuating circumstances.

Other determining factors are the size of the supervisor's department and the state of the technology employed. The larger the number of people supervised, the more likely one should use the legalistic approach and settle for matching the letter of the penalty to the rule. She or he isn't necessarily more heartless or less aware of the dangers of distributing justice by formula. It's simply that the supervisor lacks any intimate knowledge of the subordinates' personalities as well as the time to pursue the path of the well-tempered reprimand.

The point about technology places the average supervisor in a shabby light. However, it's a point that must be made. Take the case of two supervisors. One is in charge of forty-seven spinners in a textile mill, doing unskilled, repetitive jobs that anyone can master within a week. Contrast this person with the supervisor in charge of a ten-person maintenance crew in a chemical plant, skilled craftspeople all, who have spent years mastering the intricacies of the complex, expensive equipment they keep in good working order. Which supervisor is likely to apply discipline without punishment, and which will meticulously fulfill the requirements of the hot-stove rule? Make no mistake: Positive discipline takes time, patience, and plenty of thought. The easy way out always is to follow the letter of the law, and this is the way that comes naturally to many supervisors with employees whom they feel can readily be replaced.

MORE LIMITATIONS ON
THE SUPERVISOR'S FREEDOM OF ACTION

In discipline, as in so many matters, the bosses call the tune and the lowly first-line supervisor has little choice except to dance to the tune set for him. If there is any leeway, one will tend to cultivate the disciplinary style that wins favor and approval from superiors and avoid the style that results in disapproval or retaliation.

We remember the successful division head of a successful organization—in five years of his stewardship, the division had tripled its sales and quadrupled its profits. He reflected, in a rare moment of introspection, "I've always thought of my employees as the enemy." To be sure, he was seldom that explicit about his views, but nonetheless they permeated the organization. When an employee was suspected of any offense, "guilty until proven innocent" was the attitude a boss was expected to take, and if guilt was proved, the maximum penalty was the mandatory one except on those occasional instances when the division head reversed a subordinate's verdict, abandoned consistency, and indulged in a sentimental and quixotic gesture.

Finally, there's the situation, becoming less common over the past decade but predominant in unionized plants, where supervisors have lost most of their power to administer discipline. In many corporations, higher management holds that discipline is too important to be left to supervisors. Serious cases of discipline in the union plant—those involving work standards, frequent garnishment, work stoppages, organized gambling, and similar problems—are the province of the labor relations specialist, armed with suitable training, an overview of the situation, and, purportedly, greater objectivity. Even in areas like insubordination, absenteeism, and careless performance, where there is nominally more leeway, the supervisor is frequently obliged to consult with superiors, perhaps the general supervisor or the personnel adviser, before making a decision. And when a decision coincides with theirs, it holds. In rare cases discipline is housed in a straitjacket. The only hope of preserving the always fragile contract is to fall back on an exhaustive enumeration of violations and penalties, with no discretion left to anyone. Justice without mercy or common sense, which is what this approach is all about, sometimes keeps the peace.

We are aware that we have listed these last limitations on the supervisor's freedom of action as if they were hateful. And no wonder—that's the way we feel about them. However, we recognize that they are sometimes necessary. In the normal plant or office setup, the supervisor with tact, patience, and judgment can accomplish much more by applying discipline without punishment, by postponing punishment until the time when discharge is the only alternative, or, as a minimum, by following the requirements of the hot-stove rule.

The trouble is that this procedure requires time, patience, the willingness to be reasonable, the ability to compromise—and on both sides. The totally intransigent employee, whether badly advised or hostilely motivated, will frustrate the efforts of the most determined supervisor. If it's only one or two who are at fault, the effort justifies the failure. However, when the basic agreement, the implied contract to work, has broken down and what you have is a continual conflict between what the boss can exact and what the employee can get away with, it takes an autocratic, uniform hand to achieve even minimum results. Our only caveat would be the feeling that past supervisory laxness, indifference, or overseverity probably have had a lot to do with bringing about the conditions under which other supervisors have lost their power over discipline. The sins of the fathers—it's an old, old story . . .

ORDER GIVING

Why do we write about order giving right after discipline? What's the association? Is it simply that disobeying orders frequently gives rise to discipline?

Not at all. The similarities run deeper and are more subtle and more significant. We have already seen that much discipline fails in its avowed purpose—to motivate the employee not to repeat the offense. In turn, many orders fail in their avowed purpose—to motivate the employee to do what the superior wants. Punishment alone seldom suffices to motivate workers to mend their ways, and the obligation to obey is frequently insufficient to make them accept orders from superiors. Punishment and obedience are flimsy crutches for the same basic reason: They ignore the realities of human nature and rely on fear to the exclusion of any other motivator—and fear cows one person at the cost of inflaming five. Whatever it may do for the ego of those who choose to use it, as a motivational tool fear is a demonstrated failure.

That order giving is a complex process is something many managers, especially those at the first level where the content of the order itself appears direct and unambiguous, fail to appreciate. Their reasoning is simplicity itself: "It's part of my job to give orders to my subordinates, and it's part of their job to carry them out—that's what we're both paid for."

A lot of research and observation, as we have suggested, tells a different story: Subordinates do not automatically obey an order because it comes from someone with the authority to issue it. Between obligation and obedience, other forces supervene. Many orders are tacitly accepted only to be so radically changed in their execution that the boss can scarcely recognize his or her brainchild in the end result.

Guidelines for Complying with Orders

To what forces are we referring? What happens in the interval between the giving of the order and its execution? Why do employees, on occasion, resist and twist orders? About forty years ago, Chester Barnard, whom we mentioned earlier as a rare combination of practicing theorist and successful operating executive, laid down four conditions that must be met before an employee can carry out any order from a boss.

1 The order is and can be understood.
2 The order is consistent with the purpose of the organization as the employee understands it. In other words, the employee will resist in some fashion an order that he or she perceives as bad or stupid from the organization's viewpoint.
3 The order is compatible with the employee's personal interests as a whole.
4 The employee is physically and mentally capable of carrying it out.

Points 1 and 4 are obvious, although they have contributed their share of headaches to many managers. Let's concentrate on number 3—it accounts for the most serious instances of noncompliance with an order and is by far the most difficult point for most managers to comprehend and cope with. Yet, until a supervisor has grasped something about the circumstances under which a subordinate will subvert an order despite the usually considerable risk involved (the boss sooner or later will discover that his or her order has been flouted), the problem can be attacked only with threats that are sometimes successful but more often impotent. One frequent cause of resistance to an order is that it contradicts a subordinate's own idea of what constitutes a fair day's work. Let's consider the case of a train crew handling 150 trains a day. By taking a number of shortcuts, they completed the work in 6 hours—with the remainder of the time being devoted to loafing and sleeping. When management found out what was happening, the decree went out: Handle 200 trains a day. It's not difficult to guess what happened next. The crew resorted to the rule book and followed each rule to the letter. They worked a full 8 hours but somehow only processed fifty trains. Common sense triumphed: Management gave up its notion of 200 trains a day, and the crew went back to its old and comparatively productive ways.

The Indifference Zone

Of course, in this example, the members of the crew drew courage and strength from collective action. A solitary employee would be far less likely to engage in so blatant a defiance of the intent behind management's order. Nor do we wish to exaggerate by claiming too much for the similarity between punishment and the obligation to obey. Punishment, as it relates to the goal of discipline, is almost always self-defeating because it is almost always resented. Not so with the obligation to obey and the goal of order giving. To explain the difference, we will use another concept of Barnard's—"the zone of indifference." (See Figure 6-2.) Once the employee has accepted the authority of the organization, including that of the immediate superior, in exchange for certain material and/or psychic benefits, she or he carries out many orders. An order is obeyed, first, because it is recognized that there is a general obligation to accept orders, and second, because the specific order doesn't challenge a sense of personal interest—it lies within the zone of indifference. Also, she or he weighs, consciously or subconsciously—and we suspect the process is usually subconscious—feelings of attraction, repugnance, or indifference to the order against the overall satisfaction with her or his position in the organization.

Let's look, for example, at the matter of overtime. To the secretary with a very active social life and no pressing need for extra cash, overtime may be a fighting word. It's well outside her zone of indifference and she will use every stratagem she can think of to avoid it.

Subordinate accepts orders within these limits

Above this limit likely to be censured by informal group, violates own norms, requires "excessive effort," personal discomfort

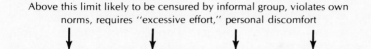

Acceptable, fulfilled orders tend to fall within these limits

Below this limit would be doing less than "obliged" to do in return for receiving salary and accepting the job—minimally acceptable performance

FIGURE 6-2 Zone of indifference

To another secretary, overtime may be an unappreciated chore but her hours after five aren't that full—besides, she was warned that there might be overtime before she accepted the job. It's within her personal zone of indifference. Therefore, she makes no special effort to escape it.

About one thing we can be fairly certain: Any order that changes the employee's frame of reference about what constitutes a fair day's work is likely to be resisted. Suppose that an office manager suddenly told her office clerk to clean the copying machine every two weeks. The clerk had been accustomed to cleaning it every two months—that's what it said in the manual. It was a messy, unpleasant job and one that he regarded as cruel and unusual punishment—to be ducked at almost any cost. We suspect that he might quit rather than conform to that particular order. Of course, if the circumstances were different, his reaction might have been different, too. Let's say that a service representative from the manufacturer had just inspected the copier and had recommended that it be cleaned every two weeks, a suggestion based on the company's experience with thousands of similar machines over several years. Let's further suppose that the manager had called in the office clerk and let him listen to what the service representative had to say. The office clerk probably would have accepted the order—and if he hadn't, it would indicate that there was something radically wrong in the relationship between him and his boss—which leads to an important point.

The process which determines where a particular order falls in the employee's zone of indifference—outside, within, or on the line—is subtle and complicated. Many factors enter into it: The employee's conscious and rational perception of self-interest; respect for the boss and faith—or lack of it—in the boss's credibility; interpretation of what the boss says in giving orders, which, in turn, depends on how he or she relates the boss's words to past experiences and concepts. Here is an example, actually oversimplified despite its length, of supervisor A endeavoring to get subordinate supervisor, B, to understand a problem and comply with an order.

A SIMPLE LITTLE PROBLEM

Supervisor A: (saying) Good to see you back. How are things going? It's been a long time—

(thinking): I've got to warm him up a bit before getting down to business.

Subordinate B: (interpreting received meaning) I wonder what's up.

(saying): Oh, OK, I guess, not much new except people pushing you all the time. You're lucky, Alice, being in that nice office.

(thinking): I am sure she didn't drop by to pass the time of day and get away from that nice office. I'd better let her know I'm busy and not very happy with this job.

Supervisor A: (interpreting) There he goes, complaining again. I wonder if I should soft-soap him a little or get down to business.

(saying): That's the way it is. They want those files right away and don't care who came first and how busy the other person may be. But what are you going to do—that's just the way people are. I've got to get over to see the big boss soon, but first I wanted to get you started on setting up a special file for these accident cases involving minors. Remember we talked about it last week? Now I think I know just how we should do it. This might be a good day for a dry run and I can stop by tomorrow to see how it's going.

(thinking): Much of what I give you comes from the big boss, so don't blame me. This is really an order I am giving you, you know I never just say "do this" or "do that." Dip into your memory and bring out what I said before, because what follows relates to that.

Subordinate B: (interpreting) There she goes again, throwing her status around. Now let's see what she wants. Oh, yes, I remember that discussion last week and how she wants a duplicate file by both age and sex for those under twenty-one.

(saying): Shoot! I remember. But don't forget I've got to fit this into all the other things I am doing today, so don't expect miracles. This could be like last Tuesday, when I promised to get those lists done but never got to them.

(thinking): I hear you and I remember—so go ahead. But don't hold me to a time schedule. Get your random-access memory working too and associate this extra task to the extra task I got last week. I'll do what I can, but no miracles performed here.

Supervisor A: (interpreting) Oh, boy, another excuse. He's getting ready to let me down.

(saying): Sorry to say this, Beck, but this really is rush. I've got to get the forms printed after we see what the files are like and all that has to be done by next Monday. You know I get you out of as many unnecessary things as possible. You and I really talked them out of converting everything to hanging files. That really was a great battle and we won it because we stuck together on it.

(thinking): I'm not just a fink. We've been through a lot together and I believe in reasonable work loads. We stick together on a lot of things—after all, this is our department, yours and mine.

Subordinate B: (interpreting) Alice is a pretty good supervisor—we really showed what a fighting pair we could be in the hanging file matter. Boy, that was a good battle! It showed the rest of this organization that this department is nobody's patsy.

(saying): OK. Give me the word on this.

Supervisor A: (saying) You recall that system of filing by age and sex we tried out last year, don't you? This is just a slight modification, using a lesser number of categories. Here, I've put them on this sheet—

(thinking): Shift your thinking to that system you finally mastered a year ago that unfortunately we had to discard because we needed the file space. If you can remember that, all the rest will be easy because this is going to be exactly like that, with a few very simple modifications.

Subordinate B: (thinking) I guess we did do something like this last year, but I'll be damned if I can remember anything about it. That was nine or ten months ago at least, maybe longer.

(saying): Yeah, I guess I remember.

Supervisor A: (saying) Well, on second thought maybe we'd better go over the whole thing.

(thinking): That was a pretty weak yes he gave me, so I guess I'll have to start from scratch—he's dubious, I can tell.

Subordinate B: (interpreting) I am glad she has the good sense to be clear on these things. I know how angry she gets if anything is done wrong, even if it's her fault for not making it clear in the first place.

(saying): Let me sit down and get some paper out to make notes, and give it to me slowly.

(thinking): Remember, you're usually rushing off some place and don't take the time to give me a full description.

Supervisor A: (interpreting) I wonder if he just wants to make a big deal of this, or is he really trying to take it seriously?

Comments on the Case

We can see how far removed this dialogue is from giving instructions to a computer. There are lots of anticipated and unanticipated byways, and there is the need for redundancy and for analogy. The listener is tying in what he hears with what he already knows, and, if the sender listens carefully, he is revealing what he doesn't know.

The superior, supervisor A, made one big error when she invoked the wrong symbol—the big boss—in an effort to get off the hook on the order. Subordinate B interpreted the remark in an entirely different way—as an attempt on his boss's part to throw her weight around—and it made him feel more negative about his boss and more resistant to the order. The turning point in their interaction came when the boss's reference to the joint battle against the hanging files invoked the symbol of past solidarity and changed the emotional climate between them. After that, the subordinate was willing enough to accept the order. What was required, and fortunately was supplied, was the boss's perception that the subordinate's "I guess I remember" meant the reverse of what he said on the surface, that it would take a detailed clarification before the subordinate understood and could comply with the order.

One missing element in the case is any reason for the order, any explanation as to how the change embodied in it would benefit the unit, the overall organization, or the employee. The subordinate is free to conclude that it's simply a case of management caprice at work, of change for change's sake—at his expense.

As a general rule, to give an order without explaining why breeds resistance. Take the by now classic tale of "boiler scale" on a destroyer during World War II. Even in a danger zone, the captain could never get a much-needed five knots over the maximum rated speed because of the mysterious boiler scale. He got the needed knots only when he dramatized the importance of extra speed by having a blow-by-blow description of each engagement sent over the public address system to the men in the engine room. Once they knew the reason why, the boiler scale disappeared and the captain got his five knots.

One final point about the case: The supervisor was conscious of not giving her subordinate a direct order. The closest she came to it was her statement, "I wanted to get you started on setting up a special file" and so on. What about this approach? We would say that it was about right. Manners do count. Most subordinates appreciate an order couched as a request—not a blunt "do this" or "do that"—and few fail to perceive that the request has the force of an order. Some managers go to the other extreme: They present their orders as suggestions and are surprised and unhappy when their subordinates disregard them. Part of the confusion springs from an honest misapprehension: The subordinates took the suggestion at its face value. Part of it comes from the fact that many subordinates do not respect the boss who pussyfoots in giving an order. As Professor Whyte of Cornell points out, "Most men have no respect for the supervisor who gives orders timidly and with uncertainty." Of course, the context in which the order is given counts for something. A request that would be readily understood as an order (although not necessarily accepted) when made by a bank officer to a subordinate would be completely ignored on the docks if it passed from a loading boss to a stevedore. In the latter case, the request would probably have to be a direct order—with a few obscenities to underscore the point.

CONCLUSION

In our discussion of discipline and order giving, we have seen that each manager should begin by discarding any illusions he or she may have about the rationality of a human being—although he or she might well search for consistencies in a human's irrationality. Rationality and self-interest would indicate that the employee who's been laid off for three days for excessive absenteeism should turn over a new leaf—yet, typically, he or she won't. Rationality and self-interest would indicate that the office clerk will start cleaning the copying machine every two weeks, once the failure to follow orders has been found out. Yet the chances are probably fifty-fifty that the clerk will continue to defy the order.

Discipline based on punishment fails 99 times out of 100 because the employee resents the punishment and therefore rejects the efforts to reform him or her. Order giving, based on the subordinate's obligation to obey a higher authority, frequently fails because it, too, is based on fear of the consequences of *not* following the order. Most orders receive a measure of compliance because they fall within the individual employee's zone of indifference. But when we examine the factors that determine the zone of indifference, we uncover a potpourri of emotions and attitudes—perceived self-interest, loyalty to the superior and to the organization, belief in the credibility of the superior and respect for him or her as a person and a technician, plus literally dozens of other elements, tangible and intangible, that contribute to that general state of mind known as job satisfaction.

In other words, success in handling discipline and order giving is something no manager can take for granted. All it takes is intelligence, intuition, prolonged and patient observation of people and events, a horror of easy answers and quick solutions, a reputation for credibility and fairness, a strong dose of humility—and a lot of luck.

THE EDUCATION
OF GREG HORNING:
FEBRUARY 21

Apparently, Rick had not felt like winning when he woke up on Monday—his output had been below standard. But since he'd been on the new machine, he'd consistently turned out more than Kilpatrick had. Greg had kept his eyes open—the others seemed to be leaving Rick alone—and Kilpatrick had been working slowly and sullenly, but without too much griping at his new job. By yesterday, Greg had decided that they would all adjust to the changes without a lot of trouble and that everything would be all right.

But when he came back from a late lunch this afternoon, he found all work stopped. Everyone was standing around Kilpatrick's new station, looking at his machine, handling malformed pieces which were supposed to be spools, and talking at once.

"What's the matter? What happened?" Greg yelled, rushing over.

Creegmore, who had been bent over examining the temperature dials on the machine, straightened up and answered Greg. "Ted's just had a little trouble with his machine, that's all. Helen had to go over to check something with Jeannette for a minute and Ted was watching the machine until it jammed . . ."

"Jammed! You mean the machine's not working at all? What's going to happen to the shipment we're supposed to get out by tomorrow?"

"They'll just have to sit on their asses and wait for it, that's all." Phil Martello volunteered this sarcastically. "Look. We'll have to get maintenance in here to fix it and you know those guys. We'll be lucky if they get it going in a week."

Greg looked at the pile of faulty spools lying beside the machine. "My God, Ted! How could you let that much stuff come off your machine without seeing it was no good?"

Kilpatrick just stood with his hands in his pockets, saying nothing. Again, it was Creegmore who answered. "All right, now, Greg. Take it easy. It wasn't his fault. You know we don't stop to check each piece. Besides, it's Helen who does the checking, and I told you, she had to step away for a minute. Now, if you'll just calm down, I can tell you what happened." He took Greg by the arm and drew him aside, explaining the situation slowly and in a low voice.

It seemed that the main temperature knob, which was supposed to be pre-set, had been loose for months. They had complained that it needed to be fixed, but maintenance never would cooperate. Today, the vibrations in the room had finally caused the control to shift to a high enough temperature to grossly deform the pieces. One of them had gotten stuck and caused the backup, so that now the machine was not working.

"But why didn't Kilpatrick catch it sooner?" Greg persisted. "I don't care what you say, Henry. It was carelessness. Pure damn carelessness."

"Now, listen, Greg . . ." But Greg felt that he had allowed Creegmore to patronize him long enough.

"Look, I've spent enough time listening to your excuses for Ted. Now get back to work and get the others going, too. We have to make up as much of that shipment as we can. Send Ted in to see me."

Greg started toward his office. Creegmore seemed about to follow, then changed his mind. Instead, he went over to say a word to Kilpatrick, who, with his hands still in his pockets and his head down, followed his supervisor into his office.

The two men, both standing, confronted each other across Greg's desk. "Well, Ted, what do you have to say for yourself?"

"It wasn't my fault, Greg. That control's been ready to go for months now. Henry knew it, and I remember the old foreman, before he left, he . . ."

"Never mind that, Ted," Greg interrupted impatiently. "You were supposed to be watching the dials."

"Yeah, but, Greg, you can't have your eye on everything at once. I was watching the other settings because it was a new batch of polyurethane I'd just put in. That dial that went—that's not supposed to change and . . ."

The older man went on with his explanation, but Greg was not really listening. When he had gone out to the shop, his first thought had been that the men had manipulated the dial purposely to sabotage the shipment. But that didn't make sense. If they had planned it, Kilpatrick wouldn't have been the scapegoat; they would have rigged Rick's machine. No, it had been an accident, all right, and now Greg was pretty sure he knew why it had happened.

"Where'd you have lunch, today, Ted?" he asked abruptly.

"Huh? Why I went over across the way. I always go to that place across the way with the other guys. But what's that got to do with . . ."

"That place across the way—it's a bar, isn't it, Ted?"

"Well, yeah, I guess so. A bar and grill. But . . ."

"Look at you, Ted. You're all red in the face and you stink of liquor. This whole office stinks. I think you drank your lunch and you came back here drunk and didn't know what the hell you were doing!"

"Now, wait a minute, Greg. I . . ."

"That's it, Ted. You're lucky I'm not firing you. You were drunk and you were negligent—knob or no knob—and there's no excuse for it. I'm giving you a three-day layoff so you can go home and sleep it off. Now get out of here. I don't want to see you again 'til next week."

Kilpatrick's face had been red; now it was redder. His mouth worked open and closed without any words coming out. Then, his hands back in his pockets, he slumped out.

Greg went over to the window. Kilpatrick had gone straight to Phil Martello, who was listening with his mouth tight in anger as Kilpatrick talked. Creegmore started over to them, but Martello was already striding toward Greg's office. He threw open the door.

"Look, kid, I don't know who you think you are, and what's more, I don't give a damn." Martello spoke quietly, but his anger seemed to make the words reverberate in the small office. "We've got a union in here—in case you didn't know—and we're not going to stand for this kind of thing. You just try proving a charge of drunkenness. He had three beers—I was there, so don't tell me—I've seen him put away a dozen without missing a step."

"Now, hold on a minute, Phil . . ."

"You just hold on a damn minute, yourself. Ted Kilpatrick may not be the sharpest man in the crew, but he's been here over thirty years, and if you think you can give him the shaft just because you don't like him, you've got another think coming."

"That's not it, Phil. He . . ."

"You just shut up and listen to me, buddy. I'm telling you this officially as a union representative and you listen to me good. We'll fight you on this all the way through. You'd just better forget this whole thing ever happened or you're beat before you've even started." Stopping to breathe hard, Martello glared at Greg. Greg ran his hand over his face.

"All right, Phil. All right," said Greg very slowly, getting a grip on himself as he spoke: "We've all been angry. Maybe I should think about it a little more."

"Yeah. You think it over and you think it over right," Martello shot back, the door knob in his fist. "If you don't, I'll make you look like a jackass. And let me tell you—it'll be my pleasure." He slammed the door and was gone.

Greg passed his hand over his face again. Those union people sure could put the pressure on. But he'd put the pressure on them too—maybe too much. Kilpatrick had a pretty unimpressive record, but he'd never had any accidents before.

"Yeah," Greg muttered to himself, "maybe I was too rough on him. Maybe he wasn't drunk, but he sure reeked of booze."

It might have been the kind of accident that could happen to anyone. Greg decided to call Ed Briscoe in maintenance and check it out.

"If that dial really could have gone out of kilter by itself . . ." Greg sighed deeply.

181
ADMINISTERING POSITIVE DISCIPLINE

QUESTIONS
1 Why do you think Greg refused to accept Creegmore's explanations?
2 In talking to Ted Kilpatrick, at how many points did Greg deviate from the "hot-stove rule"?
3 Do you feel that Martello's position toward Greg was justified? What about his tone?
4 What mistakes did Greg make in handling the situation?

BEHAVIORAL EXERCISE

Two people are needed for this exercise. One takes the role of the supervisor who has asked a subordinate to be sure to come in on time the next morning in order to begin an important project with a tight deadline. The other person takes the role of the subordinate, who arrives two hours late. The supervisor (since this problem has occurred before) must try to cope with this disciplinary challenge to his authority by confronting the subordinate. The subordinate, on the other hand, ought to assume that some terribly unexpected "problem" arose that morning which was responsible for his or her being late.

The two confront each other as the supervisor, who has impatiently been waiting to begin this urgent project, sees the subordinate coming in two hours late. (Note: The subordinate did *not* stop to explain the lateness, but went right to work.)

Discuss this situation in front of students or colleagues and evaluate how well the supervisor handles the subordinate, and whether or not the employee's motivation to improve has been helped or injured by the confrontation.

BIBLIOGRAPHY

Black, J., *Positive Discipline*, AMACOM, New York, 1970.
Feinberg, M., *Effective Psychology for Managers*, Prentice-Hall, Englewood Cliffs, N.J., 1965.
Miner, J., *The Management of Ineffective Performance*, McGraw-Hill, New York, 1963.
Steinmetz, L., *Managing the Marginal and Unsatisfactory Performer*, Addison-Wesley, Reading, Mass., 1969.

READING

The Theory of Authority*

CHESTER IRVING BARNARD (1886-1961)

Barnard was a rare combination—in the United States there has been no equal—of the extremely successful executive and theorist on the executive process. He was, at various times, president of the New Jersey Bell Telephone Co., Director of Relief in the state of New Jersey, president of the Rockefeller Foundation, and head of the U.S.O. during World War II (incidentally, according to him the most difficult post he ever held in his life). He wrote only two books, but one of them, *The Functions of the Executive*, from which the selection is taken, is still one of the most valuable books written on what it takes to be a twentieth-century manager. Barnard tells it the way it really is—and tells it in a way that the reader can use to enrich his own understanding.

Barnard was associated personally and intellectually with Mayo, and the work of each man complements the other. Mayo's accent, as dictated by his studies, was on the small industrial work group at the operator level. Barnard took the whole organization for his province but similarly stressed the importance of the informal organization. A quality that distinguishes Barnard from Mayo was that he had the subtler and the deeper mind. But let's consider one more example—Barnard's discussion of leadership in his second book, *Organization and Management.* He defines leadership as "the quality of the behavior of individuals whereby they guide people or their activities in organized effort," by which he both denies the existence of leadership with a capital L and at least implies that leaders are made as much by conditions as they are by innate abilities. And he cautions us that leadership is a perilous undertaking for "that (selection) which is made by formal authority we call appointment (or dismissal), that by the informal authority we may call acceptance (or rejection). Of the two, the informal authority is fundamental and controlling." Working from that basic insight, Barnard lists the five qualities of leadership in descending order of importance—on first glance a surprise ranking—as (1) vitality and endurance, (2) decisiveness, (3) persuasiveness, (4) responsibility, and (5) intellectual capacity. We haven't the space to summarize his discussion of the five qualities, and no summary could do it justice.

So far this has sounded like a fan letter for Barnard—and so far

*Reprinted by permission from Chester Irving Barnard, *The Functions of the Executive*, Harvard University Press, Cambridge, Mass., 1938, pp. 165-170. Copyright © 1938 by the President and Fellows of Harvard College.

it has been. Barnard, let's admit, has his arid and unattractive side. The man himself was pompous; he had the self-conscious air of one who had walked with the captains and the kings. He wrapped his rare perceptions in the intellectual window-dressing provided by Pareto's theory, a process that added nothing to the substance of his thought and prevented many from understanding it.

Finally, Barnard was an elitist, one of those from Plato on down who felt that decisions on large and complex issues were the natural monopoly of a few who were qualified by experience and brains. For the proof, read his essay "Riot of the Unemployed" in which he describes how he manipulated the leaders of the unemployed into accepting his diagnosis of their problems and which he sums up with the words "I do not think I had ever before made a purely personal accomplishment the equal of this."

However, having redressed the balance, let's end positively. Barnard has less fire in his belly than Mayo or Taylor, much less humanity than McGregor, Rogers, or Bennis, and the least engaging style of any of our classic management thinkers; against this, he has one pretty potent advantage—he thought more deeply about management on the basis of more direct experience than the rest.

As for his books, first *The Functions of the Executive*, Cambridge, Mass., Harvard University Press, 1938: We recommend skipping Part I which is pretty much window dressing à la Pareto. Of the second, *Organization and Management*, Cambridge, Mass., Harvard University Press, 1948: We recommend especially Chapter II, "Dilemmas of Leadership in the Democratic Process," Chapter III, "Riot of the Unemployed," and Chapter IV, "The Nature of Leadership."

The necessity of the assent of the individual to establish authority for *him* is inescapable. A person can and will accept a communication as authoritative only when four conditions simultaneously obtain: (*a*) he can and does understand the communication; (*b*) *at the time of his decision* he believes that it is not inconsistent with the purpose of the organization; (*c*) *at the time of his decision*, he believes it to be compatible with his personal interest as a whole; and (*d*) he is able mentally and physically to comply with it.

(*a*) A communication that cannot be understood *can* have no authority. . . . Now, many orders are exceedingly difficult to understand. They are often necessarily stated in general terms, and the persons who issued them could not themselves apply them under many conditions. Until interpreted they have no meaning. The recipient either must disregard them or merely do anything in the hope that that is compliance.

Hence, a considerable part of administrative work consists in the interpretation and reinterpretation of orders in their application to concrete circumstances that were not or could not be taken into account initially.

(b) A communication believed by the recipient to be incompatible with the purpose of the organization, as he understands it, could not be accepted. Action would be frustrated by cross purposes. The most common practical example is that involved in conflicts of orders. They are not rare. An intelligent person will deny the authority of that one which contradicts the purpose of the effort as *he* understands it. In extreme cases many individuals would be virtually paralyzed by conflicting orders. They would be literally unable to comply—for example, an employee of a water system ordered to blow up an essential pump, or soldiers ordered to shoot their own comrades. I suppose all experienced executives know that when it is necessary to issue orders that will appear to the recipients to be contrary to the main purpose, especially as exemplified in prior habitual practice, it is usually necessary and always advisable, if practicable, to explain or demonstrate why the appearance of conflict is an illusion. Otherwise the orders are likely not to be executed, or to be executed inadequately.

(c) If a communication is believed to involve a burden that destroys the net advantage of connection with the organization, there no longer would remain a net inducement to the individual to contribute to it. The existence of a net inducement is the only reason for accepting *any* order as having authority. Hence, if such an order is received it must be disobeyed (evaded in the more usual cases) as utterly inconsistent with personal motives that are the basis of accepting any orders at all. Cases of voluntary resignation from all sorts of organizations are common for this sole reason. Malingering and intentional lack of dependability are the more usual methods.

(d) If a person is unable to comply with an order, obviously it must be disobeyed, or better, disregarded. To order a man who cannot swim to swim a river is a sufficient case. Such extreme cases are not frequent; but they occur. The more usual case is to order a man to do things only a little beyond his capacity; but a little impossible is still impossible.

Naturally the reader will ask: How is it possible to secure such important and enduring coöperation as we observe it in principle and in fact the determination of authority lies with the subordinate individual? It is possible because the decisions of individuals occur under the following conditions: (a) orders that are deliberately issued in enduring organizations usually comply with the four conditions mentioned above; (b) there exists a "zone of indifference" in each individual within which orders are acceptable without conscious questioning of their authority; (c) the interests of the persons who contribute to an organization as a group result in the exercise of an influence on the subject, or on the attitude of the individual, that maintains a certain stability of this zone of indifference.

(a) There is no principle of executive conduct better established in good organizations than that orders will not be issued that cannot or will not be obeyed. Executives and most persons of experience who have thought about it know that to do so destroys authority, discipline, and morale. For reasons to be stated shortly, this principle cannot ordinarily be formally admitted, or at least cannot be professed. When it appears necessary to issue others which are initially or apparently unacceptable, either careful preliminary education, or persuasive efforts, or the prior offering of effective inducements will be made, so that the issue will not be raised, the denial of authority will not occur, and orders will be obeyed. It is generally recognized that those who least understand this fact—newly appointed minor or "first line" executives—are often guilty of "disorganizing" their groups for this reason, as do experienced executives who lose self-control or become unbalanced by a delusion of power or for some other reason. Inexperienced persons take literally the current notions of authority and are then said "not to know how to use authority" or "to abuse authority." Their superiors often profess the same beliefs about authority in the abstract, but their successful practice is easily observed to be inconsistent with their professions.

(b) The phrase "zone of indifference" may be explained as follows: If all the orders for actions reasonably practicable be arranged in the order of their acceptability to the person affected, it may be conceived that there are a number which are clearly unacceptable, that is, which certainly will not be obeyed; there is another group somewhat more or less on the neutral line, that is, either barely acceptable or barely unacceptable; and a third group unquestionably acceptable. This last group lies within the "zone of indifference." The person affected will accept orders lying within this zone and is relatively indifferent as to what the order is so far as the question of authority is concerned. Such an order lies within the range that in a general way was anticipated at time of undertaking the connection with the organization. For example, if a soldier enlists, whether voluntarily or not, in an army in which the men are ordinarily moved about within a certain broad region, it is a matter of indifference whether the order be to go to A or B, C or D, and so on; and goings to A, B, C, D, etc., are in the zone of indifference.

The zone of indifference will be wider or narrower depending upon the degree to which the inducements exceed the burdens and sacrifices which determine the individual's adhesion to the organization. It follows that the range of orders that will be accepted will be very limited among those who are barely induced to contribute to the system.

(c) Since the efficiency of organization is affected by the degree to which individuals assent to orders, denying the authority of an organization communication is a threat to the interests of all individuals who derive a net advantage from their connection with the organization, unless the orders are unacceptable to them also. Accordingly, at any given time there is among most of the contributors an active personal interest in the maintenance of the authority of all orders which to them are within the zone of indifference. The maintenance of this interest is largely a function of informal organization. Its expression goes under the names of "public opinion," "organization opinion," "feeling in the ranks," "group attitude," etc. Thus the common sense of the community informally arrived at affects the attitude of individuals, and makes them, as individuals, loath to question authority that is within or near the zone of indifference. The formal statement of this common sense is the fiction that authority comes down from above, from the general to the particular. This fiction merely establishes a presumption among individuals in favor of the acceptability of orders from superiors, enabling them to avoid making issues of such orders without incurring a sense of personal subserviency or a loss of personal or individual status with their fellows.

Thus the contributors are willing to maintain the authority of communications because, where care is taken to see that only acceptable communications in general are issued, most of them fall within the zone of personal indifference; and because communal sense influences the motives of most contributors most of the time. The practical instrument of this sense is the fiction of superior authority, which makes it possible normally to treat a personal question impersonally.

7

CONTROLS, INCENTIVES, AND APPRAISALS

LEARNING OBJECTIVES

1 Recognize why controls are equally important to both superior and subordinate in performing their respective jobs.

2 Be able to cope with the difficulties of designing good controls that will not injure the work flow.

3 Predict employee response to different kinds of controls and to the unintended "cues" supplied by the managers, including how employees seek to "beat the system."

4 Describe how to apply an MBO system to different kinds of organizational positions and know its likely limitations and problems.

Most new managers take as obvious what turns out to be one of their most difficult challenges. A critical element in every manager's job is assessing and influencing how well an employee is doing his or her job. This responsibility turns out to be a good deal more problematic than common sense might suggest.

Unfortunately, this element is made needlessly complicated by the different words and concepts that managers use for essentially the same problem area: influencing and appraising performance. Such measures as production totals, quality levels, turnover, and absenteeism are designed to tell the manager how employees are doing.

But controls also involve *rewards* and *punishments:* Subordinates are usually rewarded, directly or indirectly, when they do well (in other words, are productive) and punished when they show up badly (when they show up late, for example, or not at all). Also, rewards are central to the general subject of *incentives,* that is, extra pay for additional performance. And, in the field of personnel administration, concern with making employee *appraisals* (often involving the filing of formal appraisal documents for each subordinate), giving *merit salary increases,* and deciding on *promotions*—all have their bases in management's evaluation of and influence on subordinates. After all, there is no point in going through all these procedures if you don't think that they will influence people to try to look better, to do those things which bring approval, and to avoid those things which are likely to be followed by punishment.

Thus controls, incentives, appraisals—what have you—all deal with getting employees to move away from undesirable work patterns in the direction of more desirable behavior. But to use any of these techniques, we must know the answers to these questions.

1 What is desirable job behavior?
2 Is the employee demonstrating this behavior?
3 How and when should the supervisor communicate his or her evaluations to employees?

THE SUBORDINATE'S WORLD OF APPRAISAL: IMPLICIT CONTROLS

Every one of us in the world of work and in the community is deluged with requests, rules, temptations, and deterrents which influence what we should do with our time. At least for most people—again both at work and outside—there is neither time enough, energy enough, nor will enough to do everything we might do or are asked to do. Here is one employee's list of the decisions and choices she evaluates in expending her seven and a half working hours. (She is a claims adjuster in an insurance company.)

> Management has told us we should handle twenty claims a day. One way I can reach this total is to avoid the really tough cases and shift these up to my supervisor.
> My fellow employees often urge me to do less than twenty to prove to management we are overworked.
> Sometimes if I hurry I approve or disapprove claims that I would settle differently if I had more time; I am not sure whether this makes much difference or not.
> I am often asked by the accounting department and our customer relations department to answer inquiries, and I question how much time and energy I should devote to these outside requests.
> If you want to do a really thorough job on some cases, it means a dozen phone calls, lots of checking in files, and even consulting with the more experienced adjusters. How thorough should I be?
> I often am asked by those less experienced than I to help them, too.
> I ought to spend some time reading some of the old files and policy statements here in the office to improve my ability to do this job. Also, I ought to be studying up on other subjects to qualify for a promotion.
> I've been asked if I wanted to take over temporarily—while the woman who handles the job has her baby—a claim review job. It's hard work and very demanding, and I don't know whether it's worth it for a couple months.
> The company wants you to keep your desk neat at all times and everything put away in files. If I do this, I work slower because it means constant filing.
> You're only supposed to have one customer record out of central filing at a time. If I take several, I can work on another while I am waiting for some information on the first.
> I have a typist working for me and I can let her fill in some of the more routine things, or I can meticulously spell out every detail.
> I've got some ideas on how this job could be improved, and I wonder whether it's worth trying to get the company to listen.

This short list of one employee's choices could easily have been made longer if we had wanted to be exhaustive (in both senses of the word). But it is long enough to show that an employee's use of his or her day is obviously not dictated by some explicit job assignment. What you emphasize and deemphasize, what you do quickly or indifferently, what you concentrate upon, what rules or norms you follow and which you ignore, when you are responsive to the requests of others and when you turn them aside, when you seek to introduce improvements in the job or in yourself, and when you concentrate on the here and now—all are choices that you, as an employee, make. They are not predetermined by the organization or the definition of the job. Even on relatively programmed jobs, there will be a good deal of room for maneuvering.

The Supervisor Provides Clues

While there are other influences on these choices (such as the informal group and the personality differences that we have already discussed), one of the major determinants will be the supervisor's own actions. What does the manager emphasize or deemphasize? What is rewarded or punished—or ignored? What is watched closely and what, indifferently? Many times, managers are not aware of how they cue employees as to what is worth doing and what is not—in a world where you can't or won't do everything that conceivably might be done on any particular job.

A bank teller learns that, while his boss talks a lot about being pleasant to customers, the one thing that really makes him fuss is inaccuracy. So he is brusque at the window but spends a great deal of time counting his cash.

There is no workbreak scheduled during the day, but employees walk over to the cafeteria in threes and fours every day—and nobody says anything.

Chris Ames worked on his lunch hour and a little during the workday to develop a new fixture that would save setup time, but it wasn't successful. In the process, he broke a tool bit and the supervisor roundly criticized him for "wasting time and company property."

A salesclerk spent a great deal of time calming an irate customer who claimed that the store had shipped her the wrong size purposefully. The clerk was overheard by the buyer, who called her into his office to commend her. He also wrote a letter for Employee Records, indicating that this clerk handled difficult human relations problems with aplomb and dedication.

An engineer devoted a great many hours to preparing a special report and came up with some very startling conclusions that would save the company money. She even worked on it at home on her own time, concentrating harder than she ever had before. The report was two days late and she was sharply criticized. A few months before, she had done a perfunctory job on another assignment but turned in the report two days early. She was told she had done fine work.

A programmer notices that the people who get promotions appear to have several things in common: They don't wear "mod" clothes, they are neatly groomed, and they use standard English. Their work in many cases is less good than that of others who aren't promoted.

In every one of these instances, it is not difficult to deduce the conclusion that will be drawn by the employee regarding what "really counts around here," what can be safely ignored, and what must be repressed if at all possible. Gradually, as employees stay on a job, their performance will be shaped by these positive and negative reinforcements.

It may be helpful to conceive of a job as a large, shapeless, flexible mass of plastic which gradually begins to assume a fixed form as the employee receives "inputs" from the supervisor.

Unconscious Guidelines

And many of these inputs are not even consciously given: Often, a manager will be preoccupied with other matters when an employee presents a solution to a particularly difficult problem. Contrariwise, a manager will be upset by other things when an employee appears to have ignored a rather minor rule or request. In the first instance, the absence of commendation and recognition may well teach the employee that real dedication doesn't count for much. From the second reaction, one is likely to conclude that trivial matters are more important than serious ones and that appearances count more than substance.

Therefore managers can't afford to let down their guard. They must constantly ask themselves, "What is my action—or inaction—communicating to subordinates in terms of what is relatively most important to me (and their job future here), and what is of secondary or even no importance?" Managers cannot minimize their responsibilities for shaping the highly amorphous, plastic "glob" of job requirements into a desirable job pattern. They can't afford to leave their explanations of these requirements to chance or to abstract written or spoken descriptions of the job. There are just too many possible bad choices, bad in terms of the overall welfare of the department, that can easily be made by the employee.

From the employee's point of view, working is a continuous learning experience which transforms an ambiguous environment into an understandable one. There are a large number of inputs coming from disciplinary actions, from promotion decisions, from merit increases, from the supervisor's frowns, smiles, and positive responses, and from many other things. Employees must make sense of this confusing array of "directions" by coming to some conclusions with respect to what's worth doing, what is better ignored, and what should be avoided at all cost. Then they are comfortable because their world is predictable, and most of us want to be able to predict the consequences of our actions (or inactions). Of course, we are also saying that what employees perceive as the "real" world, what they have learned from experience—which always speaks in a louder voice than the supervisor's printed or verbal directions—may not be what the managers expect them to perceive.

Thus, nothing the manager does can be ignored because it is likely to affect this learning process, particularly during the more formative stage when either the employee or the boss is new and the worker is looking for hidden cues as to what is appropriate. The old cliché just happens to be true, "Do as I do, not as I say." Employees often ridicule management efforts to appraise their performance in the abstract. The following list of performance degrees for the factor "adaptability," taken from an "underground" employee-appraisal form, may illustrate our point about employee skepticism:

Far exceeds job demands: *Leaps tall buildings with a single bound*
Exceeds job requirements: *Must take running jump to leap over tall buildings*
Meets job requirements: *Can leap over a short building*
Needs some improvement: *Crashes into building when attempting to jump over*
Does not meet minimum performance: *Cannot recognize building at all, much less jump*

Now let's turn to the other side of the equation: the supervisor's problem with assessing and controlling performance.

THE MANAGER'S WORLD OF APPRAISAL

We have been concentrating on the employee's efforts to "psyche out" his or her job world and make it predictable—to distinguish the real payoffs from the phony demands and requirements. The other side of the coin is even more critical—the manager's effort to find out what the employee is doing and how well he or she is doing it. Although such appraisal may appear easy, we shall see that it is not.

The process of appraisal is the subject of management controls, as they are formally called. Controls measure how well prescribed plans and activities and tasks are being performed. We shall look closely at how this is done, but first one ought to ask the question: What purposes are being served by these measurements, these controls?

Why Does the Manager Utilize Controls?

1 He knows that he is always in the role of a teacher or trainer, as we have seen. His communication to employees that he has seen something he likes or dislikes—in other words, his feedback—will affect significantly what an employee learns about the real job requirements.

2 She wants to know where work is progressing badly in order to be able to intervene, to do something to get the job or coordination or employee morale back where it should be. This contingency aspect of every managerial job is central to good supervision. There is the brighter aspect too, that is, knowing where things are going well so that the manager doesn't have to spend scarce supervisory time on these situations and can devote her efforts to the problem areas.

Note that there can be a conflict here with point 1. Even though a subordinate is doing well and doesn't require the boss's attention, as we have seen, there may be need for the manager to tell an individual that she recognizes this good performance, and thus reinforce it.

3 The manager needs to be able to summarize the performance of subordinates in order to make sensible personnel decisions on salary increases, promotions, transfers, and the like. These actions must be consistent with a continuous observation of performance or employees will feel there are serious injustices. Unfortunately, injustice sometimes does occur because managers haven't kept good records of what they have observed. Such an oversight also means they will have a difficult time justifying their personnel decisions to others. Furthermore, actual observations of performance are a good check on the effectiveness of management's selection techniques. Is the manager a good judge of employee potential? The answer is given when a supervisor compares his or her predictions, say before hiring, with what is observed later. Where there are major discrepancies, one's selection critieria had better be changed!

4 Under some circumstances, the manager may want to tie monetary rewards to the controls. Employees may receive a bonus based on how much they sell, how high they keep quality, how many units they produce, and similar achievements. These are called incentive plans, and they depend upon the manager's ability to give quantitative dimension to job performance.

5 The manager also uses controls to spot undesirable trends. All human beings possess a well-known characteristic which is both a curse and probably a salvation: We are adaptive to our environment. Sit in a noisy room for a few minutes and you no longer hear much of the noise. Get a $35-a-week raise and in a few months the elation is gone and it seems as if you've had it forever. This same pattern of accommodation to conditions occurs in the work situation. An employee gradually arrives later and later, the work area gradually deteriorates, and performance gradually declines. If there were not reasonably objective standards, each of these trends, if it were gradual enough, might go undetected.

These, then, are five quite distinct managerial purposes served by controls. All are important, needless to say, but we shall concentrate on points 1 and 2. Let's look at the first of these more closely.

Training Employees with Reinforcement

Psychologists speak about learning taking place as a result of rewards and punishments, positive and negative reinforcements, For example, if every time a laboratory technician thoroughly washes the equipment after finishing a test run, the supervisor remarks on that being a necessary and well-done procedure, this job pattern will become ingrained. Psychologists also refer to *one-to-one reinforcement,* meaning that the reward is forthcoming every time the behavior is demonstrated. Similarly, an employee can learn not to waste time thoroughly washing the equipment (assuming that step isn't necessary) if the supervisor rebukes the subordinate for dawdling at the washing stage. This is an example of negative reinforcement, of course.

Unfortunately, forgetting—*extinction,* as it is technically called—also occurs quite quickly under one-to-one reinforcement. If the supervisor neglects to encourage desirable behavior and if the habit is clumsy or difficult to maintain, it may soon be forgotten, that is, extinguished. On the other hand, if the supervisor uses *random* reinforcement, extinction is very slow. By that we mean that the supervisor doesn't always smile or nod approval when a thorough washing job is done but does so when present during this operation, say several times a week.

Sometimes we teach employees bad habits by random reinforcement without being aware of this. Take the case of the manager who complained that one key employee often forgot to lock up the drawing materials and files before leaving. On being questioned, the manager admitted that the employee sometimes asked to leave things that way after working right down to the last minute if the employee had a pressing engagement downtown. In effect, the employee was learning that not locking up was all right.

One-to-one or random?

The major advantage of random reinforcement over one-to-one reinforcement is that extinction or forgetting is very slow even after the praise (or punishment) stops coming. So it is a good method of thoroughly and deeply ingraining a pattern of behavior. The disadvantage is that learning takes place much more slowly with its use. The obvious answer is to combine the two: use one-to-one at first when new behavior is being learned, and gradually shift over to random reinforcement. For example, to "fix" good typing habits, reward each perfectly typed letter for a few weeks, then sample the correspondence at random times after that.

An important note of warning here: one-to-one reinforcement will be ineffective if it requires the supervisor to stand over the employee and watch every move. Such close scrutiny is overbearing and often interpreted as distrust. And, of course, the time required for the manager would make the process wasteful.

Managers, then, should remember the following principles of reinforcement: *One-to-one* means fast learning, fast forgetting; *random* means slow learning, slow forgetting. There are two elements that we have neglected in this discussion of learning (sometimes called "conditioning theory"). They are the magnitudes of the rewards and punishments, and the differences between them.

Magnitude

Supervisors often think that if a little is good, a lot is better. This is really not the case. In fact, overrewarding and overpunishing have deleterious effects associated with their use. There is a good deal of evidence that employees who receive excessive praise or very large salary increases grow uneasy as a result of feeling that they are getting more than they deserve. (Psychologists use the term "cognitive dissonance" to describe this effect.) They are not sure that they can live up to the high standards expected of them. Similarly, excessive punishment is deeply resented and may produce an opposite effect from the one intended, that is, a determination to get back at those responsible. (Recall our discussion in Chapter 6.)

Of course, magnitude is a subjective, not an objective, quantity that depends upon the employee's expectations. In regard to magnitude of reinforcement, we can talk about three different levels:

1 *Undetectable level:* The amount of reinforcement given is below some threshold of the employee's expectation, so it isn't even recognized. For example, after working for several weeks to finish a difficult assignment, the employee hears the boss say, "Thanks a lot, Charlie!" Or an employee earning $200 per week is given a $5-a-week increase. Both these actions are too small to be considered rewards and may even cause resentment because they are below expectations. They certainly don't serve to reinforce desirable behavior!

2 *Normal level:* The affirmative and negative comments, encouragements, and disciplinary actions that follow employee actions are as expected. We have already described this level as part of the supervisor's training and reinforcement function.

3 *Excessive level:* The rewards or punishments seem so large that they cause the employee to become nervous or resentful because of their magnitude.

Subordinate perception: reward or punishment?

Individual expectations are so crucial to the way the employee perceives the action, of course, that the supervisor who intends to give a reward may be providing punishment or vice versa. A small reward may appear so unfair that the employee feels he or she is being disciplined in some way. On the other hand, an employee who gets only a mild rebuke for producing low-quality parts may figure "it's worth it" to avoid the effort of doing good work. (A major confrontation was anticipated with the supervisor when the bad work was detected.) Thus a positive reinforcement was given by the superior, who thought he was doing just the opposite.

Another danger in excessive use of rewards is that employees become conditioned to expecting them and even expect more each time. (This is another element in favor of random reinforcement.)

Managers should also remember that rewards and punishments are not just equal and opposite. For example, punishments, when compared to rewards, are more likely to have undesirable by-products when used as learning prods. As we all know, they create hostility toward the giver and the desire to fight back at what is perceived as the enemy (as emphasized in Chapter 6.)

Particularly when the threat of punishment is very great, the worker may even become paralyzed with fear and be unable to accomplish anything. This can sometimes be observed in very delicate craftwork where the employee knows that a slight mistake will ruin a very expensive die and might even result in being discharged. The worker may sit for hours before being able to resume work. The rule of fear is not usually a productive one. The same thing happens when a student is numb with fear of a final examination: The possible punishment (having to take the course over again with the same instructor!) seems overwhelming.

Further effects of excessive threats of punishment can be seen in many departments in which subordinates "fudge" data to avoid admitting job problems. Many managers are deceived as to the true state of affairs in their departments because employees can usually find ways to make the figures lie.

> A department head had been relaxed about production quality in the die-casting group because it had not varied over several months. He learned later that the supervisor had neglected to note the shift in the type of work being performed. The workers were now producing very easy parts where the rejection rate should have been substantially under the 5 percent rate which had been acceptable when they were working on highly complex and intricate parts. He also learned that the same supervisor was hiding rejected parts in paper scrap barrels. This behavior followed an announcement by middle management that any increase in scrap would have serious repercussions on the jobs of the supervisors involved.

A manager who is very much worried about a problem or anxious because of pressure from the boss is always tempted to threaten subordinates with dire consequences if he or she doesn't get what is thought to be appropriate behavior. Aside from being rather childish, such threats may have the opposite effect to the one desired. Furthermore, the actual imposition of the penalty, should the desired behavior not be forthcoming, can have further repercussions. For example, if the employees are unionized, the union will likely have "a good case." Moreover, whether there is a union or not, penalties tend to unite work groups into a cohesive antimanagement force.

Now to turn briefly to the subject of how to evaluate employee performance.

OBSERVING EMPLOYEE BEHAVIOR— KNOWING WHAT TO MEASURE

The supervisor wants to be assured that the employee is not doing things that are either unproductive, wasteful, or liable to cause later problems. Many times, it is necessary to observe the work in process because mistakes in work method or carelessness will subsequently be hidden from view. Slovenly filing, for example, may not show up until a document is sought. Poor welding or soldering may be spotted only in a later testing procedure, after much labor and material have been wasted in assembling the component.

To learn whether the employee is using proper methods and diligence, the supervisor makes periodic checks. Because employees are likely to behave differently under observation, and because it is very costly (as well as demeaning) to continuously watch subordinates, good supervisors learn to sample behavior. Rather than walking through the plant or office at predictable times, they adopt a random method of checking what people are doing and how they are doing it.[1] During their random appearances, they can note how many people are working, how many are idle, whether safety equipment is being properly used, if working instructions are being followed, and a number of other factors. Often work in process is scrutinized to see whether it is being handled properly. In the case of salesclerks, listening to the conversation between the customer and the clerk will give some idea of whether tact, responsiveness, and selling ability are being employed.

But of course such watching and waiting is costly in time, and no matter how carefully done, it is somewhat abrasive from the point of view of the employee. This explains why workers seek work locations that are out of the direct line of sight of the supervisor's desk, prefer the night shift where the supervision may be limited, or take "outside" jobs like selling and landscaping where they are on their own a good deal of the time.

Some jobs and some industries inherently have good measures of performance which the supervisor can use in judging whether employees are doing a good job and which eliminate the need to watch them. For example, in retail selling the supervisor may be able to tell a good deal by the actual cash register and accounting records. One can tell what quantities of what kinds of merchandise a clerk is selling— perhaps even how much repeat business (are there any loyal customers?) and how many returns were made. Furthermore, there may be many employees in similar jobs in both this and other stores, so meaningful comparisons can be made in performance. (This is not true, of course, where a job is unique, a condition that makes appraisal very difficult.) Also, retail selling jobs often lend themselves to an incentive system whereby the employee is motivated to work hard (because of direct financial gain) without constant supervision.

The same may be true on a simple machining operation. The supervisor merely checks the records of the quantity produced and the number of rejects for quality and concentrates on those workers who

---

[1]This type of investigation is formally called the "ratio delay" method, and there are specific statistical tools that help a supervisor to know exactly when and how often to appear. Under a very precise system, what everyone was doing at that particular time is recorded. Using statistics from these records, a close prediction of the pattern total of the day for all employees can be made.

are exceptions (those employees whose work falls outside the acceptable quantity and quality limits).

Unfortunately, however, it is often more difficult than this to design controls which truly measure all aspects of performance in which the supervisor may be interested. For example, an employee may be careless about a work area, fail to maintain a machine, or devote all efforts to relatively easy and straightforward tasks while "goofing off" on the tougher jobs. But this employee produces excellent quantities on all the easy jobs. Measuring such a performance is more complicated than simply counting!

Balance of Incentives

The amount of intervention required from the supervisor may also depend upon the balance of incentives in the situation. It may be instructive to contrast two types of industry in this regard.

In what has come to be called continuous-processing or automated plants (such as some chemical factories), employees work most when something has gone wrong. If they handle their jobs intelligently, foresee problems, diligently check the processing control records, and do good preventive maintenance, they may well have considerable time to themselves. Thus, for a good part of the time, the more they produce, the less they work! Both management and the workers are ahead when there isn't a great deal of effort expended.

Contrast this with a more traditional factory, where the harder the employees work, both the more fatigued they may become and the greater the advantage to the company. Here, the employee and the supervisor may have almost opposite incentives. The supervisor wants more work, the employee wants less. To make matters worse, in the automated plant, labor costs, as such, are a quite small part of total costs—most of the expenses are for equipment. In the traditional factory, labor costs are very significant and management is much concerned with how hard employees are working.

Of course, there is an even greater extreme. Many professionals, such as doctors and professors, get such satisfaction from their jobs that they always push themselves to do more (even to the detriment of their health). Their internalized incentives (plus the early programming contributed by their training and experience) mean that they require almost no supervision from their superiors.

Elusive or Changing Measures of Performance

Some managers believe that employees work harder if they are kept guessing as to how they are being evaluated. So they keep changing their standards. This way, all are kept on their toes and can't relax thinking that they know what to concentrate upon and what to ignore.

Such an attitude naturally destroys employee confidence in the supervisor and can also lead to a great deal of wasted time. Listen to this comment by a credit analyst:

> Karl plays his cards close to his chest as to what he is looking for in these reports we are preparing. So every week we all get together and compare what he has said to each of us about our reports. We purposefully introduce a lot of stuff we don't think is useful to see how close he reads them and what he'll "bite on." They take a lot more time this way—much of it wasted—but believe me we're going to figure this guy out once and for all.

To see how destructive changing performance standards can be, it is worth looking at some studies of animal behavior. Scientists have shown that you can induce psychotic states in animals by using ambiguous stimuli which lead to reward or punishment. More specifically, psychologists condition an animal to know that jumping or pawing at a circle will give him a food pellet whereas jumping at a long oval will bring him a punishing electric shock. Gradually, the researchers change both shapes to a more elliptical one. Now it is difficult for the animal to discriminate between the stimulus that provides a reward and the one that brings punishment. At this point, the animal often "breaks down" and shows psychotic symptoms.

MANAGEMENT BY OBJECTIVES (MBO)

Recognizing the importance of controls, many organizations have established formal programs that require all their managers to work with subordinates to develop performance standards that will motivate effectively. These "MBO" programs, as they're called, are based on the following principles:

1 Employee performance will be higher when clear, unambiguous standards exist in contrast to simply being instructed to "work hard," "do your best," or "follow instructions."
2 Standards that are reasonably high elicit better performance than standards which are very easy and quite low. (Obviously standards that appear very difficult to attain or are unreasonably high will not be successful.) However, the interesting research finding is that

people do respond positively to reasonable challenge, combined with the knowledge that their supervisor has confidence in their ability to attain high levels of performance.

3 These standards should be established by joint consultation between boss and subordinate rather than simply by having the boss impose them. The manager's objective should be to get the subordinate to propose what he or she thinks are sensible and likely-to-be-attained objectives. (In fact, research also often suggests that individuals often will set *higher* standards for themselves than would their superiors.)

4 Motivation to meet these "targets" is maintained by frequent and regular feedback by the boss in which recent performance is reviewed and assessed. Ideally the subordinates themselves are able to report on how well they have achieved the goals they set. (For some objectives, such feedback will be devoted to progress reports, for others it will be possible to assess whether or not the objective has been met fully.)

In summary, MBO requires quantitative, jointly established work standards which will provide challenge and which are reinforced by periodic feedback sessions.

The objectives, of course, are derived from the employee's job responsibilities and may well differ for different employees. Here are a few examples:

An insurance claims adjuster agrees that every claim or inquiry crossing her desk will receive a telephone or written reply within 48 hours and, at least 5 percent of these will receive some answer within 24 hours.

A secretary proposes to reduce the photocopying charges she incurs by 15 percent (by greater use of carbons and checking carefully on how many copies are actually required).

A laboratory technician believes he can handle an average of forty routine tests and fifteen of what are defined as nonroutine tests per day.

During the feedback session, the employee and her manager may agree that the standard was too high or too low or that progress has been delayed by some new factor—which then may become a new "objective." For example, the lab technician above did not meet the standard after the first month because one of the major pieces of equipment he had to use was out of service several times. Since breakdown was related to care in usage, the technician agreed to "limiting equipment breakdown to under 6 hours per month."

Cautions in the Use of MBO

There is little question that MBO has become one of the best known and most widely used new management tools in recent years. Organizations find that providing objective "targets" initiated by subordinates themselves is an important source of motivation. Further the process of target setting and evaluation of the results encourages a healthy superior–subordinate relationship. And the discussions are reality-based, focusing on job performance rather than dealing with vague generalities like, "How's the job going?" or "Got any problems I should know about?"

But there are some limitations surrounding MBO that should be recognized.

1 While MBO is usually conceived as a method to increase the subordinate's sense of participation in goal setting, in determining the standards by which he or she will be judged, that is not an inevitable result. MBO, as George Strauss has pointed out, can also be a means of exercising tighter and more centralized control.[2] Managers can go through the motions of asking subordinates what they think are reasonable, sensible "targets" while, in fact, imposing these standards on them. This is often called "masterminding"—giving the impression of allowing someone else to make a decision while you really force them to make the decision you wanted all the time.

2 Some important aspects of the subordinate's job may be difficult to convert into quantitative results; there are more qualitative parts of jobs. For example, a subordinate may have to build good relationships with a customer that will not immediately show up in higher sales or help handle complaints in a patient manner that builds difficult-to-measure "good will." MBO should not be used in such a way as to eliminate concern for these less measurable or more intangible responsibilities. The manager must find ways of maintaining subordinate interest in the parts of the job that are not included in the MBO measures.

3 There is always the danger that MBO may encourage subordinates to do their jobs in such a way that their performance is improved, but at the expense of others in the organization.

The Feld Hospital had an outpatient clinic with high patient costs. Under an MBO program, the clinic manager set a high standard for a number of patients that would be treated each day. The standard was met by limiting patient service to only one "ailment" per visit. As a result patients were

---

[2] George Strauss, *MBO: A Critical View*, University of California at Berkeley, Reprint #359, 1972.

required to make more appointments, overloading the admissions office and the quantity of patient records increased dramatically which created problems for the billing department. Thus clinic productivity appeared to increase while all the service departments were experiencing heavier work loads and patients were burdened with the need to make extra trips to the hospital.

4 Meeting the target is not the sole job requirement in most cases. An example may be useful here.

Phyllis Cohen asked her administrative assistant, Jack Picco, what he could propose to reduce the costs of office supplies. He said that he could probably cut monthly costs by at least 20 per cent by more careful shopping and getting bids on larger quantities of some supplies. Phyllis has to be sure that in meeting his goal, Jack has received proper training in company policies concerning purchasing. In this case, the company has a number of rules it expects every purchaser of outside supplies to follow:

a Purchases cannot be made from a supplier who employs relatives of those authorized to approve purchases.

b Where possible 10 percent, at least, of all purchases should be made from local suppliers and preferably those operated by minorities.

c No more than one month's supply of any material should be inventoried without special approval from the chief accountant.

d There should always be at least two suppliers of every resource used with regularity.

One of the strengths of MBO is that is focuses on results, not means or methods. It provides a strong incentive to improve performance as distinct from concentrating on the procedures surrounding the job. However, organizations do have to meet multiple objectives and no department is an "island." Successful MBO assumes that subordinates can be delegated broad responsibilities because they are adequately trained and thus familiar with company policies and procedures. A supervisor can delegate when he or she has reasonable assurance that the subordinate will do the task in a manner consistent with both the boss's and the organization's values.

No more than any other management tool, is MBO a panacea. However, when used intelligently it can improve both efficiency and subordinate motivation. It combines an emphasis on clear, quantitative controls with employee participation in goal setting.

OTHER PROBLEMS WITH CONTROLS

Managers must be aware that employees are very sensitive to controls. They adjust their behavior accordingly, although the adjustment may not be what the manager hoped for. As we shall see, managers have to be very careful to select measurements that do not encourage responses that are destructive of the work organization. Inadvertently, many managers do, in fact, utilize such poor controls.

Output quality may be lowered

Here are some examples of destructive influences:

Certain employees were encouraged to produce as many units as possible by being told that their production was the primary measure of their effectiveness and by being offered extra pay (incentive piecework) for what they produced above a given standard. Gradually management discovered that the employees were becoming very careless about how much material they used, about keeping their equipment well-maintained and their work areas cleaned. Quality was a continuing problem because, in rushing the job, employees produced a great deal of marginal work.

Other organizational problems emerged. When management changed the material from which the parts were produced, the workers wanted the standard lowered (to enable them to get to bonus earnings more quickly), claiming that the new material was harder to handle and slowed down the machines. Also, when management attached new feeding devices to the machines (to lessen employee effort and make high production easier), the workers fought against management's raising the standard. When management argued that it wasn't fair to pay workers for the additional production that would be possible because of the new feeders (which were quite expensive), the employees charged that this was just a trick to lower their bonus.

In short there are dangers in poorly chosen controls and incentives. They may cause employees to neglect unmeasured or unpaid-for parts of their job. And they may create additional sources of antagonism between employees and their manager over what is a fair standard and what can be changed in the work environment.

Competition versus cooperation

There can be many other destructive results. An employee who is being measured and rewarded for doing a job in a certain way may become less cooperative with fellow workers. If strongly motivated by the control and/or the reward, this employee may ignore their requests for help or for minor modifications in what he is doing that will make his work more consistent with their jobs.

Under strong incentives, employees can even begin to fight with each other over who gets the easiest or more lucrative jobs. A supervisor described a personal experience like this:

> I've had an awful time supervising these store clerks; they would kill each other if I gave them a chance to rush the big spenders who come in. At the same time, they all manage to be busy when a poorly dressed customer comes in and argue whose turn it is for fear that they'll be wasting time and losing commission. Each blames the other for not taking time to straighten up stock because they're too busy trying to write up sales.

In clothing plants, one can even see hair-pulling and fist fights over the distribution of new work, since some sewing jobs are slightly easier and permit more bonus earnings. Employees, like the managers themselves, are under strong controls, and they learn to pass the buck.

> I got sore when those parts didn't fit—those people were speeding so just to make bonus—so I didn't see anything wrong with throwing them in the tote box and letting the next group down the line sort them out. After all, I lost time because of the machinists' selfishness and I can't be expected to worry about the next group.

Among sales representatives, one finds high-pressure tactics to make the sale and indifference to customer-servicing needs after the sale that result from supervisory pressure for higher performance. Several years ago, the telephone company found that carefully measuring how many connections were made by central-switchboard electricians (who did the rewiring for changed telephone numbers) spurred them into making more connections, but at the expense of quality. The old wire, from the previous connection, was not removed effectively, and after a few months, the back panels of the switchboard became so filled with old, unconnected wire that extra staff was necessary just to clean it out.

Managers are not immune to this single-purpose emphasis. On production lines, the typical end-of-the-month competition to meet production quotas often encourages managers to "bleed" the line—to push everything in process through and leave nothing in the line to begin the next month's work. They also engage in what is called "balloon squeezing"—trying to prove that costs ought to be assigned to departments other than their own.

> I was putting great pressure on my key workers to keep welding costs

down. I discovered that they were having the welders paint over weld defects that then wouldn't show up until the assembly or test operations— someone else's department. Then the other department's budget would get socked for the rework labor cost and my people would come out smelling like a rose.

Good controls take time

An old-fashioned and fallacious view of bonus and incentive plans is that they relieve the supervisor of a good deal of time-consuming responsibility. This view assumed that employees motivated to earn extra money would now take care of both themselves and their work. But it doesn't work out that way, as we have seen, because incentives create their own supervisory problems.

Employees emphasize the most "profitable" parts of their job and ignore other aspects which may be critical to the flow of work and coordination between jobs. They argue with one another and with management over who has the most lucrative assignments, and they are reluctant to accept any procedure, equipment, or materials changes which may injure their earnings potential. There are really more, rather than fewer, supervisory problems with incentives.

This does not mean, however, that incentives have no value. There may be a number of routine jobs that can be very well defined, that are highly autonomous (others don't depend closely on them) and that the employee cannot easily distort. Under these circumstances, the constant reward-reinforcement provided by "beating quota" can and does encourage greater productivity. Thus the worker who learns that greater productivity is rewarding consistently tends to repeat this behavior. And incentives may provide some job satisfactions that would be nonexistent on many dull, routine types of jobs. There can be on-the-job pride and pleasure coming from the sense of winning economic payoffs. But there may be fewer such jobs than the manager imagines or hopes, as we shall now see.

OUT-OF-CONTROL CONTROLS

Sometimes managers become angry when they detect that employees are finding ways of "beating the system," that is, of looking good under the control being utilized but hurting the job. Rather than admit to poorly chosen controls, the supervisor blames the employee and starts issuing more and more rules to circumscribe what an employee can do. They require time to enforce and complicate the work situation.

Incentive workers, in an effort to produce more, were wearing out tool bits at an extravagant rate. The supervisor decided that an employee would have to sign a special form to get a tool bit from the storeroom. Also, if the employee got more than one bit per day, the form would have to be countersigned by the supervisor. In a short time, employees complained that the standard rate on the job should be loosened bcause there was always a line filling out forms at the storeroom. Also, there were long arguments over whether the excess wear on the bits was due to poor maintenance on the machine, poorer quality steel, or just employee carelessness. The supervisor became embroiled in these discussions and in approving tool-bit requests to the point that nearly one-third of the day was devoted to this process, which had required no supervisory intervention before the incentive plan was introduced.

It is often worthwhile to reconsider whether the right controls are currently being used before instituting more complicated rules and procedures. Furthermore, employees are very adept at finding their way around almost any new rule or procedure, if you make it advantageous for them to do so.

What Is Good Supervisory Performance?

Of course, managers also get appraised by their superiors, and the same problems arise as with nonmanagers—finding good measures that will motivate better performance. The most frequently used measure is that of costs. A supervisor who keeps costs within the budgeted amounts is considered to be doing a good job. Costs are also a function of quantity of output. Since most of the department's costs are fixed—wages, electricity, equipment—the "cost" of the department's output depends on how much work the employees turn out.

In most industrial operations, cost accounting has developed "standard costs" for every item produced. If the standard cost of an item is 45 cents and the supervisor's department can make it for 43 cents, he is a hero. But if he makes the same item for 49 cents, he is a bum. Sounds fair enough, and it would be, except for two things. First, cost accounting is far from an exact science—figures may never lie, but they're only as accurate as the input from the frequently fallible and occasionally devious industrial engineers who set the standards in the first place. Second, standards may be too "light" or too "loose" because of an error, or occasionally they may be too "tight" because the industrial engineer feels its her job to build pressures for top performance into the standard. In these instances (and they're common), the supervisor is either penalized or rewarded by the defective standard, and higher management gets a false picture of his performance.

Figures never lie, but sometimes they omit—and omissions frequently conceal the true facts of performance. Any attempt to measure performance through statistics fails to get at the whole truth because some elements of the supervisor's performance are very difficult to measure, and others, such as the supervisor's success in maintaining the morale of his department, resist statistical measurement. These inherent weaknesses of statistical controls have two consequences, both of them unfortunate for the supervisor and higher management. Superiors get a picture of the supervisor's performance that is distorted and that doesn't reflect his real value to the organization. The supervisor, in an effort to impress higher management, concentrates on those areas of his operation where success can be quantified and where it is certain to be recognized—and, he hopes, rewarded.

Then we have the areas, such as morale, that most supervisors tend to neglect—and for good reason. Because such areas are so hard to measure, higher management has no yardstick with which to judge the supervisor's performance. So it usually overlooks them completely when the time comes to hand out pay and perquisites. Good employee relations are something a supervisor may get around to worrying about when costs are in line, production is up to snuff, and the scrap rate is well within the allowable limits. Developing subordinates is a similar area. The personnel department exhorts supervisors to develop their employees for positions of greater responsibility and usefulness, but we rarely hear of supervisors' receiving bonuses or other forms of explicit recognition for developmental prowess. Until they do, we expect that they will continue to goldbrick on their developmental function.

When statistical data are the prime means of evaluating success or failure, supervisors, like their employees, will sometimes go a long way to show up well on paper. Figures never lie but they can be "adjusted." In one department, workers tossed defective parts into trash cans, with their supervisor's full knowledge and tacit approval. The reject count, naturally, was below average. In another department, the supervisor came back alone at night to collect the rejects and dump them into a local quarry. In the morning, there would be nothing to count in the trash cans.

And figures are juggled. An engineering supervisor in an electronics company, whom we know, recently submitted a quarterly budget that allotted many worker-hours to a project that was nearly finished, and assigned only a few hours to a project, already way over its budget, that needed many more hours to complete. The supervisor's reasoning was obvious: The juggling wouldn't cost the company any more money, and unless higher management found out the truth (which was unlikely), it would get him off the hook.

Buckpassing

Buckpassing is also endemic in operations which emphasize statistical controls. Whenever parts turn out defective, there is always controversy about which department should be charged with the cost of repair. And the bigger the charge, the longer and louder is the controversy. In one organization, for example, a dispute over one big error lasted two months. The supervisors of the departments most likely to be blamed waged a continuous campaign to prove their innocence. Each supervisor blamed the others, since no one wanted the error on his or her record. In consequence, the supervisors spent hundreds of hours arguing and debating among themselves. The big boss, unable to pinpoint the responsibility for the error, finally gave up and allocated it to "general factory loss."

Trading off

As we observed previously, the supervisor is the person in the middle, caught between pressures from above and below. How is this dilemma resolved? Frequently, a supervisor trades off privileges in areas higher management isn't concerned about or won't discover for a production level higher than could be obtained from employees without these concessions. For example, one supervisor in a welding department lets employees bring in transistor radios—the kind with an ear plug for silent listening. And they are allowed to play cards on their lunch hour—contrary to company rules, and this supervisor even supplies, free of charge, day-old crullers from a local bakery to sweeten up their coffee breaks.

The Context of Measurements

We want to emphasize the importance of placing statistical controls in the proper context, of not mistaking any part of the performance for the whole. Measure such items as production runs and reject rates—fine. But higher management should not neglect to measure, by means of turnover rates, attitude surveys, and direct personal observation, the *human* efficiency of the supervisor's operation too. Nor should it fail to measure the third element of any supervisor's performance—his or her personal contribution to the organization and his or her own growth potential. Superiors should consider and evaluate the suggestions an employee has submitted, any ideas contributed at meetings, the courses he or she has taken, the qualities of judgment and initiative shown in handling day-to-day decisions. In other words, does the supervisor go beyond conformity and use judgment and initiative?

A SYSTEMS VIEW OF CONTROLS

Essential as controls are, we should be alert to the difficulties of both establishing and using them. If they go awry, they can be detrimental to the overall organizational system and to individual production. We have already described two tendencies relating to their use:

1 Managers are likely to employ, as a measure of job performance, aspects of the job which are easiest to count objectively. They are apt to ignore aspects of the job that are more difficult to measure. Unfortunately, many of the latter job elements contribute to coordination and cooperation between jobs and to real productivity as distinct from individual "scores." This is a systems view of jobs and of controls.
2 Employees are quick and alert to sense where the real payoffs are and to respond accordingly. These responses to incentives and controls can introduce very real distortions into the organization.

What must managers do to avoid these destructive aspects of controls? Think carefully about the jobs being appraised in terms that we dealt with in Chapter 4. Rather than starting with what is available to measure, what is countable, start with the job and all its interrelationships. Is the employee performing a job which is truly an independent one or a job that relates closely to the jobs being performed by others? What are the most critical elements in a job which will affect the total performance of the work system for which the management is responsible?

In most cases, the supervisor will find that a job requires more diverse behavior than can be measured by a single yardstick or single number.

In some cases there may not be neat, objective measures available, for example, in assessing an employee's helpfulness to coworkers. However, workers need to know that their behavior is being observed, and they should be able to detect positive reinforcement from the supervisor when they act commendably in this area. In other cases, managers may shift their measures from the individual to the group. It may be better to encourage cooperation by measuring the group's total production—thereby stressing collaboration—than to set up competition and fighting among its members.

Often a manager emphasizes effort when accomplishment should be emphasized. Maintenance workers in one plant were measured in terms of how many repairs they made per week. Later, the measure was shifted to how little downtime there was for the equipment. Now, maintenance employees were encouraged to keep things going. Often, in the past, a worker would see a minor malfunction in a piece of equipment that was still operating satisfactorily. One would get credit, however, not for preventive maintenance but only for fixing a broken machine when asked to do so. Now, however, if the worker spent a few minutes adding oil or tightening a belt or removing an obstruction, the equipment might not break down at all. In effect, the worker worked less hard by using intelligence and alertness, and management got more overall production than when employees were measured on the basis of how hard they worked.

On college faculties, teachers who have to obey the "publish or perish" commandment tend to neglect teaching. Even though teaching performance is harder to measure objectively, there are a variety of ways to sample student opinion and to detect the teachers whose classes are either readily filled up or consistently avoided. When the professors know that teaching also is being measured, they devote energy and care to this part of the job.

Controls and the Introduction of Change

Another aspect of a systems view of controls is the manager's use of time. As we have said, the manager depends on one type of control to tell where something is going wrong which may require attention. Quality is falling off on the stitching machines, absenteeism is climbing among the younger workers in the department, squabbling is increasing among employees over job assignments. Each of these measures should bring the manager into action to get the system back to its normal operations: quality up, absenteeism down, intragroup squabbling down. Sometimes it might require seeking out a deeply buried problem (using good interviewing techniques). At other times, it may be necessary to give an order such as "Send that machine down to the repair shop and transfer the work to that idle equipment." The important thing is to take action to get the system going.

The good manager also keeps track of where she is spending her time. How often must she talk with John about absenteeism? How often is that machine breaking down? Where she finds problems that are taking her time consistently and that seem to recur again and again each time she thinks she has them solved, this is a signal that there is a more fundamental problem in the situation.

In a sense, the manager learns from this type of control. It measures his own use of time and shows that his intervention is not working. Perhaps the employee is unsuitably placed or the equipment is the wrong type for the job. These time-consuming areas require a major investment of work hours to solve once and for all. The manager may have to initiate a series of discussions with the employee, with the personnel department, and even with the union steward concerning a transfer of the wayward employee. Or he may have to undertake many long talks with the boss and the chief engineer to convince them that the machine is the wrong type for the work required of it.

Many managers are loath to invest extra days or even weeks in problems that have already cost them a great deal of time and effort. Yet, these are just the problems which require significant organizational changes if they are to stop being a drain on the supervisors' scarce time and energy resources.

Therefore, the good manager seeks out, by the systems type of control, the real trouble spots in the department. He or she then initiates, difficult as it may be, the process of organizational change, to eliminate the time drain caused by recurring problems. All managers, even those at the bottom of the executive ladder, have a responsibility to keep changing their organization as these recurring problems show themselves. Identifying and solving them is the mark of the successful manager.

CONCLUSION

New managers are often told that employees resist change. As we have seen in previous chapters, there are a number of instances in which they do so. But managers also need to remember that human beings are enormously flexible. They are constantly learning—that is, they are adjusting to the rewards and punishments that they find in their environment in such a way as to improve their lives. An adage of learning theory, called "the law of effect," is worth emphasizing: Behavior is repeated which provides rewards and tends not to be repeated when it is punishing.

Thus employees are very responsive to the rewards and punishments they find on their jobs. In fact, they engage in a great deal of "search behavior" to smoke out the real (as distinct from verbalized-by-the-boss) rewards and the real punishments. After all, the job situation is very ambiguous. The employee is typically asked or told to do many things that he or she doesn't have time or energy to do thoroughly. There are countless rules, norms, and practices (initiated by the company or the work group) which may not be mutually compatible. So one has the problem of finding one's way in this maze.

Unfortunately, managers tend to forget that everything they do communicates rewards and punishments to employees. In the employee's eyes, formal controls, appraisals, salary increases, promotions, discipline, incentive pay, words of praise and criticism—all are summed together. From all these, employees deduce what is worth doing, what must never be done, and what they can get away with. Managers must always keep in mind the total impression they are communicating.

On the other side, the manager has to find ways of adequately assessing employee job behavior in order to accomplish a number of distinctive management responsibilities. These are:

1 To train employees through adequate reinforcement
2 To determine where one's own supervisory intervention is required
3 To have the knowledge necessary to make personnel decisions on such actions as merit increases and promotions
4 To pay equitable bonuses or incentives when appropriate
5 To detect undesirable trends before serious damage is done

For all these purposes, the manager needs realistic information about employee performance. Naturally, perhaps, there is a tendency for managers to look only at those aspects of a job which are easiest to measure or appraise. They may neglect aspects of the job that, though more difficult to measure, may contribute significantly to total systems performance. This can lead to serious distortions as employees seek to "look good" in terms of what is being measured and slight those aspects of their jobs which are not measured.

From a managerial point of view, the controls that a manager uses to appraise employee performance thus become one of the most critical determinants of that behavior. In effect, managers have much more influence over employee behavior than they sometimes imagine. They can change this behavior more easily than they think—by changing controls.

What we have been describing is not much different from what happens in the classroom where there is an overemphasis on grades produced by a final examination. Rather than learn the material in the course, the student may spend all his or her time trying to figure out the instructor's special interests and the questions that are likely to be asked. Everything one does has to help "beat" that exam. Still worse, when students are told that the class will be graded "on a curve," meaning that one student's grade will go down if someone else does better, they won't even help each other learn. Every teacher and student faces the problem that some objective measure of performance is useful feedback and provides a summary of accomplishment needed by both sides. Yet overemphasis on a single measure, say a final exam grade, produces deleterious effects on both classroom and out-of-the-classroom behavior. This is one reason why, in recent years, there has been growing emphasis on programmed self-instruction in which there are built-in continuous feedback and reward and punishment directly related to the total learning process.

The manager must be careful, then, not to use as a primary control or measure of performance the most convenient statistic or objective measurement in the situation. This type of measure often neglects the total system in which the employee's job is embedded and fails to motivate a person to do his or her total job. The manager must therefore find a number of measures of performance to give adequate weight to all the duties and responsibilities associated with a given employee. These measures are essential to employee motivation.

THE EDUCATION OF GREG HORNING: MARCH 4

Greg's call to Ed Briscoe hadn't proved anything one way or the other, but it had made Greg think of something he hadn't been aware of before. Those knobs could loosen up by themselves sometimes, Ed said, but whatever it was, he wasn't going to let his crew get stuck with the blame. They had too much to do—they couldn't be expected to run all over the plant every time a knob rattled. Ed's loyalty to his crew struck Greg. He'd been expecting his group to support him; now, he suddenly saw that it could work both ways.

Still, if he reversed his decision, he'd look awfully foolish. Maybe he should check with Al Sykes, head of personnel. By the time Sykes finished raking him over the coals, Greg conceded he deserved it.

"You just don't pick someone who's been with the company for over thirty years as a fall guy," Sykes told him. "Not when there's a union in the shop. These people stick together—and with the amount of proof you had, you'd have to be out of your mind to think you could make it stick. You'd better do something to get yourself out of this mess—and fast."

So the morning after the accident, Greg had called Kilpatrick at home. He admitted to being hasty in his judgment and apologized for having accused Kilpatrick of being drunk. He told Kilpatrick to forget about the layoff, but since his machine wasn't functioning he might as well take the day off. Kilpatrick surprised Greg by saying, no, he'd rather come in. His wife had him doing odd jobs around the house anyway, and if he was there he could at least work with one of the other men and help make up for the lost time.

The reactions of the others surprised Greg, too. They'd pitched in making up the time on that rush order—they'd only lost a half a day getting it out. Greg had appreciated that and he'd told them so. During the next few days, Helen had called him over a couple of times to check pieces with him. They talked a little and she told him about her son who was majoring in business administration at college. "He's just about as pigheaded as you," she'd said, and they'd both laughed. Then there was that morning when he'd come in with the new tie—a wide one, with red, white, and blue stripes. Jeannette had called out to him in the same teasing tone she used with the men on the floor, "Hey, boss! You getting Rick to buy your clothes for you?" He blushed and grinned and they all had laughed.

Gradually the crew was becoming more friendly and relaxed. Greg found that he was relaxing too. Furthermore, he was beginning to see that there were better ways of tackling his big, unsolved problem— increasing production by 25 percent.

As the crew was starting back to their machines after the midmorning break, Greg came out on the floor.

"Before you get back to work, I thought we might have a talk." He felt a little nervous, remembering the other "talks" he had had with his crew, but they had interested expressions on their faces and some of them were looking around for a place to sit.

"Sure, Greg. What'd you have in mind?" Phil Martello said.

"Well, Phil. I'll tell you. You all know the trouble I'm having with the big boss upstairs about our output. He's really on my neck for more production from this department, and I thought you people might have some worthwhile ideas about how we can get more out." He looked around the group, waiting. Martello was the first to speak.

"Gee, Greg. I don't know. I just don't know. We work damn hard. Now I don't know what more we could do. Of course, the materials they give us these days aren't what they used to be and there's always something going wrong with the machines. I mean, look at what happened with Ted's a couple of weeks ago . . ."

"And what about the materials handlers?" Helen cut in. "You know how they're always putting the tote boxes in the wrong place. And can you ever find one of those guys when you need them?"

"Well, you know I've tried to talk to them, Helen," Creegmore said. "They just won't cooperate. Now that I think of it, the mixing department does whatever they can to mess things up for us, too. Like you say, Phil, the plastic they been sending us is lousy quality."

"OK. Let's back up a minute." Greg put in with evident exasperation. "So far all the complaints have been with other departments. What about what goes on right here. Every thing can't be the fault of another department. What can we do ourselves to get more work out?"

"Well, as I was saying, Greg,"—this was Phil again—"we do a fair day's work for a fair day's pay. In fact, we probably do a hell of a lot more than we get paid for right now. I don't see how we can do any more."

"Besides, Greg," Jeannette added, "what's the good of the men turning more pieces out when Helen and I—we get backed up with the flashes and the sorting and packing and all of that. If you put too much pressure on the men, they get careless, and that means more work than we can handle. See what I mean?"

"Now wait a minute, Jeannette," Phil broke in. "Don't you start blaming us. As I say, we do a fair day's work. And if we were more careful about the rough edges we'd have to slow down. Henry and Rick, now, it'd be easier for them to turn out more where they've got the larger machines."

"Hold on, now, Phil," Greg said. "No one is *blaming* anyone. We're just trying to figure out where our problems are so we can get rid of them. As far as the other departments go—I'll get to work on them and see what I can do. But what about us—that's the big point—we've got to cooperate too. Right?" He looked around the group. Creegmore and Alfred shrugged their shoulders, but the rest nodded or smiled.

The crew went back to work and Greg returned to his office. Not that the meeting went out of his mind—for the rest of the day the same questions about the crew's complaints kept popping up. How much of it had been buckpassing and an attempt to duck the pressure? How much of the griping was legitimate? And even if it was, what could he do about it? Most important, under these conditions, could they really do anything much to speed up output without sacrificing quality? It looked like a real can of worms.

QUESTIONS

1 It is easy for most employees to convince themselves (and to try to convince others) that they are working very, very hard (regardless of how hard they are working) and that their supervisor doesn't realize how conscientious they are. Is Greg here helping to give his people an overinflated view of their own accomplishments?
2 How can Greg reinforce positively their accomplishment associated with "pitching in" and getting out that rush order without agreeing with everything they say?

3 Are there any "internal" incentives on these jobs, associated with the way the work is done, that Greg is not conscious of that either encourage or discourage good performance?

4 Given the nature of this work group and the work they are doing, what elements of employee performance should be discussed only with individuals and what elements should be discussed with the group as a whole?

Behavioral Exercise

List the controls that might be used to evaluate the following jobs, and ask yourself which ones would improve performance and which ones might injure performance or have undesirable side effects:

1 A hospital nurse
2 A college faculty member
3 A bus driver
4 A photocopy machine operator who "services" a large number of departments

BIBLIOGRAPHY

Kellogg, M., *What to Do about Performance Appraisal,* rev. ed., AMACOM, New York, 1975.

Kreitner, R., "PM—A New Method of Behavior Change," *Business Horizons,* December 1975, pp. 79–86.

Melcher, A., *Structure and Process of Organizations,* Prentice-Hall, Englewood Cliffs, N.J., chaps. 9–10.

Newman, W., *Constructive Controls: Design and Use of Control Systems,* Prentice-Hall, Englewood Cliffs, N.J., 1975.

Reddin, W. J., *Effective Management by Objectives: The 3-D Method,* McGraw-Hill, New York, 1971.

Thompson, P., and G. Dalton, "Performance Appraisal: Managers Beware," *Harvard Business Review,* 48:149–157, January-February 1970.

Whyte, W., et al., *Money and Motivation,* Harper & Row, New York, 1955.

READING

Self-Control through Measurements*

PETER F. DRUCKER (1909-   )

Now at Claremont College, formerly a professor at New York
University's Business School, a prolific author, constant lecturer, and
peripatetic consultant, Drucker is very much with us. A principal
reason for including him in our selections is the sheer celebrity of
the man: he has written more words on management that have
been read by more people than any living man. Yet it's not the only
reason for choosing him. If we were compiling a selection of
twentieth-century sermons, we would not include one or more by
Billy Graham merely because he had reached so many people,
including some in the highest places. Quality is our first criterion.
And Drucker has it.

Yet writing about him is a puzzlement. Unlike all the other
thinkers quoted in the selections, he has no central point of view,
no unifying theory that he has pursued with more or less constancy
throughout his career, no commitment to a specific method of
discipline. Part of the answer lies in a paradox: Although Drucker is
probably the best-known management specialist, he is not, as he is
the first to admit, a behavioral scientist. His formal training is in
economics, but he classifies himself as a journalist—and what is
sufficient for Drucker should be sufficient for us, too.

It is as a journalist that Drucker deserves to be understood and
appreciated. He is critic, not creator; the man of uncommon
experience and inspired common sense who exposes the fallacies
or improves on the insights of minds more original but less
balanced than his own.

We cited inspired common sense as one of Drucker's qualities.
Here's an example, drawn from *The Practice of Management,* in
which Drucker describes the limitations of operations research and
all its techniques with these words: "They cannot determine what is
the right question. They cannot set objectives for the solution. Nor
can they set rules. Similarly, the new tools cannot make the
decision concerning the best solution; they cannot by themselves
make a decision effective. Yet these are the most important phases
in decision-making."

There is nothing, or very little, that is original here. Most of the
points have been scored separately by previous critics at inordinate
length in the most constipated prose or reluctantly conceded by
operations researchers themselves. What Drucker did was to state
all the major reservations and do it with unequaled clarity and
brevity.

* Reprinted by permission of the publisher from Peter F. Drucker, *The Practice of Management,* Harper & Row, New York, 1954, pp. 130-133.

In all fairness to operations research, let's add that Drucker went on to discuss the very real contributions that operations research could make to the decision-making process.

We hope that we have indicated something about the sources of Drucker's deserved popularity. For the rest, let us recommend you to his books. We have listed only four out of eleven, but they're all worth reading.

The Practice of Management, Harper, New York, 1954.
Managing for Results, Harper & Row, New York, 1964.
Technology, Management and Society, Harper & Row, New York, 1970.
Management Tasks, Responsibilities, Practices, Harper & Row, New York, 1973.

The greatest advantage of management by objectives is perhaps that it makes it possible for a manager to control his own performance. Self-control means stronger motivation: a desire to do the best rather than just enough to get by. It means higher performance goals and broader vision. Even if management by objectives were not necessary to give the enterprise the unity of direction and effort of a management team, it would be necessary to make possible management by self-control.

So far . . . I have not talked of "control" at all; I have talked of "measurements." This was intentional. For "control" is an ambiguous word. It means the ability to direct oneself and one's work. It can also mean domination of one person by another. Objectives are the basis of "control" in the first sense; but they must never become the basis of "control" in the second, for this would defeat their purpose. Indeed, one of the major contributions of management by objectives is that it enables us to substitute management by self-control for management by domination.

That management by self-control is highly desirable will hardly be disputed in America or in American business today. Its acceptance underlies all the talk of "pushing decisions down to the lowest possible level," or of "paying people for results." But to make management by self-control a reality requires more than acceptance of the concept as right and desirable. It requires new tools and far-reaching changes in traditional thinking and practices.

To be able to control his own performance a manager needs to know more than what his goals are. He must be able to measure his performance and results against the goal. It should indeed be an invariable practice to supply managers with clear and common measurements in all key areas of a business. These measurements need not be rigidly quantitative; nor need they be exact. But they have to be clear, simple and rational. They have to be relevant and direct attention and efforts where they should go. They have to be reliable—at least to the point where their margin of error is acknowledged and understood. And they have to be, so to speak, self-announcing, understandable without complicated interpretation or philosophical discussion.

Each manager should have the information he needs to measure his own performance and should receive it soon enough to make any changes necessary for the desired results. And this information should go to the manager himself, and not to his superior. It should be the means of self-control, not a tool of control from above.

This needs particular stress today, when our ability to obtain such information is growing rapidly as a result of technological progress in information gathering, analysis and synthesis. Up till now information on important facts was either not obtainable at all, or could be assembled only so late as to be of little but historical interest. This former inability to produce measuring information was not an unmixed curse. For while it made effective self-control difficult, it also made difficult effective control of a manager from above; in the absence of information with which to control him, the manager had to be allowed to work as he saw fit. . . .

This should not be misunderstood as advocacy of low performance standards or absence of control. On the contrary, management by objectives and self-control is primarily a means to obtain standards higher than are to be found in most companies today. And every manager should be held strictly accountable for the results of his performance.

THE
COMMUNICATIONS
PROBLEM:
BEING
UNDERSTOOD

LEARNING OBJECTIVES

1 Understand how important communication is to the manager's success and how much time should be spent on it.

2 See what can be done to close the communications gap.

3 Consider the pros and cons of communicating orally and in writing.

4 Grasp the problem of noncommmunication—why it exists and the problems it leads to.

5 Appreciate the importance of the credibility gap.

6 Determine how the supervisor acquires credibility.

MISS OTIS REGRETS

"Helen, there are a few things I want you to do while I'm away," said Charley Pringle. "First, there's that hydraulic pump for Drysdale Oil. Call Tom Watkins, the company's plant manager, and remind him that I promised speedy delivery on the Drysdale order. It's a big account, and if we ever lost it. . . ."

"Yes, of course I'll call Mr. Watkins," replied Helen Otis. "Just how do you want me to put it?" she added in a tentative tone.

"Oh, by the way, before I forget, there's a little favor. It's Mrs. Pringle's birthday on Thursday. Call up the florist and order a couple of dozen roses—come to think of it, she likes amaryllis—claims they go with the living room rug. Get that, Helen? I'll be in the doghouse if you forget."

"Oh yes, Mr. Pringle."

At this point the telephone rang and Charley Pringle had a couple of minutes' conversation with a sales representative about some of his problems. Helen Otis sat silent meanwhile, with her pencil poised in midair.

"Where were we? Of course. The Drysdale order. When you call Tom, remind him, in case he's forgotten, just how important Drysdale is to us. No, maybe you'd better not. If you put too much pressure on Tom, he really gets his back up. That man cares more about keeping to his schedules than he does about satisfying customers. A good engineer, but no businessman."

Helen nodded her head sympathetically.

Aftermath

A week later, Charley Pringle came back, after a swing around the Northeast, to find a telegram from the Drysdale company requesting immediate delivery of the hydraulic pump and threatening to cancel all its business unless it received the shipment within forty-eight hours. Charley pressed the interoffice buzzer till the blood ran to the tip of his index finger.

"You rang, Mr. Pringle?" said a distraught Helen upon entering

"Yes, I rang, Miss Otis—just to see whether you were alive and alert," Charley added sarcastically. "What happened to the Drysdale order? Didn't you call Tom Watkins and tell him to give top priority to that order? Drysdale had to have that pump."

"I called, of course. But I'm sorry—that wasn't quite the message I got across. I said you were concerned about the order and would appreciate whatever Mr. Watkins could do to get it out."

"That's what you said!" Charley leaned back in his chair and groaned.

JANE HENNING PUTS THINGS STRAIGHT

"You're probably wondering, Henry, why we're taking the chrome off the valve and making a few other changes," said Jane Henning, twenty-eight years old, an industrial engineer, with a reputation for being whip-smart.

"Yes, I've been curious," replied Henry Schmidt, aged forty-three, a production foreman, proud of his department and of his own competence.

"Well, I'll keep it short and sweet. We ran the whole process through the simulator—computer, I mean—and found that by substituting plastic for chrome, we could make big cost savings at a very small decrease in performance. A slight increase in the obsolescence factor would have been desirable too, but that we decided to forgo—at least for the time being," added Jane, brightening a little.

"OK, I've got it," replied Henry. "We make something cheaper and we make more money."

"That's not really it, Henry. We've cut out a few features, but mostly the chrome. Our market researchers have checked—chrome doesn't count. Nine out of ten customers have indicated a willingness to accept plastic as a substitute, particularly if it means a price reduction, which it can." Henning underscored her words. "Got the picture?" She ended, with uplift in her voice.

"Got the picture," answered Henry.

Aftermath

Henry faced the crew. "What's the score, Hank?" asked Roy Le Blanc, the senior operator. "Yeah, what are they trying to put over on us?" chimed in George Williams, another operator.

"Well, it's like this," Henry began slowly and with some reluctance. "We had it pretty much figured. They decided to make more money out of the valves and found out that they could get away with it by making them poorer. Wish I could read it any other way. Any way you look at it, the company comes out ahead," finished Schmidt glumly.

"Are we going to get some of the dough?" Roy asked.

"Yeah, what about that?" a chorus arose from the rest of the crew. Schmidt shrugged his shoulders.

HOW IMPORTANT IS COMMUNICATION?

Sound exaggerated, these two caselets? Yes, but not by much. Both situations are repeated not once, but hundreds of times—not every week but every day. The boss is disorganized, distracted, contradictory, and ambiguous, as he was in "Miss Otis Regrets," or arrogant, remote, uncomprehended, and uncomprehending, as she was in "Jane Henning Puts Things Straight."

Do breakdowns in communications such as these matter? To any manager, at any level, the answer must be "Yes." The typical manager spends at least 60 percent of the time communicating. One manager, observed for a period of thirty-five days, for example, had only twelve periods when she spent fifteen minutes of her time *not* talking, while another study found that in one English company, executives spent, on the average, 80 percent of their time talking. In short, communication counts.

Drucker drives the point home:

> The manager has a specific tool: information. He does not "handle" people, he motivates, guides, organizes, people to do their own work. His tool—his only tool to do all this is the written or spoken word or the language of numbers. No matter whether the manager's job is engineering, accounting or selling, his effectiveness depends on his ability to listen and to read, on his ability to speak and to write—in other words, on his overall abilities as a communicator.

For managers, the communications process involves much more than simply expressing their ideas accurately and precisely, difficult as that may be on occasions. Nine-tenths of the time, when they communicate on the job they're not gossiping—they're working. What they have to say is a prelude to action—telling people what to do or trying to persuade them to do it. Or else they're on the receiving end of some instructions or some persuasion. In all these cases, the communication is intended to have a direct consequence.

That's why it's so important for any communication to be understood correctly and that's also why understanding is never enough. To be effective, a communication must fulfill three requirements: It must be *understood*. It must be *believed*. And, finally, it must be *accepted*.

Therefore, when we talk, in this chapter, about barriers to communications and what the supervisor can do to overcome them, we will consider in turn the three types of barriers: barriers to understanding, barriers to credibility, and lastly, barriers to acceptance.

Now that we've established the importance of communications to the supervisor—and for that matter to every level of manager, let's go back to our cases and analyze what went wrong in both of them, how the communications barriers present could have been bridged, and what the cases tell us about communications barriers in general.

The Communications Barriers in the Otis Case

Our sympathies to Helen Otis. As a communicator, Charley Pringle was an abysmal failure. He made just about every mistake in the book. In the initial formulation of his instruction, he committed the always fatal error of making the key word ambiguous. Disraeli wrote that "words are but empty vessels into which I pour meaning." Fine—but what Charley Pringle meant by "speedy" might mean something else to Helen Otis and something else again to Tom Watkins, the plant manager. When Helen pleaded for clarification—"Just how do you want me to put it?" was a distress signal born of confusion if we ever heard one—Charley ignored her and digressed to a totally different topic, ordering flowers for his wife's birthday. When he finally got back to what Helen Otis was supposed to say to Tom Watkins, he told her one thing, only to retract the instruction in the next sentence. Finally, when Helen had relayed her version of the communication to Tom Watkins and failed to obtain the result Charley Pringle intended, he gave way to self-righteous indignation based on his fanciful recollection of his conversation with her. As with many of us, Charley's memory served as a defense mechanism that absolved him of any responsibility. What he should have told Helen was that she and he and Tom Watkins could divide the blame between them.

Our little tale has several morals, first among them being the importance of avoiding ambiguity in communications. Don't use slippery words with multiple meanings, such as "speedy," "faster," "slower." Instead, use phrases with unmistakable meanings. "Give this order top priority," was what Charley Pringle remembered after the fact as his message to Watkins. "Give top priority to the Drysdale order" was much more calculated to get action on the order than the "speedy delivery" of his spoken message. Still better—more urgent and less ambiguous—would have been "I promised delivery on that pump within forty-eight hours." Maybe Watkins would have ignored the communication, but certainly he would have understood it. To take another example, if a supervisor were dissatisfied with the pace of a grinding-wheel operator, there would be small chance of having the operator achieve a satisfactory rate by merely saying, "Go faster." However, if the goal were expressed to the operator in revolutions per minute, the operator might or might not make it, depending on aptitude, attitude, and other factors, but at least the supervisor's goal would be understood.

The other morals to be drawn from "Miss Otis Regrets" are simpler and more obvious: Not only say what you mean, but mean what you say. In other words, one compounds the chance of being misunderstood if, like Charley Pringle, one contradicts oneself and changes a communication in midstream. As a corollary, it's important for managers to plan any communication in advance: (1) to make sure that they know their major theme, (2) to minimize the chances of having to contradict themselves because they haven't thought out the impact of their communication, and (3) to help ensure that their communication will be clear and that they won't leave anything out.

A Simple Instruction?

Maybe this strikes you as much ado about very little. However, experience has shown that managers, and the rest of us, too, have difficulty in getting across even relatively simple instructions. To dramatize the point, one Midwest corporation conducted the following exercise in its management-training program. The trainer drew five squares on a sheet of paper and kept the paper hidden. Then one of the executives was asked to draw square 1. Next the trainer described where square 2 was in relation to square 1 and repeated this with squares 3, 4, and 5, the object being to have the executive draw the five squares to look exactly like the ones the trainer had drawn. What happened? The trainer repeated the experiment many times. But only in a small minority of cases was there success in communicating a simple picture of five squares. In short, never underestimate the difficulty of communication.

One final moral from "Miss Otis Regrets": Don't interrupt a communication with irrelevant digressions. Of course, interruptions are frequently unavoidable. The supervisor is the person in charge of putting out fires. The phone keeps ringing, people keep breaking in to report on emergencies—in brief, interruptions are part of working life. At least a supervisor can avoid what Charley did and not be the person responsible for interrupting the communication. When Charley Pringle launched into his digression about his wife's birthday flowers, he further compounded the confusion of an already rattled Miss Otis. It would have served him right if Tom Watkins had gotten an amaryllis plant!

PSYCHOLOGICAL BARRIERS TO COMMUNICATION

The basic psychological barrier to communication is inherent in the nature of language itself. Strictly speaking, we can't convey meaning.

All we can do is convey words. The real meanings of words are in the minds of those who speak them and in the minds of those who hear them, not in the words themselves.

The implication, then, is that the full meaning of any word or any communication (a communication being merely words strung together in sequence) never appears until it is placed in its context. And what do we mean by context? Nothing less than the total personality and experience of listener and speaker—their experience of the language, their knowledge of one another, the frame of reference from which they view the communication, their mood at the precise moment when the communication is formulated and received. Looked at in this way, successful communication appears to be what it in fact is—a real achievement!

Our communications-receiving apparatus (sense organs) and brain works like a combination converter and filter. Instead of hearing what people say, we hear what our minds tell us they said, which may be the same thing or may be something very different. That we convert what we hear into something relevant to our own past experience—and our recent past at that, and not the speaker's; that we filter what we hear through layers of bias shaped by group, class, age, race, education, and occupation; that we distort or filter out altogether everything that doesn't fit in with our preconceived notions; that we continually convert sentiments into logic—all give some measure of the problems involved in communicating.

Are you skeptical about people interpreting messages differently according to their past experience? Try a little experiment with yourself. Pretend you're a supervisor and further pretend that you're observing a group of your subordinates laughing heartily. You don't know the cause of the laughter—all you know is what you see and hear. What message comes across to you? There are three common reactions to such a situation, and yours may be one of them:

To managers who believe work must be unpleasant in order to be productive, the laughter communicates that time is being wasted, and that maybe the assignments are too easy.

To managers who believe that contented employees work harder, the laughter communicates that they are succeeding as managers.

To managers who are personally insecure, the laughter communicates the likelihood that the workers are making fun of them.

Even if your reaction is different, we think you will concede the point:

The same simple situation could convey very different messages, depending on what the listener brought to the situation.

Here's a simple example. The manager tells an employee that the company has lost some important jobs. The employee filters the message through his own experience. In the past, whenever his company has lost business, he has been thrown out of work. So what he hears the manager say is "You can expect to be laid off in the near future." When he comes in two weeks later and announces that he has taken a job with a competitor, the manager is shocked and surprised to hear that he thought his job was in danger.

What Happened to Jane Henning?

Our second little case, "Jane Henning Puts Things Straight," offers an example of communications block at the psychological level. When Henry Schmidt agreed that he had gotten the message, he wasn't consciously trying to deceive Jane Henning. It was just that the message he received was not the one that Jane was trying to convey. There were two messages, not one, and they differed greatly from each other.

Why the difference? Why couldn't Jane get through to Henry? What were the barriers to effective communication between the engineer and the supervisor?

A simple answer goes a long way toward explaining the problem. Jane and Henry belonged to different groups (what the psychologists call reference groups), identified themselves with different values, and shared different perceptions.

As an industrial engineer, Henning belonged to a group that traditionally has been obsessed with efficiency. To find a way of making any product that will (1) save substantial amounts of money while (2) diminishing the utility of the product only slightly as well as (3) having no negative effect on the sale of the product—this is the goal of every industrial engineer. Schmidt caught Henning in a moment of full professional pride.

From his perspective, Schmidt viewed the situation very differently. His pride was in his job, not the company. He identified with the work group he headed, not the overall organization—an identification common to most first-level supervisors. He was proud of doing quality work and he wanted to keep doing it. When Henning said that "chrome doesn't count," she obviously hadn't polled Schmidt or his crew. To them, the use of chrome had an emotional—if you will, a symbolic—significance. It meant, among other things, pride of product, aesthetic satisfaction from the job, the determination to be best even if it cost a little more. What Henning dismissed—the use of chrome—was something that had added to the self-esteem and contributed to the job satisfaction of Schmidt and his crew. They cared little about what the market researchers said and even less about the computer's judgment. The message they received was that their jobs were being diminished and they were being involved in short-changing the customer with no hope of profiting themselves. We would wager that under these circumstances, Schmidt and his crew would see to it that not all of the savings anticipated by Henning were realized. Similar situations in industry have frequently led to similar disappointments.

CLOSING THE COMMUNICATIONS GAP

So far, we have emphasized the difficulties and complexities of communication, and we're not going back on anything we said. However, we also don't want to give the impression that most communications are inherently destined to be misunderstood and that communication is always a frustrating and usually a futile process. It doesn't always have to be that way, as almost every effective manager has learned. Feedback is what makes most of the difference between an effective and an ineffective communicator. What do we mean by feedback? How does it make such a big difference?

Using Feedback

A large group of management trainees listened intently as a trainer gave them elaborate instructions on how to arrange five dominoes in a certain pattern. But they were not permitted to ask any questions. In another room, trainees received the same instructions, and they were allowed to ask the instructor as many questions as they pleased.

What happened? In the first room, only three trainees were able to arrange the dominoes correctly. In the second room, only four trainees did *not* arrange them correctly. What do you think accounted for the difference in performance? The answer is pretty simple: Feedback, the term adapted from engineering, refers to the ability of certain machines to check on their performance and to correct it, if necessary. The thermostat, for example, regulates the amount of furnace heat on the basis of feedback, in this case, the temperature of the room.

Norbert Weiner, who did some of the key pioneer work in applying the principles of electronic communications to human communications, observed in words that deserve to be writ in gold, "I never know what I said until I hear the response to it." In other words, you can't really know what you've communicated until you've gotten the feedback. What was true for Weiner is true for all of us. Only feedback can tell us what we're communicating or, in fact, whether we're communicating at all. Maybe the listener is tuning our messages out.

There are two prerequisites for successful feedback. A little feedback, of course, is better than none at all. But the more feedback the better. If a supervisor wants listeners to repeat what they think the manager said, they shouldn't be limited to yes or no responses, but instead should be encouraged to say as much as they want.

Maximum feedback also requires face-to-face communication. Only when managers can experience direct feedback from receivers can they really know what receivers are hearing and they are failing to hear. Managers can catch the telltale gesture, the nervous cough, the turned-down corners of the mouth that indicate the existence of the real meaning receivers are giving to the words. There's a world in a wink, while memos can't frown. Written communications generally leave much unrevealed and unsuspected.

Let's return for one last look at our two examples, Pringle and Henning. Neither bothered to get any feedback, and therefore neither one had any way of being sure that what they meant to say had been communicated. Of course, the motivations underneath the failure to communicate were different. Charley was simply a well-intentioned bungler, or at worst a self-satisfied egoist. When Helen Otis plaintively inquired, "Just how should I put it?" Charley ignored the distress signal and went on to the next subject that absorbed his attention, the flowers for his wife's birthday. He assumed, as many managers have done, to their subsequent distress, that Helen understood what he said, the connotations as well as the words.

Jane Henning was different. Her failure to communicate, together with her failure to obtain any feedback, was rooted in the same sentiment: indifference born of intellectual arrogance. Basically, she didn't care what Henry Schmidt thought of the change. If he agreed with it, maybe it would make a little difference on the shop floor, but the change had already been approved by the unbribable tribunal—the computer and the market researcher. Henry's opinion, in Jane Henning's context, was relevant but trivial.

Is feedback the complete answer to surmounting the barriers to communication? By no means. It's the biggest part of the answer, but as there are other facets to the communications problem, so too are there other solutions. Actually, two additional problems are interrelated with feedback.

The Medium and Message

One is the problem of medium: Should the supervisor communicate orally or in writing? In one sense, we recognize that the question is immaterial. Several studies have shown that supervisors communicate orally dozens, sometimes hundreds, of times daily in situations which leave them with no choice as to whether the communication should be oral or written. We'll restrict ourselves to the limited opportunities where the choice exists. In our discussion of feedback, we've already indicated that nothing, but nothing, can take the place of verbal communication. Yes, but on occasion it's imperative to reinforce verbal communication with a written follow-up. On what kind of occasion? Thereby hangs a story.

A manager we know put a certain price tag on her own worth, a combination of self-esteem and her reading of the marketplace. A job turned up which fitted her, but there was a problem: The salary was short—within the target range of her goal, but still short. She was honest with her prospective employer, confessed her deep interest in the job together with her hesitation because of the salary. In response, as she understood it then and later, she got a commitment to a salary figure upon employment, plus a raise six months later, that would bring her up to her concept of the going rate for her services. Six months later, no raise. The problem wasn't the quality of her work but contingencies. Her raise was "dependent upon how well the company was doing," a qualification which either had never been made or had been filtered out. In disgust, she quit. And no wonder, given her belief that her boss had reneged on a promise.

The lesson of this little tale? In matters which are important to the subordinate and therefore particularly susceptible to misinterpretation, the supervisor should follow up any verbal communication with a written confirmation. Of course, there are other circumstances when a supervisor should reinforce an oral communication with a written follow-up: When the communication is so lengthy, complex, or technical that the subordinate with the best will in the world would be likely to forget or misinterpret it, even if it is understood on first hearing. The supervisor, in preparing the written version, can take advantage of the feedback to get the full message across by stressing those elements which people had difficulty in understanding.

Directing the Message

Another communications problem related to feedback is the question of layers of communication: How many intermediaries can there be between the communicator and the eventual recipient of the communication before the message is twisted and lost? An experiment conducted a few years ago at Bell Telephone Company sheds light on the probable answer.

Six people took part. The first person viewed a picture, received two minutes to memorize the details, and was then told to describe what he had seen to a second person. The process was repeated with the third, the fourth, and the fifth participant. By the time the message came through to the sixth person, it was almost impossible to recognize the picture from the description.

Given most people's propensity toward inattention and their capacity for misinterpreting one part of the message and filtering out another part, the only sensible rule for the supervisor to adapt is this: If the communication is important, tell it to the person directly affected and do it face-to-face so you can get immediate feedback. Put even one person between yourself and the recipient of the communication and you are asking for trouble. Like every rule, it has its necessary exception—time is short, the need to communicate is urgent, and other communications have a higher priority. Even so, the supervisor should follow up at the earliest possible opportunity to make sure that the other party has in fact received the intended message.

THE NONCOMMUNICATION

As a final barrier to communication being understood, let's consider the case of the message that was never understood because it was never delivered in the first place. Lest you think we're talking nonsense, we quickly add that we're talking about communications dictated by necessity and common sense but withheld by subordinates from the bosses who needed the information. The machine looks as if it's headed for a major breakdown, the employee doesn't like the partner whom the boss has hired for the job, the secretary sees a better way of batching the work—all are matters which the boss needs to know but frequently never hears. One study of a business organization concluded that it was common for most subordinates, particularly among the nonmanagement ranks and the first two levels of management, to withhold large amounts of need-to-know information from their superiors.

The status barrier

What's the explanation for this wholesale failure to communicate? Obviously, different subordinates have different reasons. One factor, however, is present in every situation: the status barrier. The supervisor worries so much about what the boss is thinking that minimal attention is given to what subordinates are thinking. The subordinates, for their part, care what the boss thinks, all right, but the status barrier inhibits their initiation of any contacts that aren't compulsory. Several studies have shown that bosses continually overestimate the number of meaningful contacts they have with subordinates. And since information channels have never really developed, subordinates are naturally reluctant to communicate anything which could in any way have a negative effect on their relationship with their bosses. In some cases, obviously this reluctance is increased by other factors such as dislike and distrust of the boss, dissatisfaction with the overall job situation, or the influence of norms established by the group. It's significant that a study of boss-subordinate pairs found the fullest and most accurate communications occurred between a boss and a trusting subordinate who didn't want to get ahead.

The old credibility gap

Getting communications understood correctly, as we have stated previously, is only part of the story. For any communication to be effective, the recipient must also believe and accept it. We subscribe fully to the words Whyte wrote a number of years ago in the book *Is Anybody Listening?*: "Only with trust can there be any real communication, and until that trust is achieved, the gadgetry of communications are so much waste effort. Study after study has pointed to the same moral: Before employees will accept management 'facts' they must first have overall confidence in the motives and sincerity of management."

How does the supervisor acquire a passport of credibility? Rigid adherence to two principles will carry you most of the way: You should tell the truth when communicating and be sure that actions support your words. There can be short-range advantages to lying or at least in not telling the whole truth as you know it. However, sooner or later you are almost certain to be found out. And once lost, a reputation for credibility is almost never reclaimed.

Credibility is independent of position. Union members sometimes will believe in management pronouncements; people will believe even their enemies in war once they've established their reputation for credibility, as the British Broadcasting Company demonstrated in World War II. During the bleak years, the BBC had given the whole grim tale of defeats and disasters to its listeners. When the tide turned, Europeans of all nationalities tuned in to BBC and accepted its claims of a German rout—a well-deserved bonus of establishing a reputation for credibility.

The second point is just as obvious and just as important: What supervisors do communicates to others more strongly than anything they say. To the extent that their actions contradict their words, they will be judged by others as cynics trying to manipulate people or as people without integrity in whom no one should put any trust.

HOW DOES THE SUPERVISOR ACQUIRE CREDIBILITY?

We'll discuss the full ramifications of the problem in Chapter 11, when looking at boss-subordinate relations. Suffice it to state here that the boss should always bear in mind the barrier that status erects to open channels of communication between superior and subordinate. The boss has responsibility for initiating most communications—by necessity and by default.

Employees have eyes and ears. They can judge, usually with a high degree of accuracy, the fit between what the manager says and any previous actions. Take, for example, the supervisor who had always looked the other way where safety violations were concerned, believing (rightly or wrongly) that following the safety rules to the letter would interfere with meeting the production quotas on which he was really judged. Suddenly, he holds a safety meeting in which he talks tough— threatens to throw the book at safety violators. What message gets across to his subordinates? Probably not that he means what he says but that he is going through the motions because someone upstairs is concerned about the department's safety record. Furthermore, there will be real surprise and resentment if the supervisor proceeds to ferret out the violations at which he has previously winked and to punish the violators.

The irony is that this same lack of credibility can attach itself to quite sincere efforts on a manager's part to improve relations with subordinates—and sometimes thwart the efforts. We cite, for example, a manager of accounting, known behind her back as "the calculator" because of her cold, standoff manner in dealing with subordinates and associates. She was packed off for five days to a sensitivity-training program in which she learned the virtues of involvement with other people and of openness in dealing with them. The experience took, and she returned determined to remake her attitudes in dealing with people.

And she gave it the old college try, soliciting the reactions of people whom she had previously ignored, giving frank and full explanations of why she favored a particular course of action, being genuinely friendly and interested. The trouble was that no one met her halfway. Her overtures were greeted with suspicion, her explanations were regarded as symptoms of previously unsuspected weakness, and her requests for advice were pretty much ignored. After a short time, she reverted to her old mode of action, thereby confirming the suspicions of those who felt all along that she was up to something. Of course, the story could have had a different ending if some of her associates had also participated in sensitivity training or if the manager had persisted longer with her changed behavior. Over time, her associates would have found the new look credible and accommodated themselves to it—with gratitude and mutual profit.

Tone—Words and Gestures—Expresses Attitude

We won't attempt a variation on McLuhan and contend that the tone is the message. But the *tone* of any communication, whether verbal or written, has a lot to do with whether or not it is believed and accepted.

Sometimes we even communicate, without words, things we don't mean. If the manager has been stopped by a police officer for speeding on the way to work, any general irritability toward subordinates unlucky enough to be around—at least for the next hour or so—may "tell" them that the boss is dissatisfied with their work. Of course, that isn't the intention. But a raised eyebrow, a cold manner from someone who is usually warm, the measured tapping of fingers on a desk top—all convey a message just as surely as words do.

Humor in communications is also a risky device. Managers have to be sure of their ground in advance. Otherwise, they run the risk of having people feel that they don't take the subject seriously—or a much graver danger—that they don't take them or their interests seriously. In either case, the message will be discounted.

Emotionalism and the appeal to fear are also dangerous in a communication. They're likely to boomerang and have the exact reverse of the desired effect. Consider the results of a study in which three different groups of high school students listened to three different lectures on dental hygiene. The first lecture pointed out the consequences of neglecting teeth in harrowing terms and stated that neglected teeth led to "pain, disease, and body damage." The second lecture was moderate in tone, while the third avoided any reference to unpleasant consequences. All three lectures contained the same basic information and recommendations. The first lecture may have caused the most worry, but the third got results. The first group apparently resisted or resented the threat and tuned out the message—a phenomenon that sheds light on the relative failure, to date, of the campaign to intimidate the American public into giving up cigarettes.

Let the facts speak for themselves

By contrast, a sober and low-key presentation of the facts will help to create a climate of credibility. When the office supervisor, for example, announces the details of the company's new major medical plan, it is advisable not to tell employees how generous the new plan is but, instead, to let the facts speak for themselves. The employees have a pretty good idea of what similar and competing companies offer. If it's generous, they can see it for themselves, and if it isn't, the attempt to make it appear so will add an unappetizing dimension to an already unhappy situation.

The manager who makes a policy of letting the facts speak for themselves sooner or later is in for a bonus. She will face a situation, on occasion, in which she lacks the facts or can't disclose them, but assuming the condition is temporary, she can fall back on the mechanism psychologists call "transference." In this case, belief in the fact will be replaced by belief in an individual—the supervisor involved. "If she says it, that's good enough for us" will be the collective reaction from her subordinates.

One final word on tone: Arrogance is an enemy of credibility. We know a man with ability, a big reputation in his field, and considerable powers of articulation, but somehow many of his communications, even when they are correct, are disbelieved by the people whom he is addressing. The explanation is the arrogance of tone in his communication, conveying to the listener that his opinion is not worth considering, that his views, whenever they diverge, contain not a shred of substance. No matter how right our friend is, the egos of his listeners compel them to reject the message. We're reminded of a remark made to Ben Franklin at the close of a discussion in which he had been on the winning end, "Thee hath won thee an argument, but lost thee a friend."

Projection and Credibility

Managers who want to get their communications believed would boost their chances if they put themselves into the listener's shoes and tailored their messages to fit the vocabulary, values, and interests of the listener. Take an obvious case: You're a plant manager announcing an expanded production schedule to the work force. You don't talk, in the message, about bigger profits for the stockholders, higher salaries for management, and more promotional opportunities for the executive staff. Instead, you will talk about more job security, the opportunity for overtime, and the chance to acquire new and valuable job skills. In other words, you tailor your message to the interests of your listeners.

What happens to the manager who fails to practice projection when communicating? Consider, for example, a young college-trained supervisor who was having great difficulty getting his instructions across to the old-timers in his work crew. He would hand out very specific instructions and then discover, when he checked later, that the worker had done what he asked him to do—but that was all. The rest of the job, which the supervisor assumed quite properly the person knew all about, wouldn't be done at all. He thought his way out of this dilemma by using a little projection: He put himself in the place of the old-timers and concluded that he would resent getting detailed instructions from someone half his age, particularly when he, as an old hand, had a basic understanding of the job. When he applied this insight and started making his instructions as general as possible, his problems with half-finished jobs were over.

Of course, projection won't always turn up the answer to getting a communication believed and accepted. But we recommend its use to any manager, preferably before and certainly after delivering a communication whenever there's difficulty getting believed and accepted. Happily, most communications permit a second chance.

Credibility and the Grapevine

What about the grapevine? How does it affect the credibility of the manager's communications? First off, let's concede that the manager has to live with the grapevine that is a feature of every business. Actually, there's not one grapevine but, depending on the size of the establishment, dozens or even hundreds running up, down, and across. These grapevines, in turn, are rooted in large part in the nearly insatiable curiosity of employees generally to know the answers to questions which management has answers to but is unable or unwilling to disclose, the answers to questions which management has not yet answered, and the answers to questions which management hasn't even asked. As such, the collective grapevine fulfills an important function in informing people who are isolated from crucial information about the business—information to which they feel they're entitled. Furthermore, it has a generally unrecognized function in pressuring top

238

management to come up with answers to problems or to ask questions about problems which were exposed to the top levels of the organization only via the grapevine itself. One study of a business organization purported to show that the grapevine transmitted more information than the formal systems. We are skeptical about the possibility of measuring the volume of information carried by the grapevine, but we concede that it is an important vehicle of communication. And it's here to stay.

The grapevine presents a problem to supervisors when they have to communicate something which is at odds with what has previously been disseminated through this medium. Problem, you say? Isn't the supervisor's word the official word, and if the supervisor has a previous record as a truth-sayer, what's the problem? It isn't that simple. Experiments have demonstrated that a person is less likely to believe an official announcement if, prior to its issuance, a contradictory or conflicting rumor has been heard. However, if the official words are received first, and the rumor second, the former will be accepted. That is, a message is more likely to be understood and accepted if it's not competing with another, and potentially conflicting, message. This was, of course, the basis for brainwashing in the Korean war. Some of our captured soldiers were isolated from their buddies and exposed to repeated anti-American slogans. A milder application of the same principle occurs when executives gather for an important policy meeting at a mountain-top conference center: Without the interference of normal communications, they would be more likely to "hear" the full message of the conference.

The implications for the manager are clear. In the words of General Nathan Bedford Forrest, "Get there fustest with the mostest." As soon as supervisors are aware of an impending announcement, which all too often they themselves hear first through the grapevine, they should pressure their superiors to get all the facts out in the open before the rumors begin. There's no other way of beating the grapevine.

CREDIBILITY IS NOT ENOUGH

We don't want to equate credibility with acceptance, to con anyone into thinking that once you've established the credibility of your message, you've ensured its acceptance. As Pascal observed, "Habit is but a second nature." When the contents of a communication conflict with the habits of a lifetime, the communication will be believed but ignored. In an experiment on delegation involving a large number of middle managers playing the role of first-line supervisors, they all received pointed instructions to reveal some time-study data to their subordinates—but 54 percent of them ignored the instructions. They handled themselves according to their prior conceptions of the job and their customary styles of management. In other words, those who were generally permissive and democratic followed the instructions which the majority ignored.

Also, we sometimes reject the speaker's message out of hand because we suspect her motivations. "If she said it, it can't be so." The classic example of disregarding the message because of the source occurs in labor relations. Some union members interpret every company statement as an attempt to deceive them. Similarly, some managements regard every union grievance as a cynical maneuver to strengthen the position of the union leadership among its rank-and-file members.

One researcher clipped a cartoon from a union publication entitled "The Four Goals of Labor" and added a caption indicating that it had come from a publication of the National Association of Manufacturers. When a group of union members saw the clipping, they were all critical of it as an unfair, biased representation of labor's goals. We suspect that if you reversed the coin and clipped a statement of management's goals from an NAM publication, represented it as coming from a union source, and showed it to a group of managers, you would get a similar reaction. The supposed source would dictate the response to the communication.

Compromise and Goals

Probably nothing could have swayed the middle managers we described from sticking to their rut. Other situations, however, offer more promise that a communication will be accepted. In most cases, there's a central goal of the communication and a preferred, not obligatory, path for reaching it, unless the communicator is too much of an authoritarian or a perfectionist to recognize it. When the sender has feedback, especially from a sensitive and sensible receiver, the sender will understand that the receiver has reservations about the communication—or at any rate about accepting it unless the receiver can influence the sender. Unraveling what the receiver's resistance owes to ego and what to substance should best be left to someone else with twenty years for the task. The manager's job is clear. First, it must be recognized that if the communication isn't modified, it will probably be rejected or given lip service, which amounts to the same thing. Second, the manager must determine the ways in which the communication can be changed without damaging its substance.

Take, for example, the district sales manager who faced her sales representatives resistance to a new system of compensation and reporting on several counts. They objected that the new system, by paying higher commissions on high-volume, high-profit business, would force them to neglect business that had yielded steady commissions in the past. They also asserted that the new system would put them at the mercy of a few big accounts and that the reporting features of the new system were needlessly complicated and time-consuming. Finally, they complained that their views hadn't been sought in advance. The district sales manager, facing a real revolt in the ranks and the prospect of losing some of her best personnel, recommended to the home office that the objectionable reporting features of the new system be simplified. The core of the new system was the revamped compensation scheme; the reporting changes were a secondary feature not worth pressing for in light of the resistance. The home office accepted the recommendation and the communication was accepted, although reluctantly, by the sales representatives— partly, we think, because it had been modified to meet some of their objections. The restatement of the communication incorporated some of their reservations.

CONCLUSION

We have stressed throughout this chapter that effective communication requires more than understanding. To be effective, a communication must be believed and accepted as well as understood. Whether or not the particular communication wins this kind of reception depends primarily on the sum of all the communications that have preceded it, on whether or not an atmosphere of mutual trust and respect has developed between the manager and the people with whom he or she is communicating. Where there is mutual confidence and regard, a clumsy communication will somehow muddle through. Where there is distrust and suspicion, technique alone will never suffice.

The reason is simple enough. A human being is rational and learns from experience. Cherry compares the brain to a giant totalizer at the race track that accepts the tokens (money) from the outside world (bettors) and calculates the odds on various hypotheses (horses) to give the greatest expectation of goal attainment (profit) according to assumed standards of utility. Before a person decides which horse to bet on, he or she consults the horses' racing history and the track records and lays a bet accordingly. A horse whose record is spotty and whose performance is undependable is certain to be passed up. Similarly, the employee will neglect, ignore, or reject a communication from a boss with a bad track record for veracity and dependability.

Lastly, there is the matter of self-interest. Employees will resist, reject, or, at most, pay lip service to any communication whose contents run contrary to their self-interest as they understand it.

THE EDUCATION OF GREG HORNING: MARCH 5

Still wondering about the gripes from the crew, Greg received a call the next morning to report to Steve Phillips' office. Production had come back up that 5 percent, Phillips told Greg; in fact, the group was now doing 87 percent of standard. That was better, but it was only a beginning. Now was the time for Greg to really crack down on them—with enough pressure, he could get them up to standard and over.

Greg knew that production was inching up a little, and he was pretty sure it was because he'd eased up with the group. Pressure just didn't work in that department; Phillips was wrong—but he was such a difficult guy to talk to. Greg hesitated. He could just go along with Phillips—agree, then go back and do what he wanted with the group. As long as he got results, Phillips wouldn't give a damn how he got them. Still, there were those complaints. Greg couldn't bring the other departments in line, but Phillips could.

"Well, I don't know if it's as simple as that, Steve," he said finally. "They're working pretty well now, but they've got a lot of gripes that sound sensible to me."

"Ah, the hell with the gripes. Those people always have a beef. If something goes wrong, it's always sombody else's fault. Just don't pay any attention to them. Crack down. They'll shape up." Greg ignored the sound of dismissal in Phillips' voice and plugged on.

"They tell me that maintenance and materials handling foul things up for them. They refuse to put things where we need them to do the job right. And the machines aren't kept in good repair—when they break down it takes days to get somebody over to fix them. And then there's the plastic mixing sends us . . ."

"My God, Greg!" Phillips had been fingering through some papers; now he threw them down on the desk. "They must really be having a field day in there with this bright-eyed, bushy-tailed patsy they've got! What's the matter with you, anyway? Can't you see they're just selling you a bill of goods? Now, you go back down there, and the hell with all these excuses. I want to see the goods—you tell them to get off their fat asses and work."

There was no point trying to argue with a man like Phillips, Greg thought as he went back to his office. His mind was set in concrete. Greg was sure he was wrong, still it made things damn difficult.

"Oh, Jeannette. Hi. You want me for something?" Pacing back and forth in front of his desk, Greg had not heard Jeannette come in.

"Yeah. You see, Greg?" she held out a piece that looked all right, except that the edges were extremely rough. "This is what I was telling you about yesterday."

"Yesterday?"

"Yeah. Remember how I said if the men went faster the pieces came out all right but there was an awful lot of flashing to do on them?"

"Oh. Yes. I see. But that's a good piece, Jeannette. I wouldn't reject that piece."

"Well, that's what I mean, Greg," Jeannette said, her voice becoming more insistent. "It's too good to reject, but see how much extra time a piece like that takes—for Helen and me. It's because the men are going faster. It slows Helen and me down. If they could just be more careful. I mean, if we can't keep up with them, there's no sense in their going faster."

"Yes, I see. But I don't know what we can do about it," Greg answered vaguely. "We can't start rejecting perfectly good pieces."

"Well, I know that," Jeannette said, exasperated now and ready to leave. "Oh, never mind. This is just a waste of time. I have a whole batch of boxes to move around before I can get to doing these pieces, anyway. The handlers dumped them at the wrong end of the floor again. I just thought maybe you'd . . . oh heck—forget it."

Coming up in the elevator on his way back from lunch, Greg ran into Frank Granto from the industrial engineering department.

"You got a minute, Frank?" Greg said, putting his hand on Frank's arm. "There's something I've been wanting to ask you about."

"Yeah, Greg. Just about a minute. What's on your mind?"

"Well, it's about this materials handling business. My people have been griping about how they're always putting things in the wrong place and how that slows them down. Does it really make that much difference?"

"Are you kidding?" The elevator stopped at Greg's floor and the two men got out together. "Do you know how much time a crew can waste just lugging boxes around to where they need them?"

"It's really important, then?"

"Listen, Greg. It can make you or break you—let me tell you. It's one of the biggest keys to an effective work flow." They were at the door of the molding shop now. Frank had his arm on Greg's shoulder. "I'm really pleased that you've recognized this point, Greg. You're one of the few guys outside of our department who does. We're always trying to hammer it into the supervisors' heads, but they never listen."

"Yeah, Well, I guess that's a big problem everywhere, Frank," Greg said, smiling. "Everybody talks and no one listens."

Frank smiled back. "You've got a point there, too, Greg. Well, listen. I've got to get going. If there's anything else I can help you on, let me know."

"Thanks, Frank. See you."

Greg started into the shop, thinking. Maybe if Jeannette didn't have those boxes to move, she'd be able to keep up with the flashing. If her gripe was legit, maybe the others were too. Obviously Phillips wasn't going to help. Greg would have to see what he could do on his own.

Phil Martello stopped Greg as he went by: "Got a second, Greg, I want to talk to you."

"Sure, Phil, what's up?"

"It's Ted Kilpatrick. You know he's a pretty old guy and some of the rows are getting to be too tough for him. What about if we change machines when the going gets too rough for him?"

"I don't know, Phil. I appreciate your wanting to help out, but . . ."

"I know how you feel Greg, about people doing their own work but this way you would be getting more production—I would be taking over the jobs that Ted is the slowest on."

"I see what you mean," said Greg after a minute's hesitation. "Okay—let's give it a try."

"Sure thing, Greg."

"One other thing, Phil. I appreciate your thinking of production as well as Ted. That's something we can't have enough of around here." Greg put his hand on Martello's shoulder and smiled. Then he went into his office to call Ed Briscoe in materials handling.

QUESTIONS

1 What connection do you think there is between Phillips' handling of Greg's complaints and Greg's handling of Jeannette's complaint?
2 How would you describe Jeannette's message to Greg as he heard it?
3 What's the significance of Greg's conversation with Granto for the first case?
4 Why was Greg able to communicate effectively with Granto but not with Phillips or Jeannette?

BEHAVIORAL EXERCISE

The problem is to communicate the exact form of the diagram reproduced below. The communication is to be undertaken in two ways. First, don't allow people to ask questions, and have them turn their backs to you so you can't see their facial expressions and they can't see the diagram. Then repeat the experiment, only this time allow the other people to ask questions. Then compare how long each communication took and the degree of accuracy.

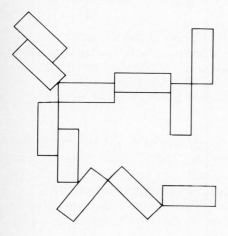

BIBLIOGRAPHY

Karlins, M., and H. Abelson, *Persuasion: How Opinions and Attitudes Are Changed*, 2d ed., Springer, New York, 1970.

Leavitt, H., *Managerial Psychology*, rev. ed., University of Chicago Press, 1968.

Nirenberg, J., *Breaking Through to Each Other: Creative Persuasion on the Job and in the Home*, Harper & Row, New York, 1976.

READING

Dealing with Breakdowns in Communication— Interpersonal and Intergroup*

CARL R. ROGERS (1902-   )

Professor of psychology successively at Ohio State, Chicago, and the University of Wisconsin; now Resident Fellow at the Western Behavioral Sciences Institute; practicing psychotherapist for two generations; and through the medium of several books and numerous articles, therapist to humanity—that would be a fair measure of Carl Roger's career.

Yet it would be far from a full measure of what he has accomplished. More than any man living—and probably dead—he has taught people the meaning of communication and a good deal about how to achieve it. The principles and practices he first developed in order to help the neurotic and the disturbed to accept themselves, to grow, and to change, have proved equally valuable in breaking down the communication barriers between more normal people to help them to accept each other, to grow, and to change.

Rogers wrote that therapists are most effective if they (1) are transparently real in their relationships with their clients, (2) accept the client as a separate, distinct person, and (3) are empathetic in their understanding, see the world through the client's eyes. Substitute supervisor or manager for therapist and employee or worker for client, and the same criteria are equally valid for any meaningful communication between boss and subordinate.

That communication between managers and subordinates has made substantial progress in the past generation (and we believe it has), and that many managers have learned the value in sensitive situations of nondirective counseling and the nondirective interview, of "listening with a third ear" (listening for the implied as well as the stated meaning of what is said), is directly due to Carl Rogers and his techniques. As such, a generation of managers stands profoundly in his debt.

Still we haven't done Rogers complete justice. There is more to his thinking than an attitude toward communication and a hatful of communication techniques for overturning barriers and establishing mutual understanding, valuable as that certainly is.

Rogers, in the most profound sense of the word, is a social philosopher, a man who has assigned to himself no less a task than battling with the nature of humanity as defined by two millennia of Christian thinkers—original sin and all that—and buttressed by Freud with his bleak concept of the id and substituting in its place the scientific finding that the innermost core of human-

---

* Reprinted by permission of the publishers from Carl R. Rogers, *On Becoming a Person*, Sentry Edition, Houghton Mifflin Company, Boston, 1970, pp. 329–334.

ity's nature is "basically socialized, forward-moving, rational and realistic." It is possible to applaud the effort, even if one is not convinced by the evidence.

As a social philosopher and practicing humanist, Rogers is preoccupied with the current and future role of the behavioral sciences, which he sees as a great force for good or evil. Here's the choice as he sees it: "We can, if we wish, choose to make men submissive, conforming, docile or . . . we can choose to use the behavioral sciences in ways which will free, not control; which will bring about constructive variability, not conformity; which will develop creativity, not contentment; which will aid individuals, groups, and even the concept of science, to become selftranscending in freshly adaptive ways of meeting life and its problems." Rogers, of course, comes down on the side of the angels.

As for his books, the best known, the most available, and probably the best is *On Becoming a Person*, Sentry Edition, Houghton Mifflin Company, Boston, 1970. Also recommended is *Client-centered Therapy*, Houghton Mifflin Company, Boston, 1951.

I would like to propose, as an hypothesis for consideration, that the major barrier to mutual interpersonal communication is our very natural tendency to judge, to evaluate, to approve or disapprove, the statement of the other person, or the other group. Let me illustrate my meaning with some very simple examples. As you leave the meeting tonight, one of the statements you are likely to hear is, "I don't like that man's talk." Now what do you respond? Almost invariably your reply will be either approval or disapproval of the attitude expressed. Either you respond, "I didn't either. I thought it was terrible," or else you tend to reply, "Oh, I thought it was really good." In other words, your primary reaction is to evaluate what has just been said to you, to evaluate it from your point of view, your own frame of reference.

Or take another example. Suppose I say with some feeling, "I think the Republicans are behaving in ways that show a lot of good sound sense these days," what is the response that arises in your mind as you listen? The overwhelming likelihood is that it will be evaluative. You will find yourself agreeing, or disagreeing, or making some judgment about me such as "He must be a conservative," or "He seems solid in his thinking." Or let us take an illustration from the international scene. Russia says vehemently, "The treaty with Japan is a war plot on the part of the United States." We rise as one person to say "That's a lie!"

This last illustration brings in another element connected with my hypothesis. Although the tendency to make evaluations is common in almost all interchange of language, it is very much heightened in those situations where feelings and emotions are deeply involved. So the stronger our feelings the more likely it is that there will be no mutual element in the communication. There will be just two ideas, two feelings, two judgments, missing each other in psychological space. I'm sure you recognize this from your own experience. When you have not been emotionally involved yourself, and have listened to a heated discussion, you often go away thinking. "Well, they actually weren't talking about the same thing." And they were not. Each was making a judgment, an evaluation, from his own frame of reference. There was really nothing which could be called communication in any genuine sense. This tendency to react to any emotionally meaningful statement by forming an evaluation of it from our own point of view, is, I repeat, the major barrier to interpersonal communication.

But is there any way of solving this problem, of avoiding this barrier? I feel that we are making exciting progress toward this goal and I would like to present it as simply as I can. Real communication occurs, and this evaluative tendency is avoided, when we listen with understanding. What does this mean? It means to see the expressed idea and attitude from the other person's point of view, to sense how it feels to him, to achieve his frame of reference in regard to the thing he is talking about.

Stated so briefly, this may sound absurdly simple, but it is not. It is an approach which we have found extremely potent in the field of psychotherapy. It is the most effective agent we know, for altering the basic personality structure of an individual, and improving his relationships and his communications with others. If I can listen to what he can tell me, if I can understand how it seems to him, if I can see its personal meaning for him, if I can sense the emotional flavor which it has for him, then I will be releasing potent forces of change in him. If I can really understand how he hates his father, or hates the university, or hates communists—if I can catch the flavor of his fear of insanity, or his fear of atom bombs, or of Russia—it will be of the greatest help to him in altering those very hatreds and fears, and in establishing realistic and harmonious relationships with the very people and situations toward which he has felt hatred and fear. We know from our research that such emphatic understanding—understanding *with* a person, not *about* him—is such an effective approach that it can bring about major changes in personality.

Some of you may be feeling that you listen well to people, and that you have never seen such results. The chances are very great indeed that your listening has not been of the type I have described. Fortunately I can suggest a little laboratory experiment which you can try to test the quality of your understanding. The next time you get into an argument with your wife, or your friend, or with a small group of friends, just stop the discussion for a moment and for an experiment, institute this rule. "Each person can speak up for himself only *after* he has first restated the ideas and feelings of the previous speaker accurately, and to that speaker's satisfaction." You see what this would mean. It would simply mean that before presenting your own point of view, it would be necessary for you to really achieve the other speaker's frame of reference—to understand his thoughts and feelings so well that you could summarize them for him. Sounds simple, doesn't it? But if you try it you will discover it is one of the most difficult things you have ever tried to do. However, once you have been able to see the other's point of view, your own comments will have to be drastically revised. You will also find the emotion going out of the discussion, the differences being reduced, and those differences which remain being of a rational and understandable sort.

Can you imagine what this kind of an approach would mean if it were projected into larger areas? What would happen to a labor-management dispute if it was conducted in such a way that labor, without necessarily agreeing, could accurately state management's point of view in a way that management could accept; and management, without approving labor's stand, could state labor's case in a way that labor agreed was accurate? It would mean that real communication was established, and one could practically guarantee that some reasonable solution would be reached.

THE COMMUNICATIONS PROBLEM: LISTENING TO AND UNDERSTANDING OTHERS

LEARNING OBJECTIVES

1 Understand what's involved in listening with a "third ear."

2 Grasp the principal uses of the nondirective interview.

3 Master the principles of the nondirective interview.

4 Consider a battery of techniques that fine tune the art of listening.

5 Review the communications pitfalls in the appraisal interview and how to overcome them.

6 Evaluate transactional analysis as a communications tool.

In this chapter, we're going to talk about the other half of the communications process—and the more difficult half: listening. Certainly, getting messages across to other people is difficult enough. However, we would argue that receiving messages from other people is even more difficult, if we mean by this finding out what is really on their minds.

A large part of the problem is that people don't spend enough time listening. They think that they are communicating with other people when what they really do is talk a lot without taking the time to get the feedback to what they said. In fact, they take the echo-chamber approach to communication and settle for the illusion of it. They hear only themselves as their words are thrown back to them by the listener. Feedback, as we have stressed, is important, but there's much more to listening than that.

We agree with Whyte that "the art of listening remains one of the most overlooked tools of management," and we would add, one of the most important. The reasons why people spend so little time listening are fairly easy to identify. Some are too self-centered; it is impossible for them to concede the importance of what anyone else has to say. Some are too insecure; they're afraid that, if they listen long enough and hard enough, they will discover unpleasant truths about themselves. Some are pressed for time; they recognize that listening is a time-consuming process and they feel the return doesn't justify the investment. Finally, some shy away from listening because they feel it is an art which they haven't mastered.

Listening and Understanding

Many of those with reservations about listening as an unmastered art are correct. Effective listening is an art which involves the development of a certain attitude, the skilled control of a definite strategy, and a set of techniques. Once the manager has understood this, intense concentration, repeated practice, and a high degree of intuition will do the rest.

Listening with a "third ear" comes under the heading of concentration and even intuition. It sounds formidable but it's simply the recognition that there's a hidden content in many communications that can only be inferred by the listener. But how does the manager listen with a third ear? She's no psychiatrist, but actually, all she needs is a hunch. The other person's statements somehow don't sound convincing. She senses a buried meaning, so she probes for it. Joe might come in to quit because he was "just fed up with the job." But he didn't seem able to give any details of his dissatisfaction. Under these circumstances, the manager would search for clues, asking herself such questions as "Was his chance of promotion really the issue? Family troubles? Me as a boss?"

As we have discussed, symbols sometimes block effective communication. One case occurred in a large manufacturing company, when a new sales manager asked his sales representatives to compute certain correlation coefficients on the basis of their sales records. The job was easy, but the resistance to doing it was terrific. How come? After a lot of digging—that is, listening—the sales manager found out that, three years previously, an authoritarian and thoroughly disliked supervisor had tried to introduce the same technique. Ever since then, it had become a symbol of oppressive supervision to the sales representatives. Once he had solved the mystery, the sales manager withdrew his request temporarily and waited for his group to develop confidence in him. Then he reintroduced the technique and met with no opposition.

How can the manager tell when symbols may be blocking communication? If there is extraordinary, unexpected resistance to a proposal, for example, it's a tip-off to look for some symbolic meaning.

As for the attitude the effective listener needs to develop, take the case of Tim Hardy, a cool, dependable lathe-operator who had demonstrated over the years his ability to juggle a number of rush jobs at once. Suddenly, all this changed. Hardy started performing like a robot, stopping his machine and changing his specifications each time he received a high-priority order even if there were only one or two pieces remaining on the earlier job. The result, after a time, was a huge backlog.

Hardy's boss was tempted to try for a quick solution: bawl him out for not using more common sense and tell him to get back on the ball, or else. It could work, but on the other hand, it could lead to mutual name-calling and the kind of defiance which would leave his boss with no choice except to discipline Hardy or even fire him.

Instead, his supervisor took time out for insight. She kept her cool, determined to find out what was underneath Hardy's behavior, and ultimately got to the truth. Hardy felt, and with justification, that other operators were getting long-run orders which could be run automatically. He felt discriminated against, and in retaliation he practiced a form of malicious obedience that raised havoc with production schedules. The story had a happy ending. The unfair work split was unintentional—Hardy's boss had been handing out assignments by quality and quantity and neglecting complexity. Once the inequities were corrected, Hardy's performance returned to its previous level.

What do we mean when we contend that Tim Hardy's boss adopted the right attitude for effective listening? On the surface, Hardy's behavior was outrageous, indefensible—you name it. Yet the boss managed to rid herself of any preconceived notions, to suppress the natural temptation to harangue Hardy. Instead, she kept her cool and determined to get at the facts even when they pointed, as they did, to her own shortcomings as the root of the problem. Of course, effective listening alone is not enough. There would have been no happy ending unless Hardy's boss had straightened out the inequities which lay at the base of Hardy's action.

THE NONDIRECTIVE INTERVIEW

Hardy's boss was actually using some of the techniques involved in the nondirective interview, a form first practiced in industry by researchers during the Hawthorne experiment. Since then, it has been used by legions of personnel specialists and line managers to get at the reality underneath the surface of what people were saying and doing.

What is the nondirective interview? How does it differ from the usual interaction between boss and subordinate that is our major focus in this book? And what functions does it perform? The interview is called "nondirective" because, by contrast to most boss-subordinate exchanges, the initiative lies with the employee, not with the boss—with the person being interviewed, not the interviewer. The employee does nine-tenths of the talking and the boss does the heavy listening.

What does the nondirective interview accomplish, for example, that can't be accomplished in the typical boss-subordinate interview? How does it differ from the one where the boss begins with a set of assumptions, poses a set of direct questions framed to confirm or modify these assumptions, and concludes with a decision or solution based on the initial assumptions plus whatever additional facts the questions have uncovered?

The primary uses of the nondirective interview are threefold:

1 It is a uniquely effective device for getting at what is really on someone else's mind. The direct-question approach may produce honest responses, but they are bound to be partial and they are likely to be constructed with an eye to pleasing or at least placating the boss (if the boss is the interviewer). In other words, the direct-question approach never gets at the whole truth and infrequently achieves only the truth.

There are also many occasions when a manager recognizes that there is no ready-made set of assumptions. All the manager knows is that there is a problem with an employee. The cause of the problem is something to be determined during the interview with the subordinate. Under these circumstances, the manager has no choice but to practice patient and prolonged listening.

2 The nondirective interview forces the person being interviewed to think out loud about job problems, to organize them more clearly, and to think about them more deeply and differently. "I've never really thought of it that way before" is a phrase that often comes from an interviewee who has achieved new insights in the process of reorganizing and redefining problems.

All this has great significance for the interviewer, who's hoping—really betting—that the subordinate will arrive at a solution and that it will be one that a manager can live with. The manager knows the truth of what Bobbie Burns wrote: "He who is convinced against his will, is of the same opinion still." Therefore, the manager would vastly prefer a solution reached by the subordinate to the one the manager might feel compelled to dictate personally.

3 The process of getting things off one's chest frequently enables the subordinate being interviewed to achieve what the ancient Greeks called "catharsis"—a feeling of relief when a channel has been provided to funnel off frustrations even though the basic cause of the frustrations may remain.

Conducting a Nondirective Interview

So much for functions. Now let's talk about the nondirective interview itself and the three stages characteristic of each one: feelings, facts, and solutions. Almost every employee goes into a nondirective interview emotionally worked up. The interviewer should give the employee plenty of opportunity to blow off steam, partially, as we suggested earlier, to encourage catharsis and partly because feelings color facts. The manager is not likely to reach a satisfactory solution of any problem until the employee can look at the facts rationally.

Of course, feelings themselves are facts and, on occasion, constitute the essence of the problem. We know of a case where the number one reason for the slump in a typist's performance was an intense dislike of the office manager. The causes of the dislike remained murky, but the feelings were very real and very strong. About all the manager could do, when the interview disclosed such feelings, was to tolerate the hostility without responding to it and to discuss the possibilities of a transfer in the near future.

From emotions to solutions

The previous paragraph suggests an obvious point. The three stages of the nondirective interview are not watertight compartments. Feelings are facts, and the factual stage of the interview is scarcely devoid of emotion. Both stages hopefully build toward a satisfactory solution in the third stage. What distinguishes the stages from one another is the emphasis in each one and the differing degree of initiative played by the interviewer—in our discussion, the boss—in each one.

In the first stage, the manager plays a primarily passive role. She has little or no idea of what will be forthcoming. She listens, accepts what the employee tells her, and urges the subordinate to keep talking. In the second or factual stage, her role becomes somewhat more active. Building on the indicators provided in the first stage, she seeks additional facts from the subordinate, her criteria being those facts that point to a viable solution of the problem, or she takes the initiative and provides facts drawn from her own knowledge. In the third, solution-reaching stage, the manager's role differs widely. As we now know, ideally the subordinate personally reaches a solution which the boss has merely to approve. It is not always possible for the boss to be that nondirective, however. Sometimes it is imperative for a manager to step out of character because the subordinate is unwilling to come up with a solution with which the manager and the organization can live.

Let's assume, for example, that the problem under discussion is habitual tardiness—Jones is 30 minutes late almost every day. (Remember the discussion of *tone* in Chapter 6, which looked at this same problem.) The facts are: no alarm clock, unpredictable bus schedules, and insufficient sleep. For management, the only acceptable solution is for Jones to get to work at least roughly on time. Among the means toward that end are: Jones buys an alarm clock, Jones joins a car pool, and Jones makes a practice of getting eight hours a night sleep. Because Jones won't accept the latter two suggestions, he doesn't buy the solution. At this point, the manager would have to be directive—to assume charge and indicate that Jones has no choice but to take steps (the particular steps are up to him) that will solve the problem in a way satisfactory to management. Our example, happily, illustrates the exception, not the rule. In most cases, the subordinate does reach—with a subtle assist from the boss—a satisfactory solution to the problem.

LISTENING TECHNIQUES

The professionals who first developed the nondirective interview built into it a few techniques (gimmicks, if you will) which they found helpful in getting people to speak freely and fully, techniques from which many managers have profited.

Setting the stage
The first is not really a gimmick but an exception to the rule that the boss should be nondirective in the early stages of the interview. It's up to the manager to set the stage, to define the subject which the interview will cover. Otherwise, time is likely to be wasted in pointless discussion or aimless small talk that only increases the tension, anxiety, and frustration level of an already overwrought subordinate. If the reason for the discussion, for example, is that Ted's production record last month was down by 20 percent, the manager should begin with the simple statement, made in a nonemotional, unthreatening way, "Let's talk about your production record." Once having focused on the subject the interviewer might not make another remark as lengthy for the next 20 to 30 minutes. Ted should be given the chance to air his feelings and to state all the facts of the situation as he sees them.

At the same time, the boss can't sit numb and dumb while Ted talks on. Responses should be limited but carefully thought out, and the manager should rely heavily on the psychologists' advice on the use of two devices, the reflective summary and the probe.

The reflective summary
In the reflective summary, the boss or any other interviewer summarizes the gist of what the interviewee has said or has been trying to say, being careful to avoid any words or phrases that would imply a judgment, favorable or unfavorable. For example, the boss might say something to Ted like "You say the speeds on your machine are hard to control." The simple statement accomplishes several things: (1) It shows Ted that the boss is listening, (2) it reassures him that the boss has passed no value judgments on what he has told her, (3) it gives him a chance to correct the boss if she has misunderstood what she has heard, and (4) it shows Ted she's interested and encourages him to go on with his story.

The probe
The probe serves a different but related purpose. It encourages employees to tell the boss or interviewer more about something that's been said, even if the employee appears reluctant to expand on the remarks. In other words, the interviewer's antennae send out an alert that pay dirt may have been hit and the boss wants to hear more.

Let's assume that Ted has had his say about the defective speeds on his machine. The boss has said nothing, although convinced that the real explanation for the decline in the subordinate's production is still to be heard. Then Ted tacks on the comment that "It wouldn't be so bad if everything else around here worked." He has dropped a clue, and whether or not his boss ever gets to the root of the problem may depend on what is done with the clue. An indignant "Where do you get off—'if everything else around here worked' " would cause Ted to clam up, become defensive, and effectively terminate the interview. The most helpful follow-through would be to repeat, "If everything else around here worked," in a neutral tone of voice and wait for him to pick up the ball. If Ted ignores the invitation to expand on the remark, the manager still can't ignore the clue. She has to resort to something more direct, such as " 'If everything else around here worked'—tell me what you mean. I'm interested," and hope for the best, by which we mean Ted's honest answer to the question, not his politic one. What may be gnawing away at the employee may be the fact that he was overlooked for a promotion to a job in which the boss wasn't even aware he was interested. Ted is bottled up—to himself and to others—and the boss is so removed that it might take an hour or more and the peeling off of several layers of meaning and feeling before they could arrive at the truth of the situation. Once they hit bedrock, they may or may not solve the problem, depending on the boss's ability to provide the opportunity for Ted to be considered at least for an adequate substitute position or to persuade Ted that he will be best off staying where he is. Perhaps Ted needs recognition as much as he needs a promotion.

THE MANAGER'S "THIRD EAR"

Listening is a basic tool for every first-level manager. But listening alone is not enough. Managers must not only convey that they are listening sympathetically and closely for the implied as well as the stated meanings, listening with the third ear. They must also set their listening in a framework wherein they both get the truth and can help the employee to reach his or her own solution to the problem. Hence, the nondirective interview.

This type of interview, in turn, depends on skills that are painfully acquired. Practice a little introspection and consider the moral attitude requisite for a successful nondirective interview. Abandoning preconceived notions, taking in facts without attributing praise or blame, accepting personal criticism without fighting back or even betraying annoyance, and standing patiently by while a person slowly and painfully works out a solution that you reached three days previously—doing all this tests the temper and tries the soul. Yet, it's part of the formula for conducting a successful nondirective interview.

The other requisites for the effective nondirective interview don't sin so much against doing what comes naturally—they're just hard work and they require extraordinary concentration. Managers must use reflective summaries and probes to make sure the facts are all in before they attempt to help the employee reach a solution. If that doesn't work, if the employee can't or won't recommend a solution satisfactory to the manager and the organization, the manager has to try for a joint solution. And as a last resort, after listening as carefully as possible to catch the cadences and gradations of reservation, the manager has to dictate the organization's solution—and hope the subordinate will live with it.

THE PERFORMANCE APPRAISAL INTERVIEW

Let's illustrate some of our points about listening and really understanding what the other party has to say by referring to the performance appraisal or performance review, a device that has been standard operating procedure in most corporations for over thirty years. In the more progressive organizations it's undergone an evolution from a technique that focuses on evaluating previous performance to a strategy for motivating employees to improve their future performance. The two goals have always been present, but over the years managers have come to realize that they are by and large counterproductive: The process of telling a man or woman what's wrong with his or her previous performance has aroused feelings of anxiety, conflict, and hostility—along with a minimum of commitment to improve in any specific ways.

Consider what happened several years ago when employees in fourteen different companies in fourteen different industries were surveyed. In response to a question about the guidance and correction they received from the appraisal interview, employees gave the following answers: "very helpful"—5; "somewhat helpful"—21; "little help"—35; "no help at all"—39. In short, the interview failed to achieve its prime objective with almost three-quarters of those responding.

Reactions such as these have become commonplace. Cumulatively over the years, these reactions have resulted in redefining the purpose of the appraisal interview as well as in restructuring the interview itself. The emphasis has shifted from a judicious apportionment of praise and blame for previous performance to the establishment of mutual commitments by both manager and subordinate aimed at achieving specific future performance objectives. In the process, managers have come to acknowledge that in most cases some of the blame for subordinates' poor performances is their own; they have failed to train adequately, provide sufficiently clear instructions, have set vague or contradictory goals, have appeared aloof, indifferent, and inaccessible, and so on. Blameless supervisors are about as rare as faultless subordinates. The emphasis in the appraisal interview has shifted; it has become, in theory at least, a problem-solving, goal-setting discussion in which the manager and subordinate agree on (1) what the manager can do to help the subordinate meet his or her objectives, and (2) what the subordinate personally agrees to do to meet these objectives. Obviously, in the new model appraisal interview, it is more important than ever to listen to what the subordinate has to say and give him or her plenty of opportunity to say it.

Preparing for the Appraisal Interview

Managers should never go into the appraisal interview cold. Few managers do. However, they frequently do the wrong homework in preparation. After all, it's still going to be necessary to discuss instances of below-par performance in the interview even though these instances are used as a base to build future objectives and plan improvements.

How does the manager avoid the potential conflict inherent in any discussion of poor performance? Most of the answer lies in the way the manager handles the actual interview. However, the right kind of preparation also helps. By the right kind of preparation we mean a problem-solving discussion based on *facts*—and plenty of them: facts that disprove the tendency to write off any praise as insincere, and more importantly, facts that depersonalize any discussion with the employee of where mistakes were made and why. One problem, of course, is remembering the facts. Most managers would have little trouble in remembering for a week or two certain things about a subordinate's performance. Beyond that, they would find it difficult to recollect any but those episodes of striking excellence or ineptitude. There's one remedy that some managers have used that is not too time-consuming: They keep a daily log, or at least a weekly log, in which they record key incidents in each employee's performance. Backed with this log book, they are in good position to conduct problem-solving sessions based on facts, not impressions.

Two further steps also help to set the stage for a fruitful discussion. In reviewing the record of the subordinate's performance prior to the interview and noting anything that indicates subpar performance, the manager should stop and ask: "In what way did I contribute to this record? Was there anything I did or omitted doing that helps to explain why Mary didn't do better than she did?" We recognize, of course, that asking these questions doesn't ensure accurate and insightful answers, but it's an indispensable first step.

The supervisor, at the same time, needs to set the stage and define the boundaries of the interview in advance with the subordinate. It doesn't have to be elaborate—maybe a few brief words like this:

> Mike, I would like to get together with you on next Tuesday, if that's all right with you, to discuss where we have been and where we want to go. I've had some thoughts on where I went wrong from time to time, and I hope that you will do a little soul searching of your own before Tuesday morning. If we both do our homework in advance, I'm sure that we can cover a lot of ground and have a useful discussion.

These remarks presume, of course, that the existing superior-subordinate relationship is reasonably good before the interview. The right homework beforehand and the proper strategy during the interview won't go very far in salvaging a relationship that has already gone sour.

Conducting the Interview

The primary goal of the interview, of course, is the joint identification of problems and the joint discussion of how to solve them. The supervisor has identified in advance the area or areas to be concentrated on, the specific objectives to be achieved, and some action steps that should be considered by both the supervisor and the subordinate as a means of reaching these objectives. The situation is made easier if the organization has a formal plan of managing by objectives. Then the manager and the subordinate have a previously worked-out set of objectives and plans for achieving them as the basic foundation for discussion during the appraisal interview. In essence, they will answer two questions: Have the objectives mutually agreed on during the last appraisal session been achieved?; and to the extent that they weren't achieved, what went wrong? The success of such a discussion depends, in large part, on the manager's being willing to consider the possibility that he or she may have contributed to the subordinate's partial failure, and asking, searchingly and sincerely, to what extent is the failure my responsibility? What things have I done that I should not have done, and what things have I left undone? However, there is another issue to be dealt with—the overall appraisal of the past six months' or year's performance.

Where does the appraisal belong? Before or after the problem-solving discussion? We believe that the answer depends on whether the subordinate's overall performance is good to excellent or average to inferior. If it is good to excellent, there's always a chance that the subordinate will not know that the manager is aware of this fine performance. Beginning an interview by telling the subordinate of the high opinion you have of his or her work will tend to make the subordinate more receptive to the problem-solving part of the interview. If the subordinate's overall performance leaves a good deal to be desired, the reverse strategy is in order. If the subordinate is hit straight off with a predominantly negative assessment, even one supported with plenty of evidence, the appraisal may be resented and resisted or accepted and a defeatist attitude adopted. In either case, the problem-solving discussion is likely to be aborted. However, if the predominantly negative, or at best neutral, appraisal is postponed until after the problem-solving discussion, the subordinate will find it easier to accept its validity because of the agreed-on joint strategy (manager and subordinate) for resolving the principal problems.

As for the problem-solving part of the interview, there are a number of dos and don'ts that the manager wants to keep in mind. Do try to get subordinates to identify (1) what their biggest problem is and (2) what they feel you should do to help them solve it and (3) how the subordinates personally intend to solve it. Tone, of course, counts for a lot. The manager must be friendly, interested, and objective, assuming the role of coach and counselor, not judge and jury. When employees feel they can be candid with the boss, experience has shown that they can be accurate and merciless self-critics. A simple opening statement such as "You've given some thought to your job problems over the past few days. Does any one problem strike you as being serious?" may be all the manager needs to launch the discussion on a fruitful course. When the conversation lags or needs to be moved in a specific direction, the manager may resort to the techniques of the reflective summary and the probe that we just outlined.

    Dick (aggressively): Heck—I just can't get the hang of that new machine. *(A long pause follows.)*
    Fred: You say the new machine keeps giving you trouble. (In other

words, I accept what you say and I want to hear more. Maybe I have a few ideas of my own as to what went wrong, but I want to hear from you. You are the expert.)

Of course the echo isn't foolproof. Dick's response may be a reverberating silence, in which case the boss will have to get more directive and ask Dick why he is having trouble getting the hang of the new machine.

Let's take a quite different case. Mabel Choate, who is the chief time-buyer at Tinker, Tombey, and Tamper, a medium-size advertising agency in Boston, has a secretary, Pat Grasso, who is willing, cheerful, and able—with one exception. Her stenography—well, "rusty" would be a charitable word. She should be able to take sixty words a minute, but twenty is more her speed. Mabel doesn't do too much dictation, but when she does, each session is an ordeal. The sticky part of Pat's performance appraisal, obviously, is going to be the discussion of her shortcomings in taking dictation. Here's how part of the conversation went.

> *Mabel (with obvious relief)*: You say that you know that your dictating skills are way below par. I'm relieved that you recognize it.
> *Pat*: It's true, Mabel. But you don't help very much. You have a habit of letting your voice trail off at the end of sentences. Sometimes I don't understand you at all.
> *Mabel (sounding a little petulant)*: Maybe you're right. But I have had several secretaries before you, and you're the first one to bring it up. (The others, of course, didn't have to make excuses for poor work.)
> *Pat*: I don't know about them. I just know that you don't speak very clearly to me when you dictate.

Mabel was lucky or smart. Pat was candid about her weakness. Then Mabel proceeded to blow it. The comment about her relief at Pat's admitting her weakness was gratuitous and likely to be resented. Mabel's unwillingness to consider that some of the problem may be her fault—her "Maybe you're right" carried no conviction—was a major tactical error. Mabel should have asked herself before the session whether she was part of the problem. Do I talk too fast, slur my words, forget to finish sentences, trail off at the end of sentences, and so on? Even if she believed that Pat was incorrect, she should have admitted the possibility that she might be right and promise to be more careful in the future. More than that, Mabel should have made a mental note to ask during the next few dictating sessions whether or not Pat was having any trouble understanding her, and she should urge Pat to indicate to her whenever she wasn't being clear. As it is, the prospects for a productive session are dim. Quite understandably, Pat is angry, and she is unlikely to take any positive initiatives on her own or respond favorably to any initiative from Mabel. At best, Pat will pay lip service to any recommendations from Mabel as to how she might improve her performance.

What should Mabel have done? Obviously, she should have taken Pat's criticism to heart, even if it came as a surprise. Then she should have waited for Pat to explain what she intended to do about her trouble in taking dictation. Of course, the manager cannot count on the subordinate's coming up with a plan. To recognize a problem is not tantamount to perceiving a solution. Still, the manager should avoid giving a solution. Instead, he or she should search for alternatives which will suffice to solve the problem. With Pat, it might be a brushup course at a secretarial school (the quickest, surest, as well as the most expensive solution), a self-administered home-study course, or having someone, a boyfriend or roommate, help Pat practice taking dictation when she's not on the job. The point is that subordinates are more likely to buy the solution when it is to a considerable degree their own solution. Although the idea wasn't the subordinate's in the first place, there was the freedom to choose among alternatives.

One last point about choosing objectives and solutions: whenever possible, quantify them. Of course, this is easier said than done. If you're talking about a subordinate who needs to cooperate better with fellow workers, you can see it, and you can feel it. But try to measure it! To return to our example, Pat could certainly quantify her objective—increase her dictating speed from twenty to, maybe, sixty words per minute with no more than two mistakes per minute.

What are the advantages of specificity? When the objective is achieved, there's no room for doubt or denial. The manager can recognize the achievement and reward it in an appropriate fashion; whereas the subordinate can get the certain sense of satisfaction from having achieved a goal that the boss had also agreed upon as necessary and reasonable.

TRANSACTIONAL ANALYSIS

In recent years transactional analysis (TA), a new way of looking at what people say and do to each other, has gained tremendous popular attention and acceptance. Two books on the subject have each sold over one million copies, and TA has been the subject of countless meetings, courses, and seminars.

What is TA? How can it help the supervisor do a better job of understanding subordinates? How does it relate to the other communications devices that we have described earlier in this chapter?

Transactional analysis views the human personality as being made up of three parts or "ego states": the Child that reflects our experiences as a child, the Parent that reflects our experiences with the various authority figures in our lives (the most important of which are our experiences with our parents), and the Adult, or rational ego state in which our behavior is based on an analysis of the facts. At various times a person's behavior reflects the predominance of one of these three ego states. Nevertheless, with most people, either the Child, the Parent, or the Adult is primarily in command at all times. TA identifies four life positions (see Figure 9-1) that shape the way we react to other people:

1 *I'm OK—you're OK.* These people have Adult ego states and Adult attitudes in dealing with other people. They assume in their transactions with others that people are rational individuals with whom they can have a mutually advantageous relationship. Self-esteem and esteem for others characterize such people.

FIGURE 9-1 Impact of life positions on employee behavior

1 I'm OK—you're OK
- Communicates freely
- Learns willingly
- Solves problems by mutual consultation
- Feels equal with others

2 I'm not OK—you're OK
- Communicates defensively
- Learns slowly, needs constant reassurance
- Solves problems by asking others to solve them
- Feels inferior to others

3 I'm OK—you're not OK
- Communicates aggressively
- Learns with difficulty
- Solves problems unilaterally, almost automatically
- Rejects other people's ideas
- Feels superior to others

4 I'm not OK—you're not OK
- Communicates hostility
- Learns with difficulty, prone to repeat errors
- Doesn't solve problems, succumbs to them
- Feels alienated from others

2 *I'm OK—you're not OK.* The Parent dominates in such a person. This person is suspicious and distrustful of others and will attempt to dominate any relationship.

3 *I'm not OK—you're OK.* The Child has taken control. Such an individual is submissive to authority and wants to be told what to do in every situation.

4 *I'm not OK—you're not OK.* A negativist who views himself and the rest of the human race as children. Relationships with other people are characterized by apathy, indifference, and withdrawal.

The favorite TA word is "stroke." According to Muriel James, one of TA's chief propagators, "In any transaction, there is a stimulus which is a stroke, and a response which is also a stroke. Some are negative. Some positive. Obviously some pairs of strokes are complementary, some crossed." The interaction, for example, between an Adult supervisor and an Adult subordinate is going to result in complementary strokes, while the Parent supervisor who tries to threaten or coerce an Adult subordinate into bettering a production record will produce cross strokes—and genuinely unsatisfactory results.

Transactional analysis also identifies a series of games that people play as determined by the dominant ego states. Parent supervisors and Child subordinates will frequently resort to such games as "Blemish," "Kick me," or "Stupid." The nature of these games is obvious from their titles. Child subordinates are much given to "Yes, but" in which they think of every possible reason for not accepting the responsibility for their actions. Such games may sometimes afford considerable psychological satisfaction to the players. Why else would they persist in playing them? But they consume vast quantities of time that could otherwise be used more constructively.

How do supervisors detect the prevailing ego state? And what can they do to foster the Adult state, which TA assumes is the optimum, for all personal interactions? Some tip-offs are provided by the individual's body language. The Parent may look over the rim of her glasses, have his hands on his hips, or even point an accusing finger; the Adult will make regular eye contact and the Adult's head will tilt slightly to convey the appearance of active listening; and the Child may exhibit drooping shoulders, a scowl, or pursed lips. Even more indicative are expressions that appear most frequently in a conversation: with the Parent, phrases such as "You should," "You ought," "You must," "Don't tell me," and "You always"; with the Adult, "Aha, I see," "I see your point," "How do you feel about," and "What is the alternative to"; and with the Child, "I want," "I wish," "If only," "One of these days,"

"It's not my fault," and so on. As for the games people play, supervisors need to become aware of the frequency with which games are played—and this includes themselves as the players.

What can the supervisor do about a subordinate, for example, whose ego state is that of a Child and who is much given to playing such games as "Kick me" or "Stupid"? If the supervisor has been in the habit of playing such games with the subordinate, it's time to confront the problem that he or she personally may have an I'm OK—you're not OK life position. In any case, it should be recognized that it takes two to play a game. If it's an unproductive game like "Kick me" or "Stupid," one can refuse to kick the subordinate and use the Adult ego state instead. Another authority on TA, Vincent Albano, asserts that "if you continue to use your Adult, the chances are that the employee will feel incongruous in using his Child and will sooner or later start transactions from his Adult."

Or take the game of "Yes, but" that looks on the surface like an Adult—Adult game with the subordinate supplying one seemingly rational explanation after another for the failure to get something done well, or done at all, but this is really a Parent—Child game which typically winds up something like this:

> *Boss:* Your production on the new drill is way off.
> *Phil:* Everyone's complaining about that new drill.
> *Boss:* Maybe, but you're the only one whose production is still below standard.
> *Phil:* Well, the person who explained the new steps wasn't very clear.
> *Boss:* It was the same person who explained it to all the others. If it wasn't clear, why didn't you say so?
> *Phil:* Maybe I'm just dumb.
> *Boss:* I'm beginning to see your point.

At which point, the boss is playing the unhappy Parent and the chances of working with Phil's Adult to take steps to improve his production become pretty dim. If the boss had "kept cool" and discussed specific steps that Phil might take to improve his production, including having the same trainer or a different one go over the steps again, he might have called upon Phil's Adult, and there might have been some realistic hopes for improvement.

How do we evaluate TA? Is it a fad that will eventually fade away without leaving a trace? It's too early to tell. It is possible to argue that TA is merely a method for fixing new labels to what people had known intuitively all along. Maybe so. But just this process of raising the level of consciousness to feelings about interpersonal transactions helps us to recognize those transactions for what they are, and is an essential first step in doing whatever needs to be done to improve them.

It's true that you don't basically change a human being's nature— short of the psychoanalyst's couch or a traumatic experience. Many employees—and their bosses too—are locked into the games they play so deeply that the consciousness raising provided by TA will make no difference. The games will continue. On the other hand, surface interactions can bring about changes in surface behavior. With other individuals, the behavior patterns displayed in the games they play are not that deeply ingrained. Supervisors who recognize the game for what it is, and who, in refusing to play, try to use their Adult to evoke a parallel response may succeed in changing the subordinate's behavior.

In other words, we view TA and the techniques associated with it as modest but useful tools that add a new and positive dimension to the other methods for understanding and communicating with people that we have discussed in this and the preceding chapter.

CONCLUSION

Almost ninety years ago, William H. Vanderbilt, in response to a reporter's question about the public's reaction to a move he was contemplating, replied, "The public be damned!" On any honesty index we would rate Mr. Vanderbilt tops. And he got away with it—there were no strikes, no rider boycotts of his railways. He died a few years later, the richest man in the United States, unloved but unchallenged.

Today's managers are in a very different position. Even if they felt like William H. Vanderbilt, they couldn't say, "The employee be damned." They have no choice but to listen—to listen hard and sympathetically—and to catch the subtleties of what their subordinates are telling them so that they can retain and motivate them.

THE EDUCATION OF GREG HORNING: MARCH 18

A couple of days before, Greg had remembered that it was time for Jeannette Greely's annual merit rating. Arrow Plastics was small, but it practiced most of the commonly accepted personnel techniques— merit rating being one of them.

Greg scowled into his yellow pad. What should he say to Jeannette? More important, what was she doing wrong? And what could he say that would make her perform better?

OK, on the whole he was pleased with Jeannette. Of course, she and Helen had been up in arms when he separated them and moved them closer to the machines and the operators. But they had quit griping. And her general attitude had improved recently. She had been almost motherly. "Well, she's old enough to be my mother," Greg mused.

There was one thing about her that disturbed him—and this also went for Helen. They either failed to tell him at all about a defective part, or they waited until a whole bunch had piled up and then dumped them into his lap. With production still down, the last thing he could afford was a hefty scrap rate. He had to make Jeannette see how important it was to report any defects to him on the double. This was something for which he wouldn't take any excuses like "There's no time"—"Well, she would have to make the time," thought Greg. And no sneaking around and leaving a bunch of parts while he was at lunch—and with no explanation—as both Helen and she had done more than once. Well, I have to go out and tell Jeannette about her interview and ask her to do some thinking about it. She's been here six years, so it's hardly anything new. Of course, it is her first go-round with me.

"Come in Jeannette," Greg was on his feet and smiling. "Sit down and make yourself comfortable. I want to make this as easy as possible for both of us. Want a Marlboro?" he said, passing the pack across the desk to Jeannette.

"No thanks, I have my own," Jeannette replied in a tone more relaxed than Greg's, but not as resolutely affable.

"Well, I guess that I'm judge and jury. And I can't help admitting that I'm pretty self-conscious about it." The remark was followed by a quick, nervous smile.

"I'm an old hand, Greg. Shoot! What do you think about how I'm doing. I'm interested," the last phrase said slowly—and with obvious sincerity.

"Well, first off, in general I like your work. You and Helen are both pros. You know what to do and when to do it. No one has to tell you you're on the ball. The others all respect you. When you reject something—even though it might look bad for them—they don't give you an argument."

"Let's face it, Greg, once in a while they do. Of course, they're practically never right," Jeannette added quickly. "But seriously, Greg, I'm no paragon. Don't save up the bad news. What am I doing wrong? What don't you like about my work? Or are you going to recommend me for a 20 percent raise?"

"With the department at 87 percent of standard—not a chance. Seriously, we're a team. And until the team pulls what the brass thinks it should—and incidentally, I agree with them," the last words uttered a bit defensively. "There will be no recommendations for increases from me until we meet standard. And I mean it."

"I was only kidding, Greg. I know the score as well as you do."

"Well, I just wanted to set the record straight. What can you do better? I can tell you one thing. And it's no small matter either. You can let me know anytime there's a defective part—not wait until there's a mess of spoilage. We have a couple of new workers on the line, and scrap is running higher than ever. That's why it is so important for you to let me know. I've spoken to you and Helen about this before, but it hasn't done any good. What about it, Jeannette? Can I count on you?"

"I guess so, Greg, but it will just slow me up some more. What with all the flashing I have to do with the others going faster, the running around trying to find the right boxes, and going back and forth to Helen's station to see what she thinks about rejecting a part—she's even more of a pro than I am—time is one thing I don't have much of."

"All right, Jeannette. Score one for you," Greg replied. "I think the others are working sloppier, not faster, but that's not the point. I separated you and Helen and moved you closer to the machines and the operators because I thought it would speed things up. It's been two months, and it hasn't. Apparently, I was wrong. Would it help if I moved Helen and you back to your old work stations?"

"It would sure help, Greg, but don't expect miracles," Jeannette added in a flatter tone.

"The age of miracles is over. And I might point out that one reason the new setup didn't work out is that neither you nor Helen brought me the borderline cases as I asked you to do." Greg's voice was beginning to get an edge to it. ("You make a concession," he thought, "and all you get is a big fat whine in return.")

"Look, Greg. I'll do my best. You can't ask anything more of me than that." The edge on Jeannette's voice was a match for the one on Greg's.

"Sure, sure, Jeannette. Forget my crack—it's all water over the dam," Greg said, running his hands a couple of times through his mop of blond hair. "I was just concerned that you be sure to check with me anytime you get a defect. Defects are unavoidable, but not doing something about them is inexcusable."

"Absolutely, you're right."

"One other thing. I'm not God Almighty when it comes to defects." ("Maybe this is something that's bugging her," thought Greg.) "With my training, I can sometimes spot what's wrong. But sometimes I can't. In that case, I will have to contact Frank Granto or one of his people. The point is the importance of spotting the problem and, as early as possible, getting to the heart of it. Can I count on you, Jeannette?" Greg asked in an upbeat tone.

"You can count on me, Greg." The answer was even but flat.

QUESTIONS

1 Is there anything else that Greg should have considered doing that would help Jeannette to comply with his request?

2 How well did Greg handle his concession to Jeannette?

3 In the light of their past history, was Greg's admission about his relative lack of expertise likely to be satisfactory to Jeannette?

4 Over all, how would you rate Greg's conduct of what obviously is only a part—although a key part—of the merit-rating interview?

BEHAVIORAL EXERCISE

The purpose of the exercise is to give the class practice conducting a nondirective interview—proceeding through the three stages, using the probe and the reflective summary along the way, and, we hope, emerging at the end with a mutually acceptable resolution of the problem.

The problem is this: Marilyn Hornstein, a generally efficient and likable clerk-typist had one prevailing fault—she found it very difficult to get to work on time every Monday morning. She wasn't the essence of punctuality the rest of the time, but Mondays were in a class by themselves. Never before 9:30, although work started at 9 o'clock, and frequently not before 10 o'clock. A few inquires from Jean Saudek, her supervisor, had been responded to with a muffled "I'm sorry," a wan smile, followed by "I must have overslept—I'll make it up," together with no disposition to follow up the matter further.

Sure Marilyn was a good and willing worker, Jean thought to herself, but enough is enough. At Acme Books, a wholesale book seller, Monday is the busiest day. Besides, Marilyn was the youngest employee in the department, and the other women resented her getting away with her tardiness, at least that's how it looked to them. A few of them had begun to come in late themselves on Mondays. Jean had to talk to Marilyn and get things out in the open.

The instructor should ask for two volunteers and then send them out of the room. Review the principles and procedures of the nondirective interview with the rest of the class, and ask the class to take notes on the course of the interview. The student taking the role of Jean Saudek will be asked to use the nondirective interview to bring about a successful resolution of her problems with Marilyn. At the conclusion of the interview (30 to 35 minutes), the class should try to answer the following questions:

1 Did Jean Saudek follow the rule of spending most of the time listening, especially during the early stages of the conversation?
2 Did Jean give Marilyn adequate time (and encouragement to express her feelings)?
3 Did Jean set the stage in a definite, but nonthreatening, way?
4 Did she get the opportunity to use the probe and reflective summary? If so, did she use them effectively? If not, why not?
5 Did Jean do an effective job of drawing out the facts? If she didn't, how does Marilyn share the responsibility for the failure?
6 What about the solution to the problem? Was Jean able to persuade Marilyn to come up with it herself? To the extent that Jean had to be directive, what evidence do we have that Marilyn is likely to abide by the solution?

BIBLIOGRAPHY

Chapple, E., and L. Sayles, *Measure of Management: Designing Organizations for Human Effectiveness*, Macmillan, New York, 1961, chap. 7.
Walter, O., and R. Scott, *Thinking and Speaking; A Guide to Intelligent Oral Communication,* Macmillan, New York, 1973.
Leavitt, H., W. Dill, and H. Eyring, *The Organization World,* Harcourt, New York, 1973, chap. 5.
Whyte, W., *Organizational Behavior,* Irwin, New York, 1969, chaps. 6, 12, and 14.

READING

One-Way versus Two-Way Communication*

HAROLD LEAVITT (1922-   )

Traditionally psychologists sought to measure individual characteristics, everything from eye movements and finger dexterity to interpersonal skills. Harold Leavitt represents the new breed of social psychologists who moved away from the individual and began studying industry and organized human work efforts in the period after World War II. In fact, he is one of the very few such academically trained psychologists who have also sought to employ experimental methods to simulate real organizations.

He received his doctoral training at MIT at a time when that institution was literally packed with creative, outstanding social psychologists, including Douglas McGregor, who sought to solve real world organizational problems. Perhaps the most distinguished was Kurt Lewin, a German refugee who showed how psychological theory could be adapted to harnessing the inherent power of small groups to motivate individuals to change their behavior. At the same time Alex Bavelas, a student of Lewin's, was seeking to design experiments to test the likely effect of different kinds of group structure on group productivity and decision making. Leavitt melded these two influences in a classic and widely cited research study of group problem solving. Utilizing innovative techniques to simulate different kinds and numbers of communication channels, Leavitt was able to simulate different organization structures. He helped further demonstrate what Lewin had shown earlier, the power of participation in improving both satisfaction and effectiveness. (However, the groups in which members could communicate more freely with everyone were not necessarily the most efficient structures for some kinds of problems.)

While communication and small groups fascinated Leavitt, he also spent a good deal of his time looking at larger organizations as a management consultant. Thus his later work is more concerned with the impact of larger structural forces and of technology on both work efficiency and human satisfaction.

After his famous communication studies at MIT, he wrote one of the best known textbooks on organizations, with a social psychological base: *Managerial Psychology* (University of Chicago Press, 1964). More recently he was the senior author of a text that sought to analyze and describe modern organizations, including their computers and management scientists: *The Organizational World*, with William Dill and Henry Eyring (Harcourt, 1973). Both of these books show the social psychologist's ability to move from the individual to large structured groups.

---

* Passage from Harold J. Leavitt, *Managerial Psychology*, The University of Chicago Press, 1964, pp. 141-143.

Leavitt taught first at his own school, MIT, then at Carnegie-Mellon, and has been a professor at Stanford University's Graduate School of Business for more than a decade.

His wide-ranging mind, his training in experimental methods, and his interpersonal skills, learned from the psychologists who pioneered sensitivity training and encounter groups at MIT under Lewin, represent a unique combination for a scholar of organizational behavior.

Essentially our problem is to clarify the differences between these two situations: (1) One person, A, talking to another, B, *without* return talk from B to A; versus (2) conversation from A to B *with* return conversation from B to A. The differences can be clarified best by testing one method against the other. Here is such a test situation:

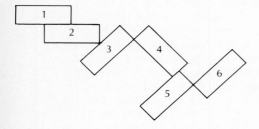

The pattern of rectangles shown here is an idea you would like to tell some B's about. Suppose you try to communicate it *in words* to a half-dozen of your friends who are sitting around your living room: Assume that the rectangles touch each other at "sensible" places—at corners or at midpoints along the line. There are no touch points at any unusual places. All the angles are either 90° or 45° angles; there are no odd ones. This pattern of rectangles is an idea comparable perhaps to a complicated set of instructions you may have to give to a subordinate or to the definition of a policy that you would like to pass along or to the task of explaining statistical quality control to a sales manager. This idea can be communicated to others under (1) one-way or (2) two-way conditions.

If you are the communicator, these are your *one-way* instructions:

1 Turn your back on your audience so that you cannot get visual communication back.

2 Give the audience blank sheets of paper, so that they can listen

and draw exactly what you are communicating. Ask them to try to draw as accurate a picture of the pattern of rectangles as possible.
3 Describe the pattern of rectangles to them *in words* as fast as you can. The audience is not permitted to ask questions, or laugh, or sigh, or in any other way to communicate back to you any information about what it is receiving.

This game is a good parlor game, if you can find some people to try it on. Try it, time it, and then check the accuracy of your communication by determining whether or not your audience has drawn what you have described. If they received what you tried to send, so their pictures match the test picture, then you have communicated. To the extent that their pictures do not match the one in the drawing, you have not communicated.

Two-way communication can be tested for contrast in the same way. The same rules apply, and here is a similar test pattern:

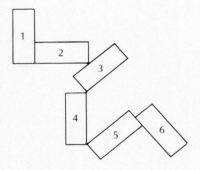

This time the basic job is the same, to describe the pattern verbally so that the people who are listening can draw it. But here are the differences:

1 This time you may face your audience.
2 They are allowed to interrupt and ask you any questions they want to at any time they want to.

Try it this way and time it. The differences between what happened the first time and what happened the second time are the differences between one- and two-way communication. (The order in which the two methods are used does not matter.)

4

Under experimental conditions these findings have emerged from this game: (1) One-way communication is considerably *faster* than two-way communication. (2) Two-way communication is *more accurate* than one-way, i.e., more people in the audience correctly reproduced the drawing under two-way conditions. (3) The receivers are more sure of themselves and make more correct judgments of how right or wrong they are in the two-way system. (4) The sender finds himself feeling psychologically under attack in the two-way system, because his receivers pick up his mistakes and oversights and *let him know about them*. The receivers may make snide remarks about the sender's intelligence and skill, and, if the receivers are trying very hard and taking the task seriously, they may actually get angry at the sender, and he at them. (5) The two-way method is relatively noisy and disorderly—with people interrupting the sender and one another, with the slowest man holding up the rest, and so on. The one-way method, on the other hand, appears neat and efficient to an outside observer, but the communication is less accurate.

10

LEADERSHIP: HOW THE SUPERVISOR MOTIVATES SUBORDINATES

LEARNING OBJECTIVES

1 Recognize that leadership depends on matching the behavior to the situation—and that no two situations are exact duplicates.

2 Appreciate that the successful leader must cope with many elements.

3 See that effective decision making is a key element of leadership.

4 Determine the conditions and the degrees under which a supervisor should share decision making.

5 Divide supervisory styles into three general types—general, autocratic, and pragmatic—and consider the situations under which each is likely to be effective.

6 Appreciate that another key to leadership is achieving a reasonable balance of "inputs" and "outputs" between supervisor and subordinate.

7 Realize that the supervisor should strive for synchronization in any contacts.

8 See that the supervisor uses status and power to protect subordinates.

The subtitle of this chapter fulfills an important function: It emphasizes that leadership does not exist in a vacuum—that whether or not the supervisor is a leader depends on his or her ability to motivate subordinates. To be sure, the authority conveyed by being the boss means that the boss is the formal leader to whom subordinates report. The supervisor has the authority to issue orders and give directions. Subordinates, in turn, have the obligation to implement these orders and follow these directions. But as the previous chapters have sought to make abundantly clear, these statements embody a view of superior-subordinate relations that is naive, one-sided, and wrong.

The effective supervisor is the man or woman whose presence makes a positive difference. Who a person is and what that person does contributes to satisfactory morale and productivity. The task is formidable. The supervisor must determine the behavior that is appropriate to the situation—and remember, no two situations are exactly alike.

For his or her influence to be effective—and the supervisor motivates by influence and/or example, not fiat—the supervisor must possess not one but several antennae. As Tannenbaum and Schmidt summed it up in a classic article,

> The successful leader is one who is keenly aware of those forces which are most relevant to his behavior at any given time. He accurately understands himself, the individuals and the group he is dealing with, and the company and broader social environment in which he operates, and certainly he is able to assess the present readiness for growth of his subordinates. . . . The successful leader is one who is able to behave appropriately in the light of these perceptions.[1]

A tall order! Little wonder that effective leaders at every organizational level are in short supply.

Effective supervisors are made, not born. A researcher in the area of leadership who had left it for 15 years remarked that he felt he had been away 15 minutes—so little progress had been made. And if he were talking about a significant theory supported by convincing evidence that the theory worked, he would have been correct.

Various researchers took off from Carlyle's assertion that some people are born leaders and assembled a list of traits that all effective leaders had in common, such as energy, self-confidence, intelligence (but maybe not too much intelligence), decisiveness, persuasiveness,

---

[1]R. Tannenbaum and W. Schmidt, "How to Choose a Leadership Pattern," *Harvard Business Review*, March-April 1958, p. 101.

and so on. Each researcher came up with a personal laundry list. The problem was that the attempts to validate the various laundry lists turned out to be useless as indicators of how to select a leader or how the effective leader should behave once selected. Sometimes leaders with the requisite traits succeeded; sometimes they failed. In any case, the correlations between the traits and the behavior that marked the success or failure were too indistinct to be useful.

A more ambitious effort conducted by researchers at Ohio State classified all leaders into two broad categories (not necessarily exclusive) of leadership style:

1 Consideration—a dimension that reflected the degree to which the leader is considerate of the persons he or she leads.
2 Initiation of structure—a dimension that reflects the degree to which the leader organizes and defines the superior-subordinate job relationship. The leader plays a large part in determining the who, what, and when of the job.

As we mentioned, the two styles are not exclusive. Leaders who are sensitive to the needs of their subordinates could be high on initiation and still show consideration in their initiations. And if the subordinates, in turn, were people who didn't place a high value on autonomy, on doing their own thing, they might respond positively to such a manager. In general, however, it's not possible to label one style or the other as consistently more effective. Generally, morale seems higher with a considerate employee-centered style. But productivity is the more important variable for any manager. And as we have seen before, there's little correlation between morale and productivity. The manager who craves to be liked, who always remembers the line that "love flees authority," is likely to end up with a bunch of low-producing, highly contented slobs.

FIEDLER'S CONTINGENCY THEORY

An ambitious research effort is the one conducted by Fred Fiedler and his associates over the past dozen years to determine the existence of basic leadership styles and, more importantly, to discover which leadership style is appropriate in what situation. According to Fiedler, there are no born leaders—merely people with the potential to be successful leaders under certain conditions or resounding failures under other conditions.

What are the basic leadership styles? How do you determine what kind of leader an individual will make? How do you go about slotting the leader into the situation in which he or she will be effective?

Fiedler identifies two basic leadership styles as task-oriented or relationship-oriented, reminiscent of the Ohio State division into consideration-oriented or relationship-oriented. To determine leadership orientation, a test should be administered in which one identifies the least preferred coworker (LPC). The leader, claims Fiedler, who identifies his or her least preferred coworker in relatively favorable terms, "not a bad person, really—we just couldn't see eye-to-eye," is relationship-oriented; whereas, the leader who paints the least preferred coworker in bad terms, "a no-good idiot," for example, is task-oriented.

How do you go about matching leaders to situations? A relatively complex job is depicted graphically below. (See Figure 10-1.) The other major element in the theory is the degree to which the leader has control and influence—what Fiedler calls "situational favorableness." This, in turn, is measured on three subscales: leader-member relations, task structure, and position power. Leaders have more control and influence if (1) their members support them, (2) they know exactly what to do and how to do it, and (3) they are in a position to reward and punish their subordinates. Over fifty studies conducted by Fiedler have

FIGURE 10-1 Schematic representation of the performance of relationship- and task-motivated leaders in different situational favorableness conditions

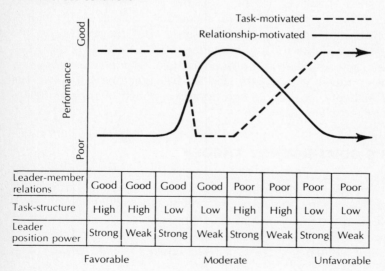

Leader-member relations	Good	Good	Good	Good	Poor	Poor	Poor	Poor
Task-structure	High	High	Low	Low	High	High	Low	Low
Leader position power	Strong	Weak	Strong	Weak	Strong	Weak	Strong	Weak

Favorable	Moderate	Unfavorable

found a consistent relationship: Task-oriented leaders tend to perform best in situations in which their power and influence are either very high or very low, while relationship-motivated leaders tend to perform best in situations in which their influence and power are moderate.

Where do we go from here? What are the implications of Fiedler's contingency model for leadership selection and leadership training? If a leader is ineffective, there are two remedies: Change the motivation structure or change the situation. Fiedler pretty much despairs of the former approach: "I don't really think that you can make someone who is cold and businesslike into a warm, cuddly leader in the course of a few hours or a few days." Precisely. What can be done is to change, or at least recognize, the situation and move the leader into a situation in which she or he can be effective. If personalities can't be changed, work on the organizational variables.

> The relationship-minded Baker has just been transferred to manager of the housewares department—a sore spot—from the book and record department where his performance had been outstanding. Only housewares is a different kind of turf. His inexperience is working against him; he couldn't restructure the job if he wanted to. Several old-timers resented his appointment and stirred up the rest of the group against him, so the job is low on support. And the mass of red tape that restricts raises and promotions weakens his power. Obviously, Baker's situation is unfavorable, and he is likely to fail unless steps are taken to correct it. Like doing what? Baker can share his decision-making power with others in the department, a move that is congenial to his basic style and should increase his support among the group. He can start reading everything he can about merchandising in his new area—a step that should influence his ability to structure the task. By doing this and other things, soon Baker can help and be helped to change the situation to the point where it is moderately favorable. Of course, he must avoid equally changing the situation to the point where it is highly favorable—at which point his performance presumably would decline. Fiedler sums up his leadership formula thus: "If you avoid jobs in which you are likely to fail, you are bound to be a success."

How seriously should we take Fiedler? How valid are his ideas? Certainly Fiedler has made a contribution in stressing the importance of the interaction between the individual and the situation in understanding effective leadership. He has also attempted to pinpoint some of the more important variables. On the other hand, it is difficult to go all out for his theory. The least preferred coworker scores measure attitudes, not basic personality structure. It's difficult to use Fiedler's

280

CHAPTER 10

theory to justify his conclusion that personalities come in more or less immutable molds. Again, by his own admission, LPC scores measure priorities or goals, not leadership behavior. In some situations, the high LPC leader might be quite single-minded about achieving the task.

At the empirical level, Fiedler is like Herzberg. Every experiment conducted by him and his associates has validated the theory; in experiments conducted by outsiders, some have tended to validate the theory, while others have tended to disprove it. The disparity provides further ammunition for the skeptic.

VROOM'S CONTINGENCY MODEL OF DECISION MAKING

The other leadership theory that has attracted a lot of attention in recent years is Victor Vroom's contingency model of decision making. Unlike Fiedler, Vroom believes that leaders can learn to lead, that they can modify or enlarge their repertoire of styles to match their growing awareness of which style is appropriate in certain situations. Vroom concentrates on a single dimension of leadership—decision making— and within that dimension, on a single issue—the degree to which the leader shares decision making with subordinates as a group. As Vroom sees it, there is no across-the-board resolution of the problem. It all depends on the situation. Sometimes the leader should make a decision autocratically; sometimes the decision should be made in a highly participative way; and sometimes it should be made in between these two.

Vroom and his associate Philip Yetton have developed a highly sophisticated and complex model—a kind of decision-making tree—to guide the manager in choosing how to approach any given decision. Vroom identifies five basic modes of decision making. (See Figure 10-2.) In AI, the manager makes the decision without consulting subordinates; in AII, the manager gets information from subordinates before making the decision. In CI, the manager consults subordinates individually and gets their suggestions before making the decision; in CII, the advice seeking takes the form of a group meeting. Finally, in GII, the leader abdicates the decision making and functions as the chairperson of a meeting that seeks a consensus as to what should be done.

What style works best under what situation? Again, it's a question of balancing several considerations and answering several questions:

How important is quality in the decision?
Does the manager possess sufficient information to make a high-quality decision?

Is the problem structured?
Is acceptance by subordinates crucial to effective implementation?
If the manager personally makes the decision, is it reasonably certain that the subordinates will accept it?

FIGURE 10-2 Decision process flowcharts (feasible set)

A   Does the problem possess a quality requirement?
B   Do I have sufficient information to make a high-quality decision?
C   Is the problem structured?
D   Is acceptance of the decision by subordinates important for effective implementation?
E   If I were to make the decision by myself, am I reasonably certain that it would be accepted by my subordinates?
F   Do subordinates share the organizational goals to be attained in solving this problem?
G   Is conflict among subordinates likely in preferred solutions?

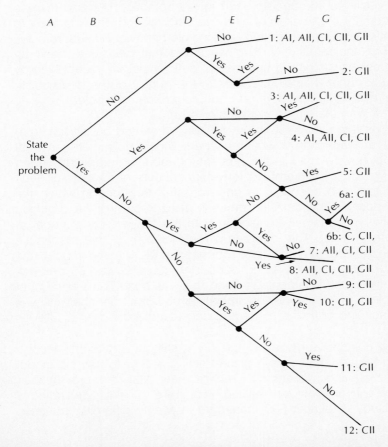

Do subordinates share the organization's goals to be attained in solving this problem?

Will there be some conflict among subordinates as to which is the best solution?

In most cases, more than one decision process squares with the model. "There is considerable evidence," asserts Vroom, "that the time required to make a decision . . . increases with the intensity of involvement or participation of subordinates. Thus a time-efficient model [which he terms Model A] would select the most autocratic alternative within the feasible set, a choice that would be clearly indicated in crisis or emergency situations in which one seeks to minimize the number of man-hours that enter into making the decision." However, Model B, the developmental model, opts for the most participative process within the feasible set. Not only is there a likelihood that participation may improve the quality of the decision and its acceptability, but also there is an enhancement of the skills of all those participating which is likely to lead to better informed and more responsible behavior by subordinates in the future. Incidentally, Vroom has found that decisions made by managers usually go wrong because of deficiencies in acceptance by subordinates rather than deficiencies in the quality of the decision. In short, the decision looked good, but subordinates wouldn't buy it. Therefore, it was the wrong decision after all.

What about the validity of Vroom's theory? It started out as a normative theory, a description of what managers should do rather than what they did do; however, it's in the process of acquiring empirical underpinnings. Vroom has assembled forty-six accounts of successful decisions and forty-two accounts of unsuccessful decisions in which the manager specified the decision process used in solving the problem. (None of the managers were familiar with the Vroom-Yetton model at the time they made the decision.) The finding? If the manager's method of dealing with the case corresponded with the model, the probability of the decision being dubbed successful was 65 percent. Not an overwhelming percentage—and this was based on a handful of cases subject to plenty of contamination because the analysis was after the fact and after the managers had learned the model. Still it's suggestive.

For more conclusive evidence, the jury is still out on Vroom's theory. Vroom and his associates have given training in how to use the model to several thousand managers in recent years. Has it improved their batting average on decision making? They are currently designing a follow-up study of almost 200 managers in twenty different countries, which, we hope, will answer the question. In the interim, it's clear that Vroom and company have made a contribution. Successful decision making is perhaps the most conclusive single index of a successful leader. The degree of participation the leader grants subordinates, in turn, has a lot to do with both the quality and acceptability of the decision. As we have seen in Chapter 5, participation has its pluses and minuses—a discussion that roughly parallels the points made by Vroom in his decision-making rules. We would add only one caveat: the intelligence of the group. A leader who faces a stupid group should hesitate to use participation even when the rules indicate that acceptability is important. A consolation might be that it is generally easier to bully the less intelligent than the bright. In any event, Vroom's theory is useful. He has made a suggestive diagnosis within a limited framework of the existing styles of leadership. And his diagnosis should help managers to become more aware of the considerations to be taken into account in any decision-making situation. Of course, we don't expect any manager to make a schematic analysis à la Vroom before a decision is made—although it might be a good idea with any important or ticklish decision. Nevertheless, a general awareness of the factors that Vroom postulates should increase the manager's understanding of the situation and contribute to better decisions.

CONTINGENCIES—CONTINGENCIES

So far we have established that the situation's the thing. The behavioral style that works with the leader in one situation can spell disaster in another. All right. Then the key to effective leadership must be to somehow classify situations and to point out those in which one style of leadership is effective and another one ineffective. This approach works up to a point. It works well with the extremes.

Close supervision is the appropriate and effective style for some types of work and work groups, whereas general supervision suits other work groups. Within the same organization or even the same office or plant, the same dominant style, whether permissive or close, may be just right in one area, tolerable in a second area, and destructive in a third. As Professor Leavitt of Stanford University put it, "The degree of latitude or control that is applied to a particular function is being selected more and more in order to expedite that function. Large organizations cannot be managed as unified wholes with a single managerial strategy equally appropriate for its varied subsections."

Is the Job Repetitive or Creative?

Let's apply this to a couple of supervisors and the different functions they perform in the same level of job. Brad Mason is a hatch supervisor working the piers in Seattle. Every ship that docks presents different problems. The winches, hatches, booms, and tackle, even the people down the hatch—all are different with each ship. Getting the cargo unloaded calls for a quick, undogmatic mind and a method of getting things done by showing people what has to be done and then giving them the proverbial rope. The tasks are unique, ill-defined, and dispersed. Brad Mason practices general supervision—otherwise, he's dead.

Sally Epstein has a quite different job. She is in charge of customer inquiries for Helpers A-Day, a large credit-card organization. Nine-tenths of the inquiries fall into relatively few categories and are answered with a form response. Any other approach would lead to inconsistencies, spiraling costs in handling, and general chaos. Sally knows the rules and makes random checks on a set schedule to make sure they're being followed. She has the job laid out in front of her and follows it every step along the way. She doesn't ask for advice because she doesn't need it. Sally Epstein practices close supervision—otherwise, her job makes little sense.

Obviously, we have indulged in hyperbole. Few people have jobs that dictate a style of supervision as precisely as those of Mason and Epstein, but the point still holds. Most supervisors have subordinates whose work falls somewhere between the two broad categories: repetitive and creative. In the repetitive job, employees repeat the same task over and over again for extended periods of time. Their tasks are usually routine and unchallenging, and the emphasis is on perserverance and discipline, self-imposed or otherwise. In the creative job, employees apply their skills to more demanding tasks that are usually varied, challenging, and longer in duration. Contrast, for example, the typical assembly-line worker versus the electrician in the maintenance department. Would anyone argue that the same style of supervision will be equally effective in both cases?

There is one study—unfortunately it's unique—suggesting that what we might call the general style of supervision is the most effective style. The study conducted at General Electric Co. showed that the most effective leader—as judged by the bosses—was the leader who practiced general supervision. OK, but what does this mean? It means that managers are more likely to (1) do work different from the work of their subordinates, (2) focus on long-range rather than short-range problems, and (3) spend a lot of time on on-the-job training.

The General Electric study observed:

> The least effective foremen spent the greatest percentage of their time finding immediate solutions to short-range production problems, while the most effective foremen spent the greatest percentage of their time on activities which involved planning and organizing the longer-range aspects of the job. The less effective foremen spent more time checking on work progress or status, securing materials, supervising materials or production movement, and similar activities which successful managers apparently delegate. Probably because of their greater emphasis on training employees, their belief in their abilities to carry out their assigned tasks without checking and greater success in organizing the work of their groups, better foremen did not find it necessary to continuously check the conditions in their area.

Here is a summary of the findings on how the two groups of GE foremen spent their time.

| | Foremen | |
Activity	Effective	Ineffective
Production	20%	40%
Personnel administration	23%	12%
Equipment and methods	14%	8%
Quality	6%	6%

There were similar differences in the pattern of communication between supervisors and their work groups:

| | Foremen | |
Type of communication	Effective	Ineffective
Giving *specific* work orders	3%	15%
Giving *general* work orders	5%	1%
Passing information to the group or engaging in two-way discussions with members of the work group	67%	47%
Receiving information from workers	25%	37%

The study comes to this conclusion:

> When the more effective foremen found it necessary to give direction to the work of their employees, they would do so in a general way, giving explanations and suggestions, but leaving details of method and sequence up to the worker. The less effective foreman, on the other hand, gave a far greater number of direct work orders, without explaining why a job should be done, or how the specific order related to the overall work pattern.

Managers who practice general supervision develop a climate in which workers feel free to bring their problems to them. In this atmosphere, subordinates ask for help and information when it is needed, thus reducing the supervisor's need to give instructions. As one foreman commented:

> As far as getting action is concerned, it doesn't make much difference whether you *tell* a man what to do or he *asks* you. But it makes all the difference in the world how he feels. So I try to be available for questions instead of telling people.

The GE study found that effective foremen were aware of this difference: "The lower-rated foremen spent more time seeking information from others, while the higher-rated foremen spent more time answering requests for information," as well as in improving their relations with their bosses, staff sections, and other departments. Here is a summary of how these supervisors spent their time.

	Foremen	
People dealt with	**Effective**	**Ineffective**
Staff and service people	32%	20%
Own subordinates	19%	17%

Limitations of General Style

On the surface, the conclusion might be that the general style of supervision is the one best style. Admittedly, it's the way in which we would like to be supervised, but that's an incidental consideration (and a desirable admission). The evidence suggests that the general style of supervision works best, if at all, under a fairly complex set of conditions.

1 *When the work group itself is basically intelligent and interested in the job.* There is an obvious degree of difference in the delegation that is feasible among nurses in a hospital and inmates in a prison. More important is the distinction involved in the recent research by Lorwin and Craig in which the quality of work done by trainees varied in relation to how the managers acted toward them. With the more competent trainees, the managers practiced general supervision. In contrast, with the duds—in this case, contrived failures unknown to any of the participants—they practiced close supervision. The authors' conclusion: "Studies that have shown leadership styles causing employee reactions may have had things backward; in fact, employee behaviors and attitudes were influencing the styles of leaders."

2 *Where it is a high-status job.* Here's another important distinction—a matter of power and status. Assembly-line workers have little pride in their skills, no feeling of importance within the organization, and even little sense of self. Their relatively small self-confidence comes from their sense of mobility, but within these limits they still can be bossed and even pushed around. This is not the case with maintenance electricians. Their superior economic position, sure knowledge of the scarcity of their skills, and pride in their craft combine to give them a firm sense of their strategic position within the organization—and generally a determination to exploit it for whatever it's worth. Few supervisors would attempt to practice close supervision with maintenance electricians—and those that do probably do not succeed.

3 *Where consistency and coordination are relatively of minor consequence.* For a dramatic contrast, compare the auto assembly-line worker and the college professor. With the assembly-line worker, standardization and conformity are the be-all-and-end-all of the job; with the professor, conformity, at least in theory, is the enemy of excellence and performance.

4 *Where technology encourages discretion.* Again, the auto assembly-line worker is at one end of the spectrum. At the other end are the surgeon in an operating room, an aircraft pilot, and a ship's captain. The time spent with the boss is also a factor. A study of parcel delivery service showed that drivers, who spent only minutes a day with their boss, preferred an autocratic boss, while the people who handled parcels wanted a less authoritarian supervisor.

5 *Where subordinates desire responsibility.* As we have seen before, people—and employees are people—vary greatly in their desire for responsibility. For the four or five employees who desire more responsibility, more autonomy, and so on, there is at least one who wants only a routine job—and a closely supervised one at that. To cite just one example, out of the five original women in the relay assembly experiment at Hawthorne, two had to be replaced early on because they failed to respond positively to the extra autonomy and responsibility on the job. A study of two hospital wards further highlights the distinction.

The first head nurse (Ms. Smith), although courteous, was uncompromising with nurses who violated regulations. She insisted that conversations be kept to a minimum and handed out detailed work assignments to her subordinates. The second head nurse (Ms. Rogers) had a more informal, almost kidding relationship with her subordinates. She consulted with them about problems and changes and succeeded in developing a strong feeling of camaraderie on the floor.

You might suppose that all the nurses would have preferred Ms. Rogers' floor to Ms. Smith's—but they didn't. The hospital let nurses choose which floor they wanted to work on; both floors were quite popular, but with different groups of nurses. In general, the older nurses liked the security of Ms. Smith's floor, where everything went according to a predetermined routine. As one older nurse put it: "I honestly feel I need a responsible person nearby to supervise me. I need guidance and therefore I prefer to work where there is fairly close supervision. . . . I like to do things in an orderly way. . . . [On Ms. Rogers' floor], things are done too sloppily."

Most of the younger nurses, however, preferred the independence permitted by Ms. Rogers.

6 *Where general supervision is a consistent pattern.* It's an unfortunate truism that more important than any manager's style of leadership—especially that of a first- or second-level manager—is the general style of leadership that prevails in the organization. A manager who attempts general supervision in an organization that practices an autocratic style is an anachronism on the road to disaster. Consider the study reported by Morse and Reiner in which an insurance company experimented with general and closely supervised styles among similar groups of employees. What were the results? Over the short run (the study lasted only a year), productivity improved in both groups—however, per employee, productivity was slightly more in the closely supervised group where the average work load was also increased. More to our point, when the employees exercised delegation in an area that higher management, to put it mildly, believed was inappropriate—they decided they wouldn't work for a couple of days—the experiment was terminated along with the services of the vice-president responsible for initiating the experiment.

The Autocratic Style of Supervision

Can the autocratic manager be an effective leader? Are there any work situations in which leaders who practice close supervision can use their roles as the prime dispensers of rewards and punishments to motivate their subordinates? Or does this combination always tend to depress morale and lower production?

There is little question that an autocratic behavior style is the preferred style among many managers, that they combine a low tolerance for ambiguity—a preference for a stable and highly predictable environment that they control—with a high tolerance for unpopularity or, at least, an indifference or insensitivity to the symptoms of unpopularity. Given the choice between being loved or being feared, they would opt for the latter every time.

We are familiar with one such autocratic manager. Let's call him Charlie Brink, who is editor-in-chief of a small and reasonably successful book publishing house that concentrates on "how to" books for various specialized consumer audiences.

Charlie is into everything. In his typical 80-hour work week, he has the time to make all the important decisions. Constant pressure is maintained for production—and more production. His decisions are unpredictable. Favoritism runs rampant. Christmas cards are sent to the loyalists on his staff—those he thought he could count on personally—the rest are ignored. Turnover is predictably high; so are the incidences of psychosomatic ailments like ulcers and migraine headaches. Back-biting among subordinates frequently devours sizable chunks of the work day. Yet higher management is, by and large, quite pleased with Charlie's performance. Fewer people are turning out more manuscripts. Turnover is at a record high, but costs are low. Higher management is probably more aware of Charlie's unpopularity than he is, but they are content to look the other way. Charlie seems set in his ways—and in his job.

How come? What are the conditions that have made Charlie Brink's style of leadership quite effective in maintaining production? First, higher management is understandably more cost-conscious than quality-conscious. With this kind of material, it's the sizzle that sells, not the quality of the steak. Charlie's style inhibits creativity and imagination, but these are qualities not much in demand in this kind of operation. Editorial personnel are generally loners, capable of plenty of griping but with little capacity for cohesive action. There's also a surplus of people with medium-grade editorial skills—a buyer's, not a seller's, market. Finally, there's the presence of the resident "workaholic," who is willing to endure the number of hours necessary to make this kind of supervision reasonably effective given the other elements in the situation.

A distinction should be made, as David McClelland points out, between the autocratic supervisor preoccupied with personal power, as Charlie is, and the autocratic manager concerned with institutional power. The former is like the affiliative manager who views leadership as a popularity contest that must be won and cares more about the happiness of particular individuals than the well-being of the whole group. In their behavior, both of these managers constantly violate the concept of fairness: affiliative managers by consistently favoring those with whom they have developed close personal relationships and the personal-power-driven managers by rewarding not compatibility but personal loyalty—defined as the almost automatic acquiescence to their ideas and directions. Neither type of manager gives top priority to performance, although the personal-power-driven manager usually manages to confuse the issue by identifying loyalty as performance.

The institutional-power-driven manager, in contrast, gives top priority to performance and is perceived by subordinates as being fair in the distribution of rewards and punishments. This manager's perception of "their just desserts" closely parallels their own; she or he practices what George Homans calls distributive justice.

It's also unfair to classify the institutional-power-driven manager among those who practice autocratic management. Quite the contrary, these managers, whom McClelland identifies as the people you need if you want to maximize both morale and productivity ("Where productivity and morale are primary goals, the power-driven manager does the job best"), are more inclined to practice general supervision. He found that 63 percent of the best managers preferred the helping hand to the authoritarian order. True, they had strong power needs, but they had learned to express them in a noncoercive way.

What can we say about autocratic management? It can be made to work—under certain conditions—although high performance seldom goes with it. It works better in the long run than in the short run. It works better (1) with white-collar workers than with blue-collar workers; (2) when too many people are chasing too few jobs; (3) with routine jobs than with creative jobs; and (4) when the job is tightly program-med by definition or when a manager has the time, drive, and energy to oversee the details of each assignment.

Pragmatic Supervision

In a sense, we're talking about the suppressed style of supervision, more practiced than written about and more written about than admit-ted to. And never—but never—found in the organization manual. Many managers who practice pragmatic supervision actually would prefer to practice general supervision; however, the situations in which they find themselves are unfavorable.

As a general rule, general supervision works best—if indeed it works at all—under conditions in which subordinates work voluntarily, even cheerfully, toward the objectives of the organization. To assume that such conditions usually hold, as George Strauss points out, is naive.

> It [the philosophy of internalized motivation] is somewhat idealistic. It assumes that somehow the needs of the organization and the needs of the individual can both be maximized at the same time so that what is good for the one will be good for the other. Clearly, this rarely, if ever, is the case. Normally there must be some kind of tradeoff. Employees will want more satisfaction, management will want more production, and where the balance is to be poised between the two is a matter to be solved by bargaining, not by scientific evidence![2]

The pragmatic manager uses the trade-off as the heart and center of an approach to management. As we have said, preferences and predispositions may lie elsewhere—toward a general, or even toward an autocratic, style of supervision. But a sense of the situation per-suades a manager to do otherwise. Maybe there is no way of enriching a job and providing intrinsic satisfactions, or maybe higher manage-ment couldn't care less about job enrichment—many higher manage-ments don't. And the possibilities for participation are unpromising. Or the manager may face a cohesive work group such as the ones described in Chapter 5 that combine status and strategic skills with a conscious determination to exercise their clout to the utmost. Under either set of conditions—the inability to provide internal motivators or the inability to pressure subordinates into production—the manager must fall back on implicit bargaining as the best available tool. In return for a satisfactory level of production—satisfaction generally

[2]George Strauss and Leonard R. Sayles, *Personnel: The Human Problems of Management*, 3d ed., Prentice-Hall, Englewood Cliffs, N.J., 1972, p. 134.

being defined on the low side—the pragmatic manager offers a variety of favors, exceptions, and privileges.

> Jane Boutwell arrived at 11 A.M. when she knew that her boss needed a report that she had been working on finished by 10 A.M. "Boy, the connections from Staten Island were lousy this morning," she said, accompanied by a wan smile. Her boss, Susan Smith, thought to herself, "She must have had quite a night if she can't come up with a better excuse than that." But she said nothing to Jane, only responding with an equally wan smile. After all, most of the time Jane was a good worker. Why rile her by doubting her excuse. Live and let live. That's what we try to do.

> "Uh, oh. Here comes young Casanova again," Bill Boulger thought as he saw Steve Guardabassi walking down the aisle headed for his office. A couple of weeks ago, Steve had asked if he could use his phone—"The call is kind of confidential," he added with a wink. Bill said sure, took the hint, and left the office while Steve called someone, presumably a lady, and presumably not his wife. Bill knew what the request was going to be before Steve opened his mouth—it was the fifth or sixth time in two weeks. "Maybe it's time to tell this tomcat off," Bill mused to himself. However, like Susan, Bill said nothing. Steve, although young, was the informal leader of his group and one of the best metal-polishers in the shop. A good person to have on your side.

Of such stuff are favors made—extra-long, unscheduled coffee breaks; quitting a little early if the quota is met; toleration of questionable lateness and suspect absenteeism; on-the-job visits among subordinates; and even, as the previously cited foreman did, buying coffee and doughnuts for an especially nettlesome bunch of subordinates. Fair? No. Other managers in other departments may not feel the need or resist the pressure to grant similar favors to their subordinates. Necessary? Frequently, yes. Some form of implicit bargaining, in which the level of output and the conditions under which people work are decided through an unwritten agreement between a manager and subordinates, is often the price of acceptable output and reasonably harmonious labor-management relations.

Summary

The previous description should have made one thing clear: There is no one set of management behavior that adds up to effective leadership under all climates and conditions. There is a time for general supervision, a time for pragmatic leadership, and even a time when autocratic leadership can be reasonably effective.

If leadership effectiveness were merely a popularity contest, the indications are that general supervision would win hands down. For example, a survey conducted several years ago by Scott Meyers among more than 1,300 managers in all levels at Texas Instruments showed an overwhelming preference for a developmental manager (roughly, one who practiced general supervision) over a reductive manager, regardless of the manager's values or style of supervision.

Preferences are one thing; results are something else—and something different. In their book, Marrow, Bowers, and Seashore, a trio of authorities prominently identified with the cause of participative management and general supervision, concede that "the 'goodness' of any particular social organization and of any particular set of guiding principles for social progress lies not so much in its own inherent merit as in its utility for the effective use of work facilities and work process resources."[3]

In other words, the decision to employ general, close, or pragmatic supervision should depend on the requirements of the particular work situation.

We subscribe to Fiedler's conclusion: "There are a limited number of ways in which one person can influence others to work together toward a common goal. He can coerce them, or he can coax them. He can tell people what to do and how to do it, or he can share the decision making and concentrate on his relationship with his men rather than on the execution of the job. No one has been able to show that one kind of leader is always superior or more effective." Amen.

A BALANCED THEORY OF SUPERVISION

Here we are going to present another view of the supervisor's job. The emphasis will be on *how* one does on a job rather than *what* one does. The method grows out of a great deal of social science research on what is called "interaction theory" about individual personality and behavior and its major finding that human beings like a reasonable balance in their "inputs" and "outputs." (Figure 10-3 illustrates this concept.) This reasonable balance is usually accompanied by a feeling

---

[3] A. J. Marrow, D. G. Bowers, and S. E. Seashore, *Management by Participation*, Harper & Row, New York, 1967, p. 229.

FIGURE 10-3 Interactional balance

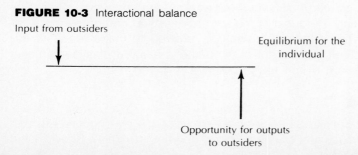

Input from outsiders

Equilibrium for the individual

Opportunity for outputs to outsiders

of well-being. When there is an imbalance, the inputs may far outweigh the outputs, the employee (or the supervisor) feels cross, imposed upon, or even angry.

But what are these inputs and outputs? Human relations, the basic building block of our working and nonworking lives, involves the interaction of people: giving and taking, talking and listening, initiating and responding. When you watch people at work, at a party, or at home, this is what you see: individuals seeking someone to listen and be responsive to them. It is as though each of us has, stored up inside, a reservoir of interactional energy that is looking to flow toward other human beings. We want to be attended to and responded to by other people.

Similarly, each of us has the capacity to take just so much of these interactional inputs. Sometimes we want to be on the giving side too. And, in fact, if there are too many inputs to us or too few opportunities for us to do the initiating, we grow restless or even hostile.

Since work is such a significant aspect of the waking day for most people, we can anticipate that people will try to utilize their reservoirs of interactional energy on the job. To be specific, supervisors have to be aware of their own efforts to balance inputs and outputs and, even more important, to balance the needs of their subordinates.

Thus many of the things we have been saying about order giving, change, communications, discipline, and other administrative problems have interactional implications. Managers who are giving orders, raising questions, and communicating new policies are using up some of their own output reservoir—and perhaps getting a good deal of satisfaction in the bargain. But they are also draining off some of their subordinates' input capacity. The reverse is also true: The boss who stops to listen to an employee's complaint or suggestion, or seeks out an opinion and lets that person talk, is providing a much-needed outlet for that employee (which may help to even out the balance in the boss-subordinate relationship).

So the wise manager seeks to provide some rough balance in the relationship with each subordinate. This doesn't mean that precise counts should be kept showing every time the manager takes the initiative in making a request of the subordinate and compares this with the number of times the subordinate is allowed to make requests for information, for help, or just for a sympathetic ear. But this does make the manager aware of the rough balance involved.

RESPONDING

Supervisors attempt to balance off these initiations by encouraging the subordinates to initiate to them. How do they do this? They make themselves approachable. It's easy to talk first about the contrary type—unapproachable supervisors. They're easy to spot. Whenever anyone tries to speak to them, to stop them for a question or comment, it is obvious that they're very, very busy and preoccupied, and they clearly communicate that they wish they hadn't been interrupted at such an important moment.

The opposite of these are the supervisors who appear to welcome employee inputs, who don't limit their conversation only to the times they have something to say. Even when the employee is interrupting something—most supervisors are pressed for time—and even when he has a silly request to make or is quarrelsome, the supervisor hears that employee out *responsively.*

All of us can distinguish between a responsive listener and one who isn't interested in us. The responsive person lets us do a good share of the talking, appears to be concentrating on what we have to say, nods frequently or says, "Yes, I understand," and shows by some questions and comments that he or she is following our train of thought and not simply pursuing his or her own. This fragment may illustrate the difference.

With the *responsive* supervisor, a scene went this way:

> *Subordinate:* No matter what I do today, I can't seem to make things go right, I don't know if it's me or this equipment or the heat in here.
> *Boss:* There are those days—I have them myself. What's gone wrong?
> *Subordinate:* Well, first thing this morning I called up. . . .

With the *unresponsive* supervisor, this was the pattern:

> *Subordinate:* (Same opening remark as above.)
> *Boss:* You know, that reminds me. I don't think you've been paying enough attention to those special orders.
> *Subordinate:* I know I sometimes forget, but let me tell you first about what happened this morning when I called. . . .
> *Boss:* Never mind this morning. Let's be sure you have that procedure down cold that we talked about yesterday.
> *Subordinate:* But can't I just tell you. . . .

Sure, what the employee had to say may not have been of any great consequence. The point is not only that the boss will never know what the employee was trying to say. More important, or at least just as much so, the boss will have lost an opportunity to let the subordinate initiate something and to show the employee that he or she is willing to be responsive. (Techniques of encouraging a person to talk are discussed in Chapter 9.) To be responsive means following rather than

leading the employee, listening rather than dominating, being interested in other people rather than being preoccupied with yourself.

Note that balancing off your inputs does not depend on why the
subordinate wants to contact you. Even after hearing the employee out,
you may not know for sure. More important, if you are adequately
responsive, you may not need to know. As an example, let's hear out
the subordinate we just cut off:

> So I called up to ask Repair Service when we were going to get that
> typewriter back we had sent last week, and the first thing I knew they were
> giving me a hard-luck story about how busy they were and how every
> department expects its work to be done first. So I told them that we're
> already one machine short, our work was being held up, and they had
> received it four days ago. They said they would look into it and get back to
> me this afternoon. But you know how reliable they are. . . .

Can you tell what he is really saying? Perhaps he wants to brag that
he was vigorously defending the department's needs. Perhaps he
wants sympathy because he has had a hard day. Perhaps he wants
the boss to express appreciation or confidence in him or to help him
deal with the outside repairman. But most important, he wants the
manager to be responsive to his initiation: his story about that morning's problem with the repairer. Even though that may be the *last* thing
the manager is interested in, and it really isn't a crucial problem no
matter how or when it is settled, the boss is letting the subordinate take
the initiative for a short period and is getting involved in the life and
world of the subordinate. In the process, he will have earned "points,"
so to speak, that will make him or her more responsive to the next
inquiry or request.

PERSONALITY DIFFERENCES

The supervisor will also have to be aware of some differences among
employees with regard to what employees require in the way of responsiveness. Here are two typical cases:

> Al Forter is always seeking you out. He has a hundred different things a
> day that seem to require your attention, or at least he thinks so. Your
> problem with Al is to keep him from monopolizing your time and to get him
> to restrain his impulse to initiate you. This means that at times you'll tell him
> you're too busy and perhaps you don't walk into his area any more often
> than you have to. Otherwise, some of your subordinates will begin to think
> you and he "have something going"—and favoritism ruins morale. Of
> course, he'll need some of your attention to satisfy that strong craving for a

responsive ear, perhaps somewhat more than others but not as much more as he wants.

Marie Incerelli is very quiet. If you leave it to her, you'll never see her because she has no social initiative. But that's bad because, without such contact, your relationship will deteriorate. So you have to go out of your way to make it easy for her to take some initiative—stopping by her work area, calling her to show her something, and then encouraging conversation.

Thus the supervisor seeks to develop a balance for different personalities, always being aware that some will demand too much and some, too little. And you must take the responsibility of making any total exchanges come out relatively even.

Internal and External Balancing

Note that this balancing involves both the initiation of the contact and the internal structuring of the conversation. The manager must learn something about how different personalities carry on a conversation in order to deal with people effectively on a face-to-face basis. Will a manager be confronting a sphinx or a Niagara Falls of chatter?

The key concept here is *synchronization*. Internal synchronization is much like the external balancing of inputs and outputs that we have been describing. Individuals want the sense of easy, smooth interactions with other human beings. That is, they don't want long periods of silence or competition with another person for the chance to talk. Experienced supervisors learn to size up each person they will have to deal with and to make minor adjustments in their own patterns of interaction to complement the interaction habits of that person.

Thus, with some people who are rather long-winded, they will have to restrain themselves because of the likelihood of cutting people off or interrupting before they are through. Other employees may be very laconic, and after the supervisor has said something or explained a new process, will only grunt or say a few words in response. Again, if the supervisor is not careful, there won't be a synchronization because he will not be prepared to fill in the gaps. With short-winded people, supervisors have to be able to speak frequently to avoid those uncomfortable (and stressful) silences when neither is speaking and both become strained.

INTERACTION AS A CONTROL MEASURE

Once managers become sensitive to these differences in customary patterns of interaction among subordinates, they are all set to measure subordinates' morale in a rather direct and unobtrusive fashion. People who are angry or disappointed almost always reveal their feelings by their interactional behavior. Of course, precisely how a person shows that he or she is upset is distinctive with the individual. But each person changes consistently when emotions change. Therefore, although one's words may seek to cover up feelings, the observant manager can penetrate the verbal facade to assess the true emotional feelings. Most of us have done the same thing (although we may not be conscious of it) in assessing the feelings of our friends and close associates. We instinctively feel when they are relatively happy as compared with when they are upset.

All that is being said is that this "instinctive" assessment can be more precise and self-conscious. Listen to this supervisor explaining how she does it:

> I know the minute I approach Heyfritz whether or not it's going to be a good time to add one of those extra jobs to his work load. If I more or less have to drag every word out of him—if he hardly responds at all when I speak to him about the weather or how his golf game is going—I know he is brooding about something. If I try to deal with him on a serious issue when he is like that, it is likely to lead to an argument because he'll hardly answer me and that, in turn, upsets me, and I start to speak more strongly and he'll mumble something about being pushed and I'll get even madder at him. This way, if I deal with him on difficult subjects when I can tell he's in good shape, there are unlikely to be any of these repercussions, which involve me in a disciplinary problem.
>
> Now, Callahan is just the opposite. When she's disturbed, I have all I can do to keep her away—she wants to blast my ear off with talk. She's not that way normally—only when something is bothering her. So when I have to go and show her a mistake she's made in filling out an order, I wait until I can hear that she's back to her normal give and take.

Thus some people become more voluble and others more reclusive under stress. Still for others, the difference between equilibrium and tension consists of more subtle changes in the way they handle interaction. In talking with them, the supervisor will notice that they are just somewhat less responsive—that is, there will be lulls or blank spots in the conversation. These are caused by the subordinate's failing to respond immediately when the boss pauses in conversation. For others, the boss will notice more interruptions and won't be able to quite finish saying something before the other person breaks in. Normally, these same people are easy to talk to—their inputs are nicely synchronized with the supervisor's inputs. The absence of synchronization is the red light that indicates trouble is brewing!

REPRESENTATION

Having covered two major supervisory behavioral patterns, initiating (or directing) and responding, we have to complicate the picture by adding a third: representation. By representation we mean the supervisor's action in getting the attention of outsiders to the problems of subordinates. That is, supervisors stand between their groups and the rest of the organization. They are the proverbial persons in the middle. Their superiors expect them to transmit instructions and directions to their people. Similarly, other department heads make requests through supervisors.

Significantly, the reverse flow is watched very closely by subordinates. Does the boss give as good as she gets? Does she defend and protect their interests, resist unfair demands, and seek to use her status and power to protect her people? Here are just a few descriptions of bosses who do this:

> We would do anything for Ms. Cary because she really takes care of us. If someone hasn't been given a new uniform on time, doesn't get a merit increase when she deserves it, is given a hard time by another supervisor, you know that within five minutes Cary will be up in the front office telling them that they can't do that to "her people." She's a real fighter when it comes to anyone trying to take advantage of us.

> Garfelli is a pretty tough supervisor. If you do anything wrong he tells you about it in no uncertain terms, and his language isn't always what they teach you in school. But most of us couldn't care less how much he shouts at us because we know that when the chips are down—when the big shots ignore us—Garfelli is right in there punching. When you work in his department, you know you have somebody who watches over your interests. So he never has to worry about us backing him up when he asks a favor; we know he has never let us down yet. He's a real scrapper.

Most subordinates know that it is a lot easier for a boss to concentrate on channeling *downward* what upper management wants than it is to channel *upward* what they want. Many managers therefore appear to their subordinates to knuckle under to the status system—to press hard downward and soft upward. They don't fight when upper management says no to a request. Many of the key decisions that affect their welfare (such as basic wage increases, work loads, clothing allowances, and some disciplinary actions) will be made outside their own departments. So they cannot expect to have a very bright future when their boss is weak-kneed and unwilling to press their demands on outsiders. Thus supervisors need to bring into balance their internal initiations and external representations, as Figure 10-3 suggests.

300

Employees recognize that an organization's resources are limited and that everyone can't win. The departments that have the best working conditions, the best jobs, and the best earnings are usually those with strong-willed bosses who expend some of their energies initiating upward. Another department may be just as deserving, but if it has too meek a supervisor, its people get less.

To be sure, a supervisor's ability to do this is dependent not simply upon his or her own energy and the courage needed to buck the status ladder, but also on the kind of boss the supervisor might have. (See Chapter 11.)

If the people at the next level of management are unresponsive, unwilling to let the supervisor initiate to them, he or she will appear impotent to subordinates. Thus upper management can help make or break a supervisor. If superiors are reasonably responsive when a supervisor says, "I need this for my people," that supervisor will be much more influential with his or her group. If they are consistently turned down by supervisors, managers will have trouble appearing to be real leaders.

Of course, the supervisor has to use good sense in performing the role of an advocate. One has to distinguish good causes from poor causes and learn how to make an effective case when representing a department. If a manager goes upstairs frequently unprepared, uninformed, or as the defender of "bad" cases, his or her demands will be more and more discounted or ignored altogether.

A manager needs to remember that subordinates are good judges of his willingness and ability to act as their representative.

CONCLUSION

There is another way of looking at all the things a supervisor handles: discipline, order giving, communications, dealing with groups, and the rest. That is, one needs to look at the overall pattern of interaction involved in any relationship with subordinates both in the group and as individuals. Subordinates will respect and follow a boss who devotes as much effort to representing their interests to outsiders, particularly upper management, as she or he does to handling internal matters. Also, they expect a manager's *responsiveness* to them to be roughly comparable with the amount of *direction* they are given. That is, managers should allow subordinates initiating to them as well as their initiating to subordinates. These three major behavioral patterns (direction, responsiveness, and representation) need to be in equilibrium if motivation and morale are to be maintained at relatively high levels.

Managers also need to be aware of individual differences in both the need and capacity of subordinates to initiate and seek responsiveness. Some subordinates will seize every opportunity to monopolize the supervisor's attention. Others will be reluctant to initiate a contact. Supervisors have to even out these differences to some extent by rationing those who initiate too much and making themselves more available to those who are unlikely to take the initiative.

These personality differences, expressed in interaction terms, help the manager to detect when an individual is under stress. Anger, fear, or hostility is shown when an individual changes his or her interaction pattern, becoming more or less active. These behavioral differences are a more reliable guide to feelings than the actual words spoken or sentiments overtly expressed.

THE EDUCATION OF GREG HORNING: APRIL 7

"Now, you see, Henry. It's very tricky here and you'd better go very slowly until you get the hang of it." Greg was out on the floor with Creegmore. The engineering department had developed a new mold which they were testing out on Creegmore's machine. It would eliminate one step in the process, but it was still in the early stages. Until they could iron out the bugs in it, it tended to break very easily. "When they demonstrated the process to me, they suggested that you hold it right here, just before it's time for the piece to come through. See?"

Greg looked up at Creegmore. "Yeah, yeah. I see," Henry said and nodded. But he was frowning and the corners of his mouth were pulling down. He obviously didn't buy engineering's suggestion.

"Unless, Henry," Greg went on, "you can think of a better way. I know you know a lot more about the actual operations than I do."

"Well, now. Let's see." Creegmore's face suddenly came alive. He bent forward to examine the new operaton. "It seems to me, if you just eased it through here instead of holding it at all, the piece would come through nice and smooth. See? Like this." Creegmore demonstrated his idea. It worked nicely—and it was faster besides.

"Say, Henry. That's fine. Better than what the engineering people said. Let's try it your way a while. If it works out, I'll tell them we've got a better method down here."

"Okay, Greg," Creegmore said, looking pleased. He started back to the job he'd been doing, but Greg stopped him.

"You know, Henry. I've been thinking about that talk we had several months ago when I first came," Greg said.

"Yeah, what about it?" Creegmore asked, his face suddenly tight again.

"Well, I think maybe you were right. Maybe industrial engineering doesn't have all the answers."

"You're damn right, they don't," Creegmore answered warmly.

"Well, look, Henry, If you can take a minute, come in and let's talk about it. I'd like to have some of your ideas."

"Now?"

"Yes. That'd be fine—if you've got the time."

"Well, sure I have, Greg," Creegmore answered quickly with a smile. "Be glad to."

"Now, for instance," Henry said, when they were settled in Greg's office. "There's the process we do on the gears. Now the job description says we're supposed to set the temperature gauge at one point and leave it that way through the whole process. But if you do that you begin to get more and more warp on the pieces when you've got a long run. Now if we vary the temperature while the run's going on—just a hair up and down—the pieces come out more regular. You see what I mean?"

"Yes, Henry. That sounds sensible. But what about the time it takes? You feel it's worth it?"

"Oh, it doesn't take up any more time. Attention—now that's another thing. You've got to watch it pretty carefully, but that's another story. And, of course, you've got to know what you're doing."

"Well, that sounds like a good idea. But what about. . . ." But Creegmore was all wound up now. He went on enthusiastically.

"And then look at what we do when the machines aren't working good. We can't get maintenance in here every time something is a little off. You know how they are—never get hold of them, anyway. Now before you told us to stick to the rules, we used to use a prod on the runners when they got out of line. It was something we developed ourselves. But we stopped using it now. But it saved us a lot of pieces. Now we either get more rejects or we have to stop using a machine sometimes and wait to have it regulated. See, these machines are almost like people—you know what I mean?" He looked at Greg, who nodded. "They all have little quirks that make them different. Those engineers don't know anything about that. Only we do—we know our own machines and we know the different things you have to do on each one to get the best output. You see what I'm getting at?"

"Yes, I do, Henry," Greg answered. "But that's one of the points of the job description, Henry. You each have *one* machine and you get the feel of it and know all the fine points of how it works. Now these refinements of yours sound good to me. I'm 100 percent for your using them." Henry smiled and started to comment, but Greg had not finished. "But this business of one person spelling another. Now that's something else—I've let Phil help you but that's a special case. If you each know your own machine other people can't get as good output from it as you can. That day Alfred came in here and you were supposed to be watching his machine. . . ."

"He had a good idea there, Greg," Henry broke in. "You ought to get him to tell you about it some time."

"Well, I will, Henry," Greg went on. "I'd like to hear everyone's ideas. But that's not my point. Now you were supposed to be watching his machine and you were way over across the room arguing about something. Now, that's what I mean, Henry. That kind of thing is bad." Seeing Henry look pleased with himself, Greg paused.

"You know, I agree with you there, Greg. But can I tell you something? I was doing your job that day. Of course, you were just fresh in here and you didn't know the ropes yet, but I shouldn't have to be haggling with the materials handlers all the time. You're the boss and you're supposed to clear all that out for us. We shouldn't have that kind of problem with them."

Greg smiled wanly, Creegmore could always make him feel a little defensive. "Let me think about that, Henry."

"Sure, Greg. You're the boss. You've got to stand up for your crew with the other departments. Take the problem we're having with the mixing department right now. They're storing more and more of their stuff in our area. Pretty soon we're not going to be able to go anywhere in here without falling over a sack of plastic pellets. It's disgusting."

"I didn't know about that."

"Well, you've seen those damn bags all over. What'd you think they were there for—decoration? They're taking advantage of us and if I were supervisor I wouldn't stand for it. You should do something about it, Greg," Henry finished, leaning over toward Greg. "They're making you look like a damn fool—letting them get away with it."

"Maybe I look like a damn fool—maybe I don't," said Greg, reddening slightly. "But you've got a point and I'll see what can be done. Thanks for the advice."

"Now the suggestions I made. . . ."

"I think we should try them. We're sort of playing it by ear—whatever works is good for the department."

"Right, Greg. I guess we see more eye to eye than I thought. I'll be getting back now. Don't forget those pellet sacks."

"No, Henry," and Greg managed a small smile. "Whatever works is good for the department," he said to himself.

The pellet problem turned out to be a bigger ball of twine than Greg had expected. When he saw Joe Barber, head of the mixing department, he found out that his predecessor had given them permission to use some of molding's space to store their plastics. Steve Phillips had also approved this allocation.

If he made any static about it, he risked causing trouble with Phillips and friction with mixing—but he had to keep good relations there. On the other hand, if he did nothing, Creegmore would think he was a coward—and the rest of the crew would probably share his feelings.

QUESTIONS

1 Point out the places in which Greg is being very responsive to Creegmore and the effect of this on Creegmore's attitudes.

2 What appears to happen to the amount people talk—the quantity of words—when the give and take is easy in conversation? Is Greg ever too responsive?

3 Can you identify any parts of the dialogue in which the easy give and take breaks down?

4 What should Greg do in relation to Creegmore if the pellet problem isn't solved? Does this mean he is not representing his group effectively?

BEHAVIORAL EXERCISE

The project is to design an advertising program to promote the sale of Pet Rocks. Sam Jones, the director of advertising, has some intuitions on the subject, but that's just what they are—intuitions, not strong convictions. Therefore, Sam tries an experiment. He divides his creative people, copywriters, artists, and so on, into three groups. To the first he says, "I want you to devise an advertising program around the general theme 'Permanent Pets.' After all, what lasts longer than a rock? And put it into a middle-class apartment setting—restricted space—the landlord doesn't like pets, the kids are out of the nest or grown-up enough not to like their parents, and so on." To the second group he gives the theme but not the setting. To the third he simply says, "Design me the best selling campaign for rocks that you can think of."

Break the class into groups of five to eight people and have an equal number of groups in each category. Give each group 30 to 45 minutes to consider the problem. When the group reassembles, or at the next class meeting, have them raise questions such as: How motivated were the participants in each group? How did the participants in the first two groups feel about the restrictions? How many people contributed ideas in each group? Did the groups reach a consensus in each case? What does the class as a whole feel is the most effective program, and why? What does this indicate about the superiority of one of the different approaches to letting the group decide?

BIBLIOGRAPHY

Ritchie, J., "Supervision," in G. Strauss, R. Miles, and C. Snow (eds.), *Organizational Behavior: Research and Issues*, Industrial Relations Research Association, 1974.

Stogdill, R., *Handbook of Leadership: A Survey of Theory and Research*, Free Press, New York, 1974.

Tannenbaum, R., and W. Schmidt, "How to Choose a Leadership Pattern," *Harvard Business Review*, March-April 1958.

Vroom, V., and T. Yetton, *Leadership and Decison-Making*, University of Pittsburgh Press, 1973.

READING

The Two Faces of Power*

DAVID C. McCLELLAND (1917-   )

David C. McClelland, professor of psychology at Harvard University
and chairman of the social relations department from 1962 to 1967,
is best known because of his work on achievement motivation. In
fact, as this chapter makes clear, he divides people into those
whose primary motivation is affiliation, those whose primary motivation is power, and those whose primary motivation is achievement.
The achievers are the artists and creative people. Generally, most
achievers are doctors, academics, and, in the business world,
entrepreneurs—all are concerned, frequently to the point of obsession, with doing the job to the best of their ability, but are relatively
unconcerned with controlling other people. What they do they
largely accomplish themselves; their satisfactions are equally personal and particular.

Everyone is in favor of achievement. Power, in contrast, has a
bad reputation. Understandably so, argues McClelland. That's because of a misunderstanding and confusion between what we call
the desire for personal power—dominance, manipulation—and the
desire for socialized power—that is, the desire to exercise influence
on behalf of other people. Successful managers, who must work
with and through other people to get things done, typically are high
in their needs for socialized—and socially desirable—power.

People who are dominated by the need for affiliation generally
make ineffective managers or supervisors. To quote the title of an
article by McClelland: "Nice Guys Make Bad Bosses." The problem? Affiliative managers are not running a department. They are
conducting a popularity contest that they feel they can't afford to
lose. They find it difficult to say no. They play favorites com-
pulsively, persuading themselves that the employee with whom they
have developed a close personal rapport is also the effective
employee. Unfortunately, this is likely to be the employee who
perceives the weakness of the affiliative manager and who takes
advantage of it, substituting sycophancy for performance.

Overall, McClelland is concerned with the decline of achievement
motivation in the United States, along with a decrease in the need
for affiliation, and a corresponding increase in the need for personal
power—trends that he finds dangerous in their implications for the
future. We are frequently described as a violent nation. He fears
that the future will surpass the past.

*David C. McClelland, "The Two Faces of Power." Copyright by the Trustees of Columbia
University. Permission to reprint from the *Journal of International Affairs*, vol. 24, no. 1, 1970, pp.
31-36, is gratefully acknowledged to the Editors of the JOURNAL.

McClelland's typology of human motivation is arresting, backed
by twenty-five years of research and study and by experiential
evidence that people, properly motivated, can be trained to shift
their basic pattern of motivation—a conclusion contrary to the
preponderance of psychological thinking.

Let us put together these bits and pieces of evidence about the
nature of power and see what kind of picture they make. The
negative or personal face of power is characterized by the domi-
nance-submission mode: If I win, you lose. It is *primitive* in the sense
that the strategies employed are adopted early in life, before the
child is sufficiently socialized to learn more subtle techniques of
influence. In fantasy, it expresses itself in thoughts of conquering
opponents. In real life, it leads to fairly simple direct means of
feeling powerful—drinking heavily, acquiring "prestige supplies,"
and being aggressive. It does not lead to effective social leadership
for the simple reason that a person whose power drive is fixated at
this level tends to treat other people as pawns rather than as origins. And people who feel that they are pawns tend to be passive
and useless to the leader who is getting his childish satisfaction from
dominating them. Slaves are the poorest, most inefficient form of
labor ever devised by man. If a leader wants to have far-reaching
influence, he must make his followers feel powerful and able to
accomplish things on their own.

The positive or socialized face of power is characterized by a
concern for group goals, for finding those goals that will move men,
for helping the group to formulate them, for taking some initiative in
providing members of the group with the means of achieving goals,
and for giving group members the feeling of strength and competence they need to work hard for such goals. In fantasy, it leads to a
concern with exercising influence *for* others, with planning, and
with the ambivalent bitter-sweet meaning of many so-called "victories." In real life, it leads to an interest in informal sports, politics,
and holding office. It functions in a way that makes members of a
group feel like origins rather than pawns. Even the most dictatorial
leader has not succeeded if he has not instilled in at least some of
his followers a sense of power and the strength to pursue the goals
he has set. This is often hard for outside observers to believe because they do not experience the situation as it is experienced by
the group members. One of the characteristics of the outsider, who
notices only the success or failure of an influence attempt, is that he

tends to convert what is a positive face of power into its negative version. He believes that the leader must have "dominated" because he was so effective, whereas, in fact, direct domination could never have produced so large an effect.

There is, however, a certain realistic basis for the frequent misperception of the nature of leadership. In real life, the actual leader balances on a knife edge between expressing dominance and exercising the more socialized type of leadership. He may show first one face of power, then the other. The reason for this lies in the simple fact that even if he is a socialized leader, he must take initiative in helping the group he leads to form its goals. How much initiative he should take, how persuasive he should attempt to be, and at what point his clear enthusiasm for certain goals becomes personal authoritarian insistence that those goals are the right ones whatever the members of the group may think, are all questions calculated to frustrate the well-intentioned leader. If he takes no initiative, he is no leader. If he takes too much, he becomes a dictator, particularly if he tries to curtail the process by which members of the group participate in shaping group goals. There is a particular danger for the man who has demonstrated his competence in shaping group goals and in inspiring group members to pursue them. In time both he and they may assume that he knows best, and he may almost imperceptibly change from a democratic to an authoritarian leader. There are, of course, safeguards against slipping from the more socialized to the less socialized expressions of power. One is psychological: The leader must thoroughly learn the lesson that his role is not to dominate and treat people like pawns. but to give strength to others and to make them feel like origins of ideas and of the courses of their lives. If they are to be truly strong, he must continually consult them and be aware of their wishes and desires. *A firm faith in people as origins prevents the development of the kind of cynicism that so often characterizes authoritarian leaders.* A second safeguard is social: Democracy provides a system whereby the group can expel the leader from office if it feels that he is no longer properly representing its interests.

Despite these safeguards, Americans remain unusually suspicious of the leadership role for fear that it will become a vehicle of the personal use and abuse of power. Students do not aspire to leadership roles because they are sensitive to the negative face of power and suspicious of their own motives. Furthermore, they know that if they are in a position of leadership, they will be under constant surveillance by all sorts of groups which are ready to accuse them of the personal abuse of power. Americans probably have less respect for authority than any other people in the world. The reasons are not hard to find. Many Americans originally came here to avoid tyranny in other countries. We have come to hate and fear authority in many of its forms because of its excesses elsewhere. As a nation, we are strongly committed to an ideology of personal freedom and noninterference by government. We cherish our free press as the guardian of our freedom because it can ferret out tendencies toward the misuse or abuse of personal power before they become dangerous to the public. In government, as in other organizations, we have developed elaborate systems of checks and balances of divisions of power, which make it difficult for any one person or group to abuse power. In government, power is divided three ways—among the executive, the legislative, and the judicial branches. In business, it is divided among management, labor, and owners. And in the university, among trustees, administration, and students. Many of these organizations also have a system for rotating leadership to make sure that no one acquires enough power over time to be able to misuse it. A Martian observer might conclude that, as a nation, we are excessively, almost obsessively, worried about the abuse of power.

It is incredible that any leadership at all can be exercised under such conditions. Consider the situation from the point of view of a would-be leader. He knows that if he takes too much initiative, or perhaps even if he does not, he is very likely to be severely attacked by some subgroup as a malicious, power-hungry status seeker. If he is in any way a public figure, he may be viciously attacked for any mis-step or chancy episode in his past life. Even though the majority of the people are satisfied with his leadership, a small, vociferous minority can make his life unpleasant and at times unbearable. Furthermore, he knows that he will not be the only leader trying to formulate group goals. If he is a congressman, he has to work not only with his fellow congressmen but also with representatives of independent sources of power in the executive branch and the government bureaucracy. If he is a college president, he has to cope with the relatively independent power of his trustees, the faculty, and the student body. If he is a business manager, he must share power with labor leaders. In addition, he knows that his tenure of office is likely to be short. Since it is doubtful that he will ever be able to exert true leadership, there seems little purpose in preparing for it. Logically, then, he should spend his time preparing for what he will do before and after his short tenure in office.

Under these conditions, why would any promising young man aspire to be a leader? He begins by doubting his motives and ends by concluding that even if he believes his motives to be altruistic, the game is scarcely worth the candle. In other words, the anti-leadership vaccine, which John Gardner speaks of, is partly supplied by the negative face that power wears in our society and the extraordinary lengths to which we have gone to protect ourselves against misused power. It is much safer to pursue a career as a professional adviser, assured some continuity of service and some freedom from public attack—because, after all, one is not responsible for decisions—and some certainty that one's motives are *good*, and that power conflicts have to be settled by someone else.

How can immunity against the antileadership vaccine be strengthened? Some immunity surely needs to be built up if our society is not to flounder because of a lack of socialized leadership. Personally, I would concoct a remedy that is one part changes in the system, one part rehabilitation of the positive face of power, and one part adult education. Let me explain each ingredient in turn. I feel least confident in speaking about the first one because I am neither a political scientist, a management expert, nor a revolutionary. Yet as a psychologist, I do feel that America's concern about the possible misuse of power verges at times on a neurotic obsession. To control the abuses of power, is it really necessary to divide authority so excessively and to give such free license to anyone to attack a leader in any way he likes? Doesn't this make the leadership role so difficult and unrewarding that it ends up appealing only to cynics? Who in his right mind would want the job of college president under most operating conditions today? A president has great responsibility—for raising money, for setting goals of the institution that faculty, students, and trustees can share, for student discipline, and for appointment of a distinguished faculty. Yet often he has only a very shaky authority with which to execute these responsibilities. The authority that he has he must share with the faculty (many of whom he cannot remove no matter how violently they disagree with the goals set for the university), with the trustees, and with students who speak with one voice one year and quite a different one two years later. I am not now trying to defend an ineffective college president. I am simply trying to point out that our social system makes his role an extraordinarily difficult one. Some structural reform of the American system definitely seems called for. It is beyond the scope of this paper to say what it might be. The possibilities range all the way from a less structured system in which all organizations are conceived as temporary, to a system in which leaders are given more authority or offered greater protection from irresponsible attack. If we want better leaders, we will have to find ways of making the conditions under which they work less frustrating.

The second ingredient in my remedy for the antileadership vaccine is rehabilitation of the positive face of power. This paper has been an effort in that direction. Its major thesis is that many people, including both social scientists and potential leaders, have consistently misunderstood or misperceived the way in which effective leadership takes place. They have confused it regularly, we have pointed out, with the more primitive exercise of personal power. The error is perpetuated by people who speak of leaders as "making decisions." Such a statement only serves to obscure the true process by which decisions should be taken. It suggests that the leader is making a decision arbitrarily without consulting anyone, exercising his power or authority for his own ends. It is really more proper to think of an effective leader as an educator. The relationship between leading and educating is much more obvious in Latin than it is in English. In fact, the word *educate* comes from the Latin *educare* meaning *to lead out*. An effective leader is an educator. One leads people by helping to set their goals, by communicating them widely throughout the group, by taking initiative in formulating means of achieving the goals, and finally, by inspiring the members of the group to feel strong enough to work hard for those goals. Such an image of the exercise of power and influence in a leadership role should not frighten anybody and should convince more people that power exercised in this way is not only not dangerous but of the greatest possible use to society.

My experience in training businessmen in India has led me to propose the third ingredient in my formula for producing better leaders—namely, psychological education for adults. What impressed me greatly was the apparent ease with which adults can be changed by the methods we used. The dominant view in American psychology today is still that basic personality structure is laid down very early in life and is very hard to change later on. Whether the psychologist is a Freudian or a learning theorist, he believes that early experiences are critical and shape everything a person can learn, feel, and want throughout his entire life span. As a consequence, many educators have come to be rather pessimistic about what can be done for the poor, the black, or the dispossessed who have undergone damaging experiences early in life. Such traumatized individuals, they argue, have developed nonadaptive personality structures that are difficult, if not impossible, to change later in life. Yet our experience with the effectiveness of short-term training courses in achievement motivation for adult businessmen in India and elsewhere does not support this view. I have seen men change, many of them quite dramatically, after only a five-day exposure to our specialized techniques of psychological instruction. They changed the way they thought, the way they talked, and the way they spent their time. The message is clear: Adults can be changed, often with a relatively short exposure to specialized techniques of psychological education. The implication for the present discussion is obvious. If it is true, as John Gardner argues, that many young men have learned from their professors that the professional role is preferable to the leadership role, then psychological education offers society a method of changing their views and self-conceptions when they are faced with leadership opportunities. The type of psychological education needed will of course differ somewhat from the more simple emphasis on achievement motivation. More emphasis will have to be given to the means of managing motivation in others. More explanations will have to be given of the positive face of leadership as an educational enterprise and will have to provide participants with a better idea of how to be effective leaders. These alterations are quite feasible; in fact, they have been tried.

11

FOLLOWERSHIP: THE SUPERVISOR FACES THE BOSS

LEARNING OBJECTIVES

1 Begin by agreeing that the first-line manager is the person in the middle—between higher management and subordinates.

2 Consider the conditions under which the supervisor can improve his or her influence by bucking the boss.

3 See the circumstances under which bypassing the boss is a viable ploy.

4 Appreciate the meaning (along with its virtues) of reverse bypassing.

5 Contemplate the "open door" and the opportunities and pitfalls it presents to the supervisor.

6 Measure the extent to which dual loyalty is a problem for the supervisor and what he or she can do to minimize its problems.

Today's supervisors live in a complex world. They must maintain good relations with their own subordinates. Between them there should be mutual feelings of trust and respect. They must perform their duties to the satisfaction of their immediate superiors, who are their prime source of punishments and rewards. They must deal on occasion with direct pressures from levels further up the hierarchy—with the expectations and demands of their superiors' bosses or people even higher. Then, too, they have frequent relations with other line and staff departments—some of the same status level, others *nominally* on the same level but actually in a position to give them orders—all of whose cooperation supervisors need to discharge their duties effectively.

These relationships would present fewer problems if the goals of the various individuals they depend on and the groups of which they are members were the same. In the broadest sense, all management groups are committed to the goal of maximum profitability for the organization. But this overreaching goal permits striking and frequently bitter divergences of opinion about how the goal can best be achieved, as well as endless power and status conflicts between managers. In these conflicts, supervisors are frequently witnesses or victims.

Among the groups with which supervisors are most intimately connected—the work groups that they lead and the higher management groups that they immediately represent—there is not even an agreement on ultimate goals. True, few rank-and-file workers want to destroy the enterprise that employs them. They feel a stake in its survival to the extent that it fulfills their personal goals—good wages, a pleasant working atmosphere, and with a different set of employees, the opportunity to do challenging, high-quality work under conditions over which they exert some control. Reasonable goals—all of them. But goals that, if fully realized, would clearly conflict with the overreaching corporate goal of maximum profit.

THE PERSON IN THE MIDDLE

More than twenty-five years ago, Fritz Roethlisberger of the Harvard Business School, in a classic article, described the foreman—the description would apply equally well to the first-line office or engineering supervisor—as "the man in the middle," endlessly subject to conflicting pressures and grievances from higher management and his own work group. Roethlisberger's description is valid for the supervisor, who is still the person in the middle. (See Figure 11-1.)

The *effective* supervisor mediates successfully between the work

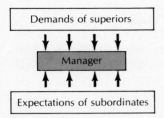

FIGURE 11-1 The one in the middle

group and management and discharges the obligations of dual loyalty—to subordinates and to the boss. The *ineffective* supervisor is
caught in the crunch between the conflicting forces, sinks into inaction
or succumbs to the pressure from one side or the other, and becomes
useless to the organization.

The picture is the same as it was when Roethlisberger wrote about it
in 1945, yet it is also altered. Wherein lie the changes? Actually, there
are three differences: (1) The controls, largely statistical, which higher
management can use to check up on the performance of the supervisor and work group are now more sophisticated, (2) the pressures
the first-level supervisor can bring to bear on subordinates are different
and generally less effective, and (3) the expectations that many employees bring to the job are higher—they want more interesting work
than the previous generations.

How does the hierarchy limit the supervisor?
In most plants and offices with more than five hundred employees,
higher management receives, on a weekly or daily basis, computer-
processed data covering every quantifiable aspect of the supervisor's
operation—pieces of paper processed by categories or components
manufactured, lost time, absenteeism, scrap, rejects, tardiness, overtime, and every other production factor. Each item is meticulously
flagged to call higher management's attention to any deviation from a
predetermined standard of acceptability. True, twenty-five years ago
higher management was receiving some of the same records. But it
received them monthly or less frequently, if at all, and the records
themselves were neither as comprehensive nor as accurate. The computer, with its ability to handle fantastic numbers of interrelated com-
putations without people and with much less possibility of error, has
tightened higher management's controls over its supervisors. Dooms-
day comes every Monday.

Affluence lessens the supervisor's power

The supervisor's position is further complicated and weakened by the decline in the economic pressures that can be exerted on work groups. Admittedly, these pressures have been exaggerated. The supervisor has always had to come to terms with the production-line workers, office clerks, and engineers who do the actual work of the organization.

In a period of relatively full employment (for the relatively skilled) and affluence among workers, the supervisor's ultimate weapon—dismissal or the threat of it—has lost most of its past clout. Certainly, supervisors can and do fire employees. But we would guess that for each person fired today, five are retained only because the supervisor can't face the task of finding replacements for them. Threats, in other words, are out—way out—and persuasion is way in, as a means of maintaining production. But there's a problem: The concessions many supervisors must make to keep people working, we suspect, are greater and, at the same time, frequently more difficult to grant because of the sophisticated controls available to higher management.

Help is on the way

The picture has a compensating side. Higher management doesn't exist in a vacuum. It is aware of the changes in the relative bargaining position of supervisors vis à vis their work force. Roethlisberger commented that "the foreman was painfully tutored to focus his attention upward to his immediate superiors and the logic of evaluation they represented, rather than downward to his subordinates and the feelings they have." The statement, largely true in the 1950s, would not be true today. The supervisor has been taught and encouraged to empathize with subordinates and even to feel loyalty toward them. Much of this new emphasis reflects the findings and teachings of behavioral scientists over the past two decades, but some also reveals a recognition, usually unacknowledged, of the supervisor's weakened bargaining position.

We recall a conversation with a senior vice president of a large New England bank, a man who skillfully concealed any inner warmth he possessed. He described with considerable satisfaction the stratagems employed by the bank to make its employees more productive, including paying 10 percent more in each job classification than its competitors. The goal of this effort: a 60 percent workday—that is, the bank's clerical force would do 60 percent as much work as the time-study people had determined they should be able to do without overexerting themselves. The vice president reported the success of the program and added complacently that other bank employees in the city were working a 50 percent day. The time-study engineers may have been mistaken—that's not important. The attitude of the banker is, and it's symbolic of the attitude among higher management generally. The big bosses don't expect the same level of production among rank-and-file employees as they did previously, and their diminished expectations have in turn lessened the pressure upon the supervisor.

THE SUPERVISOR AS IMITATOR

We talked about effective supervisory styles in the previous chapter. One problem that we saved until now is that most supervisors tend to imitate the style of supervision practiced by their immediate superiors. If they are dictatorial and distrustful, always specifying each instruction to the last detail and forever checking to see whether their orders are being followed, so are the supervisors under them. If the superior is permissive and confident, allowing supervisors to work within broad directives and interrupting only when something has gone wrong, so are they. Sometimes their sense of the situation will bail them out. But sometimes their deference to their superior will confine them to a style of supervision unsuited to the situation. Should a subordinate knowingly follow an instruction or a policy that he or she believes to be wrong? Here is how one highly effective manager handles the problem:

> My employees know they can't explain a botched job by saying, "I was only following orders or company policy." They know it is *part of their job* to endeavor to get orders or policies changed which they believe are wrong or inappropriate. This doesn't mean that they can simply ignore what has been told them, but rather that they have a responsibility to try to convince me why it is wrong in general or at least in a specific case.

Two qualifications to this statement should be noted. The flourishing of yes-people may depend in part upon the ease with which results can be measured. Where performance results are exceedingly difficult to measure, the one who can be consistently agreeable to the boss has the greatest opportunity for capitalizing on this talent. Whether the measurement of results will undo the agreeable but mediocre individual should also depend on the extent to which decisions and instructions from the boss will be reasonably adequate to cover the situations that a subordinate meets on the job. If they are, although the subordinate may appear to be getting the results, it is the superior who is really achieving them.

This discussion of yes-people has only scratched the surface of a complex subject. Our purpose here is simply to raise questions about a commonly held assumption: that yessing the boss contributes to advancement in the business organization. We have sought to point out that agreement pays off in some situations more than in others and that, in any case, it is hardly safe for ambitious executives to assume that confirmity, per se, will help them to get ahead.

Suppose our workers serving under an autocratic boss wish to increase substantially their own freedom of action—and still remain within the organization. Can anything be done about it?

The case of Wes Walsh suggests that something can be done. Walsh was superintendent of a plant who came in under a plant manager widely known in the company for his type of autocratic control. Furthermore, the offices of the two persons were within a hundred feet of each other, so that although the boss was also responsible for other plants in the area, he could keep a close watch over Walsh. Nevertheless, Walsh was able to manage his plant very much according to his own notions, with little interference from above. How did he do it?

The previous superintendent had been constantly at swords' points with the plant manager. He advised Walsh to keep away from the manager's office. "The less you see of that son of a bitch, the better you'll get along." Though Walsh and his predecessor were good friends, Walsh decided to disregard the advice. If it hadn't worked for his predecessor, why should it work for him? Instead, Walsh saw to it that he had frequent contacts with the boss—and contacts that were initiated primarily by Walsh himself. He would drop in, with apparent casualness, to report progress or to seek the plant manager's approval on some minor matter, carefully selected so that the boss could hardly veto it. Walsh was getting his boss used to saying yes to him.

Major matters required longer interaction between the two men, carefully prepared and staged. Consider the problems of the materials-reprocessing unit.

With increasing volume of production going through the plant, it had become apparent to Walsh—as indeed it had to his predecessor—that this unit was inadequate for current requirements. It was too slow in operation and too limited in capacity. This condition seriously hampered production and created a storage problem in the plant. Materials awaiting reprocessing were strewn about at one end of the operating area.

Walsh's first step was to propose to the boss that he pick a time when he could spend a couple of hours with Walsh in that plant, so that they could look over some of the problems the plant was facing. The manager set the time, and the two men spent the hours together on an inspection tour. To some extent the physical conditions the works manager saw spoke for themselves, but Walsh also supplemented these visual clues with an account of the way in which the inadequacy of the materials-reprocessing unit hampered his operations. The boss had to agree that the condition was undesirable. Eventually he asked, "What do you propose?"

Walsh was ready with a carefully worked-out proposal for the purchase of a new type of reprocessing unit at a cost of $150,000. After a brief discussion of the impact of a new machine on costs and production, the plant manager authorized the purchase. It is noteworthy that essentially the same proposal had been made more than once to the plant manager by Walsh's predecessor. Made no doubt in a different form and fitting into a different context of interpersonal relationships, the good idea had received simply a flat rejection.

So effectively did Wes Walsh handle his superior that he won a large measure of freedom from a person known throughout the works as an autocrat. And the plant manager was more than happy with the relationship. In fact, several years later, after his own retirement, he was boasting to others about how he had discovered and developed Wes Walsh! . . .

Walsh suggests these rules for approaching a big decision with an autocratic boss:

1 Prepare the ground carefully; don't just spring it on the boss.
2 Don't present the problem and the proposed solution at the same time.
3 Present the problem in stages and in such a way that no solution will be immediately apparent to the boss. This will help to assure you that he does not commit himself before you have had a chance to make your full case. Once an executive of this type has committed himself, it is almost impossible to get him to reverse his decision. If you can bring him through all phases of the problem with the solution still unclear in his mind, then your chances of getting your solution accepted are greatly improved.

It is not my purpose to suggest that Wes Walsh has discovered *the* way to deal with an autocratic boss. That would be a gross oversimplification. I cite his story only in order to show that a skillful and imaginative executive can win himself considerable freedom of action from bosses whom many would consider intolerable autocrats.[1]

---

[1] Leonard R. Sayles, *Individualism and Big Business,* McGraw-Hill, New York, 1963, pp. 170-173. (Based on an essay by W. F. Whyte.)

A LITTLE MATTER OF INFLUENCE

More important than the leadership styles supervisors use to get ahead with their bosses is the influence they have. Do other levels of management respond positively to their requests and recommendations? Do they have the skill to make effective presentations to their bosses and to other managers within the organization? In short, can they sell themselves and their ideas?

Incidentally, we feel that supervisors who practice general supervision but have little or no influence with their superiors are almost certain to destroy their influence with their subordinates. For example, a supervisor calls a group meeting to discuss the problem of how to deal with excessive absenteeism, takes the group's recommended solution to higher management, only to have it rejected out of hand. The experience is repeated several times with the same result. The group sinks into frustration and cynicism, becomes hostile and disrespectful to the supervisor, whose position is barely tenable once any impotence has been exposed.

What gives supervisors influence with their bosses? Performance is one part of the answer. Suppose a supervisor fails to measure up to the statistical indices used by top management to monitor and reward performance down the line. This is almost certain to be the subject of a confrontation between the supervisor's boss and higher management—a confrontation from which the supervisor's influence will emerge diminished or destroyed. Communication is also an important part of the answer. Success here lies not so much in the supervisor's manner of delivery or expertise in organizing the subject matter of the presentation as in the substance of the communications—what one tells the boss, and of almost equal importance, what one conceals from the boss. In subordinate-boss communications, the substance is still the message.

Maintaining Credibility

As a basic maxim of communication between subordinate and boss we commend: Tell her what she needs to know, not simply what she wants to hear, even when she has given unmistakable signs that she doesn't want to hear all the facts. We know of a case where the machinery on a conveyer line had become too light for the production load, causing frequent breakdowns and the replacement of bearings, drive belts, sprockets, and other parts. The supervisor knew a major installation was in order, but each time he approached the plant superintendent he got the Typhoid Mary treatment, and eventually he subsided. Production was being maintained at the expense of excessive overtime when the day of reckoning arrived. The plant manager called for an accounting and the supervisor was on the spot. Should he take the blame, or should he be disloyal to the superintendent, his immediate superior? He "took the count" and hoped that his superior would repay his loyalty. Who can say that he decided wrong? He owed his job to his boss. And besides, he had to balance the temporary gratitude and protection of the plant manager against the possibility of permanent hostility and continuing retaliation from his immediate superior.

We weren't surprised to hear the results of a study made to determine why some boss-subordinate communications worked and others did not. The finding of the study? The most accurate and extensive communication took place between a boss and a trusting subordinate who didn't care about getting ahead.

Empathy Works

Most bosses want the truth and appreciate it, at least in the long run—the previous case notwithstanding. In another situation with which we are familiar, the superintendent steadily resisted pressures from quality control for a lower scrap-and-reject rate on two grounds, one explicit, the other hidden. He didn't want to add the expense of hiring more inspectors to his budget, and he feared that higher-quality work would mean lower production—and production was the *idée fixe* of his boss, the plant manager. The easy position for the supervisor was to sympathize and agree with his boss. "If we went along with those goddam perfectionists in quality control, nothing would ever get out the door." However, the supervisor said nothing of the kind. He *em*pathized with his boss instead of *sym*pathizing with him, and recognizing that more inspectors would contribute to the company's—and the superintendent's—good, he took a stand in favor of adding them. In time, his pressure was influential in persuading the superintendent to modify his position. The superintendent probably never thought fondly of the supervisor for standing up to him. But he respected his integrity and recognized his credibility. People—and bosses are people too—have a deep and well-founded respect for someone who sticks to what he or she believes is the truth and who shows interest in nothing less.

Empathy Can Boomerang

Not all bosses can tolerate openness. Sometimes the truth hurts too much to accept. Take the case of the direct-mail supervisor for a magazine publishing company that sold some of its periodicals by means of premium booklets on the subjects assumed to be of interest to potential subscribers. The publisher of one magazine was a woman who preached quality to her subordinates, but who at the same time impressed her bosses by repeatedly demonstrating how costs could be cut at the expense of quality—with little or no loss of sales.

The two most recent premiums, written by hacks at bargain-basement prices, had been judged unusable by the publisher. The direct-mail chief saw the opportunity and seized it. He wrote a memo to the publisher in which he stated the case for higher-quality premiums in the strongest terms of which he was capable. Among his statements were these:

> Evidence suggests we are not competitive. We should commission premiums from people who know their subjects thoroughly, but at our rates the experts won't write for us.
>
> Premiums obtained at our price have been money thrown away. I can't resist quoting Ruskin's warning. "But when you pay too little, you sometimes lose all, because the thing you bought was incapable of doing the thing it was bought to do!"

The publisher never answered the memo or even alluded to it in any future contacts with the supervisor. Her answer came in a red-faced tirade addressed to another supervisor who had tactfully submitted a much milder document on the same general topic—the need to improve quality. (This is a wonderful example of displacement.) Apparently the publisher didn't trust her own self-control enough to risk a direct confrontation with the first supervisor, who had challenged her self-image so painfully. At any rate, the direct-mail supervisor's days of influence with the boss ended abruptly with the delivery of his memo.

The Uses of Deception

Through a frequent and painful paradox, supervisors are required to limit their communications to their bosses in order to maintain their influence with them. There are things the boss would like to know, may need to know, requires to know. But sometimes these things must be withheld from the boss so that the performance level in the supervisor's operation can be maintained at a satisfactory level. Obliged to make a choice, the supervisor has to balance his or her fears. If facts are concealed, the boss may discover the deception and penalize the supervisor—a real but indeterminate fear, since both the risks and the penalties are difficult to calculate. If one tells the truth, the price of honesty will be the impaired performance of one's work group, the almost certain loss of influence with the boss, and penalties once the performance drop becomes obvious. Faced with this dilemma, most supervisors opt for deception.

Take the supervisors described by Dalton. They were under intense pressure from higher management to increase production and driven into various departures from official procedure in order to retain influence with their bosses and win their approval.

The pay rate varied with the product specifications, and several supervisors through an informal deal with their work groups, rearranged the order sequence to permit the higher-paying orders to be run first, regardless of the scheduling. The deal, of course, was in direct violation of company regulations and threw the supervisors into conflict with production planning, which had worked out a rigid sequence for processing orders based on delivery deadlines promised to customers.

We would assume that the supervisors couldn't get away with an evasion so bald-faced. Not so. Production planning threatened the supervisors involved, who first played dumb and then contrived elaborate excuses to conceal their departures from schedule. What happened when production planning confronted higher plant management with evidence of what the supervisors were up to? Very little. Higher management condemned the supervisors' actions for the record but enforced no penalties, and the practice continued. Of course the supervisors' deal was contrary to the rules, but one fact overshadowed any other consideration: Total production in the departments that had broken the rules was much higher than it had been before.

Perhaps the supervisors had anticipated the tacit approval of higher management when they circumvented the rules, although we doubt it. Instead, when faced with the pressure for higher production, they made a deal with their workers that ensured it, then crossed their fingers and prepared to take the consequences if and when their arrangements were disclosed to higher management.

The Indispensables

Not every case of deception involves the supervisor's concealing facts from the boss because of pressures from subordinates. Sometimes it's the supervisors themselves who take advantage of their strategic position and apply pressure on their bosses to circumvent the rules. We're familiar with one case involving two copy supervisors in the Cleveland office of a New York advertising agency. The agency is notorious for the strictness and minuteness of its regulations, and the resident vice president is equally notorious for his zeal in enforcing them. One motto of the organization is that "there is no such thing as being a little bit late." Obviously, one of the VP's responsibilities was to uphold the no-tardiness rule and discipline violators.

The two supervisors systematically began to violate the rule, coming in first a few minutes late each morning, then gradually extending their tardiness to 30 or 45 minutes. The VP closed his eyes to the practice (after all, these were his most valuable employees), but after several weeks he took reluctant cognizance. The senior of the two laid it on the line—she would resign rather than obey the rule—and the VP promptly caved in.

That's not the end of the story. The two supervisors continued to do good work, thus keeping their end of the silent bargain, but the extent of their tardiness reduced the rule to a travesty. Being an hour late became standard operating procedure. Other supervisors and employees imitated the two copy chiefs, feeling that the VP would not crack down on them either, and they were correct. There was one curious side effect. Out of fear, guilt, or a combination of both, the VP became more unrelenting than ever in rigidly enforcing every last petty regulation in the shop, apparently seeking to compensate by his zeal in other areas for his backsliding with tardiness.

Bypassing the Boss

Another practice calculated to endanger relations with the boss, but one that supervisors sometimes feel justified in, or even driven to, adopting is bypassing the boss. Sometimes quick action is imperative and there just isn't time to contact the boss who's out of town or otherwise not available. One supervisor described her strategy this way: "I am always in a position of getting people to waive the formal requirements. Recently a manager said he couldn't do it without the authorization of my boss. I told him I could sign for my boss. I just had to get that approval that day. Of course, as soon as I could I went to my boss to make sure she was in agreement with my action."

Another innocent and necessary form of bypassing the boss is cutting the red tape involved in going through channels. For example, in a small manufacturing company the accounting department was located directly across the hall from research and development. Everyone recognized that scientists and engineers kept odd hours and everyone accepted this practice. What the clerks in accounting wouldn't accept and repeatedly griped about to their boss was that the clerks in R and D felt that they too were privileged characters with no obligation to keep regular hours.

What could the accounting supervisor do about the problem? If he followed the rule book, he would report the matter to his supervisor. It would travel on up the line (doubtless with the facts being distorted in the process) to the common superior of both accounting and R and D, and then down the line again till it reached the presumptuous clericals in R and D.

In this situation we suspect nine supervisors out of ten would cross the hall for a face-to-face talk with their opposite number and try to resolve the problem on the spot. Going through channels would be the last resort. It always takes time and frequently complicates the problem. Think of what would happen in a hospital if, say, an oxygen tank goes out of order. If everybody always followed channels, the nurse would report to the head nurse, who would go to the chief engineer, who would go to the repairer. The patient would probably be dead before the equipment was fixed.

Of course, supervisors who cut red tape always run the risk that what's decided upon at their level will be overruled by their superiors at one level of the hierarchy or another, sometimes on the merits of the case and sometimes out of someone's pique at being "short circuited." However, it's a risk most supervisors feel is worth taking.

THE SUPERVISOR ACTS ALONE

Not at all innocent and extremely risky is the tactic used by supervisors who make decisions on their own, overruling their bosses or ignoring them because they believe that their superiors have made a wrong decision or would do so if they had the chance. A classic case involves the origin of the phrase "turning a blind eye." Lord Nelson ignored the instruction issued by his superior to break off his engagement at the battle of Copenhagen, clapped the telescope over his blind eye—and won the battle. The problem of playing this game is that it is almost as dangerous to win as to lose. There's no possible defense in case of failure, and the best that the supervisor can hope for for making the right decision is forgiveness from the boss—and grudging forgiveness at that.

What's the worst? Take the case of a general superintendent who was asked by his boss, the plant manager, to represent him at the monthly budget review. The plant manager warned him against accepting a recommendation for a lot of costly new equipment from Vince Reilly, superintendent of building Two, but added, "Don't get into an argument with Reilly if you can help it." The meeting came and Reilly made his recommendation, but here the general superintendent departed from the script. Reilly's arguments impressed him and the others at the meeting so much that he suggested, and the group approved, a decision to purchase a single item of the new equipment to help determine whether a major investment would be justified. A week later, when the plant manager was back on the job, he vetoed the purchase and fired the general superintendent, making the undeniable point, "I spelled out exactly what I wanted you to do. If I had wanted you to do my thinking for me, I would have told you so." Our sources tell us that Reilly was right and that the compromise initiated by the general superintendent was an intelligent decision, if he had been free to ignore the human element—his boss's prejudices and instructions. He wasn't—he did—and he paid the price.

Over the Boss's Head

Now let's consider the royal flush in bypasses: going over the boss's head and appealing to a superior or even someone higher up. Nothing could be more dangerous for a subordinate. One's job invariably will be at stake. But under two circumstances, a supervisor may decide to proceed: When she feels her supervisor is incompetent and she has to secure recognition from someone else or quit; and when she believes so passionately in an idea or project which her boss opposes that she is willing to lay her job on the line for the chance to win her point.

Does it work?

An example of the first occurred several years ago in the advertising department of a large furniture company. A young copywriter, ambitious, intelligent, and convinced of her worth, found that her most original ideas and crispest copy invariably landed in the boss's wastebasket. She had decided to resign, but before leaving she tried a desperate stratagem. After all, what did she have to lose? She assembled several of the advertisements the company had run together with her own version of each ad, sent the package to the company president, and awaited the results. She didn't have long to wait. Within a week she was transferred to another supervisor, and within a month her old boss had left the company. Furthermore, she was never far from the president's eye after that. Today, she's a senior vice president and advertising is merely one of the functional areas for which she is responsible.

Another person who risked all and won was a young naval lieutenant at the turn of the century, William S. Sims. He was convinced that continuous-aim firing, introduced into the British Navy in 1898, had revolutionized naval gunnery and changed it from an art to a science. Obviously, the American Navy had to follow suit. In thirteen official reports to the Bureau of Ordnance and the Bureau of Navigation, Sims documented the case for continuous-aim firing, supporting his arguments with masses of factual data. The reactions of the naval brass? Dead silence, followed by derision of his claims and, finally, name-calling. In desperation, Sims wrote to the commander-in-chief, Theodore Roosevelt, and presented him with the evidence. The President's reaction was swift. He installed continuous-aim firing in the U.S. Navy, and made Sims inspector of target practice, a position he held for the last six years of Roosevelt's administration. Sim's personal mark had been made. He rose rapidly, and capped a distinguished career by serving as chief of naval operations in World War I.

The boss is still there

We have cited two instances where going over the boss's head paid off spectacularly, and where the game was worth the candle. These are the exceptions. In 99 cases out of 100, the supervisors who make an end run around their bosses find that, even when they get the decision they are seeking, they still have the boss to contend with. The price of their victory will be the permanent loss of whatever rapport existed between them and the boss—in the final showdown, the supervisors will have outsmarted themselves. Anthony Jay, in his book *Management and Machiavelli,* quotes Bismarck's letter of resignation from the Prussian civil service: "A Prussian official is like a player in an orchestra . . . he has to play his instrument as the needs of the conducted piece dictate . . . but for my part, I want to play music such as I regard as good—or else not play at all."

Supervisors are not Bismarcks. Lacking his spectacular abilities and iron will, they are compelled to play the music as orchestrated by their bosses. Nor is this altogether undesirable. Most managers have good reasons for taking a different position from their subordinates. Suppose they are wrong sometimes—think of an organization's cost in time and efficiency if the supervisor feels psychologically free to go over the boss's head every time he or she disagrees with a decision. And think of the effect on the morale and self-confidence of the boss if subordinates are ready and willing to undermine his or her authority whenever the spirit moves them. A degree of intimidation in subordinates, instilled by their bosses, is one price paid by a successful organization.

Reverse Bypassing

A variation of bypassing, and obviously one over which the supervisor has no control, is played when the big boss bypasses one or more levels of management to find out directly from the supervisor what is happening—for example, in the production shop or the field sales force. (See Figure 11-2.) Top management is frequently dissatisfied with the quality of reports that filter up to it and wonders what is really going on, especially when it seems to be going on badly. We are reminded of Haroun-al-Raschid of *Arabian Nights* fame who, so the legend goes, would emerge from his palace at night dressed as an itinerant traveler, and mingle with his subjects to discover what they

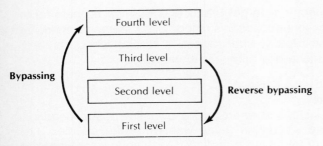

FIGURE 11-2

really thought about him and his regime. The same story told about kings and other potentates symbolizes an important fact: Status, power, and sheer size tend to isolate the top executive from the truth.

In large organizations where the top executives view operations mostly through the eyes of others, experience often leads them to distrust the evidence of those eyes. So they decide quite literally to see for themselves. Here is a description of a former president of Curtis Wright, who was famous—some say, notorious—for being his own chief troubleshooter.

> He [Hurley] seldom moves through channels. He figures that the division manager doesn't have any more idea than he has of what is wrong or the figures would not have been negative in the first place. So instead of waiting for a briefing, Hurley moves directly to the spot, right down to the machine on the floor if that is the heart of the problem. Many a division manager has discovered hours later that the boss had been in his department and long since moved on. And many department heads have discovered that an important job has been given to an employee they hardly know and without consulting them. Hurley spots a man who seems bright and says you do it. That the job may be completely unrelated to the employee's work is of no concern to him.

Effects on the supervisors
What's wrong with bosses like Hurley who cut red tape and get down to the grass roots by a direct approach to supervisors or even their subordinates? Given the way Hurley and others like him handle their bypassing of the channels of authority, a great deal. They give the responsible executive no time to take corrective action before they rush in and take over. They diffuse their energies and ultimately their authority instead of saving these assets for the problems where it is appropriate to lay them on the line. The top manager who dashes in,

unbriefed and unexpected, to take charge inevitably damages the organization from the standpoint of the supervisor. If the superior has the right answer or selects the person who can come up with it, the supervisor concludes quite logically that the big boss views everyone down through the supervisor as incompetent and to be ignored. If the big boss makes a mess out of the situation and doesn't have the answer or dumps the solution into the hands of the wrong person, this incompetence will undermine the supervisor's confidence in the whole organization. The subordinate has seen the clay feet and the image will never look the same again.

Bypassing can be a virtue, even a necessity. General Horrocks of the British Army, for example, described the circumstances under which bypassing is desirable—and his specifications can easily be translated from the military to a business organization—when the pressure is on in an emergency or when important plans are being formulated or results analyzed. Bypassing gives the person at the top a chance to evaluate the quality of younger managers, to get authentic information, and to obtain proposals and appraisals firsthand from the people who generated them. And another specification of Horrocks which is just as important in business: Always invite the person's immediate superior to be present at any discussions.

What the top person loses in frankness and openness of communication is compensated for by what is gained in retaining the confidence and the position of the superior. When a confidential session between a supervisor and the boss's superior is really called for, it is time to consider whether one of them should not leave the organization or at least the organizational unit. If they're both valuable, their relationship has deteriorated to the point where one person's potential is going to be better realized somewhere else—within the organization or outside it.

The Open Door

Finally, of course, the supervisor personally can become the victim of a bypass. Many companies maintain an open-door policy. The rank-and-file employee has the privilege of walking into the office of any manager in the organization, up to and including the president, and voice complaints or make suggestions. In most cases, however, the open-door policy is fiction. The door may be open but somehow the rank-and-file employee seldom crosses the threshold.

The reasons aren't hard to fathom. The social distance between the average hourly employee and typical higher management is too great. More important, just as supervisors hesitate to bypass their bosses because bosses are the prime source of all penalties and rewards, rank-and-file employees hesitate before they bypass supervisors. They balance, usually unconsciously, the slim chance of winning anything from their appeal against the danger of losing a great deal.

Another limitation of the open-door policy, even in organizations that sincerely subscribe to it, is the natural reluctance of higher managers to make it too effective. They are interested in creating a viable appeal channel, but they are not interested in spending great quantities of time listening to petty grievances and trivial or worthless suggestions from every clerk or assembly-line worker.

Take the case of the man in the welding shop who read in a trade magazine about some new equipment. In his role as a stockholder in the company—he owned twenty shares—he wrote the president, recommending the purchase of the equipment. In return, the welder got a warm letter from the president, commending his interest, promising to investigate his recommendation, and concluding with an invitation to communicate with him whenever there was something he felt the president should be aware of. The president's polite gesture—at least we take it as that—triggered an avalanche of suggestions. The welder swaggered around the shop boasting about his buddy Frank in Chicago. Finally, one night while under the influence, he called Frank to describe in vivid terms what he thought of his immediate boss. The next morning saw the finale—an ultimatum from the plant manager: quit bothering the president or get out.

That this case is extreme, we agree. But it illustrates an important and difficult problem for higher management: on the one hand, how to encourage the rank-and-file employee to bypass a supervisor when a complaint or suggestion is legitimate and significant, and on the other, how to discourage the employee from using the open door when the complaint or suggestion is small and has little merit.

What is the supervisor's attitude toward the open-door policy? Doesn't it worry the boss when disgruntled employees go to higher management with troublemaking problems, false charges, or tales out of school? Obviously, although the supervisor is probably even more concerned when the tales are not only unfavorable but also true.

How supervisors feel toward the open-door policy depends heavily on two factors: the degree to which they have removed themselves from their subordinates, and the approach the big boss takes with subordinates. Many times a subordinate bypasses the supervisor because he or she feels, "What's the use?" The supervisor has made it plain in the past that he or she has neither the time nor interest to listen to subordinates' complaints or ideas. The supervisor who hasn't heard from subordinates recently about any problems may be the rare but lucky person whose department has no problems. More likely, this is the supervisor who has gotten the message across that he or she doesn't want to hear that anything is wrong in the department. He or she is to be personally blamed if subordinates choose to forget that a supervisor is one of the channels through which they should go.

Making the Open Door Work

What does the boss do when approached by an employee with a gripe against the supervisor? Steer a delicate course between encouraging bypassing and sabotaging the supervisor's morale on one hand, and banning the bypassing, thereby having a disastrous effect on the workers' morale, on the other. If the subordinate hasn't already talked to the supervisor, the boss's preferred course of action is plain: Listen sympathetically but noncommittally, then refer the subordinate back to the supervisor. What if the subordinate has talked to the supervisor and the failure to obtain any satisfaction from the supervisor is precisely what has landed the employee on the boss's doorstep? What does the boss say then? Up to a point, the same script is followed, listening sympathetically but noncommittally, even if it appears obvious that the supervisor is at fault. At the end of the talk, the boss promises to talk to the supervisor and that the supervisor will, in turn, be in touch with the employee.

From there on, it is more difficult to prescribe the course of action. Too much depends on the persons involved and the circumstances. An autocratic boss, confronted by a pigheaded and stupid supervisor, might find it a necessity as well as a pleasure to administer a brutal tongue-lashing. Nothing less would take. However, even under those circumstances, the boss should take great care to see that the rank-and-file employee knows nothing about how the problem was handled. It should be the supervisor who explains the change of position to the subordinate, not the boss, and wherever possible, the decision should be presented as a case of the supervisor's having changed his mind, not of having had his mind changed for him. Obviously the employee, knowing the stubbornness of his boss and his past opposition, will suspect the true story. But the continuing authority and prestige of the supervisor requires the big boss to maintain the myth that the supervisor made the final decision. Otherwise, every decision could be challenged by anyone who disagreed with it and any position taken in the future would become untenable.

Speaking Up for Subordinates

One final problem area in upward communications casts the supervisor in a position where frank speaking may cause immediate difficulty with superiors, and silence will cause trouble with subordinates and may ultimately undermine the supervisor's effectiveness in helping management gain its objectives. We're talking about the supervisor's responsibility to protect subordinates' interests and represent them to higher management. It's the supervisor's duty to speak out on their behalf when higher management has made what they both feel is a wrong decision.

Some supervisors fulfill this role admirably. Consider, for example, what one worker said about her supervisor. "My present supervisor is the nicest person I've ever worked for. The other employees respect her also. I saw her stick her neck out with the general supervisor over work loads. She'll argue a point with the general supervisor if she thinks she is right."

However, there is considerable evidence to suggest that this supervisor is in the minority. One study conducted by the Opinion Research Corporation showed that only 12 percent of the hourly workers interviewed rated their supervisors as "good" in handling questions and complaints, and another study showed that nearly half the employees agreed with the statement that an employee who told the immediate supervisor everything he or she felt about the company would probably get into a lot of trouble. "Many employees believe," concluded Alfred Vogel, research director of the Opinion Research Corporation, "that their bosses are paid to block criticism from going up the line." Incidentally, supervisors had a very different perspective on themselves. In dealing with their employees' problems, most asserted that they "almost always" or "usually" take prompt action.

The dilemma of dual loyalty

What's the reason for the generally poor performance of supervisors in representing the interests of their subordinates to higher management? The easy answer is fear of retaliation from higher managers, the paradox being that the more credit a person gets from below, the less that person gets from above. Credit from below comes when a supervisor questions every unwelcome decision from above and protests vigorously and repeatedly any time higher management has done wrong by a subordinate. The dilemma is real enough, but let's not exaggerate its importance. The supervisor, as we have seen, has dual loyalties—to both management and subordinates—but only the most Neanderthal of managements fail to recognize the existence of this duality or attempt to monopolize the supervisor's allegiance. The more sophisticated managements know that a supervisor's duality works to their advantage even when, or perhaps most when, the supervisor's loyalties are weighted in the direction of employees. A study conducted by the Prudential Life Insurance Company indicated that out of eleven high-production supervisors, nine identified themselves more with their employees than with the company. Among low-producing supervisors, the reverse was true: Eight of them identified themselves with the company and only two with their employees. The same pattern was repeated in the attitude toward separate dining rooms for supervisors. The high-production supervisors reflected the attitude of their employees and objected to the segregation, while the low-production supervisors went along with it. The wage contract apparently buys the minimum level of performance—conscience and fear motivate employees only up to a point.

Performance beyond this point is the result of many factors, not the least of which is loyalty of the employees to the supervisor and their desire to make her or him look good. Obviously, one must earn this loyalty, and the most effective way of doing so is by representing subordinates' interests to higher management.

RECOGNITION OF DUAL LOYALTY

As we have pointed out, most higher managements are aware of and even encourage the supervisors' dual loyalty. But in some companies they don't recognize it: They rebuff the supervisors' every attempt to represent their employees' interests, frequently adding gall and wormwood by complaining that the supervisor isn't acting like "a company person." Here, we can end our search for the reasons why supervisors are not doing a better job of speaking out for their subordinates. They are not allowed to, and if they persist, they probably will lose their jobs.

The umbrella of top management's demands, however, isn't broad enough to cover all circumstances where supervisors renege on their responsibilities of representing their subordinates. Some rather ugly factors also enter into the picture—to be specific, arrogance and a sense of social distance. Most supervisors have a low opinion of the capabilities of the employees who work for them. A survey of 500 managers showed that the managers in every group rated their subordinates and rank-and-file employees well below themselves, particularly on responsibility, judgment, and initiative. When supervisors fail to speak up for employees, they are showing them how little they think of them. At the same time, they are reasserting and reinforcing their own sense of superiority. After all, if the employee's judgment were equal to the supervisor's, the issue would never have been raised.

And the supervisor is doing something else: By showing that he is 100 percent "a company man," he emphasizes his social distance from his employees. We usually think of social distance in terms more innocent or harmless—the supervisor up from the ranks stops bowling with some of the subordinates on Fridays, drifts out of the social club where some employees spend their spare time; or quits having a round of drinks at the shift's end. None of these are as dramatic as failing to speak up—this clearly emphasizes the message: "I've left those people behind. I'm 'a company person' now."

Of course, as we noted before in talking about supervisory styles, the particular styles of supervisors have less effect upon their employees than whether these styles have helped them win influence with their bosses and peers. Their skills in this area are revealed when they speak up for their subordinates. Employees respect bosses who represent their interests, but if the representations almost always fail because the supervisors' low level of performance, ineptness in handling their other upward communications roles, or both, have destroyed their influence with higher management, their repeated failures will in the end forfeit their employees' esteem. It is not enough for the supervisor to be a person of good will. Influence fosters respect; impotence destroys it.

CONCLUSION

We have seen that whether or not the supervisor succeeds with the boss depends upon a more or less happy combination of factors, several of which the supervisor has little or no control over. Take the worst of possible combinations: The supervisory style favored, in fact insisted upon, by the boss is both uncongenial to the supervisor and unsuited to the requirements of the work process and to the strategic position of the work group. The statistical standards in the department are in effect rigged against the supervisor by a hostile superior and an overzealous industrial engineering department. The supervisor, in turn, spends most of the time airing what he or she feels are the legitimate complaints of the work group to a boss with no inclination to consider its gripes sympathetically. In such situations, the supervisor obviously can't and won't win. That such a situation is atypical is also obvious.

The more typical supervisor makes do through various stratagems: using empathy frequently with the boss; telling the boss everything he needs to know but omits those things he doesn't have to know that would lessen his or her own influence; knowing where and when to extend privileges and make concessions to subordinates to get the performance the boss expects, and where to withhold them. This supervisor knows that it is an important part of the job to represent the legitimate gripes of subordinates to the boss; he or she also knows the importance of timing and delivery. In short, the successful supervisor in relation to the boss plays many roles—counselor, informant, diplomat, and deceiver—and displays skill in all of them.

THE EDUCATION OF GREG HORNING: APRIL 19

Jeannette told Greg just before four o'clock. They had done it. Not 110 percent—but for the first time the injection molding department had hit 100 percent of standard.

"Hey, that's terrific!" Greg said. "I think it calls for a celebration. No more work for today—what do you say?"

"Great! I'll go tell the others."

Greg was pleased—and proud of the crew. They were really shaping up. Creegmore, apparently, had passed the word after their talk a couple of weeks ago and it had made a lot of difference. They'd gone back to the refinements they used before Greg had enforced the rules and introduced Alfred's clamp and a few other improvements that Creegmore had come up with. If there was a little more job sharing than Greg would have liked, the results made him overlook it.

Greg had finally overcome the materials handling problem. Ed Briscoe had given him a rough time—his people just didn't have the time to go watching out for particular places to put every little thing. But Greg had fought. In the first place, by keeping their machines under careful check, his people saved the maintenance crew a lot of repair time. Perhaps Ed hadn't been aware of that. Well, he had noticed that Greg's department called for repairs less often than some of the others, but still. . . . And when you thought about it, Greg had persisted, how much extra work was it for a person to carry something just a few more yards. When you measured that against the women having to stop in the middle of something, maybe lose count on a shipment, to jump up and run around trying to find boxes—surely, Ed could see his point. Well, maybe—he'd see what he could do. It had worked, and the improved delivery system had made quite a difference.

Yes, Greg was feeling pretty cocky.

"Hey, Greg! There you are!"

"Come on in, boss! Join the party!"

"Pretty good, huh, Greg? We'll be breaking records by next week."

"How about a Coke, Greg?"

Someone had turned on a transistor radio and Rick and Jeannette were dancing. They'd come up with soft drinks and doughnuts from somewhere—the festivities were in full swing.

Greg was arguing with Phil Martello over who would win the National League pennant, when he heard his phone ringing.

"Mr. Horning? This is Mr. Phillips' secretary," the voice said when he picked up the phone. "He'd like to see you in his office right away."

"Is that how you get your people to work up to standard?" Phillips shot out at Greg when he came in. "Break for cocktails every afternoon? Why didn't you tell me? I'd have called a caterer for you!"

"Now, just a minute, Steve," Greg answered quickly. "If we were making too much noise and somebody complained. . . ."

"Nobody complained. I went by myself and saw what was going on."

"Well, if you'd have cared to come in," Greg said, his face very red, "you could have congratulated us and joined the celebration. We hit the 100 percent mark today. I thought that was worth a small sign of appreciation from me and I. . . ."

"All right. All right," Phillips answered more calmly. "I guess I should have asked you before I flew off the handle that way. But just the same, Greg, don't let it happen again. It's a violation of company rules and if it got around, it'd set a bad example for the rest of the plant. Besides, I think you were a little ahead of yourself—after all, the goal's 110 percent, isn't it?"

"I know that," Greg answered, his resentment well under control now. "But they've worked damned hard and I wanted them to know I appreciated it. After all, all I did was let them quit a half hour early and drink a Coke with them."

"Okay. But, listen. Don't you let up on them now. The target's 110— and don't you forget it. You hit that, and *I'll* throw the party."

"No," Greg said, with a small smile. "I won't forget it." He felt he'd been dismissed, but he had something else on his mind. "Steve," he said, "as long as I'm up here, there's something I'd like to talk over with you."

"Yes? What is it?" But Phillips sounded uninterested. He glanced at his watch as Greg went on.

"Well, we're having a hassle with the mixing people. They got permission from the supervisor who was here before me to store their sacks of pellets in our area."

"Yes. I know about that—I okayed it. What about it?"

"It's beginning to get awfully jammed up with those sacks and my crew is complaining."

"Your people are always complaining. Just tell them to do their work. If they don't like the decor, they can always go to work for *House Beautiful*."

"Steve! Damn it—that's unfair. They're working hard and their morale's getting better all the time. You can't expect them to work in a pigpen."

"Oh don't be so melodramatic, for God's sake! It's far from being a pigpen."

"That's not the point. They think it's a pigpen, and if they think so that matters to me."

"Are you telling me you can't get more work out of them unless we take those sacks out?" Phillips said impatiently.

"Honestly—I'm not sure. But I know it lowers morale, for one thing. For another, they waste time beefing to me about it. And how can I expect them to listen to me when I tell them it's important to keep their work stations clean and then let them work in a mess like that?"

"Maybe you're right. But even if you are, we're short on space. There's no place else to put all that stuff." Phillips got up. Obviously, he was ready to quit for the day.

"Well, of course, I don't mean that it all has to go," Greg felt that he had to close in quickly. "We can keep about as much as used to be stored there before I came on the job. And the rest of it—well, I noticed an area in the mixing shop last time I was there. They've got old parts there now that they don't use. I asked one of the workers there. They could pile them into about half as much space as they take up now and the rest of the pellets could go in beside them."

Phillips was getting into his coat. "All right, Greg. We'll see. I'll look into it and let you know."

"Good, Steve. Thanks," Greg got up, too, and went toward the door.

"And don't forget," Phillips said, following him out, "no more parties until I send the invitations."

QUESTIONS

1 How would you explain the fact that the group reached 100 percent of standard?
2 Do you feel that Greg should have checked with Phillips before holding "The Party"?
3 How would you appraise Greg's handling of Phillips?

4 In his conversation with Phillips, Greg was performing a vital function of any supervisor. How would you describe the function?

BEHAVIORAL EXERCISE

Consider the case depicted in this chapter of the conflict between the direct mail supervisor and the publisher of a magazine (page 322). You have seen what the supervisor wrote to the publisher and the outcome of the memo. Let us assume that the direct-mail chief was sincerely interested in persuading the publisher to reverse her policy on premiums rather than in putting down the publisher and exposing the error of her previous ways. Set up a role-playing exercise with two participants in which one plays the publisher and the other plays the supervisor. The supervisor's task obviously is to persuade the publisher of the merits of the case and to avoid alienating the publisher and losing the case in the process—a delicate assignment because the disastrous policy was undertaken at the publisher's initiative in the first place.

Ask two people to volunteer for the role of publisher and supervisor and give them 20 minutes to act out the roles; then repeat the process with two more participants.

After the role playing, raise the following questions with the class:

1 How successful was supervisor A in presenting the case to the boss? Supervisor B? What were the differences in the substance of their presentations?
2 What about the manner of the presentations? Which one was superior? How do you explain the superiority?
3 Did one publisher make the supervisor's job any easier? In what way?
4 In general, what insights did you derive as to the nature of boss-subordinate relationships?

BIBLIOGRAPHY

Argyris, C., F. Fiedler, and V. Vroom, "Leadership Symposium," *Organizational Dynamics*, vol. IV, no. 3, 1976, pp. 2-43.
Guest, R., *Organizational Change: The Effect of Successful Leadership,* Irwin-Dorsey, Homewood, Ill., 1962.
Whyte, W., "Structural and Administrative Innovations That Motivate People," in L. Sayles (ed.), *Individualism and Big Business,* McGraw-Hill, New York, 1963, chap. 16.

READING

The Foreman: Master and Victim of Double Talk*

FRITZ J. ROETHLISBERGER (1898-1974)

Roethlisberger, along with Mayo, is generally described as the father of the human relations movement. But when he talks about the human relations movement, he does not mean the plethora of canned programs and panaceas assembled by the naive and the greedy under the banner of human relations that sought to claim descent from the Hawthorne experiment and the research conducted by Mayo, Roethlisberger, Whitehead, and others. By the human relations movement he does not mean the alleged discovery—it was, in fact, *not* demonstrated by the Hawthorne studies— that relations between the supervisor and the worker depended on the supervisor's skill and that these relationships, in turn, determined such key factors as job satisfaction, morale, and productivity. In fact, Roethlisberger has devoted much time and energy over the past four decades to disclaiming the parentage of Hawthorne for what he describes "as the ball of wax that came to be known as human relations."

What is the legitimate scope of the human relations movement as it has appeared to Roethlisberger? What is the principal legacy of the Hawthorne studies—which is almost the same question? To him, Hawthorne was a justification of the clinical approach to studying people at work; that there was no substitute for the slow and laborious task of observing how workers actually behave in the shop; that no generalization holds water unless it has taken into account the work group as a social system; that for the investigator to ask about the morale of our plant is about as sensible as for the physician to ask about the health of the patients in our hospital. Roethlisberger emphasized that the satisfactions and dissatisfactions of the individual employees were always relative to the demands they brought to the particular situation along with the demands that the particular situation made on them.

Beyond that, he saw the principal lesson of Hawthorne as the importance to the employee of being listened to and paid attention to. And of the two, he would stress the importance of counseling to the manager, what he defined as "listening with understanding," of listening for the little things that made the big difference. In other words, Roethlisberger saw that human relations skills must always exist and be developed within a particular organizational setting in which the manager by patiently observing himself as well as observing and listening to others becomes in time—and usually it

---

takes a long time—proficient at promoting cooperation and participation. Roethlisberger was only secondarily concerned with generalities, what he calls "the search for simple uniformities"; his emphasis, instead, is on the clinical investigatory approach— on the close study of unique situations.

Most of this may strike you as commonplace and obvious, which is but one proof, and probably the most convincing proof, of Roethlisberger's status as a classic management thinker. It is the fate of the most perceptive insights of one generation to become part of the intellectual folklore of the next. So it has been with Roethlisberger. The more responsible practitioners of the human relations movement have shared his perceptions and preached and utilized his approach for a generation.

As for further reading, the following are important to any understanding of Roethlisberger's ideas: *Management and the Worker* (with Dickson), 1939 — *the* book on Hawthorne; *Management and Morale*—a better written book (obviously, Roethlisberger was the stylist of the team) but of much less significance; and *Man in Organization* (1968), a collection of essays written over a forty-year period, of which the best, such as "The Foreman: Master and Victim of Double Talk," are very good indeed.

It is in his new streamlined social setting, far different from the "good old days," that we must learn to understand the modern foreman's anomalous position. The modern foreman has to get results—turn out production, maintain quality, hold costs down, keep his employees satisfied—under a set of technical conditions, social relations, and logical abstractions far different from those which existed 25 years ago.

For one thing, he has to "know" more than his oldtime counterpart. Any cursory examination of modern foreman training programs will reveal that the modern foreman has to know (and understand) not only (1) the company's policies, rules, and regulations and (2) the company's cost system, payment system, manufacturing methods, and inspection regulations, in particular, but also frequently (3) something about the theories of production control, cost control, quality control, and time and motion study, in general. He also has to know (4) the labor laws of the United States, (5) the labor laws of the state in which the company operates, and (6) the specific labor contract which exists between his company and the local union. He has to know (7) how to induct, instruct, and train new workers; (8) how to handle and, where possible, prevent grievances; (9) how to improve conditions of safety; (10) how to correct workers and maintain discipline; (11) how never to lose his temper and always to be "fair"; (12) how to get and obtain cooperation from the wide assortment of people with whom he has to deal; and, especially, (13) how to get along with the shop steward. And in some companies he is supposed to know (14) how to do the jobs he supervises better than the employees themselves. Indeed, as some foreman training programs seem to conceive the foreman's job, he has to be a manager, a cost accountant, an engineer, a lawyer, a teacher, a leader, an inspector, a disciplinarian, a counselor, a friend, and, above all, an "example."

One might expect that this superior knowledge would tend to make the modern foreman feel more secure as well as to be more effective. Unfortunately some things do not work out the way they are intended. Quite naturally the foreman is bewildered by the many different roles and functions he is supposed to fulfill. He is worried in particular by what the boss will think if he takes the time to do the many things his many training courses tell him to do. And in 99 cases out of 100 what the boss thinks, or what the foreman thinks the boss thinks, will determine what the foreman does. As a result, the foreman gives lip service in his courses to things which in the concrete shop situation he feels it would be suicidal to practice. In the shop, for the most part, he does his best to perform by hook or by crook the one function clearly left him, the one function for which there is no definite staff counterpart, the one function for which the boss is sure to hold him responsible; namely, getting the workers to turn the work out on time. And about this function he feels his courses do not say enough—given the particular conditions, technical, human, and organizational, under which he has to operate.

Curiously enough, knowledge is not power for the modern foreman. Although he has to know a great deal about many things, he is no longer "the cock of the walk" he once was. Under modern conditions of operation, for example, there seems to be always somebody in the organization in a staff capacity who is supposed to know more than he does, and generally has more to say, about almost every matter that comes up; somebody, in addition to his boss, with whom he is supposed to consult and sometimes to share responsibility; somebody by whom he is constantly advised and often even ordered.

To the foreman it seems as if he is being held responsible for functions over which he no longer has any real authority. For some time he has not been able to hire and fire and set production standards. And now he cannot even transfer employees, adjust the wage inequalities of his men, promote deserving men, develop better machines, methods, and processes, or plan the work of his department, with anything approaching complete freedom of action. All these matters for which he is completely or partially responsible have now become involved with other persons and groups, or they have become matters of company policy and union agreement. He is hedged in on all sides with cost standards, production standards, quality standards, standard methods and procedures, specifications, rules, regulations, policies, laws, contracts, and agreements; and most of them are formulated without his participation.

Far better than the old-timer of 25 years ago the modern foreman knows how much work should be done in what length of time; how much it is worth; what the best methods to be used are; what his material, labor, and burden costs should be; and what the tolerances are that his product should meet. But in the acquisition of all this untold wealth of knowledge, somehow something is missing. In some sense, not too clearly defined, he feels he has become less rather than more effective, less rather than more secure, less rather than more important, and has received less rather than more recognition.

Interactions with many people

Let us explore further this feeling of the modern foreman. Not only does he have to know more than his old-time counterpart about the "logics" of management, but also he has to relate himself to a wider range of people. In any mass production industry the foreman each day is likely to be interacting (1) with his boss, the man to whom he formally reports in the line organization; (2) with certain staff specialists, varying from one to a dozen people depending on the size and kind of organization—production control men, inspectors, standards men, efficiency engineers, safety engineers, maintenance and repair men, methods men, personnel men, counselors; (3) with the heads of other departments to which his department relates; (4) with his subordinates—sub-foremen, straw bosses, leadmen, group leaders, section chiefs; (5) with the workers directly, numbering anywhere from 10 to 300 people; and (6) in a union-organized plant, with the shop steward. Exploring the interdependence of each of these relationships as they impinge in toto upon the foreman makes it easier to understand how the modern foreman may feel in his everyday life. A diagram may help to make this clear.

Foreman-superior

In the modern business structure there is probably no relation more important than that of the subordinate to his immediate superior.[1] This statement applies straight up the line from worker to president. It is in the relation between a subordinate and his immediate superior that most breakdowns of coordination and communication between various parts of the industrial structure finally show up. It is here that distortions of personal attitude and emotional disturbances become more pronounced. Why this relation is so important could be indicated in any number of ways. But it is clear that any adequate analysis would go far beyond the confines of this article, since it would involve a critique of modern business organization and the individual's relation to authority and, in part, an examination of the ideologies held by the leaders and executives of business.[2] It is enough that the importance of this relation and its consequences in terms of behavior, particularly at the foreman level, are matters of common observation; and it will be at this level of behavior and its associated *feelings* that we shall remain.

Personal dependence upon the judgments and decisions of his superiors, so characteristic of the subordinate-superior relation in modern industry, makes the foreman's situation basically insecure. He feels constant need to adjust himself to the demands of his superior and to seek the approval of his superior. Everything that he does he tries to evaluate in terms of his superior's reaction. Everything that his superior does he tries to evaluate in terms of what it means or implies about his superior's relation to him. Everything that his subordinates and workers do he immediately tries to evaluate in terms of the criticism it may call forth from his superior. In some cases this preoccupation with what the boss thinks becomes so acute that it accounts for virtually everything the foreman says or does and all his thinking about what goes on around him. He will refrain from doing anything, even to the point of dodging responsibility, for fear of bringing disapproval from the boss. Hours at work and at home are spent in figuring and anticipating what explanations or reasons he will need to give the boss. And the boss's most innocent and unintentional acts—failure to say "good morning," for instance—are taken perhaps to imply disapproval.

It is hard to realize how much those who are interested in improving the efficiency of industry have neglected this area. If the man-

---

[1] See B. B. Gardner, *Human Relations in Industry* (Chicago: Richard D. Irwin, 1955).

[2] See Chester I. Barnard, *The Functions of the Executive* (Cambridge, Mass.: Harvard University Press, 1938), pp. 161-184.

hours spent by subordinates both on and off the job in preoccupation about what the boss thinks were added up, the total hours would be staggering—not to mention the results this phenomenon has produced in nervous breakdowns and other forms of mental anguish. Stranger still, it almost appears as if modern industrial organization, which prides itself so much on its efficiency, has aggravated rather than reduced the amount of this preoccupation, with disastrous consequences for health and thus for efficiency. All this applies to the foreman in particular.

The crux of the foreman's problem is that he is constantly faced with the dilemma of (1) having to keep his superior informed with what is happening at the work level (in many cases so that his superior may prepare in turn for the unfavorable reaction of his superior and so on up the line) and (2) needing to communicate this information in such a way that it does not bring unfavorable criticism on himself for not doing his job correctly or adequately. Discrepancies between the way things are at the work level and the way they are represented to be to management cannot be overlooked, and yet the foreman feels obliged to overlook them when talking to his boss. This makes the foreman's job particularly "tough" and encourages him to talk out of both sides of his mouth at the same time—to become a master of double talk.

Each foreman, of course, resolves the conflict in terms of his own personal history, personality, and temperament. Some foremen become voluble in the face of this situation; others are reduced to stony silence, feeling that anything they say will be held against them. Some keep out of the boss's way, while others devise all sorts of ways for approaching him and trying to direct attention to certain things they have accomplished. And extraordinary are the skills which some more verbally articulate foremen develop in translating *what is* into a semblance of *the way it ought to be* in order to appease their superiors and keep them happy.

But, for the most part, the foreman, being loyal and above all wanting to be secure, resolves the conflict and maintains good relations with his superiors by acting strictly in accordance with his functional relations and the logics of management. In spite of what this may lead to in his relations to workers and other groups, his relations with his superiors at least are not jeopardized.

Thus the foreman, like each individual in the modern industrial structure, is in effect painfully tutored to focus his attention upward to his immediate superiors and the logics of evaluation they represent, rather than downward to his subordinates and the feelings they have. So rigid does the conditioning of supervisors and executives in the industrial structure become in this respect that it is almost impossible for them to pay attention to the concrete human situations below them, rich in sentiments and feelings. For them, this world of feeling does not exist; the territory is merely populated with the abstractions which they have been taught to see and the terms in which they communicate—"base rates," "man-hours," "budgets," "cost curves," "production schedules," and so on.

12

LATERAL RELATIONS AND EXTERNAL DEMANDS

LEARNING OBJECTIVES

1 Understand the meaning of managerial "work and be able to define the five basic types: work flow, service, advisory, stabilization, and audit relationships.

2 Predict what kinds of relationship problems will emerge in carrying out each type of managerial work.

3 Learn how to evaluate the performance of another manager and assess which parts of his or her job are being effectively performed and which parts ignored or poorly handled.

4 Be able to recognize why increased specialization *within* management makes managerial jobs more difficult to perform, particularly where one's authority is less than one's responsibility.

There should no longer be any lingering doubts: The manager's job is dealing with people. Many of these people are subordinates whose cooperation and motivation must be obtained. But many of those dealt with do not work personally under the manager. After all, one must work with one's own boss, and there will be large numbers of people in other units who affect a manager's own department. The duplicating department is getting prints back too slowly. The personnel department has not authorized a high enough salary for clerk-typists to attract a good person. The department next door is putting excessive pressure on a key person, who therefore is threatening to quit. All these situations require the supervisor to initiate and maintain relationships with a wide variety of personalities and departments.

It is easy to make two common mistakes in dealing with other people. The most obvious is to assume they are just like yourself. "If I see that getting here five minutes late in the morning is a problem, it should certainly be apparent to Mary too. After all, she knows what responsibility means."

But when we stop to think about it, of course, such an attitude is foolish. Individuals differ enormously, one from the other, in their personal makeup and in their reactions to the work situation. We cannot assume that our feelings or needs are mirrored in other people any more than we can assume that everyone will work harder if offered more money or that all employees will take criticism equally well or poorly.

Some managers go to the opposite extreme. In effect, they tell themselves that the human element is just too complex to be comprehensible. In their eyes, every person is not only different from every other person but also unpredictable. "One day Joe is as pleasant as can be to deal with, and the next day everything I say is likely to cause him to explode." Furthermore, since no two people are alike, it would appear to be an impossible task to try to understand enough about personality differences to make this insight useful in dealing with job problems. This philosophy causes many supervisors to give up when it comes to coping adequately with personality variations.

However, we have already seen that there are some common factors. For example, while individuals differ in the relative importance they place on various on-the-job sources of need satisfaction, we observed in Chapter 2 that they all have some measure of physical, egoistic, and social needs.

Obviously, working with other people in the organization is going to depend upon their different personalities. With Jim, for example, you know that you have to spend a long time beating around the bush before you tell him the problem. Frances is impatient and wants it straight between the eyes and no stalling. But working within an organization also requires understanding and predicting how an individual's reactions depend upon the *position* being played. Thus, as we shall see, as a supervisor you can come to expect certain behavior from a fellow supervisor who depends upon your department to feed supplies to his department—regardless of the personality of that supervisor.

> Greta Commins and Henry Krisky behave almost identically, although they are very different kinds of people. Both Greta and Henry are in charge of departments that service many other departments. Greta heads up the word processing department and Henry is in charge of maintenance. Both are constantly being called by other supervisors to rush their work, even to put it ahead of other supervisors' work. As service managers, they frequently become provoked at how selfish other managers are in trying to get their needs satisfied ahead of their colleagues.

Thus, whenever a supervisor approaches Greta or Henry, it will be useful to know that they both are frequently strained by these competing demands. It is easy to evoke an angry, emotional response by putting on pressure to get a specific job out first. Other managers are also liable to try that maneuver. As will be clear later, these other managers also believe that either the service manager or their "competitors" are preventing them from getting fair access to service.

In this chapter, we shall describe various managerial "positions" that may surround the supervisor. We shall also seek to show what it's like for the supervisor to fill a given type of managerial position and what it's like to have to deal with the supervisor in that position.

YOU ARE NOT ALONE

While it might be a nice prod to the ego to think that you are almost totally on your own—at least within the confines of your own department, this is just not the case. The large organization employs a number of managers, experts, technical personnel, and staff aides with whom you will have to build a satisfactory working relationship. This relationship is not simply a matter of good fellowship or the sharing of common membership in the XYZ Corporation. No, the larger company has established its structure, its patterns of work, in such a way that managers must collaborate and interact with one another. And to carry out that collaboration effectively, the manager must know the names, numbers, and positions of the other players on the team.

In fact, the personnel in an organization are like an athletic team in that everyone is playing a unique position. You'll work closely with some managers and see others only in an emergency. Some are there to watch you, and others, to help you. Your success depends upon distinguishing who does what and knowing how to work with each one in different types of "plays."

The managers, aside from your boss, with whom you'll be spending most time are:

Those who precede and follow you in the flow-of-work
Those who provide common services for many managers
Those who are available for advice and counsel on difficult supervisory problems
Those who seek to "stabilize" the larger organization by limiting your decision making
Those who evaluate or "audit" your performance in your job

WORK-FLOW RELATIONSHIPS

Most supervisors are "in the middle" in more ways than one. Of course, they must accommodate the conflicting demands of boss and subordinates. In addition, most of them find themselves between a department or group that sends them work and one to which they send work.

For example, a bookkeeping or clerical department may receive data from one or several departments on their sales or costs or orders, and in turn, it prepares reports which go to other managers. Here, it is numbers or data that are moving between departments. Physical parts or materials also "flow." The parts machined in the grinding department go to a subassembly group and, when incorporated into the subassemblies, they are moved to the final assembly and shipping department.

But, knowing what we now do, we can predict the problems supervisors will face in relating themselves to these preceding and succeeding stages in the work flow without even knowing whether it is sales figures or steel parts that are moving. Each supervisor in the flow of work will be trying to persuade other supervisors to do their work in ways that will help get the job done much as employees in a work group seek to modify one another's behavior so that they can work together easily and with minimum disturbance.

To simplify the problem, let's look at two supervisors, Homer and Chris. Homer is in charge of the receiving and storage area in a large store selling tools, hardware, toys, and general merchandise. His people also restock shelves in the selling area. Chris is in charge of the total selling area. Here are some typical problems they will face almost every day in maintaining a working relationship with each other.

From Homer's point of view:

I get a rush call from Chris that she is out of light bulbs. I've got two people out sick and the others are unloading a truck. She expects me to get my people out of the truck, get the truck driver to stay overtime, and start them picking out light bulbs, when she could have noticed she was getting low yesterday.

Chris is always telling my people that they can't leave anything in the aisles. But how are they going to load up the shelves efficiently if they can't bring a number of cartons out at the same time? She wants them to bring out one at a time, which would probably increase my labor costs by 25 percent.

The way we store things, it is a lot easier to stock the shelves in the same order that we warehouse. In other words, I want my people to restock Chris's department by moving from light bulbs, to cleaning supplies, to small tools, and so on. But Chris always has her "special list." She wants us to move from one emergency situation to another, and my people complain that they have twice as much running around to do this way.

From Chris's point of view:

I can't predict what my customers are going to buy. You suddenly get a run on some item or we run a sale and everything is grabbed up the first hour. Whenever I call Homer for help, he tells me that I am asking for things in the wrong sequence or his people are busy doing something else. After all, we're in business to please customers, not truckers or warehouse workers.

When Homer's people are working in the selling areas, they are as sloppy as can be and they don't care how much they interfere with customers.

Homer has developed a system for restocking shelves that is fine for him, but lousy for us. Why can't he arrange his warehouse supplies to fit our needs, not his?

Raising the Pressure Level

Taking both points of view, each is right. Each supervisor is making demands on the other to fit his or her own needs. How each supervisor does the work has an immediate and critical effect on the other supervisor—they are very much interdependent. How can that work-flow interdependence be converted into cooperative give and take?

In answering the question, it may be easier to look at the typical adjustments which guarantee the opposite: open conflict and mutual frustration. If Chris and Homer wish to frustrate each other, each will try to get the other to do his or her bidding by raising the pressure level. Since they are on the same organizational level, neither is the boss of the other—one can't just *order* the other to be more helpful or cooperative. But they can put on more and more pressure. This is always the first temptation when the other person is making it difficult for you to do your job.

Thus, Chris will be tempted to:

1 Go to her boss to put pressure on Homer, claiming that Homer is causing her to lose sales.
2 Collect evidence on the length of time she has had to wait for shelves to be restocked, the number of times she has had to get Homer's people to clear the aisles, the number of times they have stocked the wrong items on the wrong shelves.
3 Call Homer or one of his workers on the phone, saying a big customer is actually in the store and waiting for some piece of merchandise.
4 Try to get a rule or policy established that restocking should have priority over all other work in Homer's area.
5 Give orders to Homer's people when they are not doing their jobs as Chris thinks they should.

And what will be the result if Chris thus succumbs to the temptation to fight back? Of course you have guessed it. Homer will retort in the same ways. Pleading with the boss to defend him, putting pressure on Chris and her people, and developing evidence to prove that Chris is tardy in getting information to the warehouse—these are all methods available to Homer, too. What's sauce for the goose. . . .

In many adjacent work-flow positions, this kind of open warfare exists. Each person is convinced that the other is selfish, uncooperative, and out to embarrass the other. And since supervisors may see less of each other than do employees who work next to each other, it is easy for such conflict to persist. In fact, it is highly likely because supervisors like Homer and Chris tend to see each other only when one or the other is upset with something. Under these emotional circumstances, it is easy to blow up at the other person. Imagine your best customer has just said she is never coming back to the store because, for two days in a row, you've been out of floor paste! And here you've called the storage area three times for it. What is Chris likely to say to Homer when she next meets him?

Improving the relationship

But it is not that difficult to avoid these work-flow relationship problems—particularly when each supervisor recognizes the temptations and the pitfalls.

Each must try to build a working relationship and not wait to see the other supervisor when upset and aroused and apt to be hostile. For example, if Chris knows she has just placed a special on floor wax and that customer demands are likely to be larger than usual, she can tell Homer *in advance*. This allows Homer to make plans to accommodate the added stocking job into the working schedules of his people in the least disruptive way. In turn, if Homer knows he has some trucks coming in which will require several hours to unload, during which time his people will not be able to service the selling floor, he can give Chris advance notice.

Both can avoid seeking to force the other to cooperate by using pressure tactics such as appeals to the boss, excessive demands, and trying to prove the other is the villain. For example, if Chris is out of some item, she might ask Homer to bring over only enough items to get her through the day, or offer to send one of the clerks into the storage area if Homer will have the items ready to be carried out.

In a sense, each supervisor endeavors to build a *balanced* give and take with the other. That is, he or she knows it will be necessary to respond to requests from the other about as often as the other will have to respond. If one tries to "out-point" the other supervisor by making many requests without personally being willing to accept demands, we can predict trouble. Shortly, if not at once, the "put-upon" supervisor will start to fight back, and when he or she does, the first supervisor will become more antagonistic. Soon the two will be engaged in open conflict.

So Homer and Chris will have to find ways of accommodating to the other's needs, avoiding contacts with each other during periods when they are under great stress or emotionally upset, and responding to requests as often as they initiate them.

SERVICE RELATIONSHIPS

In some ways, service relationships are similar to work-flow relationships. Managers are dependent upon service groups to get their work done. However, unlike work flow, "services" are pooled or centralized activities which handle requests from a great many line supervisors. In a department store, the receiving and ticketing department services many selling departments by providing them with new and priced merchandise. A maintenance group in a school or factory fills requests for repairs from all over the plant just as a typing pool responds to the clerical needs of a number of managers.

By putting yourself in the place of the manager of a service group, it is not difficult to imagine the troubles. Everybody wants top priority and, as fate would have it, usually everybody comes around at the same time. It takes a great deal of personal skill and fortitude to manage the service or support group. Managers have many different people making demands upon them, but they have nobody to make demands upon. It is very much a one-way street. As we have seen in other contexts, such unbalanced jobs, where all the demands flow in one direction, are most difficult to handle.

And to make matters worse, managers always face the tendency for any minor scarcity in their service area to become a major shortage. As many managers know, there is no such thing as "a little shortage." Again, imagine yourself as the manager dependent on getting some computer runs completed by the machine room in time to give you data for the reports that top management is on your neck to complete. You hear through the grapevine that the machine room is behind in its work or overloaded, and that people sometimes have to wait 48 hours to get material back. What are you likely to do?

Most managers are apt to increase their demands in the hope that they can thus satisfy their minimum requirements. If you need the data tomorrow, you will rush in with the punch cards today, first thing, and insist that this is a rush order and must be processed today. Further, if you know that you will need some work done later in the week, you'll take that along with you so that it gets an earlier place in line. But, of course, everyone else will do the same, the minute the word gets out that computer time is scarce. Everyone "ups the ante" in an effort to avoid delays and to avoid looking bad to the boss because of falling behind schedule. The result is often an emormous logjam or bottleneck at the focal point of all these demands: the service group and the service manager. "The little shortage" becomes a major scarcity, with rationing just around the corner.

Service managers, for their part, may lose self-control and start arguing with their customers. "You aren't going to get this for a week no matter how loud you complain, and if you keep taking my time by complaining, it will probably take longer!" The manager who has expected service and not an argument is then tempted to fight back with threats of reprisal and the whole process may degenerate into a street brawl.

Planning versus Pressure

To prevent this, managers dealing with service groups have to recognize the psychological and organizational pressure which these people operate under. If you watched them closely, they would look like the harried waitress you have seen in a restaurant when everyone demands service at the same time and the kitchen can't keep up. Under those circumstances, many understanding patrons learn to help out. They don't add to the waitress's problems by demanding faster service, asking for a variety of extra things (more water, another kind of dessert, a special drink), and complaining of what they do get. Instead, they help make service easier. When the waitress comes for the order, they are ready with their decisions and don't dawdle over the menu. They may pour themselves water and even pass the plates back and forth if the waitress has put the beef order in front of the guest who ordered fish.

For her part, the good waitress can take some pressure off her position by giving patrons a realistic view of the likely service. Also, she might say that items 3 and 77 on the menu are already prepared and can be served a great deal faster than the others (assuming the patrons are indeed in a hurry). She may also suggest that they order only a main dish or carry over a drink from the bar as a means of reducing the congestion in the kitchen.

These same tactics help in any service relationship where there is a scarce resource. The managers requiring its use can avoid the temptation to add pressure on top of pressure (and to encourage retaliation against themselves, at the same time) by improvising ways to assist the service group. They can give longer advance notice of their requirements, thus permitting more efficient scheduling. They can offer to handle some of the more routine parts of the job usually performed by the service group. For example, the production manager might tell the manager of the word processing department, "Don't bother collating and stapling the reports; we'll do it here when you send the typed pages back." And they can express understanding of the difficult job being performed during peak-demand periods.

On the other side, the service manager has to accept a reasonable amount of the stress and strain that are inherent in the position. But he or she can also take the initiative in showing other managers how they can facilitate their work by timing their orders carefully, preparing the work efficiently, and doing certain things for themselves.

Most managers are not prepared to wait in line or are always fearful that someone else is getting more than a fair share. Yet getting service work done within the organization is just as much a process of give and take, of using personal and personality skills, as getting an employee to accept a difficult and unusual assignment. It is usually not simply a matter of writing out an order—except in the most routine cases. So dealing with service groups becomes both a time and an energy requirement of most managers' jobs.

One additional note on the other side of the coin: inside the service group. Because of the pressures coming in from other managers, the service manager would be well advised to protect subordinates from undue buffeting. The manager, given the supervisory status, is much better able to stand up to overdemanding colleagues than is one of the subordinates. The subordinate is tempted to agree to everything, to promise too much, and to give unrealistic expectations to other managers. Such "cooperation" only makes the situation worse for the service group and for the requesting manager as well. The service manager can more easily take the initiative in getting demands reduced or modified, dealing as he or she is with status equals, which the subordinate is not. (Consider how easy it is for the typical instructor to fend off eager students, all of whom want their papers graded yesterday!)

ADVISORY RELATIONSHIPS

Most organizations provide a certain number of experts to help the manager make difficult decisions. For example, the union claims the supervisor unfairly disciplined (with a two-day layoff) one of the workers who came in fifteen minutes late two days in a row. The personnel department is supposed to have expertise on handling both union grievances and disciplinary problems. The supervisor can go to the department and learn some of the implications of sticking to the original decision or of conceding that he or she was wrong, given the facts of the case and the current status of the union-management relationship. Or, with a mechanical problem, the supervisor may go to Engineering and get the department's opinion on whether a certain machine is worth repairing or ought to be replaced.

All this sounds both simple and highly useful to the supervisor, particularly in areas where he or she is inexperienced. Where do the difficulties occur in these advisory relationships? Maybe a supervisor's comments will suggest some of the problems:

> When I went into Personnel yesterday to ask them how to handle my worst troublemaker, Crouse, all I got was a lot of double talk, "ifs," and "buts." They said if I discharged him—these were some of the likely consequences, and if I kept him on—these were some of the other troubles I would have. I wanted them to give me a straight yes or no answer as to whether or not I could get away with sacking him. I left more confused than when I came in. Some help they are!

Advice, not answers

What has happened here to frustrate our supervisor with a personnel problem who is seeking a quick answer? It sounds to us as though the fault lies with him. He wants Personnel, with which he has an *advisory* relationship, to make his decisions for him. Of course, they (that is, Personnel) would then be responsible for the decision. If it backfired, if there were unpleasant ramifications that hurt production or caused major union-management troubles, the supervisor could say ingenuously, "Well, after all, it wasn't my decision, they told me to do it that way."

In a good advisory relationship, the adviser avoids making decisions for the line manager. This way, the line managers don't feel an outsider is telling them how to run their affairs, and they also learn how to cope with both responsibility and risk. After all, a good share of management consists of making decisions where the information is imperfect and the outcome is in doubt. A supervisor who hopes to grow in managerial stature must learn how to obtain technical advice—how to use the experience, know-how, and counsel of the adviser—and then sit back and make his or her own decision.

Carrying the Burden

Further, there will be times when one may get conflicting advice. One's boss may sometimes act as a consultant rather than a boss, and several staff departments may have different outlooks. Again, it is up to supervisors to factor in these judgments with their own judgments and come up with decisions. If it is their decision, they will be in a better psychological frame of mind to handle any of the follow-up problems. On the other hand, if they feel someone else has made the decision for them, they will be tempted to "pass the buck" for any undesirable consequences.

In the XYZ Company, the Employment Office doesn't just advise superiors on prospective job applicants—it actually selects candidates for supervisors. Crichot hired Oliphant this way after she was "advised" that he would be a good shipping clerk. When Oliphant began objecting to his work assignments the first week, Crichot got angry and refused to work with him and told her boss, "Look, I didn't want him in the first place. They put him here and I want them to take him out. I don't have the time to try to motivate him." Some weeks before, Crichot had brought in a cousin of an existing employee. The woman soon began exhibiting a good deal of tardiness, but that time, Chrichot felt responsible and worked with the new employee until she "came around."

The supervisor therefore ought not to expect an adviser to give her a final answer, but she can help substantially in coping with problem equipment, people, and procedures.

Eager Advisers: Unasked-for Advice

But some advisers want to go beyond the consultation role. In doing so, they can create, in effect, the opposite type of problem for supervisors. They pressure supervisors to try out new procedures or take on new ways of handling employees when the supervisors may be content to continue with their old ways of doing things. So supervisors have to be able to handle the overly eager, as well as the reluctant, adviser. Let's look at an example of the eager-beaver type.

> I keep having trouble with our procedures department. They want me to adopt a new filing setup and start using some new equipment they've found. While they claim it would reduce fatigue and increase my workers' output, I'm skeptical. In the first place, I would probably lose several days' work just having those people retrained. And there would be no assurances the new techniques would work any better, and this way nobody in the department is complaining. New methods always result in lots of complaints. They want me to accept all of this new stuff because it looks good on their record if they can get improvements introduced. Only, how do I know it's an improvement?

Some managers complain that staff advisers look for trouble in their departments in order to justify their being called in to offer a solution. While such fears are not always justified, it is not easy to fill an advisory slot. Here you have to wait to be asked for help. If you aren't invited to give advice, you can't be active and you can't prove to your boss that you are doing a good day's work. Having such an optional status, it is no wonder that many advisory managers do try to drum up business for themselves by finding sore spots.

Many supervisors, moreover, are either blind to the availability of such consultation services or reluctant to try anything new because it would require some short-run effort on their part. Surely one of the important characteristics of the successful supervisor is the willingness to invest time and energy (and budget) in solving persisting problems. A methods engineer tells this story:

> Carlin was a reasonable supervisor, but I could never convince him to take the time to develop a method of equalizing the difficulty of the jobs in his department or to find a way that his employees would accept as

equitable to exchange jobs. The result was that he was spending half his supervisory time arguing with workers about who had the tougher job or who should get some easier job that was coming up tomorrow or who was being favored and who discriminated against. Well, one day, he finally had a revolt on his hands; everyone just stopped working. Now his problem was so evident to him that he was actually looking for help. As a staff adviser, I know that when someone "is hurting," that's the best time to sell them on a new idea. With no production at all coming out, he called me up, and I got the people back to work by promising that we would do a major study in the department. Two weeks later, I prepared a number of options on sharing both the "good" and the "bad" jobs that were discussed by the whole department. The employees actually voted on the plan they liked best and there hasn't been a gripe since. Now Carlin probably had to spend three or four days working with our industrial engineers on this but he has saved himself 10 or 15 hours a week he used to spend arguing with his people. Some people take a long time to learn.

Thus, good advisers learn to begin selling their services and themselves by working first on areas in which the supervisor has obvious and real problems, rather than by trying to convince the supervisor that there is a problem. If they do well solving these, they will be called back again and again for other, and perhaps less obvious, problems. When the supervisor wants to be an adviser to someone, even the boss, he or she uses the same principle: Work in areas where the other person has a major incentive to try something new and to give up the old.

STABILIZATION RELATIONSHIPS

The decisions of any one supervisor can affect many or most colleague-supervisors. If supervisor A grants a 20 percent salary increase to a secretary, supervisor B's secretary, who does the same work and who has been told she is one of the best secretaries in the firm, will want the same or even a greater increase. If supervisor X decides to provide 10 percent fewer parts this week (because of vacations), supervisor Y (whose department uses those parts to make subassemblies) is going to have to cut back 10 percent whether she wants to or not. There are many such decisions that have a broad impact, and in such areas, the organization may establish a special department to control these decisions "for the greater good."

In this vein, Personnel may have to approve all salary increases. Production Control may have to approve weekly production schedules. Each supervisor will have to budget enough time and energy to work with these "stabilization" groups. For example, it may be very important to get a key worker a salary increase that at first blush will appear excessive to personnel. The manager has to be willing to explain, justify, and persuade why this case is special and why it should not set a precedent.

Obviously, supervisors won't win all these arguments, but they will win more than if they simply don't try. Just as misguided is the manager who can't understand why any limitations are necessary:

> All those people know is what is down in the rule book. They're just there to tell you no, and get paid a lot for doing it. I never waste my time explaining things to them because they couldn't care less how I personally am being affected.

But the point is that "they," meaning the managers who are responsible for these functions, do care. However, their job is the difficult one of balancing individual needs against the needs of the total organization. When they hear a well-presented, rational case and the individual need is great, they will often make exceptions.

> The company's traffic department is supposed to keep us from overpaying on transportation charges. There is a firm rule: Everything gets shipped truck or rail express unless you can convince them that the world will come to an end otherwise. I did just that. We have a finicky customer in Sacramento and we had sent him the wrong style and he said he was losing business, being out of stock. It was a small order and not much profit involved, but I felt sure we would never see that store as a customer again unless we made up for the mistakes in the last shipment. I culled our records and could show that more than half our total sales come from small customers like him and that over five years he had spent $11,000 on our merchandise. By the end of the "data," they were approving air express and even special delivery charges.

So far, we've been assuming that these stabilization departments only deal directly with the supervisor. They may also come in contact with subordinates. Under these circumstances, it's important for supervisors to demonstrate that (1) they have some technical knowledge in the area, and (2) they have some power in the situation. If they simply abdicate when subordinates are having trouble with the "rulings" of the stabilization department, they will lose the respect of their people.

Time Study and Rate Setting

In this connection, the role of time-study and rate-setting engineers provides a good example. These people are responsible for making sure that employees throughout the organization have comparable work loads and comparable opportunities to earn extra pay if the company is using incentive plans.[1]

Below is a typical exchange between an industrial engineer (time-study analyst) and a supervisor. Given this breakdown in communications and mutual trust, consider, as you read the dialogue, the impact on the relationship of the supervisor to his subordinates; the relationship of the time-study analyst to the employees; and the attitude of employees toward the fairness of the rate-setting (that is, stabilization) decisions of the time-study department. Here is the scene: The supervisor has just received official notice as to what piece rate he can pay employees on a new job. At this point, the time-study analyst who analyzed the job comes into the supervisor's office and the following discussion takes place.

Supervisor: It looks to me as if that rate is pretty tight and we are going to get a lot of gripes from the operators.

Time-study Analyst (to herself): How does he know; he hasn't even looked over the study—in fact, he probably doesn't even understand time study; he just wants to avoid any personal troubles with the workers. *(to Supervisor):* Well, I've done a careful job, and I think it is a good standard.

Supervisor (to himself): Here is another one of those know-it-all kids who thinks she has learned in a couple of days what it took me 15 years to learn. There's no use trying to reason with them. *(to Time-study Analyst):* I've already heard a number of complaints from the workers that they can never make out under this new standard. I wonder whether there might not be some factor that was overlooked in the study.

Time-study Analyst (to herself): Just as I thought, he doesn't have the ability to get his people to accept the new standard; they are so used to only doing half a job that tightening up seems unfair. *(to Supervisor):* If they would only give it a chance and really try it out, I know they could make it, but they prefer to gripe rather than work.

Supervisor (to himself): There is not much use even talking to her; she doesn't care about what happens *after* she sets the rate. In fact, she probably gets a pat on the back from her boss for the amount she increases the standard on the job; the greater the increase, the more likely she is to get a raise herself. I'm left holding the bag as far as dealing with the workers is concerned and with the new quality problems that are going to come up when they try to beat it and with more tooling breakdowns and

---

[1] Incentive plans, sometimes called piecework, provide that an employee is paid by the quantity produced as distinct from the time put in. But to pay for quantity, it is necessary to have some standard or base line. Otherwise, one employee might be able to earn $25 an hour and another only $2 an hour. To assess what an average employee might be expected to produce per hour, many companies use industrial engineers who observe employees, time them, and estimate how hard they are working. Their results show up in the form of a "rate" for a given job. Thus, a pieceworker on a punch press might be given an extra 2 cents for each acceptable unit his or her machine produces over the standard of 750 per day.

costs which those analysts never figure on. (*to Time-study Analyst*): OK. We'll see what happens but I can tell you right now we are in for trouble on this.

    Time-study Analyst (to herself): Sure, if that's the way the supervisor feels about the standard already, what can you expect from the workers? We'll have trouble from them. (*to Supervisor*): If they'll only give it a fair trial I know it's going to work out.

    Supervisor (to himself): They think they can never make a mistake! Everything was fine here until she came in. (*to Time-study Analyst*): We'll see. . . .[2]

Obviously, the supervisor finds himself in the middle, between the stabilization department (in this case, time study) and his workers. To be successful and not be torn apart by these conflicting interests and points of view, he must be able to stand up to both and be responsive to both. He must show the time-study experts that he is willing to spend time to understand their methods, their studies, and their objective of organization-wide stability, not just departmental harmony. He is also willing to dispute them when he thinks they are wrong and ready to defend their rate setting to his employees when he believes they are right. As we noted in Chapter 10, he will be willing to represent his department to the time-study people when they have legitimate complaints and he will have the courage to initiate to his subordinates and get them to accept the rate when they have no legitimate complaints. By balancing this direction and representation, he proves to both his employees and to Time Study that he is fair and responsive.

AUDIT RELATIONSHIPS

Audit relationships are like the stabilization relationships just discussed in that they involve the supervisor with other reasonably powerful managers. Audit managers are those who evaluate or appraise the work of the manager periodically in order to tell the boss and/or upper management how well he or she is performing. For example, traditional auditors like accountants are used to telling management whether a given department has stayed within its budget or how closely it is meeting standard cost targets.[3] Personnel, by looking at turnover, grievances, absenteeism, and the like, will be able to assess whether or not a supervisor has been able to build both good relationships and a department of loyal employees. Quality inspectors appraise the

---

    [2] George Strauss and Leonard R. Sayles, *Personnel,* 2d ed., Prentice-Hall, Englewood Cliffs, N.J., 1967, p. 665.

    [3] Standard costs, somewhat like piece rates, involve targets established by some expert as goals that the average supervisor ought to be able to hit. But here the target is the production cost per unit rather than the number of units produced.

quality of work completed by the department, and there may be other auditors looking at such things as safety records, housekeeping, employee morale, and the like.

But these, too, are not passive relationships. The manager may have to spend time and develop skills in explaining to each expert who is appraising the department why his or her group has fallen below some standard. In some cases, external conditions were changed—absenteeism was high because bus service was suspended during the heavy snow storm so several employees couldn't get to work. In other cases, the standard may just not be appropriate for the operation, and the manager has to try to convince the audit group to change it.

> When our value engineers came up with these new plastic parts, we had to change the sealing material. We know it won't stand the same 140-degree heat test as the old sealant, but we think it doesn't have to because the plastic will never get as hot as that metal did in actual use. Now the engineering department never got Quality Control to change its test standards—say down to 125 degrees—so we've got to convince them, hopefully with the engineering department's help. Otherwise, our reject rate is going to look like the national debt.

Sometimes, appraisal groups will be mutually contradictory. A manager is told not to use overtime for subordinates above a certain level and is also told (by another department) that if any orders are delayed more than 24 hours, it will be considered a serious supervisory error. With extra orders coming in and no extra employees, the supervisor may have the choice of looking bad on one measure or the other. And here again, managerial decision making is involved. The experienced manager knows it may be necessary to take the risk of falling below standards in some areas temporarily in order to meet standards defined in another area, which in the short run are more critical for the larger organization. This is another reason why the supervisor's boss who misuses quantitative standards to evaluate subordinates is creating trouble, as we saw in Chapter 11.

The manager has to learn to be adaptive and to shift emphasis as one or the other of these standards appears to take on more importance. During a period of declining sales and profits, anything that cuts costs may have top priority even though some traditional standards are not met. When a company is growing in a highly competitive environment, getting and keeping new customers, sometimes almost regardless of cost, may take the top-priority position.

Also, experienced managers learn that many audit groups, if they are willing to take the time to learn from them, may well help them find ways of overcoming their poor performance. After all, auditors are typically expert in the area they are surveying, they have seen many, many other departments, and they frequently prefer to correct a situation rather than issue a negative evaluation.

> We have some really great accountants. My costs were out of line and they did a complete evaluation of exactly where I was getting into trouble. I found some things that were easy to cut back and now my boss is happy as a clam. I used to think those accountants just tried to get the goods on you and couldn't care less what happened to your work or reputation. But when you take the time to sit down with them, it turns out they are very reasonable people. I learned something about accounting too, so those reports just aren't a series of numbers.

Of course, the manager has to expect that each expert auditor thinks his or her subject and area are the most important and the ones that the supervisor can't afford to neglect, whether it's personnel or costs or safety or what have you. But this attitude is inherent in any professional group that devotes itself to improving a given field. The manager has to be the generalist who balances off all these experts, each of whom wants all efforts to be concentrated on perfecting the results in the auditor's special area. So, as the balance wheel, the manager works with these various audit groups, both listens and explains, and strikes a reasonable middle course, depending upon the circumstances of the day and the departmental situation.

WHAT KIND OF WORLD IS THIS?

The new supervisor's first reaction to these complications in his work life may be, "Stop! I want to get off." There will appear to be too many people making demands upon him in addition to his boss, too many people to please or to compete with for scarce resources. He will assume that if the organization were well managed he would be given all the resources he needs to get his job done and would control them absolutely. Furthermore, only his direct boss would be telling him what to do or making requests of him.

But this is *not* an upside-down world—or organization. It is created by the need of organizations for specialization. The modern firm and the government agency need specialists in purchasing, finance, industrial relations, safety, quality, and many other fields, Many of these experts will have an impact on the supervisor's immediate world and job. This is inevitable and consistent with good management.

Thus the supervisor's job becomes somewhat less simple, less obvious, less clear-cut. The supervisor has to deal with competing requests, with competitors for scarce supplies, with occasionally contradictory requests: "Watch quality," "We need extra output" "Use that new employee even if he doesn't do such good work," and "Put that rush order ahead of your regular work—but don't neglect your regular work."

The effective supervisor is one who doesn't get flustered or disgusted with these noisy—that is, contradictory or at least inconsistent—requests. She can balance them off and maintain flexibility. This week, she may have to emphasize labor relations and devote a great deal of time to the union steward and to working out job assignments. Next week, then, she will pay less attention to union requests and push for output. She may have to use up a good part of the monthly overtime budget (during a period when cost-cutting efforts are in full swing) to meet a rush order from an adjacent department. This may leave the supervisor with little overtime for any normal needs for the remainder of the month. However, this kind of flexibility is required if the supervisor is to be responsive to the ever-changing needs and demands of the organization.

This doesn't mean that the supervisor always says yes to all requests. It is often necessary to say no or evolve a compromise with the other team: "Look, I'll give you half of what you need today if you let me have the remainder of the week to fill the rest of the order. This way, I can go to work tomorrow on handling the requests that I'll be neglecting today by helping you out."

Of course, such negotiations and compromises take time and the energy to engage in discussions. Thus, much of the supervisor's day is spent in negotiating with other supervisors who "surround" him or her in the work situation. Managers can't afford simply to agree or disagree. They must often take the time to work through an improved, one-shot agreement to cover an immediate situation in which they are blocked by contradictory requests being made upon them. Furthermore, once they have gotten their colleagues to agree to a compromise, they may have to spend more time and talk on persuading other managers to go along with the arrangement.

I said we would work continuously and as long as necessary to get that accounting report out today. But then I had to call Accounting and get them to agree to authorize overtime (which had been prohibited since last month). I also had to go next door and borrow back the two employees I had loaned the duplicating department when we had been short of work. And then I had to bring my boss up to date on all these deviations from our usual operating procedures.

The Manager—A Dynamo

To the uninitiated, this may appear like going around in circles. Each new request or compromise requires a number of other supporting agreements. Managers must keep on the move, must keep improving to accommodate to an ever-changing environment. Their jobs are not static ones in which they do the same thing every day and are successful as long as they follow instructions and keep their own people responsive to their directions. Rather, their jobs are dynamic: They must keep finding new solutions to the new balance of forces that are impacting them.

A recent study of successful and unsuccessful supervisors in a very large industrial company shows clearly that those who got ahead were those who had this dynamic view of their jobs. The ones who failed were those who were always complaining that the company "is going to the dogs":

> "I don't have enough authority."
> "There are too many bosses pushing you around."
> "The service departments don't really support you."
> "Orders keep changing; people keep changing their minds."
> "Stop all this changing and this negotiation—"
> "I want to get off this merry-go-round!"

The reason for all this change and dynamism is that many of the problems of an organization are not soluble by a simple "do-this or do-that" decision. The decision depends upon different managers and different specialists coming to some kind of tentative agreement to modify what they are doing or to concede on something that they used to feel strongly about. All this takes a great deal of interacting, communication, and many supervisory meetings:

> Our standard operating procedure is that every machine that goes out of here must spend two weeks in testing and also receive a final paint job. One of our best customers called and said he needed a machine to test out a new apparatus he was constructing. We had none available to ship him but the sales department said that "one way or another they would get him one."
> They had called us in final assembly to ask what we could do to help out. The only machine we had close to completion was supposed to have an extra-large exhaust on it. It hadn't been finished; it was waiting for the exhaust to be fabricated. So I called the machine shop and asked if they could rush out a baffle to cut down the size of the exhaust that would allow us to attach the standard fittings. Normally they would take three or four

days to machine something to order, but I know the chief machinist and he agreed, as a favor to me, to get one done this afternoon.

Then I told the sales manager that she would have to get testing and inspection to agree to waive both the final test and painting requirement, or nothing else would be worthwhile. She did it, but then testing insisted that I sign a statement indicating that I knew no reason why the machine was not safe to operate, and I got them to come down and witness a sort of "rough and ready" test we improvised on the shop floor. Then Sales and I both went to see Production Control. P.C. had to agree to change the production schedule that had come out on Monday.

They were reluctant to do so because the schedule reflected their efforts to satisfy all company customers while, at the same time, production costs were being kept down.

Rather than sending it over to Shipping to be packaged, I agreed to let the shipping people work in my department constructing a container for the machine. I made sure that they knew this was a special concession and wouldn't be repeated because I can't get my work done if those people are working in my area—we're too cramped for space.

Count the number of contacts required to get that machine out. Which do you think involved difficult negotiation? Which contacts were easy? In how many did the supervisor take the initiative and when was he responding to other pressures? What kinds of relationships were the ones with advisory, auditing, work flow, stabilization? Who was ordering whom in these relationships? Which probably took the most time?

This procedure is much more normal in most organizations than a simple follow-the-leader, every-day-is-like-every-other-day activity. Managers spend a great deal of their time working out these lateral relationships because work gets done through other managers as well as through subordinates. Figure 12-1, showing the supervisor's pressures, does not exaggerate.

CONCLUSION

Supervisors themselves have to interact laterally to get their work done. Their success in handling these horizontal relationships is just as crucial to job success as their vertical relationships with subordinates and superiors: These dealings with colleagues facilitate getting work done as information, assistance, and requests for modifications of one another's efforts are exchanged.

Now we can begin to understand how time is the very essence of the supervisor's job. The manager can't spend too much time directly observing or intervening with subordinates or he or she will have to neglect lateral relationships. On the other hand, the demands of these

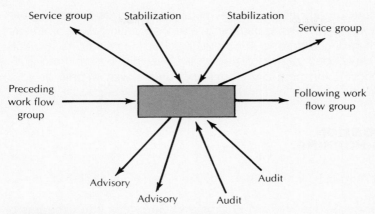

FIGURE 12-1 The supervisor's external world

relationships may be so great that one will have difficulty spending adequate time with subordinates. Effective supervisors are very conscious of this need for balance and close budgeting of their time. They realize that the secret of their successful performance is their allocation of time: How much time can I afford to train employee A, to correct or discipline B, to observe C, to handle these lateral relationships?

One final note: The individual supervisor may play more than one position. Thus a supervisor may have a series of work-flow relationships with other departments. At the same time, he or she may have a stabilization relationship with another department. (It has to get the supervisor's permission before it can change the specifications on the work it is performing.)

Because of superior technical knowledge, the supervisor may also be an adviser to one or more other groups in the organization when they get into trouble. This means that it becomes necessary to have a number of "plays" in the repertoire. The supervisor is a little like a baseball player who shifts from playing third base to shortstop, then to second base. Unlike the ballplayer, however, the supervisor may have to perform these different roles on the same day, even in the same hour, as different problems occur in the organization.

Some of these positions have higher status than others. Also, it is much more fun to audit another manager than to have to provide service. It is therefore tempting to distort your job, ignoring its less prestigious aspects so that others will be more deferential to you. Obviously, if all managers did this, there would be little service work performed and even advisory and some work-flow relationships might be neglected. Every manager learns more skills and also learns the troubles of the other person by handling all the dimensions of the job.

The modern organization can be more frustrating because a great deal of the work involves persuading and negotiating with peers as distinct from giving orders to subordinates. But the reward is a much more fully developed range of personal skills that evolve from successfully meeting the high challenges of working with people at your own level.

THE EDUCATION OF GREG HORNING: MAY 2

"This is for Aerotech, Inc. Rush it. They're one of our best customers. S.P."

The order came directly from Phillips and Greg took it to Creegmore and got him going on it. This kind of thing was no problem anymore—now that the workers were coordinated and the output was up, an emergency like this could be absorbed into the schedule without disrupting things.

But about 30 minutes later, Creegmore came in to see Greg. "I wanted to get into the job and make sure before I told you, but I'm going to run short of plastic before I finish this order."

Greg looked up, surprised. "But it's the same material you were using for the other pieces. A normal day's supply should be enough to get you through."

"Yeah. Well, a normal supply would have been enough, but those smart alecks in mixing gypped us today—I would have run out, anyway."

"Well, you get back to work. I'll see what I can do." Greg reached for the phone and dialed Joe Barber's number.

"Joe? This is Greg Horning. We've got a problem over here. It seems you delivered us a short supply today and we haven't got enough plastic to get through the day."

"That's ridiculous. We sent you what you always get." The mixing department head sounded clipped and cold.

"Well, I don't know how it happened, Joe. But my best operator was just in here and he said he was going to run out. Is there anything we can do?" Greg kept his voice firm but friendly.

"Sorry about it, Greg. But we've been having troubles over here too. Our large mixer is on the blink—maintenance has been promising to get to it for weeks, but you know how they are. Now that I think of it—we could have measured short, the way that machine's been acting up."

"Well, look. Couldn't you send over another batch right now? We've got this rush order on our hands—it's got to go right out today to one of our best customers. The orders came from Phillips this morning."

"Sorry, Greg. But there's nothing we can do. The crew's working on another plastic now; if they had to make a switch, we'd lose half a day's work. You know how that would look on the cost sheets. Cost us a fortune. Phillips would love that, huh?"

"Well, thanks anyway, Joe. I'll see what else I can do."

"Right, Greg. Good luck."

He probably enjoyed that, Greg thought, hanging up. There'd been bad blood between the two ever since Phillips had gone along with Greg's recommendations about the pellet sacks.

Well, I guess you can't win them all, Greg thought, picking up the phone again to call Ed Briscoe.

"Hello Ed. This is Greg Horning."

"Hi, Greg. How's it going, kid?" Greg had been getting along quite well with Ed lately. There'd been a good deal of give and take between the two departments. Just last week, one of the materials handlers had spilled a couple of sacks of pellets in the molding shop when he'd been coming in with a delivery. He'd been behind schedule and hurrying and run right into them. "It's all right. You go ahead—you're in a rush. One of my people will take care of it," Greg had said. He'd gotten Alfred to clean up the mess and sent the handler off to finish his deliveries.

"Well, I'll tell you, Ed. We've got a little problem here. Maybe you could help us out."

"Sure, Greg. What's up?" Briscoe at least sounded willing to listen.

Greg explained the situation, then he asked, "I thought maybe you could lay your hands on some of that 616 grade plastic. That'd do the job and I thought if there's any of it anywhere in the plant, Ed Briscoe would know where it was."

"Well, as a matter of fact, Greg, we put some of that stuff down in the storeroom a while ago. But. . . ." But Greg was ready. Before Briscoe could bring up the problems of getting it moved, Greg cut in.

"That's just great. Now what I thought was, if you could just lend me one of your workers and a truck for an hour or so, I'll send some of my crew down with the fork lift to load it. How'd that be?"

"Well, I guess I could spare you someone. Yeah. We can manage that. I'll have someone down there in half an hour."

"Thanks, Ed. I really appreciate this. Listen. We'll have to get together for lunch real soon. What do you say?"

"Fine, Greg. I'll give you a call."

Greg smiled as he hung up the phone. You can't win 'em all; on the other hand, you don't have to lose them all either.

QUESTIONS

1 Could Greg have put more pressure on Joe Barber to send him that extra material? How? With what likely consequences?

2 Under what circumstances would Ed Briscoe's reaction not have been as helpful?

3 Does it make any difference in the handling of lateral relationships that Barber is in the work flow and Briscoe is in a service capacity?

4 What should Greg do if the shipping supervisor calls to say that they will need the Aerotech order in a couple of hours if it is going to be shipped today?

BEHAVIORAL EXERCISE

Your company has just decided to add a new managerial position: director of consumer affairs. The company makes small appliances (toasters, mixers, fry pans, and so forth) and is concerned with the growing problems of consumer resistance to appliances that are either dangerous, difficult to repair, or poorly designed. The job has been described simply as one of "working with other managers in the company to make certain their products are not the subject of consumer protest or bad publicity." Describe the range of possible relationships (advisory, service, work flow, audit, and stabilization) that might evolve with other departments. How would you actually handle each one of relationships and from which can you expect some resistance? With role playing try these out with colleagues who will each take the role of one of the line managers. What will you say to the line managers when you describe how you plan to work with them in each of those five possible relationships? Get them to tell you what they think of this new addition to *their* work load.

BIBLIOGRAPHY

Lawrence, P., and J. Lorsch, *Organization and Environment*, Harvard University Press, Cambridge, Ma., 1967.

Likert, R., *The Human Organization,* McGraw-Hill, New York, 1967.

Sayles, L., *Managerial Behavior,* McGraw-Hill, New York, 1964.

READING

Techniques for Dealing with Other Departments*

GEORGE STRAUSS (1923-   )

George Strauss was trained in human relations at MIT under
Douglas McGregor, Mason Haire, and Alex Bavelas in what was
then called the Industrial Relations Section. He also took work in
social psychology at Harvard and with the group dynamics specialists that Kurt Lewin had assembled at MIT. Strauss was also trained
in labor relations and industrial economics; he thus represents the
interdisciplinary background that is very useful in management.

His early research was in the field of labor relations—how local
unions functioned in various industrial plants and in the construction
field. At this time he wrote *The Local Union* with Leonard Sayles.
From labor relations he moved to the personnel administration field
and then to general management. He has pioneered in the study of
lateral relations within management. His most famous study concentrated on purchasing agents and their dealings with other managers
who must make use of the purchasing department. He has also
looked at the role of professionals in industry and at white-collar
unionization (in government and education, particularly). He has
been a vocal and respected critic of those students of human
relations who feel that all work can be made intrinsically satisfying.

Dr. Strauss taught at Cornell and the University of Buffalo before
moving to his present position as associate director of the Institute
of Industrial Relations and professor, University of California at
Berkeley. For a number of years he has also edited the journal
Industrial Relations, and he is coauthor of two large texts: *Personnel*
and *Human Behavior in Organizations.*

Given his remarkably diverse training and his eclectic mind, it is
not surprising that his periodic reviews of the organizational behavior and management field are so highly regarded. He is one of
those rare teachers who are also researchers and noted writers; he
is also able to tie together the research and writing of others in
both a sympathetic and critical fashion. He is as generous with
praise as he is with his editor's red pencil.

Normally the agent attempts to fill requisitions as instructed. The
majority of interdepartmental contacts are handled routinely and
without friction in accordance with standard operating procedures.
Yet many difficult problems cannot be easily programmed. Other
departments are constantly placing pressure on the agent, who

---

* Reprinted by permission from George Strauss, "Tactics of Lateral Relationship: The
Purchasing Agent," *Administrative Science Quarterly,* vol. 7, no. 2, September 1962. pp. 165-167.

must take countermeasures, if only to preserve the *status quo*. And if the purchasing agent wishes to expand his power aggressively, as many do, he will inevitably run into conflict.

Understandably, then, successful agents have developed a variety of techniques for dealing with other departments, particularly when they wish to influence the terms of the requisitions received. These techniques will first be summarized briefly under five general headings. . . .

1 *Rule-oriented tactics*   *a.* Appeal to some common authority to direct that the requisition be revised or withdrawn. *b.* Refer to some rule (assuming one exists) which provides for longer lead times. *c.* Require the scheduling department to state in writing why quick delivery is required. *d.* Require the requisitioning department to consent to having its budget charged with the extra cost (such as air freight) required to get quick delivery.

2 *Rule-evading tactics*   *a.* Go through the motions of complying with the request, but with no expectation of getting delivery on time. *b.* Exceed formal authority and ignore the requisitions altogether.

3 *Personal-political tactics*   *a.* Rely on friendships to induce the scheduling department to modify the requisition. *b.* Rely on favors, past and future, to accomplish the same result. *c.* Work through political allies in other departments.

4 *Educational tactics*   *a.* Use direct persuasion, that is, try to persuade scheduling that its requisition is unreasonable. *b.* Use what might be called indirect persuasion to help scheduling see the problem from the purchasing department's point of view (in this case it might ask the scheduler to sit in and observe the agent's difficulty in trying to get the vendor to agree to quick delivery).

5 *Organizational-interactional tactics*   *a.* Seek to change the interaction pattern, for example, have the scheduling department check with the purchasing department as to the possibility of getting quick delivery *before* it makes a requisition. *b.* Seek to take over other departments, for example, to subordinate scheduling to purchasing in an integrated materials department.

13

THE
SUPERVISOR
AND THE UNION

LEARNING OBJECTIVES

1 Understand why unions get organized and how most union demands combine union and member needs.

2 Be able to anticipate how the existence of a union complicates the job of the supervisor.

3 Learn how to develop sound working relationships with your counterpart in the union.

4 Recognize how the supervisor's evaluation of individual-worker problems and complaints must take into account the union-management ramifications of any decision.

5 Learn the most frequently used behavioral skills involved in bargaining and negotiation.

6 Understand the union's political needs which determine how they respond to management initiatives.

The odds are very good supervisors, at some point in their management careers, are going to have to learn about and deal with unions. With 19 million unionized workers in the United States, even organizations which were once thought antagonistic to unions are finding that they must learn to bargain with representatives of their employees.

WHY UNIONS?

The rise of unions is not very surprising. Even though you may work for a well-established organization like a bank, a government office, or an insurance company, as an employee you are likely to experience a great number of situations where you think you've been unfairly treated. After all, how do any of us know what is equitable, fair treatment? Reflection will tell us that we all believe we work terribly hard, are underpaid or at least underappreciated, and often receive unfair assignments and even unfair reprimands. In addition to this all-pervasive sense of personal worth and personal righteousness, we always have the opportunity to look around and see others who are better off. The person next door, who hasn't had as much education as you have, works in a similar company and gets 25 percent more pay. And at the office, there are the people upstairs in the executive offices who have a lounge to take their coffee breaks, while you have to walk over to a little, untidy cart, pick up a cup, and take it back to your desk with no chance to sit and chat for a few minutes.

Unions promise employees that they will both eliminate such inequities and provide workers with more benefits than they could get by themselves. An employee can be made to feel pretty impotent when trying to bargain very hard with a whole company, unless he or she has very rare and valuable skills that are hard to replace. (There is a good deal of controversy among professional economists on whether unions actually have been responsible for increasing the earnings of American workers, but the important point is that most workers believe organized effort does help to raise wages.)

In addition, most employees have a deep-seated uneasiness about being given benefits, whether wages, improvements in working conditions, or so-called fringe benefits. They like the idea of *earning* or *winning* them. Of course, unions are not reluctant to say that they've helped workers win benefits from a not overly enthusiastic nor overly generous management. Further, employees in every organization have heard stories about the "person in department 16 who had been praised to the sky by the boss, received merit increases, and then one day was fired for a minor infraction of the rules."

As we have described in dealing with other problems of supervision, we are all uncomfortable living in a situation where there is great inequality of power. This is why adolescents and young adults are likely to rebel when their parents say "you must." They feel such decisions ought not to be made solely by the older generation. When you are totally under the control of another person because that person is bigger, stronger, or more powerful in any way—even when he or she is kind to you—you feel it is unfair. Implicitly, we recognize that where there is substantial power inequality, the good things can be capriciously and arbitrarily removed just as easily as they came.

So unions appear to provide a means of winning and holding on to benefits and of reducing the inequality in power between the individual employee and the organization. Unions also appeal as a means of dealing with difficult supervisors. They help in two ways. They bring the organized power of the group to bear against the supervisor's possible threats to discipline an employee with whom there is a disagreement. Moreover, the union provides a mechanism and a channel for getting beyond and around the supervisor and reaching the critical, decision-making upper management levels. After all, it is upper management that establishes most of the important policies that affect earnings levels and working conditions (such as prices in the cafeteria, amount of money available for salary increases, and the use of incentive systems). It is difficult even for a group of employees to walk into the office of the general manager or someone even higher and say, "We want to talk about company wage policy."

Of course, many workers join unions just because they have to. Sometimes, they are under social pressure from the group. More often, a union has established itself in the organization and has succeeded in negotiating a union-shop agreement. Under such contracts, all new workers, within a reasonable time, must join the union.

But whether reluctantly or enthusiastically formed, an existing union poses a number of challenges for the supervisor. What are these challenges and how can they best be handled?

SUPERVISORY CHALLENGES
INTRODUCED BY UNIONS

From the supervisor's point of view, the existence of a union introduces two kinds of critical changes. It influences decision making, and it affects working relationships with subordinates and union representatives.

When a union is organized, it seeks to restrict management's freedom to decide a number of questions regarding employees. The union leaders therefore negotiate a contract which specifies such things as rates of pay for specific jobs, the order in which employees will be furloughed if cutbacks are planned, and procedures that must be used if there is disagreement between one or more employees and management. Thus, management cannot freely change job structures, move people from one job to another, or alter their pay and working conditions without negotiating with the representative of the employees—the union. Furthermore, typical supervisory decision criteria (such as efficiency, equity, and eligibility for reward) have to be modified in the light of contractual limitations introduced by the union.

Impact on Decision Making

From the union point of view, these limitations on the manager's decision-making ability are needed to do two things: first, to protect employees from capricious and potentially discriminatory supervisors, and second, to protect the union's position and reputation. The union insists that its status is important because, in the long run, a strong union, with loyal members, will mean better working conditions for the workers. The following situations illustrate the most frequent and difficult types of decisions affected by the union.

Equity versus precedent

George Hingham has been coming in late for several mornings now. You can tell he has been drunk the night before and has had a hangover. You've talked with him, and he has promised to do better. You know something about him—he comes from a broken home, grew up in a very bad slum, and has been struggling to kick a drug habit. From your point of view, the facts that he works reasonably hard when he is here and had a good attendance record his first week on the job mean that he is making progress. You would like to wink at the company policy that after a tardy worker is given a verbal warning, his next late arrival calls for a day off without pay—because Hingham is making some improvement. But you know you've got another problem employee whom you have also warned and who is now testing the limits. Your boss also is very strict on these matters. He constantly tells you, "Don't look at the individual—look at the rule. We've got a union here and if you make an exception for one member, it will force you to make an exception for all. You will have established a precedent. The next time you try to discipline an employee for a poor attendance record, they'll throw in your face that he isn't one of your favorites like Hingham was, so you're giving him the business."

Ability versus seniority

The company is hitting a rough period and your boss has told you to cut back at least two employees by next week. This means a layoff of course. The person you would like to furlough is Albert Gorce. He has been goofing off for months now and does everything grudgingly. His work is just passable, so you can't charge him with anything. But the union contract is unambiguous on this score: At the time of a layoff, the person with the least seniority goes out the door first. Gorce has been around eight years. The irony of it is that the newest worker, Kaufman, is one of your best employees. He is eager and bright and does fine work. If you lose him, you are going to cripple the department because he is the one person who can handle the really tough assignments with the very critical tolerances.

The same thing may happen when the opposite type of question occurs: Who is going to be promoted? The seniority principle is less strong here than in layoffs. But consider a typical case: Jane Adams is the best stenographer you have hired and now there is an opening for an executive secretary. You think that Jane would be great on the job, but she has been with the company only eight months. On the other hand, Christine Shametz has worked in the department for several years and has been reasonably good. The union contract reads that a promotion must go to the most able person unless there are several with approximately equal ability, in which case the senior one must get the advantage. In practice, in many companies this means that the employee with greatest seniority must be offered the job unless there is someone else who is head and shoulders—as they say—above that person in ability.

So our supervisor faces a challenge: Can he or she prove beyond any reasonable doubt that Jane is superior to Christine? In most instances, there will be a number of ambiguities surrounding performance (as we saw in Chapter 7). Jane is fast and accurate and appears to be more alert. Christine can argue that she has shown her ability to handle a wider variety of assignments over the years, that she is loyal, and that she has more formal education. Furthermore, the union may imply that management is rewarding Jane because she is compliant while Christine has often spoken up when she has sensed unfairness.

Again the question is, can the supervisor prove with objective evidence that Jane has demonstrated substantially more ability than Christine?

Compensation differentials

Greg Carling has come along very fast since he was hired last year as a machinist, second class. He is very ambitious, takes orders well, and is eager to learn. You would like to reward him for his efforts, show him that you appreciate them, and try to ensure that he doesn't take a job down the street where wages are a little higher. When you propose an increase to your boss, he reminds you that the union has negotiated a rate for each job. A worker gets a raise when the union negotiates an increase for everyone or when promoted to a higher-rated job. When Carling can qualify as a first-class machinist, he gets a raise. But, unfortunately, he can't yet do a number of things which are in the job specifications for first-class work.

Does this seem unfair to you? The union admits that everyone isn't equal in performance, but it argues this way: Management might use differentials to reward their friends (for example, those who don't object to violations of the union-management contract) and punish the vigorous union activists. So the union seeks to eliminate management's ability to make distinctions among workers in a given job category.

Altruism versus due process

A manager was in the habit of giving his employees a day off now and then during the deer-hunting season and when the fishing season opened as his way of saying thank you for their help during the year. It was also his way of showing that he was "a good guy" and worthy of their respect. But one year, everyone was officially told that the company was facing some financial reverses and costs should be tightened up right down the line.

When several of the workers asked about taking off the first day of the deer-hunting season, they were told that it would be impossible this year. They said they had it coming to them—it was a "holiday" that the department had always "celebrated." The union got involved and pushed a grievance, arguing that neither the company nor its supervisors can unilaterally change employee benefits. The supervisor had established a clear precedent by always giving off that day, and if he wasn't going to continue the practice, the workers expected some other benefit in return.

Efficiency versus the contract

You observe that the persons on two clerical jobs often help each other with filing, proofreading, and running the copying machine. Three of them are called copy clerks and the fourth is a clerk-typist. You've often wondered what the rationale is for having two different job classifications anyhow, and you'd like to shift the duties around as the work load in the department changes. So one fine day, you announce that, in the future, all of them will be called clerk-typists (which, by the way, means a $4-a-week increase for the three copy clerks).

The union immediately objects that jobs can't be "eliminated" arbitrarily and implies that this is a way of reducing employment in the long run (even though no one is being dropped). Furthermore, the union representatives say that "giving a raise without consulting the union" is a device for impressing the workers with how generous the management is and how the union is unnecessary. Even though proofreading work may be declining, they want to be sure that the job isn't eliminated. "Since, in the contract, there is a salary specified for that job, you can't eliminate the job without bargaining with the union on it!"

Conclusions for the Supervisor

Thus we can make certain generalizations about the impact of the union in supervisory decision making. Obviously, supervisors have to be familiar with the agreement (the *contract*) negotiated between company and union. More and more, their decisions will be restricted by this contract and they must be sure that what they do is consistent with this document. In a sense, their effectiveness is curtailed because the best decision (in their judgment) for the unique problem (such as George Hingham's tardiness) may be inconsistent with the general rules. They must consider past practice and precedent, too. If they do something today, will it come back to haunt them tomorrow? They can't consider individuals quite as much as they used to, but they must be more responsive to the group and even to the political needs of the union leader, as we shall see.

Obviously, some supervisors are frustrated by these restrictions and they see them as foolish barriers. That is both realistic and silly. There are all sorts of restrictions on a supervisor under the best of circumstances: the boss's pet ideas, an employee's personality limitations, an old building, a cranky machine, wage and hour laws—one could go on and on. The challenge of management is to get work done in spite of, and within, these constraints. Almost no one has a free hand to do what one pleases in any organization—or even in most aspects of life.

The union just adds another set of constraints that have to be considered before the supervisor moves on a number of issues. But the existence of the union also affects *how* the supervisor moves, the *process* by which she or he gets decisions implemented.

THE BARGAINING PROCESS

If you think carefully about all the supervisor's decision-making problems that potentially involve the union, it may appear that the job has been complicated beyond reason. It will certainly seem that way if the manager tries to handle every employee grievance and supervisory decision so that problems never develop. Given all the coercive comparisons, jealousies, ambiguities, and legitimate differences of opinion and interest in any work situation, the realistic manager must anticipate that he will have to devote time and effort to working through various difficulties. Only a very naive or foolish manager expects that, through cleverness and omniscience, he or she can avoid such efforts. The real key to successful supervisory-union relationships is an understanding of the *process* through which such differences are resolved. It is this process which prevents arguments and grievances from becoming major issues which might cause strikes or slowdowns. Thus, although managers cannot avoid union problems, they can handle themselves and their responsibilities in such a way that the number of problems may be minimized and the problems that do occur will be resolved with a minimum of controversy and hard feeling.

This process involves both greater sensitivity to the need to document your decisions and actions and those of your employees, and an ability to learn to negotiate and come to terms with the departmental union representatives (the stewards).

Records, Notices, and Warnings

Many union-management disagreements involve questions about the past. Did Helen Corelli actually receive a verbal warning for being late? Did the employees who handled carbon black always receive an extra 20 minutes of wash-up time? Were two workers assigned to the large mill *only* when the machine was running extra-long pieces? Managers have to keep much better records on what happens with whom, and when, where, and how often it happens. An employee may say that he or she was never warned about coming in late unless a supervisor keeps good records and can show that the regulation had been communicated clearly and unambiguously. If there is a rule that no smoking is allowed, it is the manager's responsibility to see that everybody knows it. A supervisor can't say, "Well, they should have known it. We've had the rule for years and, after all, it's obvious that's no place to smoke!"

Managers can't get away with vague statements like "I am pretty sure I did that" or "Anybody knows that." They must find ways of documenting their actions and those of their employees. Similarly, they must keep track of the frequency with which actions occur. If an employee is allowed to repeat questionable behavior or a benefit is granted consistently, the union can claim, with justification, that a pattern or precedent has been established which *must* be continued unless the company and the union can agree jointly to discontinue the practice.

It is always helpful if the union representative is notified when anything extraordinary occurs. The representative can then feel that the manager is not trying "to pull a fast one," that he or she is being kept informed, and that he or she has the necessary knowledge to do the job as a union watchdog.

Handling the Union Representative

It should already be clear that patience and fortitude are required. There will be many problems which defy easy solution and require endless discussions which will try the patience of the manager. However, you have to be willing to listen to the complaints and arguments (even when you think you can predict exactly what will be said because it has been said many times before). Some of the listening is necessary to satisfy the union official that his status is not being ignored and that the supervisor respects his position. Listening also indicates an open mind and serves to fill the political needs of the union official, who must show he is alert and on the job. This doesn't mean, however, that the supervisor should allow endless harangues or should not terminate discussions after a reasonable time because some talkative union representatives seem to enjoy bargaining for its own sake—and many of these officials are relieved from work responsibilities while engaged in union business. There is a fine line between cutting off necessary expression and being taken advantage of.

Many times, a supervisor feels threatened by a union steward. This undesirable reaction stems from a number of factors. Many people become emotional when their decisions or actions are questioned, and some supervisors just panic when told, "You've made a serious mistake. You can't transfer that employee to another job. It's a violation of the union contract." They either feel intimidated by such a challenge or believe that their wisdom and honesty are in question.

Of course such reactions are naive because modern supervisors never have complete autonomy or independent power anyway. There are always "outsiders" who can question their decisions: their bosses, Accounting, Industrial Engineering, Personnel, Safety, and almost every other department. (A supervisor's responses to this type of challenge are discussed in Chapter 12.)

The supervisor may also be intimidated by the relationship of the steward both with the group and with higher levels of the organization. One satisfaction of management and also a symbol of successful leadership, as we have stressed before, is initiating to subordinates, giving orders, and sensing ready responsiveness. The supervisor often feels that the steward interferes with or blocks the subordinates' respect for the legitimacy of the supervisor's position.

> When I asked them to help out the maintenance crew by moving all of the empty boxes out of the way, they said the steward had told them it wasn't in their job description, it was laborer's work, and they didn't have to do it.
>
> I overheard the steward saying something to them about my having had trouble in my previous department getting along with people.
>
> The steward came over and said I shouldn't put pressure on Bozo to work overtime; it was a person's decision as to whether or not he or she wanted to accept overtime work.

There will also be times when the steward may know something that has happened in the higher echelons of the organization before the supervisor has been informed. The union chain of communications is (regrettably) shorter, more informal, and swifter than management's means of keeping everyone informed. Thus, the steward may learn that the company has just lost a critical order from one of its best customers and tell everyone she works with. When the supervisor is asked what he knows about the order and has to plead ignorance, he loses some status in the eyes of his employees.

It is easy to perceive the union representative both as a stumbling block to getting employees to respond and as a strong competitor for the loyalty of the work group. The supervisor may fear that the union actively *seeks* problems— even tries to catch him or her in some mistake—in order to dramatize to its members that it, the union, is on their side and that management is out to hurt them. In truth, however, many managers take pride in protecting their people and put a good deal of effort into representing them to outsiders. (As pointed out in Chapter 10, representation of one's subordinates is a necessary component of any leadership pattern.) Managers naturally resent any implication that they exploit employees or are indifferent to their welfare.

Control emotions

How, then, can supervisors handle this challenge to both their image and their authority? First, and most obvious, they need to recognize and control the temptation to become angry and to lash out at the union for its "unfairness." Bitter denunciations, efforts to show up the exaggerations of the steward, and complaints about "ungrateful" subordinates who forget "all I've done for them in the past" only play into the hands of an aggressive union and its leadership.

The opposite tack is much more likely to be fruitful. Accept the fact that the union does make life different and that union leaders have to try to prove themselves as active checks on unilateral management decision making. Unionized workers are likely to suspect their leaders of not being forceful enough. They tend to worry that the leader will sell out to management and that they won't get their money's worth for their dues. So the union leader is also on the defensive a good deal of the time.[1]

You can't wonder, then, that a union representative is a pretty aggressive opponent, on occasion. Remember that, although your actions may appear perfectly logical, reasonable, and fair in your eyes, they usually are seen very differently by employees. Many times the steward is simply voicing what others may be timid about saying—that you appear to be acting unfairly or precipitously.

> I really got the surprise of my life when the steward said I was browbeating employees to make bonus. Sure, I would talk to everyone who was below, but I didn't think they thought I was threatening to fire anyone who didn't get up there right away. I sometimes speak gruffly, but that's just my way. Well, it turns out that most of those young people thought I was a regular Simon Legree, just waiting to get the goods on them.

Respect the steward

If the steward knows you are willing to listen when she or he is speaking sensibly and not just emotionally, she or he can provide you with a good sounding board on some of your actions. This assumes that the steward does have the respect of the group (not always the case, as we'll see), is a reasonably well-controlled personality, and is not seeking hostility for its own sake. And, as we have said, your discussions with the steward show that you respect the steward's position as the representative of the work group. Here is a very typical case.

---

[1] See Leonard Sayles and George Strauss, *The Local Union*, rev. ed., Harcourt, New York, 1967, pp. 131-142.

I was having a great deal of trouble with O'Leary, who had a drinking problem. He would never be late and he was rarely absent, but there were many mornings when I thought he was a danger to himself and to the equipment. I had talked with him and told him that if this continued, I was going to have to take disciplinary action. When it didn't stop, I called Cabot, the steward. I told her how frequently this was occurring and that we were both going to be involved in a messy disciplinary case unless O'Leary came around. Cabot said she hadn't realized this had happened more than two or three times. Now she would keep her eyes open and check with a few of the others and see what they knew. The next week I saw Cabot again, and she said that she had learned that O'Leary was in real financial trouble—lots of debt and a wife who thought there was no tomorrow—and he did, in fact, come in pretty hung over once in a while, but the poor guy "was hurting." I told Cabot that I couldn't be responsible for his killing himself or someone else on a machine and it had to stop. She asked me if I could find out whether the company credit union might help, and when I said I would and would hold off any disciplinary action for another couple of weeks, Cabot said she would have a long talk with O'Leary. I knew that she would tell O'Leary that he would have to straighten out or the union couldn't do much for him if he got booted out since the evidence was building up. . . .

Here is a good example of a complex bargaining process at work on a very informal level. The steward gets advance notice of a problem and the sense of being respected by the supervisor. She is forewarned and also gets the chance to forewarn the employee and to check out department public opinion on O'Leary's behavior. Thus her political position is recognized and protected and she gets a chance to be involved actively. (Most union leaders get some satisfaction out of activity and out of give and take, and management can therefore make good use of their energy and need to be involved.) There is also an exchange of favors: Both supervisor and steward have the satisfaction of getting the other to be responsive. The steward proposes a postponement of any definitive action to give her a chance to do some things, and asks the supervisor to check the credit union. The supervisor gets the steward to go to work on the recalcitrant employee.

The same process may work when a layoff is necessary, when transfers have to be made, or even when new equipment is coming in. Obviously, it won't always work and the manager shouldn't expect perfection. However, there is much more likely to be agreement *before* everyone in the department gets excited and draws up battle lines.

In O'Leary's case, for example, if the supervisor had fired the man precipitously—even with good and sufficient cause—everyone in the department might have felt sorry for him and banded together to protest "the cruel injustice." Whatever the steward's own opinion about the case, she probably would have been forced to oppose the supervisor vigorously. But the problem was handled so that everyone was prepared and, had the counseling and aid for O'Leary not changed his behavior, disciplinary action would have less likelihood of being opposed.

Quiet, behind-the-scenes give and take solves many more problems than legalistic pro and con grievances. The supervisor has to spend more time and energy and invest more advance planning and forethought, but in the long run, it pays off in less lost time, less strife, and fewer open disputes. The latter are costly in terms of morale and relationships. There will still be times when there are strong conflicts of interest or when the steward will even have to fight for a case she or he doesn't believe in. But the intelligent supervisor understands that sound day-to-day working relationships with the union can withstand such interruptions.

WHO IS THE UNION REPRESENTATIVE?

So far, we've been rather vague about the union representative with whom the manager comes into contact. That was purposeful—to avoid that additional complication. Most unions have an elected representative for each major department or work area. He or she may be called a steward, committee man (committee woman), or some other name. It's their job to try to settle problems that come up in that group with the supervisor in charge of the department.

If they can't solve the problem there, they may take it to the next upper level of management or to a higher union official (likely to be elected, also). There may be still higher union officials dealing with higher levels of management in large organizations. This step-by-step procedure by which unresolved problems climb the ladders of both management and union hierarchies is called the *grievance procedure*. (The procedure is diagrammed in Figure 13-1.)

Knowing that the steward has been elected, however, doesn't tell the manager much about his leadership position in the group. Sometimes individuals are elected only because they want the job—they may not even be popular. There will be other, informal leaders in the work group whom the supervisor will also have to keep in mind because they are more influential in shaping group opinion or even in knowing group feelings. Some stewards are loud and bossy, getting a great deal of satisfaction in voicing discontent even when there isn't much of it. Others are very quiet, moderate people who speak up only when there is a real problem.

Obviously, the supervisor will learn to discount some of the loud clamorings of the troublemaker and to take seriously the problems

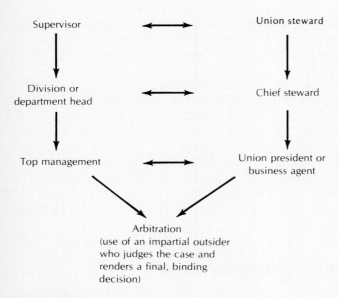

FIGURE 13-1 Typical grievance procedure

raised by the representative who is sober, is also an informal leader, or is on good terms with the group's informal leader.

To make matters more complicated, there may be situations in which one clique is strongly represented by the union steward while another clique is apathetic or antagonistic to the union. There may even be two factions vying to elect their respective candidates and seeking to embarrass each other at the expense of the supervisor.

The workers on the large drawing machines had never liked those who worked the smaller drawers. The LDs said the SDs had a soft job and they should get paid much more for their heavier work than the few cents an hour differential they now received. The steward came from the LD group. When management lost a big contract and had to lay off some workers, the steward made it clear to the supervisor that the first to go had to be those on the smaller machines. "Ours is a higher-rated job and layoffs always begin with the less-skilled workers. Even if you need less of the big machines, we can handle their jobs a lot easier than they can handle ours." Of course the SDs were just as adamant that they should stay if it should turn out that some of the large machines were to be shut down.

Thus the supervisor was caught in the middle between two contending groups. He really would have been happy with any solution, but he had to be prepared for a long series of arguments because of the intergroup conflict.

Types of Union Leaders

At times, stewards who are purely destructive will be elected. They are anti-everything and devote themselves to proving that managers are always wrong. Usually, such highly aggressive personalities are also unable to settle problems by negotiating with the supervisor. All they can do is complain. Although such negative pyrotechnics try the patience of the manager, if he or she can remain "cool," the union members will eventually recognize that this kind of steward isn't able to accomplish much beyond providing an outlet for himself or herself and perhaps for them. When they learn that the steward can't undertake the more painstaking job of working out settlements, they will replace that person with someone who is less of a firebrand and more constructive.

Then the manager must be careful not to destroy the political position of the constructive steward by doing things which create the impression that the steward is too friendly with management. Too frequent contact outside of work, socializing, and excessive friendliness can be interpreted by suspicious rank-and-file employees to mean that the steward has sold out. In fact, the supervisor ought to avoid associating the steward's name with what are likely to be highly unpopular decisions (such as the discharge of an employee for good cause) even though the steward may concur with them privately. The union representative can then be free to object, albeit weakly, to the supervisor's action. The last thing the supervisor wants is a collusive relationship which may succeed in the short run but which will surely backfire in time. At best, the membership is suspicious of the motives of its leaders.

HOW DO YOU BARGAIN?

Skilled negotiation is an art which may take years of practice to acquire. Many books have been written about bargaining techniques, but there are a few things which every supervisor can learn quickly.

1 Remember that bargaining involves give and take. You can't expect to win everything you want—even if you are sure you are right. Moreover, the union representative has to be able to show the workers that he or she has been effective in defending their interests. Therefore, extreme rigidity and a take-it-or-leave-it attitude on the manager's part is bound to lead to an impasse.

2 Don't try surprises or trickery even though they may help win in a particular grievance. In the long run, the quality of the relationship may deteriorate to the point that there will be much more trouble on other issues.

Handler suspended an employee for selling "numbers" (gambling slips) during working hours to his fellow workers. The union argued that she just had it in for Krepps; there was no good evidence other than a rumor that he sold "numbers." The supervisor refused to change her decision and the union pushed the case up through the grievance procedure over the next few months. On the last day of arbitration, Handler was present and showed a Polaroid picture she had taken which showed Krepps taking money with one hand while he had a fist full of policy slips in the other. Of course, the discharge stuck and the union looked foolish. But they vowed they would never trust Handler again. "No use even dealing with her since she doesn't put her cards on the table, but we'll make so many grievances in her department that her boss will think she's the worst supervisor in the plant."

Of course, the supervisor did nothing wrong in seeking evidence to substantiate the charge, but she should have presented it to the union at the outset. Union-management relations ought not to be conducted like the adversary legalistic proceedings in which both sides keep each other at arm's length. That's fine for Perry Mason, but not for the supervisor who still has to work with the union.

3 Try to narrow the differences by establishing as much agreement as possible on the facts in the case. "OK," a supervisor might say, "we'll agree that all employees have not been given that wash-up privilege in the past if you'll accept the fact that the grinders have been doing it for at least three years, and have always had at least 15 minutes. So the issue comes down to whether it is fair for workers on just the dirtiest jobs to get this privilege." If you try to deal with everything at once, many problems are insoluble.

4 Seek to distinguish between what the union representative considers the most vital issues and the secondary problems. For example, employees and the union can get themselves very worked up over what they consider a matter of principle and the argument will be very difficult to resolve. On the other hand, there may be secondary or less crucial issues which can be settled amicably and easily. (Of course the same holds for management.) As one supervisor tells it:

Two employees were fighting and I first insisted on disciplining both equally; I didn't care who started it. They both were going to get a two-week layoff. The union rep at first said I was a tyrant and this wasn't the kind of first offense that ought to have such a stiff penalty attached. But in talking with him, I finally learned that everyone in the department thought that there ought to be a distinction made between the instigator and whoever was caught. Anything else violated their sense of fair play. Once I agreed to consider making some distinction in penalty, the rest was easy to wind up.

The generalization is that most people find it difficult if not impossible to compromise on principle or what they see as major symbolic issues (such as acceptance of the union, acceptance of management's "right to manage," and seniority). Also, there is a tendency for the union to ask for more than it knows it can achieve, and the sooner one sifts out the more from the less important, the quicker a settlement.

5 Try to overcome a stalemate by attempting to settle the easy things first—it sometimes helps. The simple decision provides everyone with a sense of successful bargaining and moves the discussion off dead center. Save the most difficult for the end. At times, it may even be necessary to postpone for an extended time the very sticky issues.

> The steward and I tried to work out a rule that would govern who would get stuck with that messy clean-up job that comes in every week or two. It wasn't any good trying rotation because the employee whose turn it was might be tied up finishing a critical job or be taking that as a leave day. Everything else we tried either displeased the workers or I couldn't live with it, so we agreed to disagree. I would of course continue to make the decision each time and they would protest if they didn't like it. If we had tried to settle on a formula we would have been arguing from now till next year.

6 Don't reward pressure tactics—show you can hold your ground. Many times an aggressive union official will threaten to call a wildcat strike, to go over your head to upper management (to "tell all!"), to make life miserable for you, or to disgrace you by other means. If you concede under these circumstances, it will encourage continued use of threats and even stronger tactics. It is an old principle of labor relations that the only thing worse than a wildcat strike is a successful wildcat strike. Prove that reasonable give-and-take discussions are much more rewarding (in terms of good settlements) than pressure tactics and don't bargain while employees are engaged in illegal acts.

7 Similarly, don't threaten the union leader with embarrassment in front of the other workers or use other undermining tactics. As we have said, she is probably an elected official. She has to show her people that she is working hard for them and therefore has to gather in some "victories" or "winnings" to prove she is an effective negotiator.

8 Do not hesitate to conduct some bargaining quietly and in private. Many times, you or the union steward will want to try out some ideas without having either talk about it to outsiders. Some concessions the union steward may make only if they are arranged in private and if you don't quote him or embarrass him. "All right, we'll look the other way when you lay off Strickoff, if you'll agree not to push the disciplinary penalty against him. There's some justification for saying he broke his seniority during that two-year leave of absence anyhow, but that disciplinary thing would really hurt his employment record."

These kinds of trade-offs always sound illicit or even unfair if announced publicly. But bargaining does involve certain "giving in" and certain "admissions" which would prove politically unacceptable if widely announced. This is why, in international relations, negotiators insist on seclusion and often announce only the final results of their deliberations and not *how* they arrived at the settlement.

9 Try to pace your negotiations. It never hurts to spend some time in easy conversation with your union counterpart. If the debate gets too hot, it may be worthwhile to break off discussions because little of constructive value is done during periods of substantial emotionality and emotion is usually catching. Also, there may be value in giving the other person time to digest certain new information or a suggestion or even to check it out with others. In other words, don't expect an immediate yes or no on everything, and in turn, you may want to ask for time.

10 Don't give the impression that you can only say no to things, and that to say yes, everything must be checked with your boss. Under such circumstances, the union delegate rightfully concludes that it is a waste of time negotiating with you and always should immediately bypass you with requests.

USING THE UNION

At the very beginning of this chapter, we talked about reasons for unionization: the desire on the part of employees for recognition, participation, for control, and for more! Managers, if they are to be realistic, have to accept the fact of unionization. Even well-managed, generous enterprises come to be organized because no company can give its workers everything they want. Some things they *must* get—and *want* to get—for themselves through their own group.

But all this need not be solely a burden for the manager. Unionization can provide job satisfactions: an increased sense of job security, of respect and identity and assurance that one is getting a square deal. Furthermore, the supervisor can use the union in at least two important ways.

The Watchdog Effect

The union can be a kind of control system alerting the supervisor to hidden problems. Remembering that the union representative may exaggerate and may even not be a particularly good representative, there will still be many times in which the steward will bring the supervisor's attention to problems that might otherwise go unnoticed for an extended period. Often problems which are not promptly dealt with get worse and are therefore more difficult to solve than they otherwise would be. And they also hurt productivity during their festering period.

Within the laboratory technician group, there had been a story circulating for years that, back in the 1950s, technicians had received the same salary as test-cell mechanics.

But, as the story went, the head of the lab during the middle of that decade was a snob who believed that technicians were not much better than bottlewashers and she allowed their earnings to lag behind the increases granted the mechanics. Many technicians bore a real grudge and, particularly as their work load increased as a result of the expanded new product-development efforts, they resented and resisted all new job requirements.

The breaking point came when their present supervisor sought to eliminate the use of two technicians for certain procedures which he felt could be handled by one. By this time, there was a union in the lab and the union steward raised a grievance about a change in their work load, insisting that the change had to be negotiated through the union.

During the discussions between the steward and the head of the lab, this differential between themselves and the mechanics came up. The lab director was surprised by this comparison; he had never heard of this "inequity" before. In checking the records it was found that indeed there had been parity back in 1953, but after that time the test-cell mechanics' jobs had been changed substantially. Only employees with "technologist" degrees from junior colleges or special training programs could qualify and the work became substantially more demanding. The old test-cell work was gradually phased out and the new people took over tasks that had been performed by engineers.

When this was finally explained to the technicians, they became much more reasonable about their own salaries, and the grievance over the two technicians was settled quickly by a mutually satisfactory compromise. During the more demanding procedures, the old methods involving two technicians would still apply, but in other cases one technician would handle the whole thing. However, the supervisor would have to expect that such a technician would handle less jobs per day.

It should be noted that this type of problem resolution is rather typical in union-management relations. The steps are often these:

Underlying and unexpressed problems are brought out into the open. (In the above case, the 1953 salary comparison came to light.)

The process of give and take between union representatives and employees gives workers a sense of having some control over their jobs and environment.

A workable solution is evolved which incorporates some safeguards for the workers and some for management. Neither side gets what it wants completely.

Both management and the union learn something about the other's needs. (In this case, for example, management learned that the technicians were also afraid that a trend was emerging which would make their jobs increasingly demanding.)

Through the settlement, and the give and take and the release of pent-up feelings which precede it, morale—and often productivity as well—is improved.

Accepting the Decision

The second contribution the supervisor can receive from the union is greater acceptance of certain critical decisions that might otherwise be resisted or considered unfair. In the case of the laboratory technicians, for example, the process by which union and supervisor negotiated technician work-load changes served to legitimatize the final agreement. One technician was heard to say:

> You know, I thought the company was really giving us the business: getting more and more work out of us for the same pay. But I think the rule that came out of that grievance is fair to both sides. I just know that on these special tests you would need at least four hands to do it yourself, but as long as I know that we're safe on those, I'm willing to try doing the routine ones by myself.

In effect, if the relationship with the union is a good one, the union representative will sell the grievance settlement to fellow employees: "Hey look, they [management] gave a lot on this and I know we can live with the agreement. You know that if anyone tries to pull a fast one by sneaking in extra work on any of these jobs, we'll blow the whistle as we did last time. We got a good deal because, frankly, in the other labs in the other divisions, the work load is a lot higher than we've got."

Similarly, if the manager has forewarned the union representative and given him a chance to do his own investigating and perhaps cool off the hotheads in the group, the manager may well find that the union can serve as an effective channel of communication to employers.

Obviously, employees won't think that management is credible if they feel they are being "used." They need to be consulted in advance, to be given responsive answers to their complaints and inquiries, and to have their political needs accepted by supervision.

A LAST WORD

None of this discussion of management-union relationships should be taken to mean that supervisors can thus neglect their own direct relationships with subordinates. While there will be times that they will communicate through stewards and use them as sounding boards or as informal leaders, there should be more times in which supervisors continue with direct communications, counseling, advising, directing, and disciplining employees. If they rely entirely on stewards, they can both become captives and lose their own status among employees. The union is an extra channel to be used. It is not a substitute for leadership and close, direct relationships with subordinates.

THE EDUCATION OF GREG HORNING: MAY 24

The gripes from the crew about the night shift had been increasing. Greg's crew would often come in in the morning and find a lot of unfinished work left for them to do and the shop in a mess. Another gripe came frequently from the women when it came to inspecting work. The night shift had no one in particular to do their inspecting— the operators did it for themselves. According to Helen and Jeannette, they couldn't care less. They let a lot of shoddy pieces go through and the women had to reinspect the night shift's work and flash a lot of their output before they could let it pass. As a result, they wasted a lot of time redoing the night shift's work, and this really slowed the whole department's production. Greg checked the complaints and they were legitimate all right; if anything the mess was worse than they had claimed.

Greg had already tried talking to the night supervisor about the problem, but it hadn't had any effect. He was in charge of the whole plant for the night shift, and he didn't have the time to keep a close watch on any one department. So he had no choice but to leave them pretty much on their own, hope for the best, and leave the problems to the day shift foreman.

Greg was not sure what to do. He could bring the problem to Phillips' attention, but he knew better than that now. Phillips would chew out the night people, maybe fire some of them as a warning to the others. It might make them shape up, but the bad feelings it would generate wouldn't be worth it. In spite of the fact that the night shift was causing his crew trouble, they'd all join together against him if he went upstairs. It would get back to his people through the union and they'd think he'd been a fink, running to the big boss instead of handling the situation himself.

The union! That was it. This was a problem that the union should be brought into. He'd better have a talk with Phil Martello.

Martello was not exactly enthusiastic when Greg called him in to talk about it.

"I don't like the sound of it, Greg. You're putting me in the middle of a very sticky situation."

"I know it's sticky, Phil, but you've complained yourself about the mess they make. They're the worst crew in the plant and we have to take the rap. Something's got to be done about it."

"You're damned right, Greg," Phil answered angrily. But he was being defensive. "But you're the one that has to do it. You're management. Why should I do your job?"

"Listen, Phil," Greg said carefully, trying to be persuasive. He knew how Phil must feel—he knew what it was like to be boxed in. "Think about it. What could I do? I could get some of them fired and it would stick—the union wouldn't like that much, would they? Or I could get Phillips to hand out a bunch of layoffs. Your people wouldn't like that much either. There's got to be a better way. That's why I'm talking to you."

Phil smiled reluctantly. "You sure have learned a few things in five months, damn you."

Greg laughed.

"But, honest, Greg," Phil went on, shifting in his chair, "I don't know what those guys do at night. Maybe they got it good—maybe too good—but I don't know what I can do about it."

"But you do know what this place looks like in the morning. And you do know how you gripe all the time about your machine being all fouled up with dirt."

"Yeah."

"And you know the people on the night shift," Greg persisted. "Now you can talk to them, see, where I can't. You can tell them how the rest of you feel—that you're not going to fight for them because you know they've been goofing off. And you can tell them what I'll do if they don't shape up. From you, it's a friendly tip, see. A word to the wise, that kind of thing. You know."

"Yeah," Phil said, a little more positively. "I guess I could try that. I know some of the people from the union. We have a meeting next Thursday night. I guess I should tell them—they've been getting away with murder."

"You sure should," Greg said, closing in. "After all, it's our own people they're hurting. Our crew. It's not as though it was something that doesn't affect us. It does. It hurts our whole operation. And you can talk to them. You're a union steward. They'll listen to you."

"Well, all right, Greg," Phil said. But he was still doubtful. "I'll give it a try. Maybe they'll listen to me."

"Okay, Phil," Greg said. "I won't move on this until I hear from you. Let me know what happens."

"Yeah. I'll let you know," Phil said, nodding his head. "Yeah. I guess they'll listen to me. Anyway, it's worth a try."

QUESTIONS

1 Is Greg being realistic in hoping that the night shift will listen to the steward, Martello? (Are members expected to take instructions from their elected officials?)
2 At what point in dealing with the night shift could the steward best be brought into the picture?
3 What should Greg do if the steward tells him absolutely no, he won't cooperate?
4 How would you cope with Martello if he agreed to do this only if Greg would promise to get the day crew a 15-minute wash-up period in the afternoon?

BEHAVIORAL EXERCISE

You are going to take the role of a supervisor having to negotiate an increased work load with the union steward in your department. The union-management contract clearly specifies that changes in an employee's work load are a subject for union-management negotiation. You are anxious to convince the union steward that not only is the increase fair, but it's not really an increase in actual employee work effort.

The situation is as follows: Two employees have each been operating a small punch press which stamps out metal parts. In the past they have had to insert a piece of metal and press a lever which activated the press. Now the engineers have devised a gadget which allows the employee to insert the end of a rather lengthy piece of metal and the punch press will then punch and move the metal along until twenty pieces have been produced (at which point the length of metal will be used up). The company's industrial engineers find that while the machine is "processing" the metal, the employee can be feeding the second machine. In all about 3 minutes are required for the machine to stamp out the twenty parts. And, the engineers suggest that only one employee is needed to run the two machines.

The union steward has a very different view of the situation. He has seen the new gadget working. At times it malfunctions, and the metal gets stuck in the machine. The machine is also dangerous because when the metal gets stuck it can begin swinging the unused metal in such a way as to endanger anyone standing near the machine. The steward thinks the operator should be there to watch the machine full time. Even then productivity will be 35 percent higher than when the operator had to hand-feed each part. Even though the company claims it will find work for the displaced employee, there is no reason for the workers to increase their productivity 100 percent with no increase in pay and a loss of a job to boot.

Remember the industrial engineers believe that the employee will be working no harder, but that the company will get 100 percent more output from the one employee.

BIBLIOGRAPHY

Estey, M., *Unions: Structure, Development and Management*, Harcourt, New York, 1967.

Chamberlain, N., and J. Kuhn, *Collective Bargaining*, 2d ed., McGraw-Hill, New York, 1965.

Sayles, L., and G. Strauss, *The Local Union: Its Place in the Industrial Plant*, 2d ed., Harcourt, New York, 1967.

READING

Foreman and Steward*

NEIL W. CHAMBERLAIN (1915-   )

Neil Chamberlain has moved among positions in universities, foundations, and government. His career is a good example of the contribution of economists to management thinking. Like Whyte and Drucker, his work epitomizes the restlessness and breadth of the truly creative thinker. While best known for his analysis of labor-management relations, he has also sought to develop compact theories to explain the operations of the firm and management decision making. Central to much of his work is the concept of bargaining. While many of us restrict our application of negotiations to the labor-management field, Dr. Chamberlain has observed the extent to which organized groups within the firm (divisions, departments) seek to compromise their needs with the needs of the larger organization. Thus decision making, a central activity of the manager, typically involves bargaining, not simply the effort to maximize. He has also been interested in the planning process both within the firm and in government.

Some of his best-known books in these areas include *Labor, A General Theory of Economic Process; The Firm: Micro-Economic Planning and Action;* and *Enterprise and Environment.*

While serving as head of the Ford Foundation's business and economics program, he was instrumental in helping business schools introduce more behavioral science into their curriculums. He has also been active in promoting greater understanding of American institutions and methods through the American Seminar in Salzburg, Austria, which gives a seminar for young executives drawn from European companies, trade unions, and government agencies.

But the balance is not all on the negative side. Collective bargaining can be made into an effective tool by the foreman who is willing to work with it. Normally we are inclined to think of the grievance procedure as a union device, as a protest technique. The human relations people have been quite right in suggesting, however, that the grievance procedure in its bilateral stages is only one example of the consultative technique and that the sophisticated foreman can avail himself of the grievance procedure, as a consultative technique, and make it a tool for his own use. The union has provided him with a steward, the union's intent being that the steward should act as the first-line check on supervision, ensuring that the rights of union members are respected. But once the union has provided him

*Reprinted by permission from Neil W. Chamberlain, *Labor*, McGraw-Hill, New York, 1958, pp. 248-249.

with a steward, there is no reason why the foreman cannot make use of the steward for his own administrative purposes. The union steward can become a useful tool of management. Let us see how.

The one effective curb which has always been exercised over leaders is the reluctance of their followers to comply with directions. At some point, on some issue, individuals will rebel against even so-called absolute authority. Even a Hitler and a Stalin, with all their power, could not completely ignore the feelings of their followers. To secure compliance, it is necessary not to ask too much. In order for authority to remain unchallenged, its exercise must be accepted by those to whom it applies. This simple homily is relevant to authority wherever found, including that of the foreman in his shop. The foreman's command may meet with an apathetic response that robs it of its intended effect. His decision may be translated into only partially conforming behavior by those to whom it is entrusted, whose interests may be involved quite differently from the interests of the foreman and whose actions are designed to protect as best they can their own interests which have been overlooked by the foreman.

Yet it is difficult, if not impossible, for any individual to predict the likely reaction of others to his assertion of authority. All of us have experienced surprise at one time or another at the kind of hornet's nest which we have kicked up by some decision or action of ours. But for every such overt display of resistance we can be assured there are many more covert manifestations.

Under the circumstances clues to the responses of others become important management aids. If the foreman improves his under-standing of how his men are likely to react to his decisions, he can make his decisions more effective. The contemplated action which, he finds, is likely to make more trouble than he had originally expected can be modified to avoid that consequence. With respect to any change, the singleness of *his* objective may blind him to the multiplicity of effects on *others* and the accompanying protective responses evoked from others which modify or even nullify the results intended by the change. If he is made aware of these condi-tioning circumstances the proposed action can be reformulated to accommodate, at least in some degree, interests which had been neglected. As a result of such compromise, the outcome may be less desirable than had previously been *intended* but far more reward-ing than it otherwise would have been *in fact*.

Within the context of his approach to the decision-making proc-ess, the union steward can play a dual function. Not only is he the leader of the opposition, the champion of those injured by the exercise of authority, the public defender; he becomes a consultant with whom the foreman may confer, whose advice he may solicit, whose opinions he may use as a sounding board.

In the hands of an inept foreman, this approach may lead to an abnegation of authority to the steward. At the point where consultation leads to a bifurcation of leadership, with a sharing of authority between foreman and steward, the foreman's effectiveness as a leader of his men suffers. From preliminary investigations, it would also appear that shop morale declines. Men prefer to work for a foreman who is not afraid to use the authority of his position.

14

ADJUSTING TO CHANGE: PROCESS AND PROBLEMS

LEARNING OBJECTIVES

1 Understand the reasons why people resist change.

2 See that some opposition is not true resistance but bargaining to get the greater advantage from the change.

3 Consider the circumstances under which management bungles change.

4 Determine some proven techniques for facilitating change.

5 Take an overall view of the supervisor as change agent—what it's reasonable to expect that he or she can and cannot do.

6 Assess the impact of organizational development—planned systemic change.

Ours is an adaptive society. A cliché, but it incorporates a truth that has consequences for everyone living in our world. The process of technological change, the mainspring of social change in general—which the philosopher Alfred North Whitehead described forty years ago as "quick, conscious, and expected"—has greatly accelerated in the two generations since he wrote these words. Change which had been arithmetical in his day has become geometric in ours. It's a strain on the imagination to visualize the advances of the next twenty years. And if we tried, we would probably be wrong. Future realities are certain to outstrip and confound present expectations. As Herman Kahn of the Hudson Institute observed, "A study in 1937 missed not only the computer but atomic energy, antibiotics, radar, and jet propulsion, nearly all of which had been around in principle and waiting for development."

Supervisors, particularly those in industry, find themselves peculiarly the victims or the beneficiaries of change. We don't deny the facts of change in every type of organization from universities to political parties. However, it is the industrial supervisor who is in the front lines of technological change, for it is industry that has been both the catalyst and consequence of technology. "More even than machinery," as Galbraith expresses it in *The New Industrial State*, "massive and complex business organizations are the tangible manifestations of advanced technology." Industrial research and development budgets, the most accurate barometer of technological advance and of change within the industrial organization, have grown fourfold over the past thirteen years and will probably double over the next decade. It's reasonable to assume that the supervisor, who has been forced, along with the other members of the organization, to accommodate to the demands of a rapidly changing technology in the past, will have to make increasingly more drastic accommodations to meet the demands of a progressively accelerating technology in the future.

THE PARADOX OF PROGRESS

Technological change is equated with technological progress, and who is against progress? None of us, and supervisors are no exception. They subscribe to the shibboleth as staunchly as anyone—but perhaps with an extra measure of conviction. If a person works in a typical industry, he or she is supervising the manufacture of products, many of which were not on the drawing boards ten years ago. And they are made by machines which hadn't been invented twenty years ago. Furthermore, the supervisor is likely to be coordinating his or her efforts with a computer-based production-control system that was developed and installed within the past five years. The evidences of change—and progress—are all around. The supervisor has seen that many of the promises of change have been fulfilled—the plant is more productive; earnings, including the supervisor's, are up. Change has benefited the overall organization, its stockholders, even society as a whole. The company may be selling an improved product at the same price or lower, with both developments being directly traceable to technological change, a familiar phenomenon.

What is the paradox? It is that the average supervisor who subscribes heartily to the idea of change, and has seen the benefits accruing from it, has become personally opposed to many specific changes, including some from which he or she has derived tangible, and sometimes quite substantial, economic advantages. Where particular changes are concerned, the supervisor's reactions have spanned the spectrum from violent opposition or passive resistance to indifference or enthusiastic cooperation. And in the task of facilitating the adaptation to change, the supervisor has encountered a similar range of reactions from subordinates: At one time or another, most of them have responded to a proposed change with ready sympathy, sullen indifference, explicit hostility, and varying shades of emotion in between.

The Dynamics of Change

With each change, the picture is always complex and always different. The organization as a social system, whether it be an office or a factory, involves an ever shifting equilibrium of forces. The supervisor's own operation, in turn, is a miniature social system in itself, dependent on and interdependent with the larger organization, but also with its own unique and continually fluctuating equilibrium of forces. Any major change imposed from without on this miniature social system is bound to alter more or less severely the equilibrium of forces within. Of each major change, we can say what President Pompidou said of France after the general strike in May, 1969, "It will never be the same again."

The dynamics of change are also such that supervisors, in evaluating specific innovations, find themselves at different times holding quite different opinions vis à vis subordinates. Sometimes there will be essential agreement of attitude toward the change. More frequently, supervision is in the position of selling the rank and file on a change, decided upon by top management, understood and accepted at the supervisory level, but suspected by employees. Occasionally, we find the situation, a dangerous one for the organization, where supervision is in tacit collusion with the work force to oppose a change which it is formally charged with implementing. Among supervisors, a combination of lip service toward change and subtle sabotage is not uncommon.

WHY RESIST CHANGE?

Why does the same supervisor resist change on one occasion and embrace it on another? Why do we maintain that the opposite reactions may be equally rational and appropriate? Why do the supervisor and subordinates take positions toward a proposed change that are sometimes in agreement, sometimes slightly different, and sometimes diametrically opposed? And how can their distinctive positions be equally justifiable?

Let's begin by describing, in some detail, the chief categories of reasons why supervisors—and their subordinates too—resist organizational change, conceding that the categories are not self-contained and that most employees oppose a particular change for reasons which encompass several categories.

Psychological Resistance to Change

Any change that affects an individual involves him or her in a loss of security. One is trading in the familiar, the routine, the more or less mastered, for the new, the unpredictable, the to-be-assimilated. The worker in a factory, for instance, derives part of whatever sense of security that has been achieved from a sense of occupational identity. Let's assume he is a lathe operator, with a specific set of training and skills. Install a new machine which requires that he upgrade his skills— or worse and more frequent, which makes some of his previous skills redundant since it will automatically make the adjustments that he formerly made by hand—and you have undermined his sense of occupational identity.

Professor Elting Morison cites a fascinating case of pride of craft that spurred workers to resist change and thereby established the dominance of one firm over all its competitors. Between 1864 and 1871, ten Pennsylvania companies realized the superiority of the Bessemer process and imported it from England. All but one, the Cambria Company, also imported British labor. By the end of the seventies, Cambria had secured a commanding lead over its competition. How had this come about? The Bessemer process improved but the British laborers,

proud of their craft and secure in their mastery of the original techniques, adopted none of the improvements, while "the Pennsylvania
farmers, untrammeled by the rituals and traditions of their craft, happily
and rapidly adapted themselves to the constantly changing process."

Supervisors are even more likely to find themselves in this type of
bind. In one commonly encountered situation, for example, the supervisor has to adjust to a computer-monitored production-control system.
This necessarily involves her in a kind of record keeping and continuous monitoring of operations that are quite different and distinctly more
difficult than anything her job has demanded of her. Her previous
training and experience equipped her for her job as it was. The job
changes have undermined her sense of competence and also her
sense of occupational identity. It isn't the same job any longer, and
even more unsettling, she may be unsure that she is up to her new
responsibilities. Quite naturally, she does whatever she can to thwart
the introduction of the new system.

Employees and supervisors have no monopoly on resistance to
change based on feelings of insecurity. Dr. Donald Schon, in a stimu-
lating study of technology and social change, cites a number of examples of underground opposition toward technical innovation among the
same members of top management who formally and warmly endorse
innovation as a prerequisite of the organization's survival and growth.
Among his examples is a foundry under severe competitive pressure
whose new products director had been futilely exploring new product
possibilities for the past two years. The problem was not a shortage of
ideas—twenty-five promising new suggestions had been developed—
but the set of criteria specified by top management. They were so rigid
and exacting that they made product innovation impossible. On the
other hand, the company president was content to see the organization
continue its essentially sterile new product activity. Dr. Schon summarized the informal, implicit attitude of many top managements toward technical innovation thus: "It's the enemy of orderly, planned
activity. It changes everything about the business we are in. It hurts.
Let us talk about it, study it, praise it, espouse it—anything but do it."

Changes Diminish Status

A closely allied reason for resistance to change is the feeling, whether
justified or not, that innovation threatens the individual's status within
the organization. Status is a matter of comparison, and one side effect,
usually unintended, of most substantial organizational changes is the
lowering of the relative standing of one or more units of the organization, and the elevation of the standing of other units. Quite naturally the
personnel in the downgraded units are unhappy over the change.

We know of one case in a leading educational organization where the reporting relationship of the electronic data processing operation was shifted: Previously, the head of the EDP department reported to the head of Accounting but now reports to a vice president in charge of administration. Incidentally, Accounting and EDP both report to the same vice president, and the heads of the two separate but equal operations are on the same level. Obviously, the Accounting and EDP departments will continue to work very closely together, and the new reporting relationship, while not so close as the old, should help.

What happened was a rapid and drastic decline in the previous pattern of cooperation between the EDP and accounting departments. There were instances of high-handedness by some of the systems people and programmers who were feeling their oats, but the basic problem was that the personnel of the accounting department, from the top down, reacted to their loss of status and power by deciding that practically nothing the computer department did was to the accounting department's satisfaction. To changes, large and small, proposed by the computer department and previously accepted by the operating departments involved, the accounting department raised one of two stock objections: "That's the way it has been and it can't be changed," or "We weren't consulted in advance." At last hearing, the conflict continues, and many changes that would be beneficial to the organization are stalemated while the accounting department and the EDP department are nominally trying to work out their differences.

One big reason why computers in general have not been used more effectively within organizations are the changes they engender in the status relationships between various levels of supervision. Consider banks where, traditionally, the people who deal with the customers on the rugs out in front monopolize all the prestige. The "back room" was for clerks and calculators with low-status positions. Enter the computer and the back-room operation took on a wholly different coloration. Highly paid systems people and programmers, the masters of a complex and esoteric technology, were soon competing for deference, status, and power with those out front. Small wonder that, in many banks, the debugging operation has taken much longer and has proved more difficult than anticipated, and that some of the problems can be traced to resistance from managers and other personnel who resent the status changes brought about by the computer.

Change Threatens Economic Position

Many changes tend to depress the economic position of those involved in the change, either on an absolute scale or in relation to other people within the organization. Under some circumstances, violent resistance may be a logical, almost inevitable, reaction to the economic implications of the change. Frank Cousins, a prominent leader of the British Trade Union movement, commented on how appropriate the reaction of the Luddites was when they destroyed the looms over a hundred and fifty years ago. He observed: "The machine looms destroyed the jobs of thousands of hand loom weavers. They were introduced without consultation, without regard to human values, and they had dire consequences for the men directly concerned."

The Luddites, of course, faced unemployment and possible starvation as the consequence of change. Fortunately, with the options open to employees in our society, we have no Luddites. But we do have many cases of workers resisting change because it threatens—at least they feel that it does—their jobs or the size of their pay checks. The classic example is the introduction of new machinery that will increase output. In this case, unemployment is the big fear—or a change in the incentive system under which workers are paid. Speedups and lower wages are the threats perceived.

The reaction of workers to this kind of change will be largely determined by their experiences. If the introduction of high-speed or automatic machinery in the past has meant layoffs, it will be next to impossible for top management to sell employees on a different interpretation. The same holds true when previous changes in the incentive system have been followed by lower wages among incentive workers. The lessons taught by experience are usually indelible.

Resistance to technological change can be most effective. Take the case of a company, manufacturing hypodermic syringes, that developed a machine capable of increasing the production rate of the syringe bodies from 400 to 1,500 per hour. At least that's what the machine did in the manufacturer's plant. Then the union representatives looked at the new machines and predicted that they wouldn't increase production above 700 units per hour. The correctness of the prophecy should come as no surprise. The production rate of the new machines rose to about 700, leveled off, and stayed there. The environment of this story is crucial—a company with a record of poor union-management relations and of general mistrust and hostility between management and the work force. No reassurance from top management or supervision would have been believed, so the workers instead took the task of ensuring their job security into their own hands.

A positive reaction
Another kind of reaction based largely on economic grounds looks at first glance like resistance, but is actually the reverse. It is not a true opposition to the change but a conscious determination to bargain

about its conditions and to get the maximum advantages from it. Joan Woodward, in her insightful study "Industrial Organization: Theory and Practice," examined the process of change in seven firms and concluded that on the surface, the greatest opposition to change came from the most self-assured and successful individuals and groups— both managers and rank-and-file employees. However, closer scrutiny revealed that changes in the organization were viewed as opportunities to obtain either a reduction of effort, an increase in wages or both. Moreover, Ms. Woodward found these efforts were successful. "Even where they [the operators] did not get all they asked for, they managed to get something, and resistance evaporated as soon as terms were agreed."

The supervisors carried on a similar bargaining process and were similarly successful. In every case, they made top management conscious of their importance, and in at least two companies their bargaining led to concrete gains at the annual salary reviews.

MANAGEMENT BUNGLES CHANGES

So far, we have concentrated on the intrinsic, the unavoidable, reasons, given the circumstances, why people resist change. Let's switch from human nature to human frailty. Many of the problems in introducing change and much of the resistance arise because top management doesn't understand the process of initiating change and makes a mess out of it.

A little time

What's the evidence? One proof is that management chronically underestimates the time necessary to implement a major change. When the airlines began developing a computer system for customer reservations, for example, they originally estimated that the whole reservations system would take three or four years to install. Actually, it was seven or eight years before the new system was working effectively. Joan Woodward found that implementing change was a very slow process. In one firm it took nearly eighteen months (twelve meetings held at four- to six-week intervals) to resolve a bottleneck problem by changing the manufacturing layout.

A lot of pressure

Top management compounds its initial mistake by putting pressure on those people who, as seen from on high, are not working fast enough and not adapting fast enough. The result is frequently panic and almost always resentment by supervisors and employees. Management also draws the conclusion, from unrealistic estimates and consequent pressure, that the change was a mistake—or if not, it can't be made to work.

Top management obviously wants the change to succeed, so why does it habitually underestimate the time factor involved? One reason is that the big bosses and the supervisors themselves don't understand the give and take in jobs. They fail to see that most jobs require smooth, synchronized patterns of interworker and intermanagement relationships that take months to develop and months or years to restructure. For example, the U.S. Navy is able to train destroyer crews to use new electronic gear in a week or two if the ship is in port. However, because of the complicated human interrelations, it takes about six months at sea to learn to operate the equipment efficiently, smoothly, and harmoniously.

Actually, and as management usually doesn't recognize, there is no such thing as a change that's simple and compartmentalized. Changes ramify. Take the classic instance: Professor William Whyte's description of bartenders clashing with waitresses over who came first, what did you order, your handwriting is lousy, and other parries. The battle ceased when the spindle was introduced—a nail and a piece of wood on which the waitresses placed their orders. This meant that the waitresses didn't give their orders verbally to the bartenders and didn't have to compete with each other for preference, nor could the bartenders any longer resent the fact that their behavior was determined by actions initiated by the waitresses. The depersonalization revolutionized the relationship between the bartenders and the waitresses.

HOW TO FACILITATE CHANGE

If we have created the impression that it's natural and inevitable for supervisors and subordinates alike to resent and resist many changes, that is our belief and our intent. However, the problems of facilitating the introduction of change can be tackled and most of them resolved successfully by a top management with the right attitudes and the right techniques.

Let's take attitudes first. Management should never assume that it will in fact have anticipated all the problems. There's never been an organizational change of any magnitude in which anyone has predicted the full ramifications. Management should also expect that there will be resistance at all levels and that no timetable can realistically schedule its extent or the length of time necessary to overcome it. Any efforts we have seen have fallen far short of the mark in both regards.

As Joan Woodward stressed, the initiation and implementation of change is a very slow process. Furthermore, she found that, no matter how carefully and slowly the idea of change was introduced, the immediate reaction of both lower supervision and employees was to resist. Successful change requires a flexibility of mind, a patient appreciation of the problems involved, and a constant readiness to respond to challenges, criticism, and new ideas from the people who are most affected by the change.

None of these findings frees management from the necessity of doing a lot of hard thinking and careful planning before it institutes any major change. Management's inability to anticipate all its problems is no excuse for not trying to cope with as many as possible.

Change as a Total Systems Problem

What kind of advance planning does management need to do before the introduction of new equipment, new procedures, and new processes? Management must realize that change in any of these constitutes a total systems problem, to be evaluated on the basis of its full impact on all the jobs that may be affected. Management can't afford the shortcut of looking merely at what appears to be the focal point or the point at which change is actually introduced.

Alex Bavelas and George Strauss cite a vivid example of the difficulties management gets into when it neglects the total systems approach to change. The problem of how to increase productivity in the paint room of a toy factory was basically solved by giving the female workers control over their own work pace. The experiment succeeded and productivity zoomed, but in the end the solution failed because it succeeded too well. The experiment was limited to this one department, with the result that the semiskilled painters there were earning more than skilled workers in other departments. They protested so much that the superintendent revoked the new arrangements and went back to the old system. Management had forgotten that the factory, like any other organization, is an interdependent system. Incidentally, when the old system was reinstated in the paint room, production dropped drastically and within a month all but two of the eight women had quit.

What Change Does to Job Behavioral Components

Another crucial aspect of planning any change is for management to think through the effects of the change on the behavioral components of jobs. What kinds of behavior are no longer required in the job and therefore have been removed or modified? What kinds of new behavior are required?

For example, in many automated factories the new technology has virtually taken away the supervisor's old function of giving out job assignments. Yet, in some plants, supervisors continue to give such orders because they are used to this pattern of relationships. It maintained their status—and they have no viable substitute. In this case, management should aid the supervisor in developing genuinely useful new relationships with some of the staff and maintenance groups. Thus it can spare a person the need to keep to old routines that salvage his or her ego but are essentially irrelevant to the new technology.

Explaining the Change in Advance

The case for explaining a change in advance to all those who will be affected by it is so overwhelming that discussion of it seems almost unnecessary. We left it in because of the evidence that, although almost every management makes a stab at announcing changes in advance, many of them handle the job badly. Arnold Judson, for instance, in his book *A Manager's Guide to Making Changes*, tells the story of a group of women who were told six months before their company's move to a new building that they no longer would be private secretaries or stenographers, but instead would become part of a secretarial pool. End of explanation! And end of staff: Before the move was completed, 70 percent of the group had resigned. Frankly, the part of the story that puzzles and depresses us is the tenacity of the 30 percent who stayed on.

The basic principles of explaining change are few—and simple enough. Top management, and supervision to the extent of its involvement, should try, once it has identified the probable consequences of the change, to empathize with the people affected by it. Bosses and supervisors should put themselves in the workers' shoes. Then they should make a reasoned and balanced statement, preferably in a face-to-face meeting with employees, of the pros and cons of the change from the vantage point of the interests—not of the company or of top management—but of the people at this meeting. In other words, management should use the same approach in selling change that successful sales representatives have preached and practiced for generations: Tell the users what's in it for them.

Of course, there's a difference. In selling change, overstatement is more dangerous and likely to boomerang, and the maintenance of credibility is essential. It's vitally important to reassure employees, for example, that no jobs will be lost because of the change—if such is the fact. But God help the management which makes the statement, knowing that it's a lie.

Lastly, it's important to announce a change substantially ahead of its initiation. What's "substantially ahead"? We feel that depends on circumstances—on the magnitude of the change and the best estimates of how upsetting it's going to be. Certainly, far enough in advance for employees to get used to the change and to mull over its implications, and for the management to get ample feedback on their reactions, to consider their criticisms, and perhaps to modify the change in the light of these criticisms. The only thing we feel that management did right with the secretaries when planning its move to the new building was to tell them six months ahead of time.

The Case for Participation

The argument that management, in planning a change, should involve everyone who is going to be severely affected by it rests on two stools. The process of change generally calls for both an increase in orders and more frequent interaction between boss and subordinates. With these go the employees' growing sense of dependency on management and authority and their decreasing sense of autonomy and independence. In other words, the process of change threatens one's psychological security and motivates one to resist it, irrespective of the benefits it may confer.

However, if supervisors and employees are allowed to play a part in planning the change, their psychological security may actually be increased, and one basic reason for resisting the change will have been eliminated. In fact, they are likely to favor any change of which they were, even to a minor degree, the coarchitects.

The other argument for participation is that the people who will be affected by the change have a lot to contribute. They see the problems from a perspective different from management's, and they see them very closely. In fact, they will frequently spot bugs that management hasn't anticipated, and they may also see the solutions.

So much for theory. What evidence do we have that the theory works? A plethora of data is the short but accurate answer. Studies—at least the proverbial baker's dozen—are available. The role of participation in the management of change has fascinated the current generation of behavioral scientists, though it means different things in different studies.

Consultation

Successful participation occurs at several levels. The lowest consists of consultation by the personnel in charge of engineering the change with those directly affected. We know of one company where management solicited criticism from employees after moving an assembly line from one part of the plant to another. Management was flabbergasted by the number and the quality of the criticisms. The workers knew much more about the problems of exchanging and moving materials than the engineers. They also knew that the new location of certain parts made an enormous difference in their ability to do the job. Many modifications, large and small, were made in the assembly line, incorporating the employees' suggestions, and they all represented improvements over the conscientious and professional efforts of the company's engineers.

Robert Guest, in his monograph *Organizational Change*, stressed the role of consultation in the success story of a plant manager who, in three years, converted a sick operation into one of the most efficient and profitable of the company's 126 plants. The manager's role in the first few months, as he saw it, was to ask questions and to dig out ideas for improvement from the group as a whole. The process of information gathering took several forms, the principal one being the manager's face-to-face conversations with subordinates on the lower level, hourly workers, and union representatives. Ideas were then listed for the agenda of weekly planning sessions. The plant manager didn't share any power to make changes, but took extraordinary care to solicit ideas and suggestions from almost everyone in the plant before any changes were initiated.

Let the employees make decisions

A more substantial degree of participation in the management of change is seen when the problem is defined from above but the subordinates develop the alternative solutions and choose between them. Bavelas, for example, describes an effort to change the productivity level of three groups of workers in a garment factory. Two groups were given the problem of production standards but were not required to make a decision. The third group had to make a decision—and, significantly, it was the only one that increased its productivity.

Rare, in business at least, is the situation where management allows employees who are going to be affected by the change to participate both in defining the problem and in choosing the solution. Yet evidence suggests that both these levels of participation help to facilitate the introduction of change and should be more widely employed by top management than they currently are. Larry Grenier, after surveying eighteen studies of organization change, concludes flatly that "successful change depends basically on a redistribution of power in the organization"—a redistribution in which top management shares more of its power with lower levels in the organization.

The Setting Is the Thing

We wouldn't go so far as to say that change should always be supported by redistribution of power. Sometimes previous experience renders participation sterile. Take the study in the footwear department of a Norwegian factory where participation in determining work methods made no important difference in production. The explanation was simple. Sixty-four percent of the workers, relying on their previous experiences, said that they knew the rates would be reduced when they exceeded a certain standard.

And sometimes participation is unnecessary. A case in point is the "Work Itself Program," conducted by AT&T over a period of several years with many different jobs. AT&T was seeking to enrich the jobs of both employees and first-level supervision by giving the employees more responsibility and control over their jobs, and by changing the supervisor's role from primarily that of a monitor-checker to that of a consultant-trainer.

The first experiment involved 120 women, largely college graduates, who handled inquiries from shareholders, and their seventeen supervisors. The so-called achieving group, twenty-eight letter writers and their supervisors, gradually assumed more responsibility over a seven-week period, beginning with the appointment of subject-matter experts in the first week and culminating, in the last week, with the women being encouraged to answer stockholders' letters in a personal way. As the women took on more responsibility—for example, in the third week supervisors cut the verification of letters from 100 percent to 10 percent—the supervisor's role also changed from that of mother hen to that of resource person. Success was not immediate, but by the end of the fourth month, the productivity and customer service record of this group was markedly better than that of the other three groups with the same function—and it has continued to improve since then.

The striking thing is that in this and eighteen other experiments, there was no participation by anyone directly affected by the change nor was a word of explanation given. First-level supervisors simply received a series of instructions and transmitted them to their employees—instructions which revolutionized the jobs of both supervisor and subordinate. There was a minimum of resistance—one woman in the achieving group quit because she wasn't getting more money for a more responsible job. But the experiments have by and large achieved their goals—making jobs more interesting and employees both happier with their jobs and more productive.

What are the implications of the Work Itself Program for the management of change? Apparently, when the change improves the intrinsic nature of the job as the employee sees it, the time, effort, and money spent on getting participation or even on explanation are wasted. People know a good thing when they see it. And there's a corollary implication: When the benefits to those affected by the change are not so obvious or when there are distinct negatives as well as pluses, explanation and participation—at least of the consultative variety—are justified and are usually necessary as a means of minimizing resistance. Of course, there's the other justification for participation—the valuable advice management receives from employees. Even in the Work Itself Program, the women proved to be far better judges of who the true subject-matter experts were, and the supervisors reshuffled many of the initial assignments after consulting with them informally.

THE SUPERVISOR AS CHANGE AGENT: INTERMEDIARY

What precisely is the role of the supervisor in facilitating the introduction of change? With major innovations, he has little to do with the decision to make the change or with its timing and contents. In nine-tenths of the cases we are familiar with, these decisions are made by top management—the supervisor is cast in a passive role and has no more say than the subordinates. Small wonder, then, that supervisors sometimes act as accomplices with their employees in resisting a change which, as they see it, threatens their psychic or material well-being.

One point is clear in the argument of whether top management should use participation, at any rate of the consultative kind, whenever it anticipates resistance to a major change. The balance sheet shows substantial debits as well as credits. But the argument operates in spades where the supervisors affected by the change are concerned. They are uniquely qualified to understand the mainsprings of resistance to the change and to make constructive suggestions for minimizing their force. By recognizing that first-line supervision has something to contribute, top management can substantially enhance the status of the line supervisors in their own eyes and those of their subordinates—it can demonstrate to everyone that the line supervisor is not just the person in the middle, but a functioning member of management.

We have been talking about practices that are successful—but unfortunately exceptional. In most cases, the supervisor has the more modest and generally unappreciated role of helping to explain the change to those affected by it and of feeding back their reactions and criticisms to the appropriate management levels.

How skillful a job supervisors do of explaining the change depends on many factors—their skills as communicators, overall relations with subordinates, their attitudes toward the company and superiors. But the most critical element is the assistance, or lack of it, provided by higher management. Has the supervisor been adequately briefed so that the change and all its significant ramifications are understood? Does he or she know the answers to most, if not all, of the questions subordinates are likely to ask? Most important, are his or her answers to their questions as accurate as the facts allow? In other words, has higher management leveled with the supervisor? If the answers to these questions are yes, the supervisor is likely to do at least an adequate job of explaining the change.

The hardest—and most important—part of the supervisor's job is feedback. Again, the role of higher management is crucial. Key executives must encourage genuine feedback, entertaining grievances and criticisms as well as praise. They must be willing to modify the change wherever the criticisms warrant it. And lastly, they must encourage supervisors to fight for their subordinates wherever they feel their criticisms are justified.

A classic industrial relations study at IBM reinforces this last point. Several years ago, the company introduced engineered work standards for most of its production employees. In some areas of the organization, the workers accepted the standards reasonably well, and in other parts they fought them tooth and nail. What was the reason for the contrasting responses? It had nothing to do with how carefully the supervisor explained the standards or whether the employees understood them. The relevant factor was having a supervisor who would take the employees' case to higher management when they convinced him or her that the standard was wrong. Where the supervisor did not function as the subordinates' representative, they fought the supervisor every inch of the way.

Of course, the supervisors who represented their subordinates in pointing out the errors made in implementing the standards program were only doing what every textbook on human relations and supervision says they should do. But look at what actually happened! IBM would rank high in any list of the best-managed companies in the United States. Its supervisory force is probably as carefully selected and as well paid as any comparable group in the country. Yet many IBM supervisors didn't fight for their subordinates when they thought the employees were right—telling higher management that it was wrong apparently was too dangerous. We suspect that higher management's attitude toward criticism is healthier at IBM than in the average company. So the story dramatizes even more sharply the need for top management to consciously create an organizational climate in which negative feedback from any change is not merely tolerated but actively encouraged. Higher management needs to be told the truth, especially when it hurts.

At a deeper level of symbolic meaning, supervisors are uniquely qualified to report this feedback. They have a greater sensitivity than anyone else in management to the sentiments in their units that have an emotional significance far more important than their apparent real value. For example, the introduction of some complex new machine may seem to be the logical moment to compel the early retirement of a worker who has just been making the grade on the easier-to-operate equipment with which he is thoroughly familiar. It's possible that the employee himself may not resent the early retirement. But let's assume that the rest of the department will do his resenting for him. His production record isn't noteworthy, but as a person, he represents to his coworkers just about everything that is good about the organization. His forced retirement has ramifications that higher management doesn't suspect and to which the supervisor should draw its attention.

THE SUPERVISOR AS CHANGE AGENT: INITIATOR

We have stressed repeatedly the passive role of the supervisor in the initiation of any important change. However, in the implementation of some changes, the supervisor has a major responsibility for seeing that the technical side of the change works smoothly. This is in contrast to the responsibility for reporting back defects in the technique and strategy of the change to others responsible for modifying them.

What do we mean by technical errors versus errors of technique? In the IBM case, the engineered work standards, although generally correct, contained some basic faults of design, attributed to the engineers in charge, who had to correct them. These were errors of technique. In contrast, think of what happens whenever a new and complex machine is introduced into the plant or office—chaos over the short run or the long. Given a machine that is capable of the job it is supposed to do and a work force capable of operating the equipment, the time it takes a work group to adjust is largely up to the supervisor. If one anticipates the kinds of mistakes subordinates are likely to make and tells them in advance the most effective way of correcting them, the technical side of the adjustment process will run a fast course.

We know of a case of an inexperienced punch-card reader whose machine jammed frequently. Each time this happened, the unhappy reader went back to the beginning of the series and repeated the entire procedure, when all she needed to do was pull out the faulty card by hand, repunch it, and replace it. A sad chore, easily avoided: The supervisor need merely lay out a detailed recovery procedure for anticipated mistakes and make sure that every operator understands it. Of course no supervisor will anticipate all the possible errors and few employees will master all the techniques for correcting them—no matter. In the league of avoiding errors with new equipment, .600 is a fine batting average.

THE SUPERVISOR AS SOURCE OF RESISTANCE

What happens when the supervisors themselves are the source of resistance? The change will be much more difficult to install if the supervisors continue to oppose it tacitly—the ways of opposition are many, subtle, and frequently very difficult to prove. Besides, to compel supervisory compliance to a change is to threaten the whole structure of good higher management-supervisor relations.

How can top management overcome antagonism? Those in management obviously hold all the authority cards—they can order the supervisors to comply. But they may be reluctant to play their aces.

Most top managements, faced with stiff opposition from their supervisory force, find that it pays to take the long way around the problem—to employ discussion, persuasion, and participation. One classic case, reported by Marrow and French, concerned the resistance of the first-line supervisors in a pajama factory to hiring and training older workers. Research studies, conducted by a psychologist and fully supported by top management, had proved that the older workers on the payroll rated as well as, or better than, the rest of the work force by four critical criteria: hourly production per worker per day, velocity of learning, attendance, and annual rate of turnover. A representative supervisor conceded that her personal experience with the older workers in her group was favorable and agreed with the research findings, but she clung resolutely to the stereotype that older people learn more slowly, are absent more frequently, and quit after a short time. Facts succumbed to prejudice.

Higher management handled the problem by submitting the research findings to first-line supervisors in group discussions. Topics included the origin of the stereotype of older workers and the reasons for accepting it. Insights into the bias slowly developed, and after many sessions the group decided to recommend an experiment in training older workers. With the group's shift in attitude, the new policy finally became a reality.

ORGANIZATIONAL DEVELOPMENT—SYSTEMIC CHANGE

Most of what we have talked about before has centered on changing the attitudes and behavior of an individual, a work group, a department, or, at most, a unit of a larger organization. And most of it has dealt with changing individual attitudes—with answering the question: How do you motivate individuals to accept a specific change; to take a positive stance toward that change and behave accordingly; and to act in ways that facilitate rather than obstruct the change?

Now our emphasis shifts. Organizational development (OD) is concerned with changing the organization, not the individual; with behaviors, not attitudes; and typically, although not necessarily, with the whole organization or a major subunit (a plant in a manufacturing organization or a branch in a bank), not a department or a subunit. In some fifteen years, OD has grown from a small beginning into a big business. Organizations spend hundreds of millions of dollars annually on OD as a formal, organized activity. A small army of consultants is gainfully employed and, for the most part, handsomely remunerated in applying an array of remedies, under the general rubric of OD, that are designed to cure whatever ails the organization or to make the healthy organization still more effective. OD, in short, is very much in fashion. Most *Fortune* 500 companies by now have separate OD units or departments.

From where did OD obtain its popularity? Much of it is soundly based. In large part, it springs from the realization—which should have been inevitable but was a long time in getting generally recognized—that any organization, large or small, is a system, or a seamless web, and that any change of consequence within a system has repercussions throughout the entire system. To quote the old ditty, "The toe bone's connected to the foot bone; the foot bone's connected to the ankle bone; the ankle bone's. . .," and so on. (To see how the organization looks as a system, see Figure 14-1.) A key corollary: Unless the impacts of the initiated changes are anticipated, the organization is in for certain trouble. The initiated changes are likely to be dysfunctional, and over time, they will be discredited and disregarded.

There's another handle that differentiates OD—at least in the hands of sophisticated practitioners—from other efforts to change. OD reflects the belief that for any change effort to be successful, people, processes, and structures must be changed, although not necessarily at the same time or in the same order. Chris Argyris identifies four sets of independent but interacting characteristics that determine the behavior of any organization—structure and technology, leadership and interpersonal relations, administrative controls and regulations, and human control. To effect a major change successfully, it is necessary to change all four characteristics. Fragmentation spells failure.

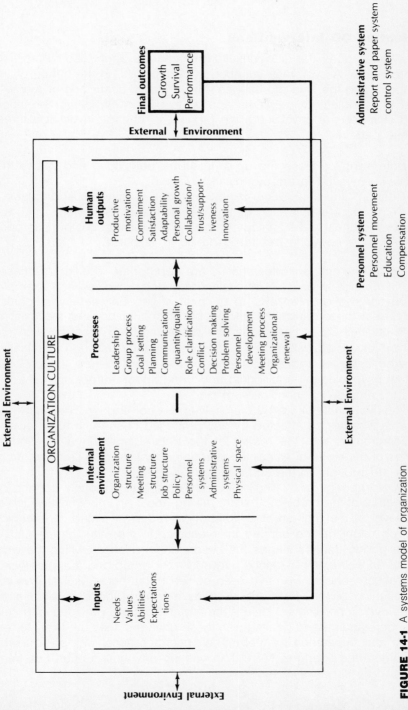

FIGURE 14-1 A systems model of organization

Effective OD Interventions

What tools does the OD consultant or change agent use to facilitate the change? As you may suspect, it all depends on the nature of the problem and the kind of changes—they seldom occur one at a time—that the problem or problems appear to call for. Whatever problems and changes are envisioned, the process of change involves a three-phase pattern:

1 Unfreezing—a loosening up of attitudes, behaviors, and values that have prevailed in the organization.
2 Change—the acquisition of new attitudes, behaviors, and values.
3 Refreezing—stabilization of the new attitudes, behaviors, and values. To change the analogy, when the old cake of custom has been broken, a new one has to be baked in its place.

Obviously, different interventions are appropriate to different phases in the change process. Unfreezing frequently involves, for example, using surveys or interviews to uncover a gap between what participants feel the organization should be or should do and the existing state of affairs. It is hoped that the process, called "confrontation" by OD professionals, will reveal such a discrepancy between identical or desired behavior and actual behavior that it will disturb the previous actual psychological equilibrium and bring about unfreezing—or a desire for change or "conviction of sin."

Surveys or interviews by themselves are not enough. The men and women who will be affected by any proposed change, in turn, have to be confronted with the results of the data—usually in a meeting or series of meetings at which the perceptual gap is revealed and problems are brought to the surface.

What happens next? The changes themselves obviously depend on the nature of the problem. If we're talking about an impoverished job at the level of the rank-and-file worker, job redesign aimed at enriching the job might be the primary intervention. On the other hand, such a redesign inevitably changes the interpersonal relations within the work group as well as the relations between work group and the supervisor. Job enrichment, as we have seen earlier in this book, usually involves a lessening of the kinds and degrees of control the supervisor exercises over subordinates. Unless the supervisors are provided with help in understanding and dealing with these changes, they are likely to feel tense and threatened by them. Their natural reaction will be to thwart or reverse the changes. More than one job enrichment effort has been aborted by supervisory resistance.

The key point is not which should come first, structural or process interventions, but the essentiality of making sure that any OD effort deals at some point with both tasks and organization structure, as well as with the interpersonal relationships of individuals and groups. People and organizations must be ready and motivated (unfrozen) in order for change to take. But unless changes in attitudes are accompanied by appropriate changes in the organizational arrangements that tend to shape behavior—such as structure, leadership patterns, and reward systems—the new attitudes may dissipate and the familiar patterns prevail.

Take one instance, the effort to establish business teams as a coordinating and integrating mechanism in the electronics products division of the Corning Glass Works. Meetings and communications were useless in making the business teams work. A simple structural change made all the difference. The reward system was changed: Now half of each member's overall performance rating reflects the employee's contribution to the business team on which he or she serves; the other half continues to reflect a performance in a functional area.

Participation and Feedback as Levers for Change

As we have mentioned before, participation in designing the solution by the people who are part of the problem helps to improve the quality of the solution. Some of the reasons are obvious. The people who will be affected by any change frequently have a lot to contribute to the solution. Also, people tend to become committed to changes they are involved in and helped to create. Another reason is subtler and less widely appreciated. Professor Michael Beer of the Harvard Business School expressed the theoretical argument better than we have ever heard it stated before.

By and large an adult's learning "takes" only after he has experimented with new approaches and received appropriate feedback in an on-the-job situation . . . In our experience, the first change was typically behavioral, not cognitive or even attitudinal. If the manager was successful in the attempt by his own subjective criteria, this would often lead to some change in attitude toward organization development, but certainly to another try. Several successful experiments led to a change in attitudes and values with respect to the management of human organizations and organizational development. Several individuals who were dead set against OD initially are now its strongest proponents.

For a diagrammatic version of this process, see Figure 14-2.

In other words, the basic model for learning, as developed by Beer on the basis of his experience as an OD practitioner, is the reverse of the customary model—from changed behavior to changed attitudes. One example, taken from the Corning Glass plant in Medfield, Massachusetts, when Beer headed up Corning's OD effort, will illustrate the point. Production employees had worked on a variety of small tasks with short-cycle times. As part of the change at Medfield, each employee assumed responsibility for turning out a substantial component. In addition, the work group as a whole determined work schedules and set their own production quotas (of course, within the framework of predetermined plant goals). Employees both set their own goals and received feedback on a daily basis as to how close they were to achieving them—a closed loop that was strongly reinforced.

The case for getting all the affected members of the organization directly involved in the diagnosis of the problem, and subsequent problems, is persuasive—but not all inclusive. There are exceptions. To emerge with and adopt the wrong solution is no contribution to effective change. Expertise has its claims, too. Sometimes the problem is such and the group is so constituted that it is unlikely to contribute to the correct answer.

Even in the case of "ownership" of the OD effort by the members of

FIGURE 14-2 Model for learning

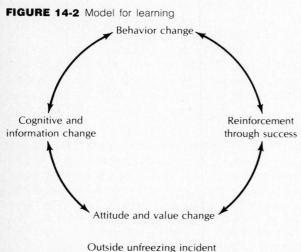

Behavior change

Cognitive and
information change

Reinforcement
through success

Attitude and value change

Outside unfreezing incident
(peer pressure, boss pressure,
or consultant influence)

the organization, that is, the feeling that they have a personal stake in the outcome of the OD effort and are committed to its implementation, participation is secondary. Success comes first. If the problem is properly defined and the interventions chosen fit, the problem of participation or the lack of it becomes irrelevant.

We have seen what happened with the correspondence clerks at AT&T. There was no participation on the part of those affected by the changes in designing the OD interventions. They weren't even told the purpose of the interventions. Still "the sweet smell of success" fueled the feelings of ownership to the point where employees began to interact on their own by suggesting which coworkers were subject-matter experts who could further help the change effort to succeed. In short, success breeds further success.

Discussion and Conclusion

What can we say about organizational development as an organization activity? Is it more effective than other change efforts which are more fragmented, less comprehensive, and much less self-conscious? Have all the hours expended and the money spent paid off?

Probably. That most of the consultants who have helped to design specific OD interventions and those managers who have commissioned the interventions are on record as being pleased with the results constitutes, in each case, less than conclusive evidence. Testimonials from self-interested individuals possess limited credibility.

The case for OD, however, remains plausible. OD conscientiously applied by committed managers and aided and abetted by experienced practitioners—and there are many around—would appear to be a substantial improvement over one-shot change efforts hastily undertaken in response to a more or less acute aggravation.

Substantial and convincing evidence of the effectiveness of OD efforts remains in short supply. Only a handful of such studies exists, among them the two Corning efforts previously cited. There is only one documented attempt to evaluate the contribution of each specific OD intervention to the total effort. No organization to date has had the resources or expertise to prove a direct cause-and-effect relationship between an OD effort and its consequences. Perhaps this is asking the impossible. Part of the problem is time. A year for an OD effort is minimal. Of the two Corning efforts, one lasted eighteen months, the other two years. A time span of five to seven years is not unusual. Given these time spans, and further given the coexistence of multiple variables in the internal and external environment, it's obvious that they have contaminated the purity of any end results—affected them negatively or positively in ways that are interesting to think about but almost impossible to measure.

On balance OD as a planned systemic approach to change, however, appears to be an improvement over the typically haphazard and uncoordinated efforts that preceded it. Obviously this does not apply to the sometimes successful efforts of snake-oil merchants in OD consultants' clothes who peddle simple nostrums as remedies for whatever ails the organization. Fortunately, such merchants are becoming rarer. Even more fortunately, the OD field is becoming increasingly populated by people who pay more than lip service to the systemic viewpoint that has been theoretically at the heart of OD from the beginning. They appreciate at one level the interrelationship between attitudes and structure and the importance of giving equal attention to each. As George Strauss has written: "Attitudinal changes may cause temporary changes in behavior, but these are not likely to last unless accompanied by appropriate changes in structure." At still another level, they perceive that the purpose of OD should be to induce managers to step back periodically and take a fresh look at the organization as a whole, its goals, and its relationship to its environment. Only through such periodic reexamination can OD ever fulfill the promise of its aspirations—we almost said its pretensions—of becoming truly a systems approach to the management of change.

SUMMARY

You have probably noticed the shift of focus in this chapter away from the supervisor and toward the actions of higher and even top-level management. The shift was a necessary one, dictated by the realities of the power situation. We continue, as we have throughout the book, to be primarily interested in the supervisor and the supervisor's role in the organization. At the same time, in discussing supervisors and their relation to any major change, we must recognize that in the process they are not the prime movers and shapers, but more frequently pawns and victims. It is decisions made several levels higher in the organization that weigh the heaviest in determining whether or not the change will be accepted and implemented successfully within the supervisor's own unit—including the decisions that will determine whether the supervisor spearheads the implementation or heads the resistance.

Not that the supervisor's role is a small one. That a person understands the ramifications of the change in the little social system which he or she heads better than anyone else in management; that he or she is the management person best qualified to empathize with the work force, to measure the depth of their criticisms and determine what modifications will overcome their reservations; that he or she knows the importance of fighting for subordinates when their criticisms are justified, is a partial measure of the supervisor's potential contribution to the change process. In short, the supervisor is a resource person with a vital contribution to make before, during, and after the change—if higher management only has the wits to use him or her properly.

THE EDUCATION OF GREG HORNING: JUNE 22

Phil Martello had never told Greg exactly what he'd said to the boys at the union meeting. Actually Greg preferred not to know anyway. But whatever it was, it worked. There were no miracles, but there was less unfinished work, fewer shoddy pieces, and generally less of a mess each morning.

Maybe this was the reason why the crew finally had achieved the goal—110 percent of standard. In the past three weeks they had hit standard once and been 3 or 4 percent over on the other two weeks.

Phillips also hadn't forgotten his promise. He called Greg to congratulate him and the company picked up the tab for the refreshments, including a big victory cake. Still Phillips, being Phillips, didn't put in an appearance at the party—too busy, he said.

Life always has its problems, though. Phillips told Greg that several customers had complained that some of the parts they got didn't meet quality specifications. Greg was sure that the reason was not because his crew was being careless or going too fast. They had installed the new mold that Creegmore had been testing back in April on all the machines, and Greg was positive that this was responsible for any substandard parts.

After all, it always took time to iron out the bugs in any new process. And that mold required special, careful handling; it was an intricate operation to get the hang of.

Greg had explained all this to Phillips and urged him to understand that it would take time to get everyone completely familiar with the new operation.

"Just wait and see," he'd stated. "In a few months we'll have any quality problems licked."

He hoped he was getting through to Phillips, but then with him you could never tell.

"What we need is an independent check in your department. Everybody is just too buddy-buddy with everyone else. I'll see whether industrial engineering can't come up with a real tough inspector."

Obviously Greg wasn't getting to Phillips. "Look, Steve, you're being unfair as hell. The reason production is up to where it is—and you're happy about it—is the fact that everyone is buddy-buddy with each other, as you put it. We're a team."

"Okay, Greg. You've done a good job. No one denies it. But I'm a production manager, not a cheerleader. And I say you need to tighten up inspections in your department."

"You're the boss, Steve," Greg said wearily, "and I guess you know what you're doing."

Still, it came as a shock to Greg a few days later when he received a memo from Frank Granto in industrial engineering, telling him that the new inspector, Sylvia Gould, would start in the molding department tomorrow and would report directly to Granto on Phillips' orders. She would concentrate on sorting and inspecting and wouldn't do any of the flashing and packing work done by the other inspectors. Furthermore, she was to be paid 75 cents an hour more than Helen and 50 cents an hour more than Jeannette.

"What a bastard," Greg muttered to himself as he read the memo for the third time and let the words sink in. He hadn't realized until now what Phillips had meant by inspection—"a spy in the department, that's what she'll be."

His next impulse was to call Phillips. Greg even got as far as dialing the first two digits of his extension. "No—that won't do any good. I'm too riled up, and Phillips wouldn't listen anyway. My only chance of convincing him is to show that it hasn't worked out. I've got to put up with it for a while."

Greg's only consolation was that the crew resented the move as much as he did. Admittedly, he didn't show any enthusiasm when he announced that a new inspector was starting tomorrow.

Sylvia had arrived after lunch. A large young woman in her late twenties, she had walked slowly and solidly through the shop, resting narrowed looks here and there but speaking to no one.

"I'm Sylvia Gould, Mr. Horning. I believe Mr. Granto told you I'd be here this afternoon." She had stood, filling Greg's doorway, and had spoken without waiting for him to look up.

"Yes, Sylvia, he did," Greg had said, taking her in and doing his best to sound cordial. "Why don't you come in and sit down for a minute so we can get acquainted."

Sylvia stayed in the doorway. "If you don't mind, Mr. Horning, I'd rather get right to work. There's a lot to be done, I'm told."

"Well, of course, Sylvia. If you'd rather that's fine." There would be no gossiping problems with this one, at any rate!

She had gone out to the shop with Greg following her. The crew responded to Greg's introductions with silence and cold stares. Sylvia had not seemed to notice. She was already examining the equipment and looking over pieces. Her eyes scanned the setup of the room.

Any minute, now, she'll be wanting to move the machines around so they'll be more convenient for her, Greg had thought. Well, I'll let the crew take care of her. They look like they can handle it.

But they hadn't been able to. They ignored her almost completely, but it had no effect. She seemed preoccupied with herself and totally uninterested in mixing. She brought her lunch and read detective stories while she ate. If she took a break at all, she went back to her reading.

Only when she felt compelled to give instructions or criticisms did she have anything to do with the others—and that was where the friction mounted.

She acted as if she were second only to Greg, saying things like "Don't do that now, Helen. You have to sort those gears before you start on that batch," or "Henry, those spools that are coming off the runner now—they're too rough. I told you—you have to fix your temperature dial a few degrees." She made it quite clear that she was a supervisor giving orders.

The reception her "orders" got was a different story: They were completely ignored or shrugged off with a "You don't know how we do things here. Ask Greg—he'll tell you." Or, "If I don't do this batch right now, we'll be behind one quota for today. Sorry about that."

Suddenly, late one afternoon Sylvia appeared at Greg's door with a petulant look on her large face and interrupted what he was doing with—"They plain won't listen to me, Mr. Horning. I don't know what to do with them."

Greg was going to ask her to come in and sit down, but she had entered and filled up the wooden armchair before he had the chance.

"You can't blame them, Sylvia," he said quietly. "They're used to taking orders from me and I don't give too many. The crew knows what they're doing and they don't need many orders."

"That's what you say, Mr. Horning," Sylvia lashed back. "They make plenty of mistakes and Mr. Granto told me to speak to them anytime I saw them do anything wrong."

"You're obviously talking to the wrong man," Greg snapped. "If you're having trouble carrying out Mr. Granto's orders, you'd better take it up with Mr. Granto."

"That's all you have to say?" asked Sylvia half in anger and half in disbelief. She apparently thought the mention of Granto's name would crumble Greg's defenses.

"That's all I have to say. Anything else I feel like saying I couldn't say to you."

The trouble, of course, Greg mused to himself a few minutes later, was that those were Phillips' orders, not Granto's. Phillips was bound to hear that he wasn't cooperating with Sylvia. And then the fat would be in the fire for sure.

QUESTIONS

1 Why do you think Phillips had the new inspector report to Granto instead of Greg?

2 Is there anything Greg could have done to make Sylvia acceptable to the group?

3 Should Greg have protested to Phillips as soon as he heard about Sylvia?

4 What about Greg's handling of Sylvia's complaint? Would you have handled her differently? Why?

BEHAVIORAL EXERCISE

The facts of the case at the International Valve Company in the motor assembly room are these: The workers, seven in number, have been used to assembling the small motors by hand. Most of the workers have specialized in assembling a particular portion, but there's a good deal of job rotation—job swapping, if you will—and generally a relaxed, informal atmosphere. Average length of employment in the room is ten years. Relations between group members are good; so is the relationship between the group and the supervisor. Output and quality generally have been deemed satisfactory, although not outstanding.

Now, everything is going to change. The assembly will be automated and machine-paced. Each of the seven workers will be responsible for a particular portion of the total assembly. Management hopes, as a result, to increase productivity by 25 percent and furthermore plans to raise wages by 15 percent. The changes, which will go into effect in about six months, have yet to be announced. Management faces the following questions (which the class will attempt to answer):

1 When should the announcement be made?
2 What points should the announcement stress?
3 What kind of reception to the news can management anticipate?
4 To the extent that resistance is anticipated, what steps can management take to soften, if not overcome, the resistance?

BIBLIOGRAPHY

Bartlett, A., and T. Kayser, *Changing Organizational Behavior*, Prentice-Hall, Englewood Cliffs, N.J., 1973.

Beer, M., "Technology of Organization Development," in M. Dunnette (ed.), *Handbook of Industrial and Organizational Psychology*, Rand McNally, Chicago, 1976.

Huse, E., *Organization Development and Change*, West, St. Paul, Minn., 1975.

Kaufman, H., *The Limits of Organizational Change*, University of Alabama Press, University, Ala., 1971.

Miles, R., *Theories of Management: Implications for Organizational Behavior and Development*, McGraw-Hill, New York, 1975.

READING

Some Strategic Leverage Points*

DOUGLAS McGREGOR (1906-1964)

Douglas McGregor began his career with a doctorate in experimental psychology from Harvard University, which might have directed him into a traditional psychology department. Instead he moved to MIT, which just before World War II established an interdisciplinary department to explore the problems of people at work. He soon attracted a number of students by his original conceptions of authority, supervision, and management. Very early he was concerned with methods of motivating people to improve their performance, which depended upon their being able to satisfy their own personal needs by working toward organizational goals. His famous "Theory Y" was an effort to show that the human potential for effective performance was much greater than most managers assumed and that both people and organizations would thrive in a freer, more flexible and open supervisory climate.

When he was offered the chance to become president of Oberlin College, he accepted the responsibility as an opportunity to put into practice his theories of management. There he pioneered in academic administration with his efforts to get both students and faculty to assume greater responsibility for administrative decisions. He then moved back to his professorship at MIT, where his influence over students and businessmen grew. At MIT he brought together an outstanding group of young psychologists including Alex Bavelas, Harold Leavitt, and Mason Haire, who made outstanding contributions to the leadership field. Further the McGregor group attracted a number of young men who became teachers of management in their own right including Warren Bennis, George Strauss, and Leonard Sayles, whose work is represented in this book.

McGregor's most famous book is *The Human Side of Enterprise* (McGraw-Hill, 1960), in which his famous "Theory Y" point of view was first developed. After his untimely death his friends and students put together some of his other work under the title *The Professional Manager* (McGraw-Hill, 1967). Through his teaching and contact with students, and his widespread consulting work and conferences with key executives, his seminal ideas on industrial leadership became an integral part of the management philosophy of literally thousands of executives in this country and abroad. It would be difficult to identify a more influential leader in this field. Interestingly, his influence was in large measure due to his own

*Reprinted from *Leadership and Motivation*, Douglas McGregor, pp. 8-17, by permission of the M.I.T. Press, Cambridge, Mass. © 1966 by Massachusetts Institute of Technology.

style of human relations, his giving of himself, and his enormous respect for his fellow human beings. Everyone who knew him responded as much to his character as to his persuasive ideas.

Physiological and safety needs

Man is a wanting animal—as soon as one of his needs is satisfied, another appears in its place. This process is unending. It continues from birth to death.

Man's needs are organized in a series of levels—a hierarchy of importance. At the lowest level, but preeminent in importance when they are thwarted, are his physiological needs. Man lives by bread alone, when there is no bread. Unless the circumstances are unusual, his needs for love, for status, for recognition are inoperative when his stomach has been empty for a while. But when he eats regularly and adequately, hunger ceases to be an important need. The sated man has hunger only in the sense that a full bottle has emptiness. The same is true of the other physiological needs of man—for rest, exercise, shelter, protection from the elements.

A satisfied need is not a motivator of behavior! This is a fact of profound significance. It is a fact which is regularly ignored in the conventional approach to the management of people. I shall return to it later. For the moment, one example will make my point. Consider your own need for air. Except as you are deprived of it, it has no appreciable motivating effect upon your behavior.

When the physiological needs are reasonably satisfied, needs at the next higher level begin to dominate man's behavior—to motivate him. These are called safety needs. They are needs for protection against danger, threat, deprivation. Some people mistakenly refer to these as needs for security. However, unless man is in a dependent relationship where he fears arbitrary deprivation, he does not demand security. The need is for the "fairest possible break." When he is confident of this, he is more than willing to take risks. But when he feels threatened or dependent, his greatest need is for guarantees, for protection, for security.

The fact needs little emphasis that since every industrial employee is in a dependent relationship, safety needs may assume considerable importance. Arbitrary management actions, behavior which arouses uncertainty with respect to continued employment or which reflects favoritism or discrimination, unpredictable administration of policy—these can be powerful motivators of the safety needs in the employment relationship *at every* level from worker to vice president.

Social Needs

When man's physiological needs are satisfied and he is no longer fearful about his physical welfare, his social needs become important motivators of his behavior—for belonging, for association, for acceptance by his fellows, for giving and receiving friendship and love.

Management knows today of the existence of these needs, but it often assumes quite wrongly that they represent a threat to the organization. Many studies have demonstrated that the tightly knit, cohesive work group may, under proper conditions, be far more effective than an equal number of separate individuals in achieving organizational goals.

Yet management, fearing group hostility to its own objectives, often goes to considerable lengths to control and direct human efforts in ways that are inimical to the natural "groupiness" of human beings. When man's social needs—and perhaps his safety needs, too—are thus thwarted, he behaves in ways which tend to defeat organizational objectives. He becomes resistant, antagonistic, uncooperative. But this behavior is a consequence, not a cause.

Ego needs

Above the social needs—in the sense that they do not become motivators until lower needs are reasonably satisfied—are the needs of greatest significance to management and to man himself. They are the egoistic needs, and they are of two kinds:

1 Those needs that relate to one's self-esteem—needs for self-confidence, for independence, for achievement, for competence, for knowledge.
2 Those needs that relate to one's reputation—needs for status, for recognition, for appreciation, for the deserved respect of one's fellows.

Unlike the lower needs, these are rarely satisfied; man seeks indefinitely for more satisfaction of these needs once they have become important to him. But they do not appear in any significant way until physiological, safety, and social needs are all reasonably satisfied.

The typical industrial organization offers few opportunities for the satisfaction of these egoistic needs to people at lower levels in the hierarchy. The conventional methods of organizing work, particularly in mass production industries, gives little heed to these aspects of human motivation. If the practices of scientific management were deliberately calculated to thwart these needs—which, of course, they are not—they could hardly accomplish this purpose better than they do.

Self-fulfillment needs

Finally—a capstone, as it were, on the hierarchy of man's needs—there are what we may call the needs for self-fulfillment. These are the needs for realizing one's own potentialities, for continued self-development, for being creative in the broadest sense of that term.

It is clear that the conditions of modern life give only limited opportunity for these relatively weak needs to obtain expression. The deprivation most people experience with respect to other lower-level needs diverts their energies into the struggle to satisfy *those* needs, and the needs for self-fulfillment remain dormant.

Now, briefly, a few general comments about motivation:

We recognize readily enough that a man suffering from a severe dietary deficiency is sick. The deprivation of physiological needs has behavioral consequences. The same is true—although less well recognized—of deprivation of higher-level needs. The man whose needs for safety, association, independence, or status are thwarted is sick just as surely as is he who has rickets. And his sickness will have behavioral consequences. We will be mistaken if we attribute his resultant passivity, his hostility, his refusal to accept responsibility to his inherent "human nature." These forms of behavior are *symptoms* of illness—of deprivation of his social and egoistic needs.

The man whose lower-level needs are satisfied is not motivated to satisfy those needs any longer. For practical purposes they exist no longer. (Remember my point about your need for air.) Management often asks, "Why aren't people more productive? We pay good wages, provide good working conditions, have excellent fringe benefits and steady employment. Yet people do not seem to be willing to put forth more than minimum effort."

The fact that management has provided for these physiological safety needs has shifted the motivational emphasis to the social and perhaps to the egoistic needs. Unless there are opportunities *at work* to satisfy these higher-level needs, people will be deprived; and their behavior will reflect this deprivation. Under such conditions, if management continues to focus its attention on physiological needs, its efforts are bound to be ineffective.

People *will* make insistent demands for more money under these conditions. It becomes more important than ever to buy the material goods and services which can provide limited satisfaction of the thwarted needs. Although money has only limited value in satisfying many higher-level needs, it can become the focus of interest if it is the *only* means available.

The carrot and stick approach

The carrot and stick theory of motivation (like Newtonian physical theory) works reasonably well under certain circumstances. The *means* for satisfying man's physiological and (within limits) his safety needs can be provided or withheld by management. Employment itself is such a means, and so are wages, working conditions, and benefits. By these means the individual can be controlled so long as he is struggling for subsistence. Man lives for bread alone when there is no bread.

But the carrot and stick theory does not work at all once man has reached an adequate subsistence level and is motivated primarily by higher needs. Management cannot provide a man with self-respect, or with the respect of his fellows, or with the satisfaction of needs for self-fulfillment. It can create conditions such that he is encouraged and enabled to seek such satisfactions *for* himself, or it can thwart him by failing to create those conditions.

But this creation of conditions is not "control." It is not a good device for directing behavior. And so management finds itself in an odd position. The high standard of living created by our modern technological know-how provides quite adequately for the satisfaction of physiological and safety needs. The only significant exception is where management practices have not created confidence in a "fair break"—and thus where safety needs are thwarted. But by making possible the satisfaction of low-level needs, management has deprived itself of the ability to use as motivators the devices on which conventional theory has taught it to rely—rewards, promises, incentives, or threats and other coercive devices.

Neither hard nor soft

The philosophy of management by direction and control—*regardless of whether it is hard or soft*—is inadequate to motivate because the human needs on which this approach relies are today unimportant motivators of behavior. Direction and control are essentially useless in motivating people whose important needs are social and egoistic. Both the hard and the soft approach fail today because they are simply irrelevant to the situation.

People, deprived of opportunities to satisfy at work the needs which are now important to them, behave exactly as we might predict—with indolence, passivity, resistance to change, lack of responsibility, willingness to follow the demagogue, unreasonable demands for economic benefits. It would seem that we are caught in a web of our own weaving.

In summary, then, of these comments about motivation:

Management by direction and control—whether implemented with the hard, the soft, or the firm but fair approach—fails under today's conditions to provide effective motivation of human effort toward organizational objectives. It fails because direction and control are useless methods of motivating people whose physiological and safety needs are reasonably satisfied and whose social, egoistic, and self-fulfillment needs are predominant.

For these and many other reasons, we require a different theory of the task of managing people based on more adequate assumptions about human nature and human motivation. I am going to be so bold as to suggest the broad dimensions of such a theory. Call it "Theory Y," if you will.

1 Management is responsible for organizing the elements of productive enterprise—money, materials, equipment, people—in the interest of economic ends.
2 People are *not* by nature passive or resistant to organizational needs. They have become so as a result of experience in organizations.
3 The motivation, the potential for development, the capacity for assuming responsibility, the readiness to direct behavior toward organizational goals are all present in people. Management does not put them there. It is a responsibility of management to make it possible for people to recognize and develop these human characteristics for themselves.
4 The essential task of management is to arrange organizational conditions and methods of operation so that people can achieve

their own goals *best* by directing *their own* efforts toward organizational objectives.

This is a process primarily of creating opportunities, releasing potential, removing obstacles, encouraging growth, providing guidance. It is what Peter Drucker has called "management by objectives" in contrast to "management by control."

And I hasten to add that it does *not* involve the abdication of management, the absence of leadership, the lowering of standards, or the other characteristics usually associated with the "soft" approach under Theory X. Much on the contrary. It is no more possible to create an organization today which will be a fully effective application of this theory than it was to build an atomic power plant in 1945. There are many formidable obstacles to overcome.

Some difficulties

The conditions imposed by conventional organization theory and by the approach of scientific management for the past half century have tied men to limited jobs which do not utilize their capabilities, have discouraged the acceptance of responsibility, have encouraged passivity, have eliminated meaning from work. Man's habits, attitudes, expectations—his whole conception of membership in an industrial organization—have been conditioned by his experience under these circumstances. Change in the direction of Theory Y will be slow, and it will require extensive modification of the attitudes of management and workers alike.

People today are accustomed to being directed, manipulated, controlled in industrial organizations and to finding satisfaction for their social, egoistic, and self-fulfillment needs away from the job. This is true of much of management as well as of workers. Genuine "industrial citizenship"—to borrow again a term from Drucker—is a remote and unrealistic idea, the meaning of which has not even been considered by most members of industrial organizations.

Another way of saying this is that Theory X places exclusive reliance upon external control of human behavior, while Theory Y relies heavily on self-control and self-direction. It is worth noting that this difference is the difference between treating people as children and treating them as mature adults. After generations of the former, we cannot expect to shift to the latter overnight.

DEFINING JOB CHARACTERISTICS

While job analyses are conducted by personnel administration specialists in larger organizations, every manager ought to be able to define the requirements of each job he or she supervises in order to facilitate training new employees, evaluating their performance, and providing them with assistance.

Job title
(Remember, many titles are not descriptive of the real duties required)

Organizational level
(Who does employee report to and salary range)

Performance requirements and skill requirements
Task and equipment responsibilities
a Work-load standards
b Maintenance standards

Analytical skills and judgment required
Manual or physical skills required; dexterity, accuracy
How job is to be performed:
a Criteria for satisfactory work—quality standards
b Criteria for requesting assistance or for identifying critical emergencies and whom to call for what
c Working relationships required with other employees in the work group or the flow of work
d How much opportunity to vary pace

Working conditions
(Any unusual physical requirements, degree of arduousness, environmental conditions such as physical exertion, unpleasant humidity, or temperature)

Promotional opportunities
(Job ladders or career lines available to those satisfactory in performing this job)

438

Qualification period
(Length of probationary period and/or length of training or apprentice-ship period required to become fully qualified on the job)

DEFINING EMPLOYEE CHARACTERISTICS

On the basis of the previous job analysis, the supervisor ought to seek to make explicit the selection criteria he would utilize when a job opening occurs. Keep in mind the temptation to add unnecessary or excessively *high* requirements which will tend to limit the number of available candidates.

Educational requirements
School level (e.g., high school diploma)
Special course requirements (e.g., algebra, manual drawing)

Experience requirements
a Jobs or tasks must have demonstrated competence in performing (e.g., at least eight months of experience as switchboard operator)
b Familiarity and experience with equipment (e.g., use of addressograph machine)

Special personality requirements
(e.g., job requires handling complaints from the general public and coping with stressful interpersonal situations)

Special physical and health requirements

EMPLOYEE EVALUATION FORM

A record such as this for each subordinate should facilitate such decisions as the following: Who should receive merit salary increases? is qualified for promotion? should be considered for discharge? needs more training or special attention? Also these semiannual reviews should be compared with initial impression of new employee in order to evaluate the usefulness of selection criteria that are being utilized.

	Almost always	Two-thirds of the time	Half the time	One-third of the time	Never or rarely	Examples (with date) and comments
Does the employee follow instructions?						
Are habits of regularity and punctuality shown?						
Is assigned work completed on schedule?						
Is quality maintained?						
Are relationships with other employees good including:						
a those in work group						

EMPLOYEE EVALUATION FORM (continued)

	Almost always	Two-thirds of the time	Half the time	One-third of the time	Never or rarely	Examples (with date) and comments
b those in preceding stages of the work flow						
c those in succeeding stages of the work flow						
Knows and follows accepted rules and procedures						
Distinguishes the relative priority of different tasks and handles them accordingly, doing the most important first						
Distinguishes between problems he or she can handle himself or herself and those which should be referred to me for assistance or decision						
Effective in detecting difficulties which will cause production or service problems and contributes to their solution						
Makes useful suggestions to improve job or work environment						
Takes on added or changed duties willingly when situation requires or when assigned work completed or unavailable						

INDEX

INDEX

Rogers, Carl, 245–248
Roosevelt, Theodore, 326–327
Routine jobs (*see* Motivation, and monotony)

Saab-Scania, 32, 36
Safety needs, 431
Sanction pattern (*see* Group, norms)
Sayles, Leonard, 7, 91*n*., 109, 145, 270, 319, 338, 361, 370, 383, 396, 430
Schon, Donald, 404
Scientific management:
  method, 10, 53–57, 433, 436
  segmentation, 68, 86, 93
  sequence, 34, 68, 85, 100
Seashore study, 134
Self-actualization, 14, 45, 433, 434
Sherman, Harvey, 89 *n*.
Short-cycle tasks, 29, 30, 101
  (*See also* Automation)
Short Interval Scheduling (SIS), 44
Sims, William S., 326, 327
Situational favorableness, leadership success, 278
Skinner, Burrhus F., 18, 146, 147
Social needs, 432
  (*See also* Job satisfaction)
Social "work environment," 12–14, 21–24, 29, 35, 44, 67, 75, 77, 99, 115, 116, 121, 124, 125, 276, 293, 347, 432
Specialization, 28, 30, 86, 346, 363, 366
Steelcraft Manufacturing Company, 43
Strauss, George, 45, 80, 109, 202, 291, 361, 371–372, 383, 396, 409, 424, 430
Strikes, 56
Structural change, top management, 424–425
Suboptimization, 123
Subordinates-supervisor relationship, 4, 7, 15, 47, 70, 87–88
  and communication, 285
  leadership, 277

Subordinates-supervisor relationship:
  and motivation, 140, 266
  and output, 135, 140
  and pair studies, 233
  and participation, 138
  and sensitivity training, 234–235
  and sharing decision making, 280
  and transactional analysis, 266
  and upward channeling, 299, 415–416
Supervision:
  appraisal of, 210, 213, 257
  credibility of, 221, 236, 237, 320, 321
  impact of, 60, 100–102, 279, 280, 293, 347
  and incentives, 13–16, 24–29, 31, 188, 198, 204–206
  and orders, 151, 170–177, 184, 185
  and orientation, 64–67
  power, 307, 311
  relationship-oriented, 278, 290, 372
  and skills, 59
  and synchronization, 275, 297, 298, 408
  and task-orientation, 278, 290
  and "third ear," 249, 250, 256
Supervisor:
  and authority, 4, 5
  and communication, 74, 186, 213, 221, 224, 230, 231, 237–248, 251, 263, 321, 334
  and compartmentalized management, 1, 408
  and control, 192, 199–210, 213, 217, 297, 315, 316, 391, 418, 435
  and discipline, 73, 77, 132, 150–170, 185
  and favoritism, 75–77, 94, 132, 289, 296, 306
  and job design, 40, 94–96, 100, 189, 191, 194, 199, 210, 214, 286, 376, 407, 420
  and role: as advocate, 300
    as agent of change, 400
    as auditor, 346, 349, 361–367
    as "bureaupath," 131